Economics: Theories and Applied Principles

Economics: Theories and Applied Principles

Edited by Luis Bender

CLANRYE INTERNATIONAL
www.clanryeinternational.com

Clanrye International,
750 Third Avenue, 9th Floor,
New York, NY 10017, USA

ISBN: 978-1-63240-947-8

Cataloging-in-Publication Data

Economics : theories and applied principles / edited by Luis Bender.
p. cm.
Includes bibliographical references and index.
ISBN 978-1-63240-947-8
1. Economics. 2. Economics--Methodology I. Bender, Luis.
HB131 .E26 2020
330--dc23

For information on all Clanrye International publications
visit our website at www.clanryeinternational.com

Clanrye International

Printed in China.

Contents

Preface

This book aims to highlight the current researches and provides a platform to further the scope of innovations in this area. This book is a product of the combined efforts of many researchers and scientists, after going through thorough studies and analysis from different parts of the world. The objective of this book is to provide the readers with the latest information of the field.

Economics is a social science which is concerned with the production, consumption and distribution of goods and services. The working of an economy and the interaction of economic agents are the key focus areas of economics. Economics has two major branches, macroeconomics and microeconomics. Macroeconomics deals with the structure, behaviour, performance and decision making of an economy as a whole. Microeconomics analyses the interaction among individuals and firms in making decision regarding the allocation of scarce resources. It focuses on individual agents and markets. Some of the other areas of study within economics are positive economics, normative economics, applied economics, Keynesian economics, economic system, rational economics and behavioural economics. This book covers in detail some existent theories and innovative concepts of economics. From theories to research to practical applications, case studies related to all contemporary topics of relevance to this field have been included in this book. It will prove to be immensely beneficial to students and researchers in this field.

I would like to express my sincere thanks to the authors for their dedicated efforts in the completion of this book. I acknowledge the efforts of the publisher for providing constant support. Lastly, I would like to thank my family for their support in all academic endeavors.

Editor

1

Organizational Conditioning of Job Satisfaction: A Model of Job Satisfaction

Marcin Wnuk[1]

ABSTRACT

Job satisfaction is an important predictor of job switching. Knowledge of the predictors of job satisfaction offers business owners and management staff the ability to shape the work environment so that the most valuable, loyal, and experienced employees can be retained in the company.

The objective of this project is to test a model of job satisfaction based on person-organization fit (P-O fit), perceived organizational support (POS), and perceived supervisor support (PSS). The study examines whether PSS directly relates to employee job satisfaction or whether P-O fit or POS mediate in this relationship. Additionally, it is examined whether POS is a moderating variable between P-O fit and job satisfaction.

The study was conducted using a sample 484 employees of a company in the IT sector.

It turns out that POS, and P-O fit to the organization are variables that act as partial mediator between PSS and job satisfaction. The relationship between PSS and POS is both direct and indirect. P-O fit is a partial mediator of this relationship, while POS is both a partial mediator and a moderator between P-O fit and job satisfaction. Among employees who POS to be high, consistency between an employee's and the organization's values is indirectly connected with job satisfaction, whereas among employees who POS to be low, this relationship is both direct and indirect. In their operations, employers should focus on shaping managers' attitudes towards their subordinates in an appropriate direction, as managers significantly influence employees' perceived organizational support and job satisfaction.

KEY WORDS: job satisfaction, person-organization fit, perceived organizational support, perceived supervisor support

---

[1] Adam Mickiewicz University, Department of Work and Organizational Psychology, Poland

Introduction

Job satisfaction is among the most commonly discussed phenomena in the psychology of business and human resource management, attesting to the importance it carries. The relevant literature treats job satisfaction as the key factor in commitment to one's job (Brown & Peterson, 1993) or the intend to quit and change it (Liu, Liu, & Hu, 2010; Park & Kim, 2009). Sources of job satisfaction among the employed are also a major focus of enquiry, so that they can be used to amplify perceived job satisfaction and thus increase employees' effectiveness and commitment and decrease motivation to quit jobs. Research conducted to date has found that perceived organizational support (Galletta,

Correspondence concerning this article should be addressed to: **Marcin Wnuk**, Adam Mickiewicz University, Department of Work and Organizational Psychology, Institute of Psychology, Szamarzewskiego street 89/AB, Poznań, Poland. E-mail: Marcin.Wnuk@komputronik.pl

Portoghese, Penna, Battistelli, & Saiani, 2011; Harris, Harris, & Harvey, 2007), supervisor support (Podsakoff, MacKenzie, & Bommer, 1996; Schaubroeck & Fink, 1998), and person-organization fit (Iplik, Kilic, & Yalcin, 2011; Narayanan & Sekar, 2009) are important elements of job satisfaction.

The aim of this article is to verify the model of job satisfaction on the basis of such organizational variables as supervisor and organizational support, person-organization fit, and the mutual relations among them. Knowledge of the organizational conditioning of job satisfaction carries significant practical value, as it offers employers a means of positively shaping job satisfaction and retaining the most valuable employees.

Literature review

The consistency between some aspects of employees' private lives and their operations at work exerts influence over the decisions and professional choices they make. Employees searching for a job select offers based on perceived and alleged consistency between their values and the values held by the company they apply to. This relationship has a two-sided character, as employers also strive for axiological consistency between employees and the organization; thus, they use tools to verify consistency between the organization's values and those of job candidates in their recruitment practices (Werbel & Gilliland, 1999).

Based on premises provided in the literature regarding attachment in the context of models of job switching, the construct of so-called job embeddedness is increasingly commonly examined (Mitchell, Holtom, Lee, Sablynski, & Erez, 2001). It is composed of three main elements that shape attachments between employees and their work environments understood broadly and is connected with the network of ties that anchor an employee to one's job. The first is concerned with relationships with co-workers and various types of actions and activities at work. The second is focused on similarities and the fit between work and other aspects of operations in one's living space. The third is connected with the ease of breaking the links enumerated above, especially if a change of job entails a change of residence. The relevant literature refers to the above elements as links, fit, and sacrifice.

In line with the concept of job embeddedness, the personal values of employees, their objectives related to their professional careers, and their plans for the future must be suited to the broad corporate culture of an organization and their own requirements for a job. An employee considers how suited one is to the community within which one is placed and the surrounding environment. In line with previous research, fit in this respect reduces intention to leave and change one's job and simultaneously exerts a positive influence on job satisfaction (Tanovaa & Holtom, 2008).

Based on the social exchange theory proposed by Blau in 1964, it may be stated that an employee perceives organizational support (POS) through the prism of one's supervisor, who is a representative of the company and personifies it. It is the direct supervisor, as the closest representative of an organization, who communicates to the subordinates the company's intentions regarding the employees. Through the supervisor, subordinates gain insight into the organizational culture, co-workers, the authority of management, the usefulness of certain skills, organizational values, and responsibility. All these elements form the construct of job fit, which is different from perceived organizational support, as the former relates to comfort experienced in an organization, whereas the latter concerns an employee's conviction that an organization appreciates one's contribution to its development and welfare (Eisenberger, Huntington, Hutchison, & Sowa, 1986). Organizational support perceived by an employee is the outcome of an employee's subjective perception of what the organization offers through one's supervisor, whereas job fit becomes stronger if the organization offers a working environment that is consistent with employees' values, professional objectives, skills, competences, and knowledge.

Perceived supervisor support (PSS) as well as fit with the company influence perceived organizational support. This is reflected in research (Dawley, Houghton, & Bucklew, 2010) in which job fit mediate between a partial intermediary between supervisor support and perceived organizational support. This means that the relationship between a supervisor's support and organizational support may have both a direct and indirect character.

Multiple studies confirm the positive correlation between POS and PSS (Hutchison, 1997; Kottke & Sharafinski, 1988; Rhoades, Eisenberger, & Armeli, 2001; Yoon, Han, & Seo, 1996; Yoon & Lim, 1999), clearly indicating the direction of the relationship between them and pointing to the supervisor's support as the predictor of perceived organizational support. For instance, in research conducted by Rhoades et al. (2001), perceived organizational perceived organizational support mediated between the supervisor's support and emotional attachment. In another longitudinal study, it was confirmed that the supervisor's support perceived by an employee influences organizational support (Eisenberger, Stinglhamber, Vandenberghe, Sucharski, & Rhoades, 2002). In research carried out by Dawley et al. (2010), job fit mediated between supervisory support and organizational support.

One element that determines job fit is values. Consistency between an employee's and an organization's values is the indicator of person-organization fit most commonly used in research. Such consistency of values indicates consistency of an axiological structure of both elements of the relationship, whose source – in line with the theory of social exchange – may be the attitude of the subordinate towards the supervisor who is treated as the carrier of values communicated by the organization. Research by Netemeyer, Boles, McKee and McMurrian, (1997) and Chen and Chiu (2008) show that a supervisor's support, as perceived by an employee, is positively correlated with perceptions that an organization's values are consistent with one's own values.

Hypothesis 1. Perceived supervisory support is both directly and indirectly correlated with perceived organizational support. The variable which partially mediate in this correlation is person-organization fit, measured by consistency between an employee's and organization's values.

Another significant variable relevant to job satisfaction is organizational support. As shown in prior research, these are two different but strongly correlated constructs (Eisenberger, Cummings, Armeli, & Lynch, 1997; Shore & Tetrick, 1991). Perceived organizational support is a generalized conviction of the existence of friendly or unfriendly attitudes of an employer towards an employee, whereas job satisfaction concerns a general assessment of various aspects of one's job (Shore & Tetrick, 1991).

In a study by Chen and Chiu (2008) conducted among employees of seven Taiwanese organizations, positive correlations between organizational support and job satisfaction were observed. Analogous results were obtained in studies conducted on 1,240 nurses from three hospitals in Northern Italy (Galletta et al., 2011), employees of one organization in the United States (Harris et al., 2007), and students of a nursing school (Gutierrez, Candela, & Carver, 2012).

Organizational support is strongly correlated with an employer's operations and policies that employees believe to be of a voluntary (non-intentional) character (Eisenberger, et al., 1986; Shore & Shore, 1995). The theory of social exchange suggests that if employees see an organization as supporting and caring, they become more willing to reciprocate through positive feelings towards the organization.

Hypothesis 2. Perceived organizational support is positively correlated with perceived job satisfaction.

Research conducted to date confirms the significant role of perceived supervisor support in perceptions of job satisfaction. Supervisors are the key link in the functioning of subordinates at work, as they create the atmosphere of work, determine relationships with employees, set aims, monitor the performance of tasks, motivate, and evaluate. All these aspects appear to have a huge influence on perceived job satisfaction.

According to Dirk and Ferrin (2002), trust of a subordinate who perceives support from a supervisor to be high is greater, which may increase one's job satisfaction. Netemeyer et al. (1997) observed a positive relationship between a leader's support and job satisfaction. Schaubroeck and Fink (1998) studied 214 employees of an insurance company in the United States and discovered positive, moderate correlations between perceived supervisory support and job satisfaction. Meta-analysis (Podsakoff et al., 1996) has shown that correlations between a supervisor's support and job satisfaction are moderate or strong.

Hypothesis 3. Perceived supervisor support is positively correlated with job satisfaction.

Another variable that is significant in job satisfaction is person-organization fit. Previous research, which has focused on employees in the public sector (Boxx, Odom, & Dunn, 1991), junior accountants (Chatman, 1991), MBA students, senior accountants, and middle management (O'Reilly, Chatman, & Caldwell, 1991), confirms the existence of a positive correlation between consistency of an organization's and an employee's values and the employee's job satisfaction and commitment to the organization. In a study of four Canadian organizations, Piasentin and Chapman (2007) showed that subjective perceptions of person-organization fit mediate between a sense of similarity and complementarity of employees to the organization and job satisfaction. In research conducted on employees of six organizations in the United States, consistency between employee and company values as well as between employees' ideal vision of the work environment and their evaluation of the current work environment were positively correlated with job satisfaction (Westerman & Cyr, 2004). This dependency was confirmed by other studies conducted on employees in the United States (Lauver & Kristof-Brown, 2001). Analogous results were obtained among employees in Spain (Vilela, González, & Ferrín, 2008), teachers in India (Narayanan & Sekar, 2009), and managers of hotels in Turkey (Iplik et al., 2011).

In line with research conducted on employees of five Turkish banks, perceived supervisor support turned out to be a moderator of the correlation between person-organization fit and job satisfaction (Maden & Kabasakal, 2014).

Erdogan, Kraimer, and Liden (2004) corroborated the mediating role of organizational support between person-organization fit and values and job satisfaction of teachers in Turkey. A moderating function for organizational support was not confirmed for other types of the person-organization fit.

Hypothesis 4. Person-organization fit is positively correlated with job satisfaction. Organizational support plays a moderating role in this correlation.

Methodology

Description of the research sample

The study was conducted on 485 individuals working in a single large organization. The participants included 97 women (i.e., 20%) and 388 men (i.e., 80%). Among responses to the survey, 21.7% were from of employees who had been employed between 1 and 12 months (short seniority), 30.6% were from employees who had been employed between 12 and 48 months (medium seniority), and 47.7% were from employees who had seniority of over 48 months (long seniority). Mean seniority was 3.06 years (SD=3.31), and mean age was 31.5 years (SD=7.75). Seventeen employees surveyed (i.e., 3.51%) had vocational education, 250 (51.54%) had secondary education, and 218 (44.95%) had higher education. Members of the management board, department directors, division and branch directors, and division and team managers composed a group of 97 employees surveyed (i.e., 20%). The number of other employees who did not hold managerial positions was 388 (i.e., 80%). The survey was anonymous. All participants agreed to take part in the study.

Research tools

The following research tools were adopted:

Identification with company values was tested using the *Person-Organization Fit Scale,* consisting of three questions (Cable & DeRue, 2002). Examples of questions in the scale are: "*My organization's values and culture provide a good fit with the things that I value in life.*", "*The things that I value in life are very similar to the things that my organization values*". Responses were provided on a 5-point scale ranging from "*I definitely disagree*" to "*I definitely agree*" and then summed up. The reliability of this tool is $\alpha = 0.90$.

The examination of organizational support was carried out with a shorter version of the *Perceived Organizational Support Scale,* comprising 8 questions. In line with the recommendation of Rhoades and Eisenberger (2002), owing to the one-factor character of this tool and a high level of reliability, the use of a shorter version appears to be legitimate. The questions used in this study were selected based on a factor analysis, with balance maintained between negative and positive statements (Eisenberger et al., 1986). Some examples of questions used are the following: "*The organization values my contribution to its well-being*". "*The organization ignore any complaint from me*". "*The organization really cares about my well-being*". "*The organization shows very little concern for me*". "*The organization takes pride in my accomplishments at work*". Responses were provided on a 5-point scale ranging from "*I definitely disagree*" to "*I definitely agree*" and then summed up. The reliability of this tool is $\alpha = 0.90$.

Table 1. Descriptive statistics of the variables used in the study *(n=485)*

	N	Min.	Max	M	SD	Skewness	Kurtosis
Job satisfaction	484	3	21	14.07	4.28	-0.42	-0.16
Person-organization fit	484	0	12	6.18	2.77	-0.31	-0.32
Perceived organizational support	484	0	32	14.11	7.00	0.06	-0.63
Perceived supervisor support	484	0	12	7.96	3.31	0.75	-0.22

Table 2. The coefficients of correlation between variables used in the study *(n=485)*

	1	2	3	4
1. Job satisfaction				
2. Person-company fit	0.56**			
3. Perceived organizational support	0.67**	0.61**		
4. Perceived supervisor support	0.56**	0.38**	0.59**	
5. Job seniority	-0.18**	-0.23**	-0.31**	-0.20**

Note:
* p≤ 0.05
** p≤ 0.01

Supervisor support was measured using the *Perceived Supervisor Support Scale,* comprising three questions adapted by way of changing the word "organization" to "supervisor" in the Survey of Perceived Organizational Support, authored by Eisenberger et al. (1986). The respondents answered the following questions: "*My supervisor cares about my general satisfaction at work*". "*My supervisor really cares about my well-being*". "*I enjoy working with my supervisor*". Responses were provided on a 5-point scale ranging from "*I definitely disagree*" *to* "*I definitely agree*" and then summed up. The reliability of this measure was estimated to be $\alpha = 0.93$

Job satisfaction was tested using the *Michigan Organizational Assessment Questionnaire* (Cammann, Fichman, Jenkins, & Klesh, 1979). This tool consists of the following three questions: "*All in all I am satisfied with my job*". "*In general, I don't like my job*". "*In general, I like working here*". Responses were provided on a 7-point scale ranging from "*I definitely disagree*" *to* "*I definitely agree*" and then summed up. The reliability of this tool was $\alpha = 0.79$.

Results

Estimations were performed using Amos software, version 23. Descriptive statistics are provided in table 1. Because variables in the model were approximately normally distributed (as both kurtosis and skewness fell in the range (-1:1)), the maximum likelihood method was adopted.

To verify goodness of fit of the model, the most commonly adopted indicators, such as NFI, GFI, CFI, AGFI, and RMSA, were used. Based on the coefficients of correlation obtained, job seniority in the current company was included in the model, as this variable was correlated with all the other variables in the model (table 2). Following introduction of this variable, job seniority was found to be directly related to perceived organizational support, supervisor support, and person-organization fit and only partially related to job satisfaction, as reflected in the final model (schema 1).

Based on the relevant literature, for a model to be considered fitted, NFI should exceed 0.90, GFI should exceed 0.90, and CFI should exceed 0.93 (Byrne,

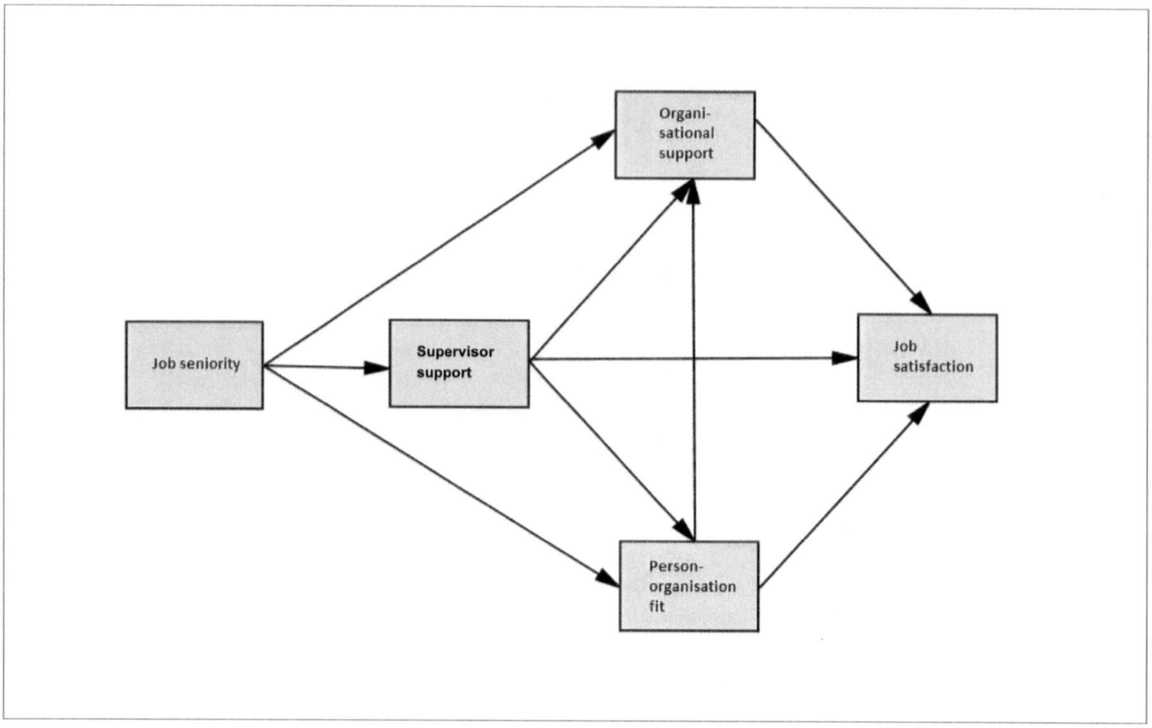

Schema 1. Model of job satisfaction based on person-organization fit and perceived organizational and supervisor support.

1994). On the other hand, RMSA should fall below 0.08 (Browne & Cudeck, 1993) and ideally below 0.05 (Stieger, 1990). In line with Kline's (1998) and Ullman's (2001) suggestion, relative chi-square should be below 2 or 3.

The values of selected indicators obtained (CMIN=1.64; p=0.202; RMSA= 0.036, NFI=0.98, GFI=0.99, AGFI=0.98; CFI=0.98) confirm a very good model fit. The total, direct, and indirect results in the case of mediation are provided in tables 3, 4, and 5.

Support from a supervisor was positively and directly correlated with person-organization fit and both directly and indirectly correlated with perceived organizational support, while the variable that acted as a partial mediator in this relationship was person-organization fit. Person-organization fit was positively correlated, both directly and indirectly, with job satisfaction. The mediator of this correlation was organizational support.

Verification of the moderating role of perceived organizational support in the relationship between person-organization fit and job satisfaction was performed using regression analysis after prior standardization of variables and estimation of the interaction term (Bedyńska & Książek, 2013).

Variance analysis demonstrated that the regression model with the interaction term is significant (F=149.55; $p < 0.001$); that is, it is well-fitted to the data. The standardized beta coefficient for the interaction effect was statistically significant and amounted to -0.07. The significance level of the R square change after taking into consideration the interaction effect was statistically significant (F=79.77; $p < 0.001$) and amounted to 0.48. This means that perceived organizational support moderates the correlation between person-organization fit and job satisfaction.

To provide additional verification of the moderating role of organizational support, Preacher and Hayes's (2008) method was applied, with respondents divided into those with high organizational support and those with low organization support. Among employees with low perceived organizational support, the influence of person-organization fit on job satisfaction (c = 0.618, t = 7.55, p = 0.0000) was reduced (c' = 0.447, t = 5.19,

Table 3. Standardized total effect between variables used in the study *(n=485)*

	Job seniority	PSS	P-O Fit	POS
Supervisor support	-0.20	0.00	0.00	0.00
Person-organization fit	-0.23	0.35	0.00	0.00
Organizational support	-0.31	0.55	0.45	0.00
Job satisfaction	-0.22	0.54	0.39	0.38

Note:
POS – abbreviation for Perceived Organizational Support
PSS – abbreviation for Perceived Supervisor Support
P-O Fit – abbreviation for Person-Organization Fit

Table 4. Standardized direct effect between variables used in the study *(n=485)*

	Job seniority	PSS	P-O Fit	POS
Supervisor support	-0.20	0.00	0.00	0.00
Person-organization fit	-0.16	0.34	0.00	0.00
Organizational support	-0.12	0.40	0.45	0.00
Job satisfaction	0.00	0.25	0.22	0.38

Table 5. Standardized indirect effect between variables used in the study *(n=485)*

	Job seniority	PSS	P-O Fit	POS
Supervisor support	0.00	0.00	0.00	0.00
Person-organization fit	-0.07	0.00	0.00	0.00
Organizational support	-0.19	0.16	0.00	0.00
Job satisfaction	-0.22	0.29	0.17	0.00

$p = 0.0000$), due to the impact of organizational support ($Z = 3.95$, $p = 0.0001$). This means that for this group, organizational support acts as a partial mediator between person-organization fit and job satisfaction. Among employees with high perceived organizational support, the influence of person-organization fit on job satisfaction ($c = 0.458$, $t = 4.78$, $p = 0.0000$) was reduced to a statistically insignificant level ($c' = 0.166$, $t = 1.61$, $p = 0.1085$), due to organizational support ($Z = 4.82$, $p = 0.0000$). This shows that for this group, organizational support totally mediate between person-organization fit and job satisfaction.

It turned out that among employees with a low level of organizational support, the fit to an organization's values is both directly and indirectly related to job satisfaction, and organizational support plays a partial mediating role in this relation. By contrast, among employees with a high level of organizational support, the fit to an organization's values is only partially correlated with job satisfaction.

Based on the results described above, it may be stated that organizational support is not only a partial mediator but also a moderator of the correlation between fit with an organization's values and job satisfaction.

Supervisor support is both directly and indirectly correlated with job satisfaction. To verify whether only a single variable – organizational support – mediate in this correlation or whether person-organization also does so, Preacher and Hayes's method was adopted (2008). Following incorporation of all the variables into the model, it turned out that the influence of supervisor support on job satisfaction (c = 0.728, t = 14.95, p = 0.0000) was reduced (c' = 0.327, t = 6.42, p = 0.0000), due to organizational support (Z = 7.24, p = 0.0000) and person-organization fit (Z = 4.72, p = 0.0000), which means that both these variables act as partial mediator in this correlation.

Variables such as age and education were not analyzed, as nearly all employees were between 25 and 45 years of age and had either secondary or higher education.

Discussion of the results

The hypothesis that person-organization fit acts as a partial mediator between supervisor support and perceived organizational support was fully confirmed. Supervisor support was directly correlated with organizational support and person-organization fit and indirectly related to organizational support through person-organization fit as a positive correlate of organizational support. The direction of the correlation between both variables also turned out to be consistent with the results of other research, indicating that perceived supervisor support is a source of perceived organizational support (Hutchison, 1997; Kottke & Sharafinski, 1988; Rhoades et al., 2001; Yoon et al., 1996; Yoon & Lim, 1999). As found in a study conducted by Dawley et al. (2010), the correlation between supervisor support and organizational support was both direct and indirect, the only difference being that the mediator of this correlation was person-organization fit.

This means that the correlation between supervisor support and organizational support is based on two separate mechanisms. One concerns the direct influence of perceived supervisor support on support from a company, as perceived by the employee. In the second case, we are dealing with a more complex process in which the employee notices the supervisor support and equates it with consistency of the employee's own values with those of the organization, compelling the employee to believe that the organization offers greater support.

The results obtained may be interpreted on the basis of the theory of social exchange, in which one party is an employee and the other an organization, with transactions between these parties made through the agency of the direct supervisor of the employee (Blau, 1964). Based on the rule of reciprocity, employees see such a relationship from the perspective of profits and losses, wondering what they gain from the organization and how they are treated by it to be able to reciprocate (Levinson, 1965). The intentions of the organization are seen by employees through the prism of the supervisor, who personifies the organization. If an activity undertaken by the supervisor as the representative of the organization is seen by the employee as favorable, it contributes to an increase of organizational support, as perceived by the employee. The power of this correlation depends on the degree to which the employee equates the supervisor with the organization. The more autonomous is the activity of the supervisor in the eyes of the employee, the lower this degree is (Eisenberger et al., 2002).

Based on the results obtained, it may be stated that organizational support is also perceived by an employee through the prism of person-organization fit, specifically, through consistency between the employee's values and those of the company. In this case as well, the supervisor appears to play the key role, as perceived supervisor support increases the employee's conviction that his or her values are consistent with the company's values, which makes the employee feel greater support from the organization. In this context, the supervisor is treated as a carrier of company values, and the perceived consistency between the organization's and employee's values exerts a positive influence on organizational support, as seen by the employee.

The hypothesis of a positive correlation between perceived organizational support and job satisfaction is fully supported, with positive correlations found between organizational support and job satisfaction. The results are consistent with results of previous research on Italian nurses (Galletta et al., 2011), employees in the United States (Harris et al., 2007), and students at a nursing school (Gutierrez et al., 2012), confirming the importance of perceived organizational support in job satisfaction. The moderate correlation between perceived organizational support and job satisfaction attests to the distinctiveness of these two constructs, which has attracted much attention from researchers in the relevant line of literature (Eisenberger at al., 1997; Shore & Tetrick, 1991). From this perspective, perceived organizational support exerts influence over only one of many aspects of job satisfaction, which is a multidimensional construct describing an organization's attitude towards an employee in terms of openness, friendliness, and care (Shore & Tetrick, 1991).

The hypothesis of a positive correlation between perceived supervisor support and job satisfaction is also supported. It turns out that perceived supervisor support is both directly and indirectly correlated with job satisfaction, and the variables that mediate this correlation are organizational support and person-organization fit. This means that a supervisor support may influence job satisfaction in three ways: through organizational support, through person-organization fit and directly. There is abundant evidence in the relevant literature confirming a positive correlation between perceived supervisor support and job satisfaction (Netemeyer et al., 1997; Podsakoff et al., 1996; Schaubroeck & Fink, 1998), indicating that satisfaction arising from cooperation with a supervisor may be important in the evaluation of job satisfaction. The two remaining mechanisms may be explained on the basis of the theory of social exchange mentioned above, where the key role is played by the supervisor, who is the most accessible representative of the company and whose activities are interpreted by an employee through the prism of the organization's intentions and not the supervisor's. This causes job satisfaction of a given employee to be seen as the outcome of organizational support and not the supervisor support, as the supervisor is mainly seen by the employee as a representative of the organization, with a role limited to serving the organization's will. Based on the relationship with the supervisor, the employee forms an image of the organization's attitude towards oneself, using the attributes of the supervisor. If this image is positive, which means that the employee sees the company as supportive, the employee feels greater satisfaction and joy from work. Otherwise, the employee feels dissatisfied with one's job.

Two elements of the third mechanism of the influence of perceived supervisor support on an employee's job satisfaction through person-organization fit were described above. An employee who experiences a supervisor support feels that his or her values are consistent with the company's values. This conviction is based on a belief that the direct supervisor – as the representative of the company – communicates these values to the employee in accordance with the intentions of the organization and not those of the supervisor. If, in the opinion of the employee, these values are consistent with one's own values, the employee is satisfied with one's job. If there is no such consistency, the employee experiences no satisfaction from the job. The positive correlation between person-organization fit and job satisfaction is the third element of the mechanism of indirect influence of supervisor support on job satisfaction. In accordance with the results, person-organization fit, as reflected by consistency between the values of these two elements, is both directly and indirectly correlated with job satisfaction. The results obtained in this study are partially consistent with prior research, which has found that either both variables are directly correlated (Boxx et al., 1991; Chatman, 1991; O'Reilly, Chatman, & Caldwell, 1991) or that the correlation between them is moderated by organizational support (Erdogan et al., 2004; Maden & Kabasakal, 2014). On the one hand, the results obtained confirm the positive direct correlations involving person-organization fit and simultaneously indicate the moderating role of organizational support. The novelty in the present context is the partial mediating role of organizational support in the relationship between person-organization fit and job satisfaction. This means that as in previous studies, an organization's values and job satisfaction is both directly and indirectly correlated (Boxx et al., 1991; Chatman, 1991; O'Reilly et al., 1991), and at the same time, the partial mediator of this correlation is organizational support, which enables person-organization fit to also exert an indirect influence on job satisfaction through perceived organizational support. The direct effect of the impact of person-organization fit is greater than the indirect effect (tables 4 and 5).

The results of this study also confirm the mediating role of perceived organizational support between the person-organization fit and job satisfaction. It turns out that for people who declare greater organizational support, perceived consistency between their values and those of the organization is not directly correlated with job satisfaction. For respondents whose level of organizational support is low, person-organization fit is both directly and indirectly correlated with job satisfaction. In the present context, organizational support turns out to be both a mediator and a moderator between person-organization fit and job satisfaction. In the relevant literature, a situation in which a single variable plays the role of both mediator and moderator is fairly rare (Baron & Kenny, 1986; Preacher, Rucker, & Hayes, 2007).

In accordance with the results of this study, job seniority at one's current job exerts an indirect influence on job satisfaction through person-organization fit and perceived supervisor and company support. This means that along with job seniority, perceived support from an organization and the supervisor as well as consistency between the employee's and the organization's values decrease, which reduces job satisfaction. Due to a lack of research on this issue, the results may be interpreted mainly in terms of mechanisms related to perceptions of the company at the beginning of a work relationship, perceptions that change over time. Throughout the first months of work, an employee is strongly motivated to fulfil one's responsibilities, is highly committed, and has great expectations regarding the organization, which gives rise to a positive image of the company and the supervisor. The employee sees the workplace through the prism of the supervisor, who is the representative of the company. As far as perceived job satisfaction, organizational support and person-organization fit are concerned, the employee builds an image of the organization on the basis of one's relationship with one's supervisor.

The results obtained confirm that the supervisor support mediate between job seniority and job satisfaction, organizational support, and person-organization fit (tables 3, 4, and 5). As time passes, the employee begins to notice all the faults and drawbacks of one's current employment situation, basing one's opinion on the relationship with the supervisor, and starts to see it as less satisfactory. This leads to a decrease in perceived organizational support and person-organization fit and consequently a reduction in job satisfaction.

Conclusions

Although the present study had a cross-sectional design, the method applied allowed us to draw conclusions on the directions of correlations between variables. The main shortcoming of the study is that all individuals surveyed were employed by one company, which limits the generalization gradient of the results to a single organization only.

The research presented has practical implications regarding the sources of employee job satisfaction. First and foremost, it demonstrates the important role of the supervisor in satisfaction derived from work by subordinates, who perceive and evaluate both the company's support and the consistency of their own values with the organization's values on the basis of their relationship with their supervisor. In this context, the attitude of the supervisor is the key element in subordinate employees' job satisfaction or lack of it. From a practical perspective, this means that employers should focus on shaping managers' attitudes in appropriate ways, as the behavior of this group of employees towards their subordinates has a decisive influence on employees' job satisfaction and hence their motivation to stay or leave (Liu et al., 2010; Park & Kim, 2009). The mechanism governing this influence has been described in detail, and possible ways of fulfilling this intention have been indicated. Apart from the direct influence of perceived supervisor support of an employee on job satisfaction, improvement of job satisfaction may occur through an increase in perceived organizational support and increased consistency between the employee's and organization's values. In this context, employers should bear in mind the overriding role of supervisors as leaders and representatives of the company, as the individuals with whom employees have most frequent contact and who create the image of the organization as a supporting vehicle for the employee and are seen to embody the values of the organization. Therefore, employers should carefully select managers who have values consistent with the organization's values and who can appropriately communicate them to subordinates. Support of managers by company owners and management boards should also foster the right attitudes among middle and lower-ranking personnel through a sense of appreciation, loyalty, and commitment to fulfilling their responsibilities.

References

Baron, R. M., & Kenny, D. A. (1986). The moderator-mediator variable distinction in social psychological research: Conceptual, strategic, and statistical considerations. *Journal of Personality and Social Psychology, 51*(6), 1173–1182.

Bedyńska, S., & Książek M. (2013). *Statystyczny drogowskaz 3. Praktyczny przewodnik wykorzystania modeli regresji oraz równań strukturalnych* [Statistical signpost 3. The statistical guide to the use of regression models and structural equation]. Warsaw: Publisher Academic Crux: School of Social Sciences.

Blau, P. M. (1964). Exchange and power in social life. New York, NY: Wiley.

Boxx, W. R., Odom, R. Y., & Dunn, M. G. (1991). Organizational values and value congruency and their impact on satisfaction, commitment, and cohesion. *Public Personnel Management, 20*(1), 195–205.

Brown, S. P, & Peterson, R. A. (1993). Antecedents and consequences of salesperson job satisfaction: Meta- analysis and assessment of causal effect. *Journal of Marketing Research*, 30, 63-77.

Browne, M. W., & Cudeck, R. (1993). Alternative ways of assessing model fit. In K. A. Bollen & J. S. Long (Eds.), *Testing structural equation models* (pp. 136-162). Newsbury Park, CA: Sage.

Byrne, B. M. (1994). Structural equation modeling with EQS and EQS/Windows. Thousand Oaks, CA: Sage Publications.

Cable, D. M., & DeRue, D. S. (2002). The convergent and discriminant validity of subjective fit perceptions. *Journal of Applied Psychology, 87*(5), 875–884.

Cammann, C., Fichman, M., Jenkins, D., & Klesh, J. (1979). The Michigan Organizational Assessment Questionnaire (Unpublished manuscript).

Chatman, J. A. (1991). Matching people and organizations: Selection and socialization in public accounting firms. *Administrative Science Quarterly, 36*(3), 459–484.

Chen, C.C., & Chiu, S.F. (2008). An integrative model linking supervisor support and organizational citizenship behavior. *Journal of Business and Psychology, 23*(1), 1-10.

Dawley, D., Houghton, J. D., & Bucklew, N. S. (2010). Perceived organizational support and turnover intention: The mediating effects of personal sacrifice and job fit. *The Journal of Social Psychology, 150*(3), 238–257.

Dirk, K. T., & Ferrin, D. L. (2002). Trust in leadership: Meta-analytic findings and implications for research and practice. *Journal of Applied Psychology, 87*(4), 611–628.

Eisenberger, R., Huntington, R., Hutchison, S., & Sowa, D. (1986). Perceived organizational support. *Journal of Applied Psychology, 71*(3), 500–507.

Eisenberger, R., Cummings, J., Armeli, S., & Lynch, P. (1997). Perceived organizational support, discretionary treatment, and job satisfaction. *Journal of Applied Psychology, 82*(5), 812-820.

Eisenberger, R., Stinglhamber, F., Vandenberghe, C., Sucharski, I. L., & Rhoades, L. (2002). Perceived supervisor support: Contributions to perceived organizational support and employee retention. *Journal of Applied Psychology, 87*(3), 565–573.

Erdogan, B., Kraimer, M. L., & Liden, R. C. (2004). Work value congruence and intrinsic career success: the compensatory roles of leader–member exchange and perceived organizational support. *Personnel Psychology, 57*(2), 305–332.

Galletta, M., Portoghese, I., Penna, M. P., Battistelli, A., & Saiani, L. (2011). Turnover intention among Italian nurses: The moderating roles of supervisor support and organizational support. *Nursing and Health Sciences, 13*(2), 184–191.

Gutierrez, A. P., Candela, L. L., & Carver, L. (2012). The structural relationships between organizational commitment, global job satisfaction, developmental experiences, work values, organizational support, and person-organization fit among nursing faculty. *Journal of Advanced Nursing, 68*(7), 1601-1614.

Harris, R. B. Harris, K. J., & Harvey, P. (2007). A test of competing models of the relationships among perceptions of organizational politics, perceived organizational support, and individual outcomes. *The Journal of Social Psychology, 147*(6), 631–655.

Hutchison, S. (1997). A path model of perceived organizational support. *Journal of Social Behavior and Personality, 12*(1), 159–174.

Iplik, F. N., Kilic, K. C., & Yalcin, A. (2011). The simultaneous effects of person-organization and person-job fit on Turkish hotel managers. *International Journal of Contemporary Hospitality Management, 23*(5), 644– 661.

Kline, R. B. (1998). *Principles and practice of structural equation modeling.* New York, NY: Guilford Press.

Kottke, J. L., & Sharafinski, C. E. (1988). Measuring perceived supervisory and organizational support. *Educational and Psychological Measurement, 48*(4), 1075–1079.

Lauver, K. J., & Kristof-Brown, A. (2001). Distinguishing between employees' perceptions of person-job and person-organization fit. *Journal of Vocational Behavior, 59*(3), 454– 470.

Levinson, H. (1965). Reciprocation: The relationship between man and organization. *Administrative Science Quarterly, 9*(4), 370–390.

Liu, B., Liu, J., & Hu, J. (2010). Person-organization fit, job satisfaction, and turnover intention: An empirical study in the Chinese public sector. *Social Behavior and Personality, 38*(5), 615-626.

Maden, C., & Kabasakal, H. (2014). The simultaneous effects of fit with organizations, jobs and supervisors on major employee outcomes in Turkish banks: does organizational support matter? *The International Journal of Human Resource Management, 25*(3), 341–366.

Mitchell, T. R., Holtom, B. C., Lee, T. W., Sablynski, C. J., & Erez, M. (2001). Why people stay: using job embeddedness to predict voluntary turnover. *Academy of Management Journal, 44*, 1102–1122.

Narayanan, S. S., & Sekar, P. C. (2009). A Person-organization fit study of college work culture and its impact on behavioural intentions of teachers. *Asia Pacific Management Review, 14*(2), 121–136.

Netemeyer, R. G., Boles, J. S., McKee, D. O., & McMurrian, R. (1997). An investigation into the antecedents of organizational behaviors in a personal selling context. *Journal of Marketing, 61*(3), 85–98.

O'Reilly, C. A., Chatman, J. A., & Caldwell, D. M. (1991). People and organizational culture: A q-sort approach to assessing person–organization fit. *Academy of Management Journal, 34*(3), 487–516.

Park, J. S., & Kim, T. H. (2009). Do types of organizational culture matter in nurse job satisfaction and turnover intention? *Leadership in Health Services, 22*(1), 20-38.

Piasentin, K. A., & Chapman, D. S. (2007). Perceived similarity and complementarity as predictors of subjective person–organization fit. *Journal of Occupational and Organizational Psychology, 80*(2), 341–354.

Podsakoff, P. M., MacKenzie, S. B., & Bommer, W. H. (1996). Meta-analysis of the relationships between Kerr and Jemier's substitutes for leadership and employee attitudes, role perceptions, and performance. *Journal of Applied Psychology, 81*(4), 380–399.

Preacher, K. J., Rucker, D. D., & Hayes, A. F. (2007). Addressing moderated mediation hypotheses: theory, methods, and prescriptions. *Multivariate Behavioral Research, 42*(1), 185–227.

Preacher, K. J., & Hayes, A. F. (2008). Asymptotic and resampling strategies for assessing and comparing indirect effects in multiple mediator models. *Behavior Research Methods, 40*(3), 879-891.

Rhoades, L., Eisenberger, R., & Armeli, S. (2001). Affective commitment to the organization: the contribution of perceived organizational support. *Journal of Applied Psychology, 86*(5), 825–836.

Rhoades, L., & Eisenberger, R. (2002). Perceived organizational support: A review of the literature. *Journal of Applied Psychology, 87*(4), 698–714.

Schaubroeck, J., & Fink, L. S. (1998). Facilitating and inhibiting effects of job control and social support on stress outcomes and role behavior: A contingency model. *Journal of Organizational Behavior, 19*(2), 167–195.

Shore, L. M., & Tetrick, L. E. (1991). A construct validity study of the survey of perceived organizational support. *Journal of Applied Psychology, 76*(5), 637-643.

Shore, L. M., & Shore, T. H. (1995). Perceived organizational support and organizational justice. In R. S. Cropanzano & K. M. Kacmar (Eds.), *Organizational politics, justice, and support: Managing the social climate of the workplace* (pp. 149–164). Westport, CT: Quorum.

Tanova, C., & Holtom, B. C. (2008). Using job embeddedness factors to explain voluntary turnover in four European countries. *The International Journal of Human Resource Management, 19*(9), 1553–1568.

Vilela, B. B., González, J. A. V, & Ferrín, P. F. (2008). Person-organization fit, ocb and performance appraisal: Evidence from matched supervisor-salesperson data set in Spanish context. *Industrial Marketing Management, 37*(8), 1005–1019.

Werbel, J. D., & Gilliland, S. W. (1999). The use of person-environment fit in the selection process. In G. Ferris (Ed.), Research in personnel and human resources management, (Vol. 17, pp. 209-245). Greenwich, CT: JAI Press.

Westerman, J. W., & Cyr, L. A. (2004). An integrative analysis of person-organization fit theories. *International Journal of Selection and Assessment, 12*(3), 252– 261.

Yoon, J., Han, N. C., & Seo, Y. J. (1996). Sense of control among hospital employees: An assessment of choice process, empowerment, and buffering hypotheses. *Journal of Applied Social Psychology, 26*(8), 686–716.

Yoon, J., & Lim, J. C. (1999). Organizational support in the workplace: The case of Korean hospital employees. *Human Relations, 52*(7), 923–945.

2

Influence of Governance Indicators on Illicit Financial Outflow from Developing Countries

Anselm Komla Abotsi[1,2]

ABSTRACT

Economic growth has traditionally been attributed to the accumulation of human and physical capital and the increased productivity arising from technological innovation. The quest to attract physical capital led to the design and implementation of policies and the building of institutions by governments of developing countries to create a congenial investment environment to attract foreign investors. The multinational corporations operating in these developing countries take advantage of these policies to profit from these countries in terms of capital through both legal and fraudulent activities. For governments and stakeholders to be able to fight this menace of illicit financial outflow, there is a need for a comprehensive scrutiny of the quality of governance indicators that enhance the activities of these multinational companies. Therefore, this study seeks to explore the influence of cross-country indicators of governance on the illicit financial flow from developing countries. This study is based on secondary data (panel) derived from the Global Financial Integrity, World Development Indicators and Worldwide Governance Indicators. The total number of developing countries included in the analysis is 139, and 1562 observations are included. Using the multilevel estimation approach, the study finds that regulatory quality has a negative and significant influence on the illicit financial flow, while government effectiveness, corruption and FDI net inflows have a significant positive effect. This finding calls for developing countries to design and implement sound policies, build effective and accountable institutions, control corruption and enhance regulatory quality to control this issue.

KEY WORDS: illicit financial outflow, foreign direct investment, government effectiveness, corruption, regulatory quality

[1] University of Education, Winneba - Department of Economics Education, Ghana; [2] P. O. Box AC 101 Arts Centre, Accra, Ghana

Introduction

Economic growth has traditionally been attributed to the accumulation of human and physical capital and the increased productivity arising from technological innovation. The importance of capital investment in the economic growth of developing countries cannot be over emphasized. Economies with positive GDP growth (elasticities greater than 0) have positive employment growth, and higher elasticities correspond to more employment-intensive growth. According to Ghazanchyan and Stotsky (2013), investment, among

Correspondence concerning this article should be addressed to: **Anselm Komla Abotsi**, University of Education, Winneba - Department of Economics Education, P. O. Box 25 Winneba, Win-neba, Ghana. E-mail: agrivetent@gmail.com

other important drivers, is a critical component of growth for developing countries. Private investment has been a major determinant of economic growth and employment in many open economies; therefore, opening markets to foreign direct investment (FDI) inflows is as beguiling as it is for trade. Bodies such as the IMF and the World Bank have suggested that attracting large inflows of FDI would result in economic development. The quest to attract FDI inflow led to the design and implementation of policies and the building of institutions, among others, by governments of developing countries to create a congenial investment environment to attract foreign investors. Some of these policies include tax holidays, exemptions on export and import duties, subsidized infrastructures, and limits on workers' rights. The design and implementation of effective tax policies is expected to allow countries to maximize the benefits of external flows by providing higher quality public services and pursuing adequate economic policies (African Development Bank [AfDB], 2012a). Developing countries have been improving their regulatory frameworks to attract more FDI inflow by opening their economies, permitting profit repatriation and providing tax holidays and other incentives (UNCTAD, 2002).

Some of these policies appear to be exploited against the very motives for which they were enacted and implemented. The multinational corporations operating in these developing countries take advantage of these polices to profit from these countries in terms of capital through both legal and fraudulent activities. Illicit financial flows (IFFs) are defined in the Global Financial Integrity (2012) report as "funds that are illegally earned, transferred, or utilized and cover all unrecorded private financial outflows that drive the accumulation of foreign assets by residents in contravention of applicable laws and regulatory frameworks". Issues on illicit financial flows have become very important with respect to the economic development of developing countries. According to Blankenburg and Khan (2012), IFFs are financial flows that have a direct or indirect negative effect on economic growth in the country of origin. Although IFFs from developing countries cannot be measured accurately, there is consensus that the amount is worth more than the official development assistance from Organisation for Economic Co-operation and Development (OECD) donor countries (Herkenrath, 2014). The socio-economic impact of IFFs on developing countries is more severe because of their smaller resource base and markets (OECD, 2013). The report by Global Financial Integrity (2013) indicates that illicit financial flows from developing countries increased by 10.2 percent per annum between 2002 and 2011 after controlling for inflation. In 2011, for example, Asia recorded the largest proportion of illicit financial flows among the regions; this represents 39.6 percent of total illicit outflows from developing countries, while developing Europe and the Western Hemisphere represented 21.5 percent and 19.6 percent, respectively. The Middle East and North Africa regions represented 11.2 percent of total outflows, on average. Although sub-Sahara Africa had the smallest nominal proportion of regional illicit outflows (7.7 percent), it has the highest average illicit outflows to GDP ratio (5.7 percent (Kar & Le Blanc, 2013). Adedze (2013) indicates that multinational corporations operating in Africa are involved in the illicit transfer of most of the $1.5 trillion they make in Africa each year back to the developed countries, hurting African economies in the process.

These multinational corporations achieve this situations ranging from "legitimate" international tax systems to dodgy accounting arrangements, according to the Adedze (2013) report. It is estimated that Africa lost over $854 billion in illicit financial flows between 1970 and 2008 with a yearly average of approximately $22 billion. Recent estimates put illicit financial outflows from Africa at $50 billion a year; this poses an economic development threat to Africa against the background that the official development assistance to Africa was $46.1 billion in 2012. A report on Illicit Financial Flows from Africa (Scale and Developmental Challenges as cited by Adedze, 2013) noted that "Just one-third of the loss associated with illicit financial flows would have been enough to fully cover the continent's external debt that reached US$279 billion in 2008." Calculations carried out by Global Financial Integrity show that the estimated illicit financial flows from developing countries are approximately ten times the total amount provided as official development assistance (Kar & Freitas, 2012). The consequence of these illicit financial flows is the aggravation of the enormous socio-economic problems confronting developing countries, since these activities constitute a drain on foreign exchange reserves and reduce tax revenue, which culminate in worsening poverty in these developing countries. The report by Purje, Ylönen, & Nokelainen, (2010) indicates that illicit financial flows from developing countries have become a major development policy issue since this act deprives states of tax revenue and disrupts the vital development of the private sector, which is recognized in the literature as the engine of growth in developing countries (Abotsi, Dake, & Agyepong, 2014), by distorting competition; this culminates in increased dependency on development assistance (Purje et al., 2010). For governments and stakeholders to be able to fight this issue of illicit financial outflow, there is the need for comprehensive scrutiny of the quality of governance indicators that enhance the activities of these multinational companies. Therefore, this study seeks to explore the influence of cross-country indicators of governance on the illicit financial flows from developing countries. The literature on the determinants of illicit financial flows is limited, although these determinants can inform policy formulation to reduce or curb the incidence of illicit financial flows. A previous study on this subject used import and export misinvoicing (components of illicit financial flow) as the dependent variables (Kar & Le Blanc, 2013); however, this study instead deploys illicit financial outflows as the dependent variable in finding the influence of relevant governance indicators on illicit financial outflows with the FDI inflow as the control. These indicators provide explicit and disaggregated information about particular dimensions of governance that are likely to influence illicit financial flow. In addition, empirical studies in explaining IFFs are generally based on the portfolio choice (PC) model; however, when the PC model is analyzed deploying only developing countries, the empirical results appear to support the assumptions of the PC model only to a certain extent (Herkenrath, 2014). The factors of the PC model have only limited explanatory power.

Using the multilevel estimation approach, this study finds that regulatory quality has a negative and significant influence on illicit financial flow, while government effectiveness, corruption and FDI net inflows have a significant positive effect. This paper continues with a literature review on illicit financial outflow and a set of potential determinant variables that influence illicit financial outflow (foreign direct investment inflow, governance effectiveness, regulatory quality and control of corruption). This work is followed by a presentation of the methodology deployed in the study. The remainder of the paper presents the results, discussion, and finally, the conclusion.

Literature review

As stated earlier, the Global Financial Integrity (2012) report defined illicit financial flows "as funds that are illegally earned, transferred, or utilized and cover all unrecorded private financial outflows that drive the accumulation of foreign assets by residents in contravention of applicable laws and regulatory frameworks". Illicit financial flow is composed of three components, which include commercial transactions, tax evasion and laundered commercial transactions; the criminal element and bribery; and finally, abuse of office by public officials (Mbeki, 2014). Empirical studies in explaining IFFs are generally based on the portfolio choice (PC) model, which attributed the massive capital outflow from developing countries to expropriation and currency losses and a reaction to comparatively low profit expectations (risks aversion) (Collier, Hoeffler, & Pattillo, 2001). According to Herkenrath (2014), the PC model does not fully explain IFFs that originate from economically successful industrialized countries as well as fast-growing emerging countries, since these flows mainly enhance tax evasion. Furthermore, to assume that these capital flows are mainly connected to the explanatory variables of the PC model (flight from economic stagnation, political instability, or the risk of expropriation) 'would make seemingly little sense' (Herkenrath, 2014). The research shows that the factors of PC model have only limited explanatory power (Herkenrath, 2014) since explained variance of their final empirical model is below 50 percent (Le & Zak, 2006). IFFs are postulated to be a consequence and a cause of development-inhibiting circumstances (Moore, 2012; Shaxson, 2010). A theoretical model of IFFs suggests a circular relationship between IFFs and development-inhibiting economic, political and social conditions (Moore, 2012). The world governance indicators reflect the views of thousands of survey respondents and public, private, and NGO sector experts worldwide on governance. These indicators also present the empirical measures of governance and thus make it possible to find the influence of these indicators on illicit financial flow from developing countries using qualitative analysis. Multinational corporations have been reported to be involved in the illicit transfer of capital from developing countries (Adedze, 2013). Based on the literature, this study reckons a set of potential quality governance indicator variables that influence illicit financial outflow. These variables include governance effectiveness, regulatory quality and control of corruption with foreign direct investment inflow as the control.

Illicit Financial Outflow

The research on illicit financial flows reveals that a source of more outright illicit financial flows is the mispricing of imports and exports to avoid duties and to the transfer monies, particularly foreign exchange, of these developing countries. Trade misinvoicing is one of the key conduits through which economic agents illegally move money out of developing countries (Bhagwati, 1974). This misinvoicing occurs because the act of deliberately falsifying invoices is illegal in most countries; therefore, trade misinvoicing estimates reflect completely illicit outflows. Another channel of illegal capital flight is via tax havens. Purje et al. (2010) suggests that most of the companies registered to tax havens truly conduct no actual activity in these places. For example, in the Cayman Islands, there is a building called Ugland House, which over 18,000 companies claim as their headquarters, whereas actually these companies conduct no actual activity in this building (Purje et al., 2010). According to Purje et al. (2010) suggests tax havens provide investors and companies with the required tailored legislation, such as banking secrecy and assisting investors with concealing their identities. The report by Mbeki (2014) shows that illicit financial flows from Africa are also attributed to aggressive tax avoidance strategies, which relate directly to the illicit outflows. Criminal activities, ranging from money laundering to drug, people and arms trafficking and smuggling, are also a key component of illicit outflows from developing countries. Commercial activities, according to the High-LevelPanel, are found to be the largest component of illicit financial flows; however, unfortunately, the global institutional framework is least developed in these areas. Resource extraction contracts that are shrouded in secrecy are another commercial source structured deliberately to deny African countries of legitimate earnings from royalties and taxes. The top 15 exporters of illicit capital are China, Malaysia, India, Indonesia, Thailand, and the Philippines in Asia, Nigeria and South Africa in Africa, Russia, Belarus, Poland, and Serbia in Europe, Mexico and Brazil in the Western Hemisphere, and Iraq in MENA (Kar & Le Blanc, 2013).

It is estimated that approximately €1,200 billion crosses state borders illicitly each year (Shaxson, N., & Christensen 2008), and the sum that leaves developing countries is estimated to comprise over half of this amount (Kar & Cartwright- Smith, 2008). The development assistance paid by rich countries to developing countries in 2008 was only one-ninth or one-tenth of the wealth that flows in the opposite direction illicitly (OECD, 2009). Between 2003 and 2012, the developing world lost US$6.6 trillion in illicit outflows; after a brief slowdown during the financial crisis in 2009, illicit outflows are once again on the rise, hitting a new peak of US$991.2 billion in 2012(Kar & Spanjers, 2014). The ratio of illicit financial outflow to GDP is a widely used indicator in assessing the adverse impact of illicit flows on an economy. Illicit financial outflows from Africa, developing Europe and Asia averaged 5.7, 5.8 and 4.1 percent of GDP, respectively, in 2011(Kar & Le Blanc, 2013). Illegal capital flight has been cited as the single most harmful economic problem for developing countries and transitional economies (Baker, 2007). A previous study on the drivers of illicit flows found trade misinvoicing to be driven largely by factors that are regulatory in nature (the export proceeds surrender requirement (EPSR) and the extent of capital account openness); one is governance-related (World Bank Control of Corruption indicator) (Kar & Le Blanc, 2013).

FDI Inflow

The pursuit to attract FDI inflow led to the proliferation of multinational companies or firms in developing countries. A major problem with respect to illicit financial flow is how these multinational firms benefit from tax holidays and then sell out immediately before the expiry period of such concessions, only to re-emerge as a new firm with a new tax holiday period. A cross-cutting issue in addressing illicit financial flows relates to the activities and practices of tax havens and financial secrecy jurisdictions, which provide a destination for illicit financial flows through tax evasion or money laundering. Multinational companies can have hundreds of subsidiaries in different jurisdictions in which they have little or no activity. Tax dodging by multinational companies accounts for two-thirds of the illegal capital flight (Purje et al., 2010). However, a common practice has been for the group to resort to declaring the most profit in the jurisdiction with the lowest taxes rather than where the profits were generated. A set of key actors in this illicit financial outflow are the multinational corporations (High-Level Panel, 2014) operating in these developing countries. A majority proportion of developing countries' tax losses is also attributed to tax dodging (evasion and avoidance) by multinational companies (Purje et al., 2010). Therefore, countries that receive more FDI inflows are more likely to experience more illicit financial outflow. Although research elsewhere found no macroeconomic factors as well as net FDI flows to be consistently significant in explaining export or import misinvoicing (Kar & Le Blanc, 2013), it is expected in this study that countries receiving more FDI inflows will experience more illicit financial outflow.

Governance Effectiveness and Regulatory Quality

The term 'governance' is broad and far-reaching, and the improvements to 'virtually all aspects of the public sector' is necessary to achieve 'good governance' (Grindle, 2004). Good governance is referred to by the World Bank as 'sound development management' and is regarded as "central to creating and sustaining an environment that fosters strong and equitable development and it is an essential complement to sound economic policies" (World Bank, 1992). Therefore, the quality of a government's policy formulation and implementation and the credibility of the commitment of government to such policies (regulatory quality) is very important in achieving good governance. According to Roy and Tisdell (1998), good governance depends on institutional structures and the economic resources available to achieve good governance. Effective government is enhanced through strong political leadership and competent public administration (AfDB, 2012b). More effective governments offer higher quality public services, attract more investment, encourage more human capital accumulation, among others, and increase the productivity of government (Mauro, 1995). The international development agencies have identified 'bad governance' as a major obstacle to economic growth and to improved welfare in poor countries (Moore, 2001). Countries provide higher quality public services and pursue adequate economic policies to maximize the benefits of external flow (AfDB, 2012a). Developing countries also open their economies, permit profit repatriation and provide tax holidays to multinational companies to improve their regulatory frameworks to attract more FDI inflow (UNCTAD, 2002). These multinational companies take advantage of these policies and exploit the system through both legal and illegal means. Mbeki (2014) suggested that to address this issue, illicit financial flow must be framed within the more technical context of political considerations. This suggestion is because of the nature of the actors involved and the 'fact that the most obvious solutions require strong political commitment and leadership'. Multinational companies may also lobby governments in the form of political campaign contributions to formulate and implement policies that will benefit them. Therefore, a country may exhibit good governance yet continue to experience high illicit financial outflow. Case studies on Brazil, the Philippines, and Russia show a relation between purely illicit flows and governance, and this relation tends to be stronger than the relationship between capital flight and governance (Kar & Freitas, 2013; Kar & LeBlanc, 2014;). The implications of illicit financial flow for resource mobilization, policy and legislation, and international geopolitics have raised concerns for governments of developed and developing countries alike (High-Level Panel, 2014). It is expected in this study that governance effectiveness and regulatory quality will explain variation in illicit financial outflow; however, the direction of influence of these variables on illicit financial outflow must be determined empirically.

Control of corruption

Corruption epitomizes the illicit use of the willingness to pay as a decision making criterion; therefore, in most cases, multinational companies make payments to public officials in return for a benefit (Abotsi, 2016).

Corruption tends to be low at higher levels of institutional quality and high at low level of institutional quality; therefore, depending on the level of quality of the institutions in the country, corruption may play the role of "sand in the wheels of commerce" or "greasing the wheels" (Abotsi, 2016). Corruption is therefore expected to have a positive impact on FDI inflow at a high level of institutional quality and a negative impact at a low level of institutional quality (Abotsi, 2016). Corruption was found by Mbeki (2014) to be a cross-cutting issue across all categories of illicit financial flows. A report by OECD (2014) states that 'high levels of corruption combined with weak institutions, and sometimes illegitimate regimes are drivers for such illicit financial outflows'. Elsewhere, research findings also show a significant link between corruption and capital flight (Le & Rishi, 2006). Corruption is therefore expected to have a positive influence on illicit financial outflow in this study.

Methodology

The study on the governance indicators that influence illicit financial outflow is based on secondary data. The data on illicit financial flow is derived from Global Financial Integrity (Kar & Le Blanc, 2013; Kar & Spanjers, 2014; Kar & Spanjers, 2015). GFI estimates constitute the most comprehensive dataset, which allows for cross-national and longitudinal comparisons over longer time periods. The data on foreign direct investment inflow is derived from the World Development Indicators (World Bank, 2013). The control of corruption, regulatory quality, and government effectiveness are derived from the Worldwide Governance Indicators (Kaufmann & Kraay, 2014). The frequency of the data is annual, and it spans from 2002 to 2013 for 139 developing countries. These indices are part of the six dimensions of governance included in the Worldwide Governance Indicators. These indices are therefore chosen not only because of their authenticity but also because of their free availability on the internet. The total number of developing countries included in the analysis is 139 from five geographical regions. These geographical regions include Asia, Sub Sahara Africa, Developing Europe, Western Hemisphere, and Middle East and North Africa (MENA).

The panel data estimation technique is employed in the estimation of the factors that influence illicit financial outflow from developing countries since, according to Ranjan and Agrawal (2011), this technique can capture the dynamic behavior of the parameters and provide more efficient estimation and information of the parameters. Many studies in economics have used panel data in their analysis using various estimation techniques including fixed and random effects. To decide whether to use a fixed or random effect model, the Hausman test is deployed in making this decision. However, the use of the Hausman test to decide which model to estimate has recently come under critical scrutiny (Bell & Jones, 2014; Clark & Linzer, 2015). The Hausman test is not a test of fixed effect versus random effect; instead, it is a test of the similarity of within and between effects. The main reason why the fixed effect model is preferred to the random effect model is the exogeneity assumption (the residuals are independent of the covariates) of the latter, which often does not hold in many standard random effect models. According to Bell and Jones (2014), fixed effect estimation models out higher-level variance and make any correlations between that higher-level variance and covariates irrelevant, without considering the source of the endogeneity. Higher-level entities in a panel study may be countries, and time-invariant variables could be the regional location. The covariates contain two parts: one that is specific to the higher-level entity that does not vary between occasions, and one that represents the difference between occasions, within higher-level entities. These two parts of the variable can have their own different effects, called 'between' and 'within' effects, respectively, which together comprise the total effect of a given time-varying variable (Bell & Jones, 2014). To solve the problem of heterogeneity bias, Bell and Jones, (2014) modeled the flexible random effect framework to correct the heterogeneity bias. Bell and Jones, (2014) posits that understanding the role of context, whether households, individuals, neighborhoods, countries or whatever defines the higher level, is of importance to a given research question. Therefore, it is prudent that one uses a random effect model that analyses and separates both the within and between components of an effect explicitly and assesses how those effects vary over time and space rather than assuming heterogeneity away with fixed effect. Therefore, this study uses the multilevel approach in exploring the factors that influence illicit financial outflow from developing countries. Multilevel models allow for study effects that vary by entity (or groups) and that estimate group level averages. Examples of advantages of multilevel models are the avoidance of sample problems with individual regressions that may be encountered and the lack of generalization. The use of regular regression ignores the average variation between entities.

The Multilevel-Model of Illicit Financial Outflow

In connection with discussions of the preceding section, the following multilevel-model (equation (1)) is proposed, where the selected variables are expected to influence illicit financial outflow.

$$\begin{aligned} &illicit\ financial\ flow_{ij} = \\ &= \beta_0 + \beta_1 FDI\_net\_inflows_{ij} + \beta_2 Control\_of\_Corruption_{ij} + \\ &+ \beta_3 Regulatory\_Quality_{ij} + \beta_4 Government\_Effectiveness_{ij} + \\ &+ u_{oj} + u_{1j} FDI\_net\_inflows_{ij} + \varepsilon_{ij} \qquad (1) \end{aligned}$$

Equation (1) depicts the value of illicit financial flow for the i th county and the j th geographical region as a function of foreign direct investment inflow, control of corruption, regulatory quality and governance effectiveness. The dependent variable is illicit financial flows from developing countries (HMN + GER) in millions of U.S. dollars; this refers to illegal movements of money or capital from developing countries. Hot Money Narrow (HMN) is "a methodology used to measure illicit financial flows recorded in the balance of payments", and Gross Excluding Reversals (GER) is a "methodology used to measure IFFs enabled by trade misinvoicing, measured the IMF's Direction of Trade Statistics (DOTS) database in conjunction with the Fund's International Financial Statistics (IFS) database" (Kar & Spanjers, 2014). Foreign direct investment refers to direct investment equity flows in the reporting economy in current U.S. dollars. The control of corruption index refers to "perceptions of the extent to which public power is exercised for private gain, including both petty and grand forms of corruption, as well as 'capture' of the state by elites and private interests". Regulatory quality refers to the "perceptions of the ability of the government to formulate and implement sound policies and regulations that permit and promote private sector development". Government effectiveness refers to the "perceptions of the quality of public services, the quality of the civil service and the degree of its independence from political pressures, the quality of policy formulation and implementation, and the credibility of the government's commitment to such policies" (Kaufmann, & Kraay, 2014). The term u_{oj} is the random intercepts for each of the j regions (it represents the deviation of country i's intercept from the overall mean intercept). The term u_{1j} represents the deviation of country i's FDI net inflows slope from the overall mean FDI net inflows slope (β_1). The worldwide governance indicator variables are transformed from their original scale, which ranges from approximately -2.5 (weak) to 2.5 (strong), to a new scale, ranging from 0 to 100 for computational purposes, to allow for easy interpretation of the results. The following formula was used: x = (a + 2.5)*20, where x is the value of the transformed variable, and a refers to the value of the original scale. This formula was also used by Abotsi and Iyavarakul (2015). This formula means that the higher a country is on the scale, the better the governance performance is in terms of control of corruption, regulatory quality and government effectiveness. The correlation matrix (Table 1) indicates that there are correlations among some of the independent variables; however, the statistical nature of panel data estimation addresses the collinearity problems (Ranjan & Agrawal, 2011). This study explores how illicit financial outflows vary with each explanatory variable holding other factors constant. The focus is not on casual interpretation; thus, endogeneity and omitted variables are not relevant to the analysis in the current study.

Results

Descriptive statistics

The descriptive statistics of the variables deployed for the study are presented in Table 2. The total observations used for the analysis is 1562. The period under study is from 2002 to 2013. The mean illicit financial outflow is 5288.49, and the standard deviation is 17122.72. This result shows that, on average, the illicit financial outflow is very large and widely dispersed within the developing countries. The result also shows that, over the period under consideration, some of the developing countries experienced negative FDI inflow.

Table 1. Correlation Matrix of Variables

	variables	1	2	3	4	5
1	illicit_financial_outflow	1				
2	FDI_net_inflows	0.8191	1			
3	Control_of_Corruption	-0.0487	0.0049	1		
4	Regulatory_Quality	0.0521	0.0889	0.6213	1	
5	Government_Effectiveness	0.0919	0.1021	0.8702	0.6939	1

Table 2. Descriptive Statistics

Variable	Observ.	Mean	Std. Dev.	Min	Max
illicit_financial_outflow	1562	5288.487	17122.72	0	258640
FDI_net_inflows	1562	4.05E+09	1.73E+10	-2.09E+10	2.91E+11
Control_of_Corruption	1562	42.71972	14.13457	13.6	85.2
Regulatory_Quality	1562	44.08707	14.58615	-3.6	80.8
Government_Effectiveness	1562	43.11216	13.92816	5	82

Empirical Results of the Mixed Model Estimation

Model Specification Diagnostics

Before a mixed model can be estimated, it is prudent to determine whether there is sufficient variance represented at a higher level to warrant the mixed approach. This determination is done by using the intraclass correlation coefficient (ICC). As a rule of thumb, approximately 10% of the total variance needs to be represented at a given level. The ICC found in the model in this study is

ICC = ((3957.4)^2)/(((3957.4)^2)+((10145.35)^2)) = = 0.132061119.

Approximately 13.2% of the total variance in illicit financial outflows can be attributed to differences between the geographical regions (i.e., level 2); this is more than the minimum of 10% expected for further modeling. Next is the random intercept model. In contrast to the ordinary least squares (OLS) regression model where the intercept and slope are both fixed and where the population parameters and individuals' variation from the predicted dependent variable are represented completely by the single error term, the individual countries illicit financial outflows are modeled with a mixed model as having a different overall level (or mean), which is represented by the random intercept according to the level 2 unit (or cluster); however, they all share the same regression slope. Random intercept models will represent the statistically problematic situation in which there are known differences on the outcome across levels of a variable that are implicitly (or explicitly) included in the sampling scheme (Gelman & Hill, 2007). To account for this difference across regions, the intercept is allowed to vary randomly (across regions). This variance would allow a slightly more accurate representation of the effect of the predictors on illicit financial outflows to be obtained. With the estimated standard deviation of the random intercepts (1313.878) in addition to the standard error (495.3016), it can be concluded that these intercepts do vary from place to place since the estimated standard deviation of the random intercepts is significantly different from zero.

The next step is to allow the slope of the regression line to take on a different value across the values of the level 2 variable. The FDI inflows predictor variable is designated as having a random slope; therefore, the slope parameter can have a variance (random coefficient models). This designation will allow FDI inflows to have a different effect on illicit financial outflows across different regions (This allows the slope variance of FDI inflows to vary randomly rather than to be fixed at zero). To determine whether to treat the slope as random or regard it as a fixed effect, there is a need to assess whether the variance of the slope is significantly different from zero. The standard deviation of random slopes on FDI inflows is more than twice its standard error, suggesting significant regional variation. Furthermore, a likelihood ratio test is deployed to test for the random intercept model and the random coefficient model. The difference is distributed as chi-square with degrees of freedom equal to the difference in degrees of freedom across the models (Gelman & Hill, 2007). The null hypothesis is that there is no significant difference between the two models. Since the result of the likelihood ratio test show that LR chi2 is equal to 166.75 with probability of 0.00000, the null hypothesis is rejected with the conclusion that there is a statistically significant difference between the models. This finding shows that the random coefficients model provides a better fit (it has the lowest log likelihood). It can be concluded that the random variance of the FDI inflows slope is different from zero. The Wild Chi-square test of joint significance reports that the null hypothesis that independent variables are jointly equal to zero at any conventional level of significance (p=0.000) may be rejected.

Interpretation and discussion of results

The results of the mixed and OLS models are presented in Table 3. The fixed effects of a mixed model are interpreted in the same way as an ANOVA, regression, or ANCOVA depending on the nature of the explanatory variables(s). However, it should be noted that any of the coefficients that have a corresponding random effect represent the mean over all subjects, and each individual subject has its own "personal" value for that coefficient. Random coefficients must be variable across groups. Conceptually, fixed coefficients may be invariant or varying across groups. The OLS results are presented only for the purpose of comparison. As stated earlier, this study only explores how illicit financial outflows vary with each explanatory variable holding other factors constant and without casual interpretation. Since the object of this study is to have an idea regarding how world governance indicators influence illicit financial flows, only qualitative interpretations of the coefficients are considered. The results show that FDI net inflows, control of corruption, regulatory quality and government effectiveness significantly influence illicit financial flow at 1%. The results show that FDI net inflows and government effectiveness variables have a positive influence on illicit financial flow; however, control of corruption and regulatory quality variables have a negative effect.

The results depict that, on average, countries that receive more foreign direct investment inflow experience more illicit financial outflow from their countries. Multinational corporations have been cited as a set of key actors in this illicit financial outflow from developing countries (High-Level Panel, 2014). It is therefore not surprising that countries that receive more foreign direct investment inflow experience more illicit financial outflow. One of the three different theories of foreign direct investments (the eclectic theory by Dunning, 1988) is the location advantages the multinational corporations enjoy in the foreign country. The specific location advantages can be divided into three categories including economic benefits, political advantages and social advantages (Abotsi, 2016). Structural market distortions such as government intervention, which affect costs and revenues, culminate into these location advantages (Harðardóttir, Óladóttir, & Jóhannsdóttir, 2008). According to Williamson (1985), the governance structure that multinational corporations choose for a venture is driven by the desire to minimize their transaction costs. It is now emerging that these multinational corporations do not only exploit their location advantages in the foreign countries

Table 3. The Results of the Mixed Model

	Multilevel_Model	OLS_Model
VARIABLES	**illicit_financial_flow**	**illicit_financial_flow**
FDI_net_inflows	9.10e-07***	7.88e-07***
	(2.60e-07)	(1.43e-08)
Control_of_Corruption	-242.5***	-304.3***
	(34.97)	(35.43)
Regulatory_Quality	-61.98***	-48.90**
	(22.42)	(23.15)
Government_Effectiveness	258.1***	317.1***
	(38.72)	(39.11)
Constant	3,969***	3,578***
	(1,070)	(855.6)
Observations	1,562	1,562
sd(FDI_net_inflows)	5.67e-07	
	(1.99e-07)	
sd(_cons)	1313.878	
	(495.3016)	
sd(Residual)	8984.254	
	(161.3164)	
R-squared		0.687
Number of groups	5	

Note: sd = standard deviation
Standard errors in parentheses *** p<0.01, ** p<0.05, * p<0.1

to reduce transaction cost but also involve themselves in activities (misinvoicing, tax haven secrecy, anonymous companies, and money laundering techniques) that facilitate illicit financial outflows.

As indicated earlier, the world governance indicators were transformed from their original scale, ranging from approximately -2.5 (weak) to 2.5 (strong), to a new scale ranging from 0 to 100 for computational purposes and to allow for easy interpretation of results. This finding means that the higher a country is on the scale, the better its governance performance. The results indicate that, on average, countries that exhibit high governance effectiveness instead experience more illicit financial flow from their countries. This finding is consistent with previous studies that found a link between purely illicit flows and governance (Kar, 2014; Kar & Freitas, 2013; Kar & LeBlanc, 2014). This finding means that the exhibition of high governance effectiveness by developing countries is necessary but not sufficient in fighting illicit financial outflow. The results also indicate that, on average, countries that exhibit high regulatory quality experience less illicit financial flow from their countries. This result means that the ability of governments to formulate and implement sound policies and regulations is paramount in the fight against illicit financial outflow. In the case of control of the corruption variable, countries scoring low on the scale are relatively highly corrupt, and those scoring high are relatively less corrupt. This finding means that, on average, developing countries that are more corrupt experience more illicit financial flow from their countries. This finding is consistent with earlier studies where panel data regressions indicate that an increase in corruption increases trade misinvoicing (Kar & Le Blanc, 2013). Le and Rishi (2006) also found a significant link between corruption and capital flight. The finding is also consistent with the High-LevelPanel (2014) conclusion that corruption is a cross-cutting issue affecting all three components (1. commercial transactions, tax evasion and laundered commercial transactions, 2. the criminal element and bribery and 3. abuse of office by public officials) of illicit financial flows from Africa.

Conclusion

This study explored the factors that are likely to influence illicit financial outflow from developing countries. Deploying the multilevel approach, this study finds that FDI inflow, governance effectiveness, regulatory quality, and control of corruption influence the illicit financial outflow from developing countries. FDI net inflows, government effectiveness and corruption have a positive and significant influence on illicit financial flow, while regulatory quality has a negative effect. This finding calls for developing countries to design and implement sound policies, build effective and accountable institutions, control corruption and enhance regulatory quality to control this issue. Global Financial Integrity suggested specific recommendations (Global Financial Integrity, 2014) that world leaders should focus on to curb the opacity in the global financial system. The recommendations address activities that facilitate these outflows such as misinvoicing, tax haven secrecy, anonymous companies, and money laundering techniques, among others. It is also expected that the announcement made by heads of the leading industrial countries and developing economies of the G20 in 2009 to end the banking secrecy of tax havens and help developing countries to benefit from "a new era of cooperation in taxation (Purje et al., 2010) will be fulfilled. In as much as FDI inflow is necessary in the development process of developing countries, extreme care should be exercised by these developing countries in the policies they enact. It is recommended that further studies on this topic should be focused on determining why countries with effective governance experience more illicit financial outflows. The study considers that there may be errors in the compilation and estimation of Global Financial Integrity data. However, in the absence of any 'better' alternative data on illicit financial outflow, this study deployed the data by Global Financial Integrity. This finding is the limitation of this study.

References

Abotsi, A. K., & Iyavarakul, T. (2015). Tolerable level of corruption for foreign direct investment in Africa. *Contemporary Economics*, *9*(3), 249–270.

Abotsi, A. K., Dake, G. Y., & Agyepong, R. A. (2014). Factors influencing risk management decision of small and medium scale enterprises in Ghana. *Contemporary Economics*, *8*(4), 397–414.

Abotsi, A. K. (2016). Theory of foreign direct investment and corruption. *International Journal of Asian Social Science*, *6*(6), 359–378.

Adedze, C. (2013). Africa is not doing enough to stem illicit financial flows. *African Agenda*, *16*(4), 14-15. Retrieved from http://www.twnafrica.org/AfricanAgenda16.4.pdf

AfDB. (2012a). *African economic outlook.* Paris. Retrieved from www.africaneconomicoutlook.org/sites/default/files/content-pdf/AEO2012_EN.pdf

AfDB. (2012b). *Development effectiveness review.* Retrieved from http://www.afdb.org/fileadmin/uploads/afdb/Documents/Project-and-Operations/Development Effectiveness Review 2012 - Governance.pdf

Baker, R. (2007, November 1). *The ugliest chapter in global economic affairs since slavery.* Washington, DC: Global Financial Integrity. Available at http://www.gfintegrity.org/press-release/ugliest-chapter-global-economic-affairs-since-slavery/

Bell, A., & Jones, K. (2014). Explaining fixed effects: Random effects modeling of time-series cross-sectional and panel data. *Political Science Research and Methods*, *3*(1), 133-153.

Bhagwati, J. N. (1974). On the Underinvoicing of Imports. In J. N. Bhagwati (Ed.), *Illegal transactions in international trade* (pp. 138–147). Amsterdam: North Holland Publishing Company.

Blankenburg, S., & Khan, M. (2012). Governance and illicit flows. In P. Reuter (Ed.), *Draining development? Controlling flows of illicit funds from developing countries* (pp. 21-68). Washington, DC: World Bank.

Clark, T. S., & Linzer, D. A. (2015). Should I use fixed or random effects? *Political Science and Research and Methods, 3*(2), 399-408.

Collier, P., Hoeffler, A., & Pattillo, C. (2001). Flight capital as a portfolio choice. *World Bank Economic Review, 15*(1), 55–80.

Dunning, J. H. (1988). The eclectic paradigm of international production: A restatement and some possible extensions. *Journal of International Business Studies Issue, 19*(1), 1–31.

Gelman, A., & Hill, J. (2007). *Data analysis using regression and multilevel/hierarchical models.* New York, NY: Cambridge University Press.

Ghazanchyan, M., & Stotsky, J. G. (2013). *Drivers of growth: Evidence from Sub-Saharan African countries* (Working Paper No. 13/236). International Monetary Fund. Retrieved from https://www.imf.org/external/pubs/ft/wp/2013/wp13236.pdf

Grindle, M. S. (2004). Good enough governance: Poverty reduction and reform in developing countries. *An International Journal of Policy, Administration and Institutions, 17*(4), 525–548.

Herkenrath, M. (2014). Illicit financial flows and their developmental impacts: An overview. *International Development Policy.* Articles and Debates 5.3. https://doi.org/10.4000/poldev.1863

Mbeki, T. (2014, March). Progress report of the High-LevelPanel on Illicit Financial Flows from Africa. Abuja: United Nations Economic and Social Council Economic Commission for Africa. Retrieved from https://www.uneca.org/sites/default/files/uploaded-documents/CoM/com2014/com2014-hlp_panel_on_illicit_financial_flows_from_africa-english.pdf

Kar, D., & Cartwright- Smith, D. (2008, December). *Illicit financial flows from developing countries 2002–2006.* Washington, DC: Global Financial Integrity. Retrieved from www.gfip.org/storage/gfip/documents/executive - final version 05-14-09.pdf

Kar, D., & Freitas, S. (2012, December). Illicit financial flows from developing countries: 2001-2010. Washington, DC: Global Financial Integrity. Retrieved from http://www.gfintegrity.org/wp-content/uploads/2014/05/Illicit_Financial_Flows_from_Developing_Countries_2001-2010-HighRes.pdf

Kar, D., & Freitas, S. (2013, January). *Russia: Illicit financial flows and the underground economy.* Washington, DC: Global Financial Integrity. Retrieved from http://www.gfintegrity.org/wp-content/uploads/2013/02/Russia_Illicit_Financial_Flows_and_the_Role_of_the_Underground_Economy-HighRes.pdf

Kar, D., & Le Blanc, B. (2013, December). Illicit financial flows from developing countries: 2002-2011. Washington, DC: Global Financial Integrity. Retrieved from http://iff.gfintegrity.org/iff2013/Illicit_Financial_Flows_from_Developing_Countries_2002-2011-HighRes.pdf

Kar, D., & Spanjers, J. (2014, December). Illicit financial flows from developing countries: 2003-2012. Washington, DC: Global Financial Integrity. Retrieved from http://www.gfintegrity.org/wp-content/uploads/2014/12/Illicit-Financial-Flows-from-Developing-Countries-2003-2012.pdf

Kar, D., & LeBlanc, B. (2014, February). *Illicit Financial Flows to and from the Philippines: A Study in Dynamic Simulation, 1960-2011.* Washington, DC: Global Financial Integrity. Retrieved from http://philippines.gfintegrity.org/Illicit-Financial-Flows-to-and-from-the-Philippines-Final-Report.pdf

Kar, D. (2014, September). *Brazil: Capital flight, illicit flows, and macroeconomic Crises, 1960-2012.* Washington, DC: Global Financial Integrity. Retrieved from http://www.gfintegrity.org/wp-content/uploads/2014/08/Brazil-Capital-Flight-Illicit-Flows-and-Macroeconomic-Crises-1960-2012.pdf

Kar, D., & Spanjers, J. (2015, December). Illicit financial flows from developing countries: 2004-2013. Washington, DC: Global Financial Integrity. Retrieved from http://www.gfintegrity.org/wp-content/uploads/2015/12/IFF-Update_2015-Final-1.pdf

Kaufmann, D., & Kraay, A. (2014). *Worldwide Governance Indicators.* Washington, DC: World Bank. Avaialable at http://info.worldbank.org/governance/wgi/index.aspx#home

Le, Q. V., & Rishi, M. (2006). Corruption and capital flight: An empirical assessment. *International Economic Journal, 20*(4), 523–540.

Le, Q. V., & Zak, P. J. (2006). Political risk and capital flight. *Journal of International Money and Finance, 25*, 308–329.

Mauro, P. (1995). Corruption and growth. *Quarterly Journal of Economics, 110*(3), 681–712.

Moore, M. (2001). Political underdevelopment: What causes 'bad governance. *Public Management Review, 3*(3), 385–418.

OECD. (2009, March 30). Development assistance at its highest level ever in 2008. Available at http://www.oecd.org/development/developmentaidatitshighestleveleverin2008.htm

OECD. (2013, December). *Measuring OECD responses to illicit financial flows*. Retrieved from https://www.oecd.org/dac/accountable-effective-institutions/IFFbrief.pdf

OECD. (2014). *Illicit Financial Flows from Developing Countries: Measuring OECD Responses*. Retrieved from https://www.oecd.org/corruption/Illicit_Financial_Flows_from_Developing_Countries.pdf

Purje, P., Ylönen, H., & Nokelainen, M. (Eds.). (2010, June). *Illegal Capital Flight from Developing Countries*. Helsinki: The Service Centre for Development Cooperation, KEPA. Retrieved from https://www.kepa.fi/tiedostot/julkaisut/illegal-capital-flight.pdf

Harðardóttir, A. G., Óladóttir, A. D., & Jóhannsdóttir, G. M. (2008). Offshoring R&D Centres to China: The case of Novo Nordisk evaluated with the OLI and OLMA frameworks. *Bifröst Journal of Social Science, 2*, 69–87.

Ranjan, V., & Agrawal, G. (2011). FDI Inflow determinants in BRIC countries: A panel data analysis. *International Business Research, 4*(4), 255–263.

Roy, K. C., & Tisdell, C. A. (1998). Good governance in sustainable development: the impact of institutions. *International Journal of Social Economics, 25*(6-8), 1310 - 1325.

Shaxson, N. (2010). *Tax havens' arguments in their defence - and why they are wrong*. Available at http://treasureislands.org/the-arguments/

UNCTAD. (2002). Trade and Development Report, 2002. Geneva: United Nations. Retrieved from http://unctad.org/en/docs/tdr2002_en.pdf

Williamson, O. E. (1985). *The economic institution of capitalism*. New York, NY: Free Press.

World Bank. (1992). *Governance and Development*. Washington, D.C. Retrieved from http://www.gsid.nagoya-u.ac.jp/sotsubo/Governance_and_Development_1992.pdf

World Bank. (2013). *World Development Indicators. Washington, DC: World Bank*. Available at https://blogs.worldbank.org/opendata/world-development-indicators013-now-available

3

Financial Vulnerability of Working Adults in Malaysia

Yiing Jia Loke[1]

ABSTRACT

Given the high and rising household debt in Malaysia, the objective of this paper is to ascertain the characteristics of a financially vulnerable individual. Financial vulnerability is measured based on two indicators: the debt-to-income ratio and the level of emergency savings for income shock. The findings of this paper show that, in addition to socio-economic factors, other factors such as risk tolerance, savings portfolio, and individuals' objectives and subjective financial knowledge can significantly explain differences in the levels of individual financial vulnerability. Using ordered probit on primary data consisting of 854 working adults aged 18–60, it is found that gender, ethnicity, income, number of dependents, age and education can significantly explain differences in the levels of financial vulnerability. Furthermore, the findings highlight the importance of continuous efforts to provide financial education to improve personal financial management. The findings also confirm that risk takers are more likely to be financially vulnerable. However, individuals who diversify their savings channels to include stock and bond holdings instead of solely saving through bank deposits are less likely to be financially vulnerable.

KEY WORDS: Indebtedness, Financial fragility, Financial literacy, Emergency savings, Personal finance

[1] Universiti Sains Malaysia - School of Social Sciences, Malaysia

Introduction

Household debt in Malaysia has been increasing rapidly in recent years, with the latest figure at RM940.4 billion (US$234 billion) or 87.9% of GDP in 2014 (Bank Negara Malaysia, 2015). This debt is the highest among its neighboring countries including Indonesia, Thailand, and Singapore. Furthermore, the debt service ratio of 44.2% indicates that approximately half of the households' monthly income is used to service debt payments. As Malaysia strives to become a high-income nation, the country is grappling with the serious problem of a growing number of bankruptcy cases, particularly among the young. Meikeng (2014) from The Star reported that the number of bankruptcy cases in Malaysia has increased consistently from 13,238 cases in 2007 to 21,987 cases in 2013. There was a significant 12% increase in bankruptcy cases from 2012 (19,575 cases) to 2013 (21,987 cases). Furthermore, Chow (2015) from Reuters also reported that there has been a significant increase in bankruptcies among those under 35 years old. According to the Department of Insolvency, a total of 24,953 people below the age of 35 had filed for bank-

Correspondence concerning this article should be addressed to: **Yiing Jia Loke,** School of Social Sciences Universiti Sains Malaysia Minden Penang 11800, Malaysia, E-mail: yjloke@usm.my

ruptcy since 2010 (Carvalho & Hamdan, 2015). In fact, approximately 47% of those between 18-35 years old are struggling financially and are living beyond their means, and 60 Malaysians are being declared bankrupt every day (Malaysian Digest, 2014).

High household debt can weaken private consumption spending particularly during an economic downturn. The problem can be exacerbated in a high interest environment as it will affect the debt repayment abilities of individuals and households. Furthermore, studies have found that a financial crisis that is preceded by large household debts will result in more severe downturns as highly indebted households and individuals will become credit unworthy as lenders tighten their loan offerings. For example, Mian and Sufi (2011) found that one of the key characteristics of the 2007/08 financial crisis in the United States was preceded by one of the largest increases in household debt in the country's history. Similarly, Chmelar (2013) also observed that household debt has a strong impact on the macroeconomic stability, the robustness of growth and the depth of the recessions. Furthermore, the high household debt to income ratio in Malaysia, which is 146 percent, is comparable to that of the U.S.A and the U.K. However, in contrast to high income nations and developed countries, the lower income levels in Malaysia raises the question of households' financial sustainability. Furthermore, while the United States and European countries share the same concern of high household debt in their respective countries, another point of concern in the issue of high household debt in Malaysia is the heterogeneity of its distribution and the direction of borrowing. Approximately 80% of household debt is by households earning higher than average income (greater than RM3,000 or US$ 748), and 46.5% is by households earning above RM5,000 (US$1,247) per month. Furthermore, the leverage ratio for households earning less than RM3,000 (US$748) ranges from 4.4 to a high of 9.6 times their annual income; many of these households obtained their loans from non-bank institutions that are outside the regulatory and supervisory purview of the central bank (Hussein, 2013). These statistics have attracted unwanted attention and raised concerns regarding the financial vulnerabilities of individuals and households in Malaysia.

Given the concerns about the increasing household debt, since 2010, the central bank of Malaysia has gradually implemented several micro-prudential measurements and introduced responsible financing guidelines for financial institutions. These new policies include changes such as raising the income eligibility requirements of credit card ownership, limiting the number of credit cards one can own, placing a ceiling on the credit limit of credit cards for cardholders with annual income less than RM36,000 (US$8977), and reducing the loan tenure for various loans (Bank Negara Malaysia, 2011a; 2011b). With the implementation of these policies, household debt moderated slightly in 2014 but remains at a high level.

The slowdown in the economy, the higher cost of living and the implementation of the Goods Service Tax (GST) in Malaysia on 1 April 2015 may adversely affect financially vulnerable individuals. The Credit Counseling and Debt Management Agency (AKPK), which was established in 2006 to help financially distressed individuals manage their debt, has cited poor financial management as the main factor for financially troubled individuals as this explains 22.7 percent of those who are enrolled in their debt management program (Malaysian Digest, 2014). More than 700,000 individuals have sought help from AKPK since its establishment; in 2015 alone, 135,000 individuals have approached AKPK to help them solve their financial problems (Credit Counseling and Debt Management Agency, 2016). As such, based on the aforementioned issues, the objective of this paper is to ascertain the characteristics of financially vulnerable individuals. This information is vital to ensure that effective educational campaigns for responsible financial management target the financially vulnerable group, and relevant intervention steps are taken to minimize the risk of bankruptcy among these individuals.

The remainder of this paper will be organized as follows: Section II provides the insights from the literature followed by a discussion on the data and model in section III. Section IV presents the descriptive analysis, while section V discusses the empirical results. The conclusion follows in section VI.

Insights from the Literature

In the existing studies, financial vulnerability or financial fragility is indicated by an inability to maintain expenses, an inability to confront unexpected expenses, and an indebtedness or a declining real household net wealth to disposable income ratio (Anderloni, Bacchoicchi, & Vandone, 2012; Clercq, van Tonder, & van Aardt, 2015; Disney, Bridges, & Gathergood, 2008; Jappelli, Pagano, & Di Maggio, 2008). In this paper, financial vulnerability is indicated not by a single measurement but is based on two indicators: the level of debt-to-income ratio and the level of emergency savings to cushion income shock. The former measures the extent of credit exposure, which reflects the existing vulnerability, while the latter measures the ability to cushion income shock, which reflects a potential vulnerability. This finding is particularly important given that nearly 50% of Malaysians' income is for debt repayment. Combining the two provides a more accurate reflection of an individual's overall financial vulnerability compared to using a single measurement, which is commonly used in existing studies on consumer indebtedness. A high debt-to-income ratio is susceptible to negative income shocks; in addition, if a consumer has weak financial preparedness for income shock, that consumer will be financially vulnerable.

The industry's rule of thumb for debt-to-income ratio is 30%, but the Credit Counselling and Debt Management Agency of Malaysia recommends the debt service ratio to be not more than 40%. Michelangeli and Pietrunti (2014) note that households with a debt-to-income ratio of above 30% are considered vulnerable. There are few studies on debt-to-income ratio per se, but studies of household indebtedness and financially constrained households are closest to it. Socio-economic factors such as income, age, education, home ownership, household structure, household net worth, financial portfolio, and regularity of income flows are widely considered in these studies, and various measurements are used to investigate the problem of indebtedness among individuals and households (Betti, Dourmashkin, Rossi, & Yin, 2007; Brunetti, Giardo, & Toricelli, 2016; Disney et al., 2008; Kempson, 2002). Generally, it is found that younger households, home ownership, lower income, and lower education increase the probability of financial indebtedness.

Emergency savings or emergency funds are commonly referred to as financial holdings that are available to cover living expenses without drastically altering the household's standard of living in the event of an income shock (Johnson & Widdows, 1985). There is debate on the adequate or minimum emergency funds that a household should have in the event of income disruption. The minimum adequacy is having funds equivalent to three months of living expenses; this is based on the average unemployment period of a worker (DeVaney, 1994; Garman & Forgue, 1997; Greninger, Hampton, Kitt, & Achacoso, 1996; Hanna & Wang, 1995). Greninger et al. (1996) found strong consensus among financial planners and educators that liquid assets for emergencies should equal a minimum of two and half to three months of living expenses. However, the rule of thumb is that consumers should hold liquid assets sufficient to cover three to six months of living expenses as this is regarded as the average period of unemployment; a laid-off worker will be re-employed in three to six months (Johnson & Widdows, 1985).

Age, years of education, marital status, ethnicity, number of dependents, and home ownership are commonly used socio-economic variables in the existing empirical studies on emergency fund holdings (inter alia, Bhargava & Lown, 2006; Chang, Hanna, & Fan, 1997; Chang & Huston, 1995; Chen & DeVaney, 2001; Hatcher, 2000; Worthington, 2004; 2005). In summary, these studies found that older households, those with higher income and educational levels, and larger household sizes are more likely to maintain emergency fund holdings.

In recent years, in addition to socio-economic factors, studies of consumer credit have included the role of financial knowledge on consumer credit. This inclusion follows from studies that have shown that financial knowledge promotes better financial decision making. For example, it has been found that those with greater financial knowledge are able to plan for retirement (Lusardi & Mitchell, 2007), participate in the stock market (Kimball & Shumway, 2006; van Rooij, Lusardi, & Alessie, 2007; Yoong, 2010), have better asset accumulation (Hilgert, Hogarth, & Beverly, 2003; Jappelli & Padula, 2011), and seek better financial service rates (Hastings & Tejeda-Ashton, 2008; Lusardi & Tufano, 2009). In terms of the effect of financial knowledge on consumer credit, Disney et al. (2008) reported that the majority of respondents have cited lack of financial literacy as a major cause of over-indebtedness. Conversely, Lusardi, and Mitchell (2009) have also added a subjective financial literacy measurement alongside the objective financial literacy measurement to investigate how it affects consumers' retirement planning. The subjective measurement of financial literacy was added to compare what consumers actually know with what they believe they know. Thus, it is important to determine if self-confidence plays as important a role as the actual level of financial literacy.

Risk aversion is also found to play a role in consumers' financial decisions such as retirement planning (van Rooij, Lusardi & Alessie, 2009), financial portfolio (Guiso & Jappelli, 2009) and level of unsecured debt (Brown, Garino, & Taylor, 2009). In the Malaysian context, there are several studies on financial strain, financial capability and in particular, financial well-being, of Malaysians, such as studies by Sabri, Masud, Karen, and Paim (2008), Delafrooz, Paim, Sabri, and Masud (2010) and Mokhtar, Husniyah, Sabri, and Abu Talib (2015) among others. However, there are limited studies that specifically examine the financial vulnerability of Malaysians. For example, in Sabri and Zakaria (2015), financial strain is measured in terms of individuals' emotional sentiments towards their financial situations such as their extent of worry regarding their ability to fulfill their financial commitments and regarding their availability of funds.

In this paper, in addition to considering socio-economic factors and financial knowledge to investigate the determinants of financial vulnerability among working adults in Malaysia, the model will include factors such as individuals' use of financial services and risk tolerance. The latter two factors are rarely incorporated into the models on consumer credit. Furthermore, by using two measurements of financial vulnerability that incorporate current and potential vulnerability, this paper is able to provide a more comprehensive indicator of financial vulnerability that has not been addressed in the existing studies.

Data and Model

Data

The dataset used in this study was obtained from a survey that was conducted in two locations (Penang and Klang Valley), which represent the Northern and Central commercial hubs of Peninsular Malaysia. Due to budgetary constraints, only two main commercial locations in Peninsular Malaysia were chosen, and only 900 respondents were canvassed. The two locations were also chosen because of the ease of access to financial services in these two locations. In other words, the targeted respondents were likely to be those with suitable access to financial services who were presented with various credit opportunities. The survey was conducted between January and March 2013. From the initial 900 respondents canvassed in the study, the final sample utilized responses from 854 respondents. Certain respondents were eliminated due to incomplete information. The respondents who participated in the survey are Malaysian working adults between the ages of 18 and 60 years old. A working adult is defined as an individual who works at least 30 hours a week. Convenience stratified sampling was used; the sample was stratified according to age bracket, ethnic group, and gender for both locations based on the Malaysian Labour Force Statictics of 2010 (Department of Statistics Malaysia, 2016) to reflect a better representation of the labor market in both selected locations. The respondents were solicited randomly in public places such as shopping malls, commercial areas, and offices. A face-to-face interview was conducted based on a prepared questionnaire. The data collected included information on respondents' financial status, financial knowledge, financial behavior and attitudes, and other socio-demographic characteristics.

Econometric Model: Ordered Probit

The dependent variable in this study is the level of financial vulnerability. The levels of financial vulnerability are defined as low, moderate, and high. Financial vulnerability is measured based on two indicators, debt-to-income ratio and funds sustainability in the event of income loss. For the debt-to-income ratio, an individual regarded as having a debt-to-income ratio within the recommended ratio of 30% or below will be accorded the value = 0 or 1 otherwise (Michelangeli & Pietrunti, 2014). Conversely, an individual who has adequate funds within the recommended level of emergency savings of at least three months or more is accorded the value 0 or 1 otherwise (Johnson & Widdows, 1985). Summing the two indicators provides the individual's level of financial vulnerability. In other words, the values of financial vulnerability range from 0 to 2 $(0 \leq v \leq 2)$, where v refers to the financial vulnerability score. For example, if an individual has a debt to income ratio of 30% and below but has emergency savings less than three months, the financial vulnerability score of the individual is equal to 1, thus putting the individual at the moderate level of financial vulnerability. Conversely, if an individual has a debt to income ratio above the recommended 30% and has less than three months' emergency savings funds, the individual's financial vulnerability score is equal to 2. Such an individual is categorized as highly vulnerable given that the individual has failed in both financial vulnerability indicators. Hence, it is clear that the dependent variable is categorical and ordinal with clear ordering. Thus, an ordered probit model is an appropriate statistical model to explain the variations in the levels of financial vulnerability among individuals (McCullaph, 1980; McKelvey & Zavoina, 1975). In general, the ordered probit is written as follows:

$$y^* = \beta' x + \varepsilon \qquad (1)$$

where y^* is the latent and continuous measure of financial vulnerability levels coded as 0, 1, or 2; β' is the vector of estimated parameters, and x is the vector of explanatory variables; and ε is the error term $\varepsilon \sim N(0,1)$ with cumulative distribution denoted by $\Phi(\bullet)$ and density function denoted by $\varphi(\bullet)$.

The observed and coded discrete financial vulnerability level, *y*, is derived from the model as follows:

$$y^* = 0 \text{ (low) if } y^* < \mu_1 \qquad (2)$$

$$y^* = 1 \text{ (moderate) if } \mu_1 < y^* < \mu_2 \qquad (3)$$

$$y^* = 2 \text{ (high) if } y^* > \mu_2 \qquad (4)$$

where μ_1 and μ_2 are threshold variables in the probit model. The threshold variables are unknown and determine the maximum likelihood estimation procedure for the ordered probit.

Variables

The explanatory variables can be broadly categorized into socio-economic factors, risk tolerance, financial knowledge and financial sophistication.

Gender, age, ethnicity, education, income, number of dependents, and home ownership constitute the socio-economic variables, while financial knowledge includes the objective and subjective financial knowledge assessment of the individuals.

Risk tolerance is measured in accordance with Hanna, Gutter, and Fan (2001), a study in which a respondent is asked if he will leave a current job that promises a guaranteed income for life for an equally desirable job with a 50-50 chance that it will double his after-tax income or that it will reduce his income by 'x%'. The respondent will be asked this question repeatedly with varying values of 'x' where x begins with 5%, 10%, 20%, 33%, and 50%. A person who is considered to have a high-risk tolerance is one who will not leave his current job if 'x' is 33% or above. In other words, for other values of 'x' below 33%, a high-risk individual will choose the new job over his current job.

The financial knowledge score is derived from the financial knowledge questions posed to the respondents. The financial knowledge questions are modified and conceptualized from various financial surveys. A total of six financial knowledge questions were asked; the concepts assessed include an understanding of inflation (Atkinson, McKay, Kempson, & Collard, 2006), interest compounding (Chen & Volpe, 1998; Lusardi & Tufano, 2009; Lusardi & Mitchell, 2009), cash flow management (Credit Counseling and Debt Management Agency of Malaysia, 2011), risk diversification (Lusardi, 2008), mutual funds (Lusardi, 2008), and the recommended debt repayments in relation to the income ratio (Credit Counseling and Debt Management Agency of Malaysia, 2011). The financial knowledge score reflects the number of correct answers. In addition to the objective assessment of the individual's financial knowledge through the six financial knowledge questions, the individual is also requested to self-assess his level of financial knowledge. This request is to distinguish between the objective and subjective financial knowledge indicators. Multicollinearity between the objective and subjective indicators of financial knowledge was eliminated, because the variable inflation factor (VIF) is found to be equal to 1.04, which is less than 10.

Respondent's financial sophistication is measured in terms of whether the respondent diversifies his savings portfolio. A respondent who saves beyond conventional bank deposits and includes investments in stocks, mutual funds or other forms of financial instruments is considered relatively more financially sophisticated and has a diversified financial portfolio.

Table 1. Selection of Variables

Variables	Description of Variable	Financial vulnerability			Total Sample	Expected signs
		Low	Moderate	High		
Binary variables (1= yes; 0 = otherwise)						
Gender	The respondent is a male	0.569 (0.496)	0.600 (0.491)	0.690 (0.464)	0.603 (0.490)	+
Chinese	The respondent is Chinese	0.435 (0.497)	0.267 (0.443)	0.264 (0.442)	0.322 (0.468)	#
Malay	The respondent is Malay	0.470 (0.500)	0.615 (0.487)	0.636 (0.483)	0.570 (0.495)	+
Indian	The respondent is Indian or others	0.095 (0.294)	0.118 (0.323)	0.101 (0.302)	0.108 (0.310)	+
Home	The respondent owns a house	0.622 (0.486)	0.443 (0.497)	0.682 (0.467)	0.539 (0.499)	+
Low income	The respondent's monthly personal income is below RM1,000	0.092 (0.289)	0.217 (0.412)	0.054 (0.227)	0.151 (0.358)	+
Low mid income	The respondent's monthly personal income is between RM1,001 – RM4,000	0.569 (0.496)	0.645 (0.479)	0.791 (0.408)	0.641 (0.480)	+
High mid income	The respondent's monthly personal income is between RM4,001-RM7,000	0.219 (0.414)	0.111 (0.314)	0.140 (0.347)	0.151 (0.358)	#
High income	The respondent's monthly personal income is above RM7,000	0.120 (0.326)	0.027 (0.163)	0.016 (0.124)	0.056 (0.230)	-
Tertiary	The respondent has tertiary education	0.445 (0.498)	0.296 (0.457)	0.279 (0.450)	0.343 (0.475)	-
Age1824	The respondent is aged between 18-24 years old	0.078 (0.268)	0.170 (0.376)	0.085 (0.280)	0.126 (0.333)	+
Age2529	The respondent is aged between 25-29 years old	0.127 (0.334)	0.183 (0.387)	0.178 (0.384)	0.164 (0.370)	+
Age 3039	The respondent is aged between 30-39 years old	0.314 (0.465)	0.312 (0.464)	0.450 (0.499)	0.334 (0.472)	+
Age 4049	The respondent is aged between 40-49 years old	0.261 (0.440)	0.222 (0.416)	0.225 (0.419)	0.235 (0.424)	#
Age 5060	The respondent is aged between 50-60 years old	0.219 (0.414)	0.113 (0.317)	0.062 (0.242)	0.141 (0.348)	-
Self-knowledge	The respondent thinks he/she has high financial knowledge	0.230 (0.421)	0.127 (0.333)	0.140 (0.348)	0.163 (0.369)	-
High risk	The respondent has high risk tolerance	0.102 (0.304)	0.120 (0.325)	0.171 (0.378)	0.122 (0.327)	+
Finst	The respondent diversifies his/her savings portfolio	0.558 (0.497)	0.416 (0.494)	0.419 (0.495)	0.464 (0.499)	-
Continuous variables						
Dependent	Number of dependents	2.149 (1.801)	1.980 (1.909)	2.395 (1.761)	2.098 (1.856)	+
Financial score	Financial knowledge score obtained (min=0; max=6)	2.707 (1.402)	2.321 (1.385)	2.450 (1.218)	2.478 (1.377)	-

Note: Std. deviation in parenthesis.
refers to reference group

Table 1. Selection of Variables

Variables	Coefficient estimates	Marginal effects on the probabilities of financial vulnerability		
		Low	Moderate	High
Gender	0.173** (0.080)	-0.049** (0.023)	0.046** (0.021)	0.036** (0.036)
Malay	0.364*** (0.094)	-0.103*** (0.032)	0.096*** (0.028)	0.081*** (0.019)
Indian	0.338** (0.138)	-0.096** (0.041)	0.088** (0.037)	0.072** (0.054)
Dependents	0.049** (0.023)	-0.014** (0.007)	0.013** (0.006)	0.012** (0.007)
Home	0.291*** (0.098)	-0.083*** (0.028)	0.076*** (0.025)	0.066*** (0.023)
Low income	0.839*** (0.248)	-0.238*** (0.040)	0.220*** (0.039)	0.180** (0.033)
Low mid income	0.903*** (0.227)	-0.256*** (0.033)	0.237*** (0.032)	0.190** (0.029)
High mid income	0.647*** (0.233)	-0.184*** (0.046)	0.170*** (0.044)	0.124*** (0.034)
Tertiary	-0.226** (0.101)	0.064* (0.035)	-0.059* (0.031)	-0.038* (0.020)
Age1824	0.401*** (0.148)	-0.114** (0.045)	0.105*** (0.040)	0.085*** (0.058)
Age2529	0.420*** (0.146)	-0.119*** (0.044)	0.110*** (0.040)	0.098*** (0.060)
Age 3039	-0.121 (0.110)	-0.074** (0.033)	0.069** (0.030)	0.051** (0.039)
Age 5060	-0.489*** (0.137)	0.139*** (0.053)	-0.128*** (0.046)	-0.101*** (0.037)
Financial score	-0.068** (0.031)	0.011** (0.021)	-0.008** (0.014)	-0.002** (0.005)
Self-knowledge	-0.227* (0.117)	0.064* (0.037)	-0.059* (0.034)	-0.044** (0.023)
High risk	0.259** (0.130)	-0.007** (0.039)	0.068* (0.036)	0.052** (0.031)
Finst	-0.163* (0.087)	0.046* (0.027)	-0.042* (0.025)	-0.034* (0.030)
LR stats: 121.96 (prob > chi2 =0.000)				
Pseudo R2: 0.720				
Log-likelihood: -785.42				
Wald test: 113.80 (prob >chi2=0.000)				

Note: *, ** and *** denotes 10%, 5% and 1% significance. Robust standard error in parenthesis.

Descriptive Analysis

Table 1 provides a summary of statistics of the survey respondents. Among the 854 respondents, the majority are moderately vulnerable financially (442; 51.7%); 129 (15.2%) are highly vulnerable financially, and 283 (33.1%) are considered to have low financial vulnerability. From a cursory analysis, males are generally more financially vulnerable than females. While males comprise 60.3% of the total sample, 69% of those who are highly vulnerable are male; in addition, only 56.9% of those who have low vulnerability are males. Chinese and Malay respondents comprise 32.2% and 57% of the total sample, respectively. However, only 26.4% of those who are highly vulnerable are Chinese, while 63.6% are Malay. This finding suggests differences in the levels of financial vulnerability among different ethnic groups. Furthermore, the summary statistics show that higher income reduces financial vulnerability, whereas 33.9% of those with low financial vulnerability are of high middle income and are high income individuals; however, 79.1% of those who are highly vulnerable are from the low middle income group. The low middle income group comprise 64.1% of the total respondents in the sample. Tertiary education appears to reduce the likelihood of financial vulnerability, whereas only 27.9% of those who are highly vulnerable have tertiary education. The average knowledge score for the total sample is 2.478; the average knowledge score for those who are highly vulnerable (2.450) is slightly lower, while the average knowledge score for those who have low vulnerability (2.707) is slightly higher than the overall total sample's average score. Furthermore, those who have high confidence in their financial knowledge comprise 23% of those who have low financial vulnerability compared to those who have high financial vulnerability (14%). This finding suggests that financial literacy and self-confidence in financial knowledge put individuals in a better position financially. Conversely, 17.1% of those who are highly vulnerable have a high risk tolerance, while only 10.2% of those who have low financial vulnerability have a high risk tolerance. Finally, 46.4% of the total sample's respondents diversify their savings portfolio beyond savings deposits; they comprise 55.8% of those who have low financial vulnerability, while 41.9% of those who are highly financially vulnerable diversify their savings portfolio.

Results Analysis

The log likelihood value for the model is -785.420, and the likelihood ratio chi-square statistic is 121.96 (prob>chi2=0.000); however, the Wald test chi-square statistics of 113.80 (prob>chi2=0.000) shows that the parameters in the model are jointly significant. Furthermore, the model has an overall predictability accuracy of 57.91%. To test whether the parallel assumption is violated, an ordered probit and generalized ordered probit regression were conducted. Under the parallel assumption, it is assumed that the correlation between the independent and dependent variables do not change with the categories of the dependent variables. If the parallel assumption test fails, the generalized ordered probit model should be used instead. It was found that the ordered probit model has a lower Akaike information criterion (AIC=1582.337) and higher Bayesian information criterion (BIC=1753.292) than the generalized ordered probit model (AIC:1608.839 and BIC:1699.066). This finding suggests that the ordered probit model is an appropriate model to use.

Table 2 presents the estimates of the ordered probit (column 2) and the marginal effects of the explanatory variables on the levels of financial vulnerability (columns 3–5). The ordered probit enables the identification of significant variables that are associated with different levels of financial vulnerability. A higher coefficient estimate (column 2) indicates a higher probability of being in the highest category of financial vulnerability (high financial vulnerability), while the converse is true for a lower coefficient estimate. The effects of the changes in explanatory variables on the probability of membership in the intermediate group (moderate financial vulnerability) cannot be inferred from the estimates of the ordered probit. As such, the discussion of the empirical results focuses on the marginal effects of the explanatory variables on the respective levels of financial vulnerability.

It is found that all socio-economic factors can significantly explain the varying level of financial vulnerability among working adults. Males are more likely to be in the category of having moderate or high financial vulnerability than females. Males are more likely to be the principal loan holder for more loans than females as they are generally socialized to be the breadwinner of the family in the Asian context (Lim, Teo, & Loo,

2003). Consequently, males will have higher debt-to-income ratios than females. The higher financial vulnerability of males than females could also be because women are more budget conscious than men, as found in Lim et al. (2003). The result supports the findings by the Department of Insolvency in Malaysia, in which the number of bankruptcy cases for men are approximately two times higher than for women. For example, in 2012, there are 13,613 bankruptcy cases reported by males compared to 5,962 bankruptcy cases reported by females. However, generally, females are found to have lower financial literacy and are weaker financially, particularly for the elderly (Hung, Yoong, & Brown, 2012; Lusardi & Tufano, 2009).

In a multi-ethnic country such as Malaysia, differences in ethnicity are found to have a significant effect on the varying disparities of financial vulnerability among different ethnic groups. The results indicate that Malays and Indians are more likely to have moderate or high financial vulnerability than the Chinese. For example, being Malay increases the probability of having moderate or high financial vulnerability by 9.6% and 8.1%, respectively, compared to being Chinese, which decreases the probability of having low financial vulnerability by 10.3%. Ethnic differences are evident in the management of personal finances; this is consistent with existing studies that show that Malays are more likely to experience credit card debt (Loke, Yen, & Tan, 2013), and Malays represent a higher number of bankruptcy cases. For example, according to the Department of Insolvency, in 2012, Malays comprise 48.41% of the bankruptcy cases filed.

It is found that greater financial responsibility puts a strain on an individual's financial vulnerability. Respondents who have a higher number of dependents and home ownership are more likely to be moderately or highly vulnerable financially. This finding is consistent with McCarthy (2011) and Kempson (2002) who found that those with young children, establishing a home and a higher number of children dependents are more likely to use credit heavily and tend to be in arrears. Furthermore, Brunetti et al. (2016) found that home ownership increases financial fragility.

Income levels have a significant effect on the financial vulnerability of individuals. Using high income (those earning above RM7,000 or USD1,746 a month) as the reference category, the results show that the lower income groups are financially more vulnerable. There are greater differences between the low income and low mid income with the high-income earners. For example, the probability that low income and low mid income earners have lower financial vulnerability than high income earners decreases by 23.8% and 25.6%, respectively, while the probability that high mid income earners have lower financial vulnerability than high income earners decreases by only 18.4%.

Education helps to reduce financial vulnerability. The results suggest that having tertiary education increases the probability of having low financial vulnerability and reduces the probability of having moderate and high financial vulnerability compared to an individual without tertiary education. Education has consistently been found to have positive effects on personal financial management (Anderloni et al., 2012; McCarthy, 2011).

Those aged between 40 to 49 years old were used as the reference group in the analysis on the significance of age on financial vulnerability. There are significant age differences for all age groups. It is found that those below 40 years old (age 18-24 years old, age 25-29 years old and age 30-39 years old) are all more likely to be more financially vulnerable compared than those between 40 to 49 years old. Conversely, those aged between 50 to 60 years old are less likely to be financially vulnerable. The findings appear to reflect the current Malaysian scenario in which there are higher bankruptcy cases reported for those aged 35 years old and below (Carvalho & Hamdan, 2015). McCarthy (2011) also found that the probability of being in financial distress increases with age to a maximum of the late 30s, after which the age effect decreases rapidly. The finding supports the life cycle hypothesis (Ando & Modigliani, 1963), in which younger working adults will tend to have lower incomes and may not have accumulated adequate assets that could be converted to liquid funds easily, making them more susceptible to income shock. Furthermore, younger working adults are likely to finance their current consumption with debt with the expectation that the debts could be repaid when their income increases in the future. Conversely, those who are older may have accumulated more savings and repaid their loans, resulting in a lower debt service ratio.

It is evident that both objective and subjective indicators of financial knowledge have a significant effect on the level of financial vulnerability. Lusardi and Mitchell (2009) who used both objective and subjective indicators of financial knowledge also found that higher financial literacy and higher self confidence in financial knowledge increase the likelihood of retirement planning. This finding highlights the importance of financial education. Financial education will equip individuals with the basic financial knowledge and boost an individual's self-confidence in addressing financial decisions.

Holding other factors constant, an individual who has a higher risk tolerance is more likely to be financially vulnerable. The results show that an individual with a high risk tolerance has a reduced probability of having low financial vulnerability of 0.7% but has an increased probability of having high financial vulnerability of 5.2%. In the existing studies on the role of risk aversion in financial decisions, it is found that those with high risk aversion have higher levels of unsecured debt (Brown et al., 2009), while Guiso and Jappelli (2009) found that those with higher risk aversion are more likely to hold risky assets and demand higher insurance coverage. Conversely, an individual who diversifies his savings portfolio beyond savings deposits is found to reduce the probability of being moderately highly vulnerable financially. Holdings of other financial instruments such as bonds and stocks appears to provide individuals with a better cushion for the availability of funds in times of emergency than those who put their savings in savings deposits only. This finding is consistent with Bhargava and Lown (2006) and Huston and Chang (1997), who found that households that are willing to take financial risks are more likely to have adequate emergency fund holdings than households that are not willing to take any financial risk.

Conclusion

This paper presents an analysis of the significance of socio-economic factors, financial knowledge, risk attitude and financial sophistication in explaining the varying levels of the financial vulnerability of working adults in Malaysia. The debt-to-income ratio and the levels of emergency savings for income shock were used to determine the overall level of financial vulnerability as the former provides the current vulnerability and the borrowing constraints of an individual, while the latter provides an indication of the potential vulnerability of the individual. In other words, the use of two measurements has provided a more holistic indicator of the financial vulnerability of an individual.

The significant age effects and ethnic differences in explaining the varying levels of financial vulnerability reflect the current bankruptcy situation in the country. Furthermore, the higher financial vulnerability of those below 40 years old are also corroborated by McCarthy's (2011) study on financial distress in the U.K and Ireland. The result that younger people tend to be more financially vulnerable is of concern as financial problems at a young age can be costly and can adversely affect an individual's lifetime financial welfare. Hence, the effort of the central bank in promoting financial education in schools and the incorporation of financial education in the school curriculum at the primary school level should be lauded and continued. As ethnicity effects are significant, a multi-lingual financial education program should be continued, and additional financial education programs could be added and expanded to target the areas with majority Malay communities. Furthermore, cultural differences could be considered and adopted to enhance the effectiveness and delivery of the financial education programs.

The financial vulnerability of low income earners requires attention. As noted by Hussein (2013), many of the low-income earners have high leverage and obtain their credit from non-bank institutions, which are outside the regulatory scope of the central bank. A "one size fits all" financial education program is clearly not suitable as the challenges confronted by low-income earners may be very different from other income groups, particularly given their lower access to financial services. Furthermore, while income poses a financial constraint on individuals, it is essential that individuals must be educated on the importance of living within their means and having a responsible financial attitude. Although the micro-prudential regulation introduced by Bank Negara Malaysia is to mitigate the issue of rising household debt, it may have made it more difficult for low income earners to gain access to credit opportunities from banking institutions. Hence, this finding is something that the authorities should examine further.

The significant positive role of education and financial education in reducing financial vulnerability is proven in this study as in other existing studies. Hence, there should be continuous effort to provide financial education to consumers to ensure that they are better equipped and more confident to address their personal finances. However, it is also important to consider the individual's appetite for risk when designing financial education modules such that consumers are alerted to possible temptations and traps. Furthermore, as the results show that diversifying one's savings portfolio is helpful in reducing financial vulnerability, consumers should be advised to diversify their savings to generate wealth. Therefore, consumers must be educated appropriately on the risk and return characteristics of different financial instruments.

Overall, the findings highlight and confirm several observations with regard to the household debt situation in the country. This paper is also one of the first to econometrically analyze the determinants of financial vulnerability of working adults that encompasses all active working age groups in Malaysia. However, for future study, more emphasis should be accorded to behavioral characteristics given that many recent studies have shown that cognitive biases can significantly affect an individual's financial decisions. Behavioral factors such as self-control and time preference could be added into the model. Unfortunately, in this paper, only a variable that proxies for individual's appetite for risk is introduced in the model; the remainder of the model focuses more on establishing socio-economic factors and financial knowledge in determining the financial vulnerability of individuals.

There are several limitations in this study. The study does not encompass all of Malaysia as it is limited to two main commercial hubs in the Peninsular Malaysia, namely, the Central and Northern regions. A nationwide study could be conducted to obtain a more representative finding of the status of financial vulnerability among Malaysians. Furthermore, future research could obtain information on the employment status of respondents regarding whether the respondent has a permanent contract or is a fixed-term contract staff as this may have an impact on respondents' financial vulnerability.

References

Anderloni, L., Bacchiocchi, E., & Vandone, D. (2012). Household financial vulnerability: An empirical analysis. *Research in Economics*, *66*(3), 284-296.

Ando, A., & Modigliani, F. (1963). The life cycle hypothesis of savings: Aggregate implications and tests. *American Economic Review*, *53*(1), 55–84.

Atkinson, A., McKay, S., Kempson, E., & Collard, S. (2006, March). Financial Services Authority Levels of Financial Capability in the UK: Results of a baseline survey (Consumer Research No. 47). Personal Finance Research Centre. University of Bristol. Retrieved from http://www.pfrc.bris.ac.uk/publications/Reports/Fincap_baseline_results_06.pdf

Bank Negara Malaysia. (2011a, March 18). New measures on credit cards to promote prudential financial management and responsible business practices. Retrieved from http://www.bnm.gov.my/index.php?ch=en_press&pg=en_press&ac=207&lang=en

Bank Negara Malaysia. (2011b, November 18). Measures to promote responsible financing practice. Available at http://www.bnm.gov.my/index.php?ch=en_press&pg=en_press&ac=140&lang=en

Bank Negara Malaysia (2015). Financial Stability and Payment Systems Report 2014. Kuala Lumpur, Malaysia. Available at http://www.bnm.gov.my/files/publication/fsps/en/2014/fs2014_book.pdf

Betti, G., Dourmashkin, N., Rossi, M., & Yin, Y. P. (2007). Consumer over-indebtedness in the EU: Measurement and characteristics. *Journal of Economic Studies*, *34*(2), 136-156.

Bhargava, V., & Lown, J. M. (2006). Preparedness for financial emergencies: Evidence from the Survey of Consumer Finances. *Journal of Financial Counseling and Planning*, *17*(2), 16-26.

Brown, S., Garino, G., & Taylor, K. (2009, November). Household finances and attitudes towards risk. Sheffield Economics (Research Papers No. 2008005). University of Sheffield. Department of Economics. http://www.sheffield.ac.uk/polopoly_fs/1.105542!/file/SERPS2008005b.pdf

Brunetti, M., Giarda, E., & Toricelli, C. (2016). Is financial fragility a matter of illiquidity? An appraisal of Italian households. *The Review of Income and Wealth*, *62*(4), 628-649.

Carvalho, M., & Hamdan, N. (2015, June 22). Becoming bankrupt before 35. *The Star Online.* Available at http://www.thestar.com.my/news/nation/2015/06/22/becoming-bankrupt-before-35-worrying-trend-of-about-25000-gen-y-msians-in-debt-over-the-last-five-ye/

Chang, Y. R., & Huston, S. J. (1995). Patterns of adequate household emergency fund holdings: A comparison of households in 1983 and 1986. *Journal of Financial Counselling and Planning, 6*, 119-128.

Chang, Y. R., Hanna, S. E., & Fan, J. X. (1997). Emergency fund levels: Is household behaviour rational? *Financial Counseling and Planning, 8*(1), 47-55.

Chen, H., & Volpe, R. P. (1998). An analysis of personal financial literacy among college student. *Financial Services Review, 7*(2), 107-128.

Chen, C., & DeVaney, S. A. (2001). The effect of life cycle stages and saving motives on the probability of emergency fund adequacy. In J. M. Hogarth (Ed.), *Proceedings of the Association for Financial Counseling and Planning Education* (pp.176-185). Columbus, OH: Association of Financial Counseling and Planning Education.

Chmelar, A. (2013, May). Household debt and the European crisis (Research Report No. 13). European Credit Research Institute. Retrieved from https://www.ceps.eu/system/files/Household%20Debt%20and%20the%20European%20Crisis.pdf

Chow, E. (2015, September 6). Bankruptcy among the young in Malaysia crimps consumption. *Reuters.* Available at http://www.reuters.com/article/malaysia-economy-debt-idUSL3N10O3QR20150906

Clercq, B., van Tonder, J. A., & van Aardt, C. J. (2015). Consumer financial vulnerability: Identifying transmission linkages that could give rise to higher levels of consumer financial vulnerability. *Southern African Business Review, 19*(1), 112-136.

Credit Counseling and Debt Management Agency. (2011). *POWER! Managing your debts effectively.* Credit Counseling and Debt Management Agency, Kuala Lumpur.

Credit Counseling and Debt Managemetn Agency [AKPK]. (2016). Lebih 700,000 dapatkan khidmat AKPK sejak 2006 [More than 700,000 has solicited services from AKPK since 2006]. Available at https://www.akpk.org.my/content/863-lebih-700000-dapatkan-khidmat-akpk-sejak-2006

Department of Statistics Malaysia. (2016). Labour force survey time series data 1982-2015. Available at https://www.dosm.gov.my/v1/index.php?r=column/ctimeseries&menu_id=NHJlaGc2Rlg4ZXlGTjh1SU1kaWY5UT09

Delafrooz, N., Paim, L. H., Sabri, M. F., & Masud, J. (2010). Effects of financial wellness on the relationship between financial problems and workplace productivity. *World Applied Sciences Journal, 10*(8), 871-878.

DeVaney, S. A. (1994). The usefulness of financial ratios as predictors of household insolvency: Two perspectives. Journal of *Financial Counseling and Planning, 5*, 5-24.

Disney, R., Bridges, S., & Gathergood, J. (2008). Drivers of Over-indebtedness. A Report to the Department of Business, Enterprises and Regulatory Reform. Available at http://www.nottingham.ac.uk/~lizjg1/file49248.pdf

Garman, E., & Forgue, R. (1997). *Personal Finance.* Boston, MA: Houghton Mifflin Company.

Greninger, S. A., Hampton, V.L., Kitt, K. A., & Achacoso, J. A. (1996). Ratios and benchmarks for measuring financial well-being of families and individuals. *Financial Services Review, 5*(1), 57-70.

Guiso, L., & Jappelli, T. (2009). Financial literacy and portfolio diversification (Working Paper No. 212). Center for Economic Studies and Finance, Department of Economics, University of Naples. Retrieved from http://www.csef.it/WP/wp212.pdf

Hanna, S. D., Gutter, M. S., & Fan, J. X. (2001). A measure of risk tolerance based on economic theory. *Financial Counseling and Planning, 12*(2), 53-60.

Hanna, S., & Wang, H. (1995). The adequacy of emergency funds to cover household expenditures. *Consumer Interests Annual*, 41, 224-225.

Hastings, J. S., & Tejeda-Ashton, L. (2008). Financial literacy, information and demand elasticity: Survey and experimental evidence from Mexico (Working Paper No. 14538). National Bureau of Economic Research. Retrieved from http://www.nber.org/data-appendix/w14538/FinLit_Appendix_20081123.pdf

Hatcher, C. B. (2000). Should household establish emergency funds? *Financial Counseling and Planning, 11*(2), 77-83.

Hilgert, M. A., Hogarth, J.M., & Beverly, S.G. (2003, July). Household financial management: The connection between knowledge and behaviour. *Federal Reserve Bulletin,* 309-322.

Hung, A., Yoong, J., & Brown, E. (2012). Empowering Women through Financial Awareness and Education (Working Paper No. 14). OECD Publishing, Paris. Retrieved from http://www.wikigender.org/wp-content/uploads/files/EmpoweringWomen-ThroughFinancialAwareness.pdf

Hussein, N. (2013, April 28). Reducing the Malaysia's debt burden. *East Asia Forum.* Retrieved from http://www.eastasiaforum.org/2013/04/28/reducing-malaysias-debt-burden-2/

Huston, S. J., & Chang, Y. R. (1997). Adequate emergency funds holdings and household types. *Financial Counseling and Planning, 8*(1), 37-46.

Jappelli, T., Pagano, M., & Di Maggio, M. (2008, October 28). Households' indebtedness and financial fragility. Paper presented at the 9th Jacques Polak Annual Research Conference, Washington, DC. Retrieved from https://www.imf.org/external/np/res/seminars/2008/arc/pdf/JPdM.pdf

Jappeli, T., & Padula, M. (2011). Investment in Financial Literacy and Saving Decisions (Working Paper No. 272). Center for Studies in Economics and Finance, Department of Economics, University of Naples. Retrieved from http://www.csef.it/WP/wp272.pdf

Johnson, D. P., & Widdows, R. (1985). Emergency fund levels of households. In K.P. Schnittgrund (Ed.), *Proceedings of the 31st Annual Conference of the American Council of Consumer Interests* (pp. 235-241). Fort Worth, TX: Amer Council Consumer Interest.

Kempson, E. (2002, September). Over-indebtedness in Britain. A report to the Department of Trade and Industry. Retrieved from http://www.bristol.ac.uk/media-library/sites/geography/migrated/documents/pfrc0203.pdf

Kimball, M. S., & Shumway, T. (2007, January 4). Investor sophistication, and the participation, home bias, diversification, and employer stock puzzles. Retrieved from http://www-personal.umich.edu/~mkimball/keio/5.%20papers/sophist3%20copy.pdf

Lim, V. K. G., Teo, T. S. H., & Loo, G. H. (2003). Sex, financial hardships and locus of control: an empirical study of attitudes towards money among Singaporean Chinese. *Personality and Individual Differences, 34*(3), 411-429.

Loke, Y. J., Yen, S. T., & Tan, A. K. G. (2013). Credit card ownership and debt status in Malaysia. *Singapore Economic Review, 58*(3), 17-44.

Lusardi, A., & Mitchell, O. S. (2007). Financial literacy and retirement preparedness: Evidence and implications for financial education. *Business Economics, 42*(1), 35-44.

Lusardi, A. (2008). Financial literacy: An essential tool for informed consumer choice? (Working Paper No.14084). National Bureau of Economic Research. Retrieved from http://www.nber.org/papers/w14084.pdf

Lusardi, A., & Mitchell, O. S. (2009). How ordinary consumers make complex economic decisions: Financial literacy and retirement readiness (Working Paper No. 15350). National Bureau of Economic Research. Retrieved from http://www.nber.org/papers/w15350.pdf

Lusardi, A., & Tufano, P. (2009). Debt literacy, financial experiences and overindebtedness (Working Paper No. 14808). National Bureau of Economic Research. Retrieved from http://www.nber.org/papers/w14808.pdf

Malaysian Digest. (2014, February 20). Debts among us: Young Malaysians are going bankrupt. The Malaysian Digest, 20 February 2014. Available at http://www.malaysiandigest.com/opinion/488936-debts-among-us-young-malaysians-are-going-bankrupt.html

Malaysian Digest. (2014, December 22). More Malaysians are spending well beyond their means. Available at http://www.malaysiandigest.com/frontpage/282-main-tile/533872-more-malaysians-are-spending-well-beyond-their-means.html

McCarthy, Y. (2011). Behavioural characteristics and financial distress (Working Paper No. 1303). European Central Bank. Retrieved from https://www.ecb.europa.eu/pub/pdf/scpwps/ecbwp1303.pdf?4ca9f70deb4b072c54015aa30aac835b

McCullaph, P. (1980). Regression models for ordinal data. *Journal of the Royal Statistical Society. Series B. Methodological, 42*(2), 109–142.

McKelvey, R. D., & Zavoina, W. (1975). A Statistical model for the analysis of ordinal level dependent variables. *Journal of Mathematical Sociology*, *4*(1), 103–120.

Meikeng, Y. (2014, April 9). Bankruptcy cases on the rise in Malaysia. *The Star Online*. Available at http://www.thestar.com.my/news/nation/2014/04/09/bankruptcy-on-the-rise-in-malaysia/

Mian, A., & Sufi, A. (2011, January 18). Consumer and the Economy, Part II: Household Debt and Weak U.S. Recover. Federal Reserve Bank of San Francisco, Economic Letter. Retrieved from http://www.frbsf.org/economic-research/publications/economic-letter/2011/january/consumers-economy-household-debt-weak-us-recovery/.

Michelangeli, V., & Pietruni, M. (2014). A microsimulation model to evaluate Italian households' financial vulnerability (Occasional Papers No. 225). Banca D'Italia. Retrieved from https://www.bancaditalia.it/pubblicazioni/qef/2014-0225/QEF-225.pdf

Mokhtar, N., Husniyah, A. R., Sabri M. F., & Abu Talib, M. (2015). Financial well-being among public employees in Malaysia: A preliminary study. *Asian Social Science*, 11(18), 49-54.

Sabri, M. F., Masud, J., Karen, K. L., & Paim, L. (2008). Personal financial wellness among Malaysian employees: Socio-demographic comparison. *Consumer Interests Annual*, 54, 189-192.

Sabri, M. F., & Zakaria, N. F. (2015). The influence of financial literacy, money attitude, financial strain and financial capability on young employees' financial well-being. *Pertanika Journal of Social Sciences and Humanities*, *23*(4), 827-848.

van Rooij, M., Lusardi, A., & Alessie, R. (2007). Financial Literacy and stock market participation (Working Paper No. 146). De Nederlandsche Bank. Retrieved from https://www.dnb.nl/binaries/Working%20Paper%20146-2007_tcm46-161161.pdf

Worthington, A. C. (2004). Emergency fund in Australian households: An empirical analysis of capacity and sources. *Financial Counseling and Planning*, *15*(1), 21-30.

Worthington, A. C. (2005). A note on households' choice of emergency finance. *Economics Bulletin*, *4*(5), 1-7.

Yoong, J. (2010). Financial illiteracy and stock market participation: Evidence from the RAND American Life Panel (Working Paper No. 2010-29). Pension Research Council. Retrieved from https://ssrn.com/abstract=1707523

Acknowledgements

Financial support from the Research University Grant of Universiti Sains Malaysia (1001/PSOSIAL/816213) is acknowledged

4

Effects of Contract and Trust on Franchisor Performance

Esther Calderon-Monge[1], Ivan Pastor-Sanz[2]

ABSTRACT

The franchisor-franchisee relationship is governed by contracts and trust. This paper analyzes how formal (contracts) and relational (trust) governance mechanisms affected franchisor performance in a service sector franchise for the period 2008¬2015. Using the SOM method in the empirical analysis, the results revealed that trust-based governance was more prominent than contract-based governance in the multi-unit franchise network and the cross-franchising network, negatively affecting franchisor performance in the multi-unit franchise network and positively affecting franchisor performance in the cross-franchising network. In contrast, contracts were more prominent than trust in single-unit franchising, negatively affecting franchisor performance. The primary practical implication is that the franchisor should prevent franchisees in the MUF network from opening new outlets in the same city and competing for the existing outlet's customers.

KEY WORDS: single-unit franchising, multi-unit franchising, cross-franchising, trust, contract

[1] Faculty of Economics and Administration of Business, University of Burgos, Spain; [2] Faculty of Economics and Administration of Business, University of Valladolid, Spain

Introduction

The literature generally addresses contracts and cooperation separately rather than considering them together within an integrated framework. Yet, an emerging academic debate is questioning whether trust-based relational governance can complement or substitute contract-based formal governance (Herz, Hutzinger, Seferagic, & Windsperger, 2016). Some authors view these two governance mechanisms as complementary, with each one compensating for the limitations of the other (Cavusgil, Deligonul, & Zhang, 2004; Liu, Luo, & Liu, 2009; Luo, 2002; Poppo & Zenger, 2002). Other researchers, however, view these two mechanisms as substitutes for one another (Adler, 2001; Bradach & Eccles, 1989; Dyer & Singh, 1998; Gulati, 1995; Granovetter, 1985; Uzzi, 1997; Wang, Yeung, & Zhang, 2011).

In franchising, the contract is the basic mechanism used to govern the franchisor-franchisee relationship (Hussain & Windsperger, 2013; Mumdziev & Windsperger, 2011; Windsperger, 2004). In addition to the contract, trust is also used as a governance mechanism (Griessmair, Hussain, & Windsperger, 2014; Gorovaia & Windsperger, 2013) Although these two governance mechanisms are used alongside one another, there is little research into how contracts and trust affect each other (Hendrikse, Hippmann, & Windsperger, 2015) and how they jointly influence franchisor performance (Herz et al., 2016). Hendrikse et al. (2015) state the

Correspondence concerning this article should be addressed to: **Esther Calderon-Monge**, Faculty of Economics and Administration of Business, University of Burgos, C/ Parralillos, s/n, Burgos 09001, Spain. E-mail: ecalderon@ubu.es

general trust of the franchisor reduce the franchisor's perception of relational risk and hence the necessity to control the network relationships by more complete contract planning, and knowledge-based trust increases information sharing between the partners and hence the knowledge base for specifying more detailed contracts. Herz et al. (2016) state the trust is a facilitator of decentralization in franchise networks, thereby increasing the positive performance effect of decision rights delegation. It therefore remains unclear how the exchange structure (i.e., the contract) and the process (i.e., trust) relate to one other and how this relationship affects franchising performance. In order to contribute theoretically to the debate discussed in the previous paragraph, this paper focuses on how contract and trust jointly influence franchisor performance into one franchise network with different sub-networks.

Franchises, interpreted as organizational networks, organize their franchisees into networks. Regardless of whether a franchise has dual distribution, the franchise network may be divided into different sub-networks (referred to in this paper as *franchisee networks*). Single-unit franchising (SUF), multi-unit franchising (MUF), cross-franchising, and franchising by franchisee-investors who hand over the running of their outlets to other franchisees are the franchisee networks considered in this research. The mechanisms governing these networks are contracts and trust. Contracts govern SUF networks, while contracts and trust govern MUF, cross-franchising, and franchisee-investor networks.

The prediction of company failure is one of the main concerns that the manager of every company must address. In the case of a franchisor, its financial performance depends on the solvency of its franchisee networks. The franchisor can also affect the financial performance and sustainability of its franchisees through the governance mechanisms that control the relationship between franchisor and franchisee. Accordingly, this paper analyzes the impact of formal (contracts) and relational (trust) governance mechanisms on franchisor performance. In order to achieve this aim, an empirical analysis of quantitative data for 113 franchised outlets of a Spanish service sector franchise between 2008 and 2015 has been carried out. A neural network algorithm yielded findings that advance the theory relating to the aforementioned debate. The findings confirm some of the key proposals of the relational versus formal governance debate. These proposals are corroborated for different franchise network structures. First, in cross-franchising, trust-based relational governance positively affects franchisor performance. Second, in MUF networks, relational governance negatively affects franchisor performance. Third, when the contractual clauses fail to adjust to franchisees' circumstances in SUF networks, formal governance through contracts negatively affects franchisor performance. The findings also contradict other theories such as agency theory, which advocates subjecting franchisees to governance mechanisms to stop opportunistic behavior from harming franchisor performance.

The value of this work is to simultaneously analyze the contract and trust in a franchise chain where its franchisees are organized in different networks such as SUF, MUF, and cross-franchising, and how these mechanisms affect the financial performance of the franchisor. The findings of this study can help franchisors decide on the right combination of governance mechanisms to expand their brands within the home market while achieving optimal performance. Improving franchised outlets' governance contributes to consolidating the franchise as a source of entrepreneurship and creator of employment. Moreover, franchisors could assess the financial situation of its franchisees in an easy and visual way, summarizing a high amount of information in a single visual representation.

The remainder of the paper is organized as follows. Section 2 develops the theoretical framework. Section 3 describes the sample and variables and explains the methodology: the self-organizing maps approach (SOM). Section 4 presents and discusses the results of the SOM analysis. Finally, Section 5 sets forth the conclusions, managerial implications, and limitations.

The franchise: A modern organizational network

The franchise, understood as a hybrid organizational form (Williamson, 1991), can be thought of as an organizational network. This interpretation illustrates and captures the dynamic nature of new corporate forms in the context of today's global economy (Weick, Sutcliffe, & Obstfeld, 2005). Franchising provides a useful laboratory for testing business ideas and complex organizational network processes within which these ideas and processes are embedded (Shane, 1996).

Franchises must have ways of controlling their franchisees, a difficult task given that the franchisor must choose between several ownership strategies within the franchise (Griessmair et al., 2014). Franchisors can exploit the same retail markets using the same business concepts by opening both franchised and company-owned outlets, or by opening franchised outlets only.

Company-owned outlets may be pilot outlets or formerly franchised outlets that the franchisor has since bought. Pilot outlets are used during the franchise's early years while the franchisor tests the business idea. Once the franchise matures, the franchisor purchases the profitable franchised outlets, converting them into company-owned outlets. Franchisors may decide to build different types of networks with their franchisees: single-unit franchising (SUF), multi-unit franchising (MUF), and cross-franchising networks. SUF refers to the "one franchisee, one outlet" format, whereas MUF refers the format whereby franchisors assign multiple outlets to each of their franchisees (Jindal, 2011). Cross-franchising refers to situations whereby franchisees operate two or more outlets with at least one of these outlets belonging to a different franchise brand. While franchisors often require franchisees to sell their products exclusively (i.e., SUF), many franchisors allow their franchisees to sell competing brand lines in their stores (i.e., cross-franchising) (Rajab, Kraus, & Wieseke, 2013). With cross-franchising, the franchisor strives to get franchisees and retailers to promote his or her brand to customers. According to Grünhagen and Mittelstaedt (2005), franchisors may opt for MUF when 1) they need franchisees to work developing markets and these franchisees enter a market because they view the franchise as an investment rather than an entrepreneurship opportunity and 2) franchisees run several outlets belonging to the same chain as an opportunity for personal development and entrepreneurship. Finally, a franchisor may have some franchisees who are investors with establishments run by other franchisees.

Franchisors use only formal mechanisms to govern SUF networks, whereas with MUF, cross-franchising, and franchisee-investor networks, they use both formal and informal governance mechanisms. The franchisor chooses the most efficient governance mechanism based on the franchise network's performance.

Trust and contracts are viewed as two important mechanisms to safeguard against opportunistic behavior and maintain cooperation (Jap & Ganesan, 2000), although other governance mechanisms exist (Rajab et al., 2013, p. 446). Trust and contracts tend to reduce goal incongruence and preference divergences among business partners, and they are widely acknowledged as essential to inter-firm collaboration (Geringer & Hebert, 1989).

Formal governance mechanism: The franchise agreement

Contracts are legal agreements between two or more business partners. They establish the legal and institutional framework and specify the rights, duties, and responsibilities of each party in a relationship (Luo, 2002). An effective contract prescribes suitable behavior by partners in the relationship, as well as protocols for distributing outcomes and penalties for violating the terms of the agreement.

Well-written contracts indicate how to handle any situation that may arise (Lusch & Brown, 1996). They reduce uncertainty regarding potential outcomes and the behavior of the parties and establish formal rules and procedures to govern the relationship. Contracts thereby limit the domain and severity of risk to which the parties of an exchange expose themselves to, while encouraging ongoing cooperation (Poppo & Zenger, 2002).

Contracts are a mechanism for resolving conflicts arising during knowledge transfer. When a dispute arises, the pertinent clause in the contract determines the legal obligations of the parties (Ring & Van de Ven, 1994). Contracts thus reduce costs and risks associated with knowledge exchange and collaboration during the relationship.

Contracts positively affect relationship performance, but the effect over the course of the collaborative process is nonlinear (Wang et al., 2011). When a contract is excessively detailed, it becomes rigid and inflexible, causing monitoring costs to rise. Furthermore, an excessively detailed contract may hinder the exchange of information between the parties of the contract in a limited area because the contract explicitly states what is and is not permitted. Using highly detailed contracts in a relationship may impede knowledge transfer (particularly tacit knowledge), prevent collaboration between parties, and may even send out signals of mistrust (Ghoshal & Moran, 1996). An overly detailed contract is therefore just as harmful as a contract that lacks detail (Wang et al., 2011). After a certain point, any additional detail in the contract may be detrimental to the relationship between the parties.

The same principles apply to the franchise agreement, which governs the franchisor-franchisee relationship. In SUF networks, the contract is in fact the only governance mechanism. An effective franchise contract prevents opportunistic behavior by both parties through clearly expressed clauses and enables the transfer of explicit knowledge (know-how) from franchisor to franchisee and the flow of tacit knowledge (market knowledge) from franchisee to franchisor. Consequently, the contract improves the performance of the franchise outlet and the franchisor.

In MUF and cross-franchising networks, the contract plays an important role in governing these networks, but trust also acts as a governance mechanism. In all cases, franchisors demonstrate a certain degree of trust in their franchisees. In MUF networks, franchisors show faith in their franchisees by letting them open new outlets. Similarly, in cross-franchising networks, franchisors show faith in their franchisees by letting them work concurrently with other franchise brands, thereby exposing themselves to the risk that these franchisees spend more of their time and effort on competing brands. Finally, franchisors also place their trust in franchisee-investors by letting them hand over the running of their outlets to other franchisees.

Relational governance mechanism: Franchisors' trust in franchisees

Trust can be studied from both sides of the franchisor-franchisee relationship—from the perspective of the franchisee's trust in the franchisor (Grace, Frazer, Weaven, & Dant, 2016) and from the perspective of the franchisor's trust in the franchisee. In this research, trust is considered from the perspective of the franchisor's trust in the franchisee. From this perspective, trust is an important informal governance mechanism that leads to higher relational rents owing to savings in transaction costs and/or an increase in transaction value (Griessmair et al., 2014). Trust represents the extent to which a firm believes that its exchange partner is honest and/or benevolent (Geysken, Steenkamp, & Kumar, 1998).

A positive experience with a franchisee during the contractual relationship signals high credibility and fairness, thereby increasing the franchisee's reputation and hence the franchisor's trust in each franchisee network. When franchisors have positive experiences with franchisees, they have a high level of trust in their partners and are more likely to select them to become multi-unit franchisees. In this case, the franchisor uses the offer of MUF as a reward strategy to screen franchisees based on their credibility and fairness in prior interactions. Therefore, the franchisee's reputation provides information for the franchisor's selection of new MUF franchisees (Gillis, McEwan, Crook, & Michael, 2011). According to Griessmair et al. (2014) this form of trust is known as knowledge-based trust.

General trust (Yamagishi & Yamagishi, 1994) can also apply to the franchisor-franchisee relationship (Griessmair et al., 2014). Under given exchange hazards, a high level of general trust means the franchisor perceives lower relational risk and hence faces lower agency and monitoring costs. These lower risks and lower costs mean that the franchisor is less likely to control the franchisees. This situation is compatible with the substitutability of formal and relational governance in inter-firm cooperation (Cavusgil et al., 2004; Gulati, 1995; Macaulay, 1963; Nooteboom, Berger, & Noorderhaven, 1997; Wang et al., 2011).

Accordingly, a franchisor with a high level of general trust and knowledge-based trust will tend to build MUF networks (Griessmair et al., 2014) and even cross-franchising networks. With cross-franchising networks, the franchisor's knowledge-based trust leads the franchisor to believe that the franchisee's positive experience with another brand can be transferred to the franchisor's brand. Furthermore, general trust leads franchisors to perceive zero or very low agency and monitoring costs related to the governance of franchisees working with another brand. Hence, with MUF networks, the franchisor's general trust coupled with the positive experience the franchisor has of managing his or her franchisees (knowledge-based trust) means that the franchisor grants franchisees licenses to run new franchise outlets. Finally, franchisors with a high level of general trust and a low or non-existent level of knowledge-based trust will tend to build franchisee-investor networks whereby investors hand over the running of their outlets to other franchisees.

As previously discussed, the franchisor's level of general trust positively affects franchisees who open additional outlets with different franchisors. Conversely, any franchisor who uses purely contract-based governance with franchisees who work with more than one franchise brand is exposed to the risk of losing the trust of these franchisees (Quinn & Doherty, 2000). Franchisors should therefore refrain from using coercive tactics to influence franchisees because such approaches harm the franchisor-franchisee relationship (Tikoo, 2002; 2005).

Environmental uncertainty must not be overlooked in the franchisor-franchisee relationship. Under high uncertainty pressure, the effect of trust and contracts on business performance may vary (Wang et al., 2011). In a context of uncertainty, it is more difficult to predict and provide for all eventualities. Even though the contract may provide for certain outcomes in the future, these provisions alone are insufficient to ensure the contract adapts to the changing environment throughout the course of the relationship (Luo, 2002).

In a turbulent environment, therefore, trust may offer way of overcoming the disadvantages of an inflexible contract-based governance mechanism. Dyer and Singh (1998) argue that as a self-enforcing safeguard, the presence of trust between business partners based on mutual commitment and shared values is more effective and less costly than creating a contract. Trust provides the flexibility to cope with inevitable uncertainties that arise in a long-term exchange. This flexibility helps mitigate exchange hazards under uncertainty and strengthens bilateral commitment to exchange-specific investments (Luo, 2002). Just as contracts affect relationship performance, the trust between business partners directly affects relationship performance (Liu et al., 2009) and financial performance (Laaksonen, Jarimo, & Kulmala, 2009).

Method, sample and variables

Method

To achieve the aforementioned research aims, the empirical study examined the financial behavior of franchisees operating outlets of a beauty industry franchise in the Spanish market between 2008 and 2015.

From an important franchisor, the empirical data from a sample of 113 franchisees were collected. By means of a Self-Organizing Map (SOM), an unsupervised training algorithm belonging to the artificial neural networks, we create a bi-dimensional map of franchisees based on the franchisees' financial statements. In this map, franchisees with the same financial situation will be placed close allowing the identification of different groups or clusters of franchisees. This first analysis can help the franchisor to identify which franchisees display financial problems or which are the most solvent. Thus, a high volume of information is summarized in a visual way. Then, once the clusters had been detected, we assessed how the different governance mechanisms applied by No+Vello are present in each of the previous established groups.

Self-organizing map (SOM)

Neural networks (NNs) represent one of the most widely used groups of models among all intelligence techniques. NNs have mathematical and algorithmic elements that mimic the biological neural networks of the human nervous system. NNs thus share similarities with the functioning of the human brain (Kohonen, 1990). NNs represent a powerful set of algorithms to find behavioral patterns (Moreno & Olmeda, 2007). Furthermore, they require no assumptions about the statistical distribution of the data, and they are not subject to the limitations of linear specifications, unlike many traditional techniques. NNs have been used extensively in business, management, marketing, production, and finance, among other fields. For example, NNs have been used to measure countries' investment risk, forecast market movements, detect failures of firms, and compute credit scores (Baesens, Gestel, Stepanova, Van den Poel, & Vanthienen, 2005; Becerra-Fernandez, Zanakis, & Walczak, 2002; Falavigna, 2012; Huang, Nakamori, & Wang, 2005). The powerful pattern classification capabilities applications of NNs made us to consider this approach in the paper where the previous applications in the franchising literature, however, are scarce.

An SOM is a kind of neural network. It is a non-supervised network that requires training. The network learns in an unsupervised way because there is

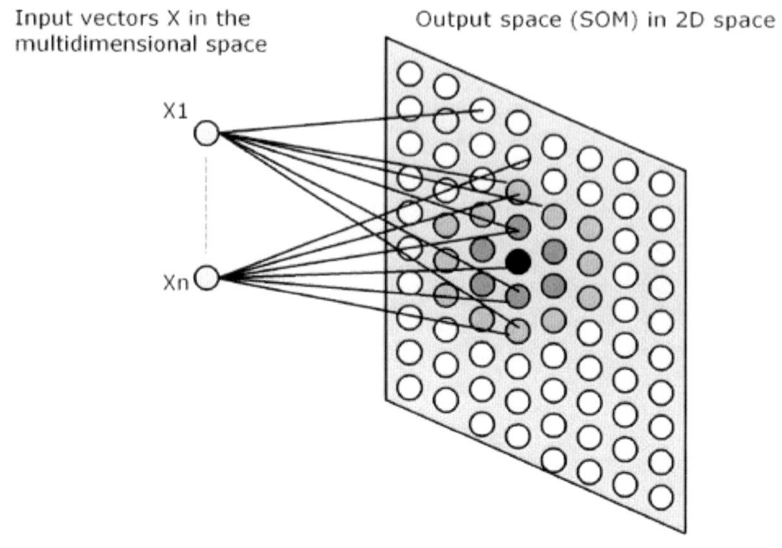

Figure 1. Graphical Representation of SOM
Source: Adapted from "The self-organizing map", by Kohonen (1990). In Procceding of the Institute of Electrical and Electronics Engineers (IEEE) Knowledge and Data Engineering Exchange, 78, 1464-1480.

no objective output. The network on its own discovers common patterns among the inputs. An SOM uses unsupervised competitive learning to form a nonlinear projection of a dataset in a reduced space while maintaining the original topology of the input space. One of the main advantages of SOMs is that they reduce the dimension of the original dataset to a bi-dimensional map in which the spatial configuration is closely linked to the statistical properties of the dataset. This means that regions that are close together in the SOM represent data that are very similar to one another in the original dataset. The converse is also true. Regions that are far apart from one another in the SOM represent data that differ greatly in the original dataset.

Figure 1 shows a graphical representation of an SOM. It can be viewed as a two-dimensional grid in which each cell in the input and output space array has a processing unit, called a neuron. Neurons of the input layer are connected to all the neurons of the output layer through synaptic weights. Consequently, the information provided by each neuron in the input layer is transmitted to all the neurons in the output layer. All the neurons in the output layer receive the same set of inputs from the input layer.

The objective of a competitive network like an SOM is to find the neuron in the output layer with the most similar synaptic weights to the values of the input layer neurons. To do so, each neuron calculates the difference between the input pattern and the set of synaptic weights of each output neuron. The winning neuron is the one with the smallest Euclidean distance between its weights and the set of inputs. The Euclidean distance is not the only measure to calculate the distance, but it is the most metric. The Euclidean distance between the neurons of the output layer and the vector of input patterns is calculated thus:

$$d_{i,j,(t)} = \sqrt{\sum_{h=1}^{k}\left(W_{i,j,h} - X_k\right)^2}$$

where X_k is the input of the k-input neuron and $d_{i,j,(t)}$ is the Euclidean distance of the (i,j) neuron in t corresponding to the input pattern for a network with i x j neurons in the output layer and k neurons in the input layer. The winning neuron is the one with the shortest Euclidean distance.

After determining the winning neuron, all neurons in the network receive an output equal to 0, except the winning neuron, which receives an output equal to 1. The weights of the winning neuron are later adjusted with a learning rule to proxy these weights to the input pattern that made the neuron win. The neuron whose weights are closest to the input pattern is thus updated so that the weights become even closer. The winning neuron is therefore more likely to win the competition in the next data entry if the input vector is similar, yet it is less likely to win if the input vector is different. Hence, the neuron becomes specialized in this input pattern.

The following equation proxies the weights of the wining neuron and the neighborhood function neurons:

$$W_{j,i,k}(t+1) = W_{j,i,k}(t) + \propto .\left(X_k(t) - W_{j,i,k}(t)\right)$$

where α is the learning ratio, $X_k(t)$ is the input pattern in t and $W_{j,i,k}(t)$ is the synaptic weight that connects the k input with the neuron (j,i) in t. The neighborhood function makes it possible to update the weights of the winning neuron and the neighbor neurons to localize similar patterns too. The neighborhood radius decreases with the number of iterations of the model to achieve a better specialization of each neuron.

The SOM model converges according to Gladyshev's theorem (Lo, Yu, & Bavarian, 1993). At the end of the training process, the SOM makes it possible to visualize the multivariate dataset in a two-dimensional graph, helping researchers infer topological relationships in the original dataset.

The model

The SOM Toolbox for MATLAB (Vesanto, Himberg, Alhoniemi, & Parhankangas, 2000) was used to train the SOM where the input data is the financial information for each of the different franchisees. Some parameters must be defined when training an SOM. Setting the size of the map or the number of units or neurons in the SOM is important. A common rule of thumb in the SOM Toolbox defines the number of units in the map as 5√N, where N is the number of observations in the dataset. Accordingly, the map in this study consisted of 54 units. We used a hexagonal grid sheet structure with the following default ratio for the side lengths: √(λ_1 / λ_2), where λ_1and λ_2 are the two largest eigenvalues of the autocorrelation matrix. The map units are connected to neighboring units on the grid by a Gaussian neighborhood function.

The data were normalized using logistic normalization (Pyle, 1999). Scaling the variables is especially important in SOM because the algorithm uses the Euclidean distance to measure the distances between vectors.

After it has been trained, the SOM creates a set of prototypes in a two-dimensional grid representing the original data. The SOM preserves the original topology, reducing data complexity. The aforementioned map with 54 units is then clustered into several groups of neurons with similar prototypes or low distances among the neurons. Detecting groups in the map helps assess patterns among the franchisees belonging to each group. The clustering process of the SOM can be performed quantitatively using a clustering technique taking into consideration the codebook or the final weights once the map has been trained. We used the K-means algorithm to cluster our trained map. K-means is one of the most well-known unsupervised algorithms because it is robust and easy to implement. Nevertheless, K-means requires the desired number of clusters to be established beforehand. We therefore ran the K-means algorithm nine times, setting the desired number of clusters each time to a different integer from 2 to 10. The Davies-Bouldin index (Davies & Bouldin, 1979) provided an indication of the best solution. The Davies-Bouldin index is a function of the ratio of within cluster variation to between cluster variation. The smaller the Davies-Bouldin index, the better the partition.

Sample and variables

This section provides an overview of the franchisor and the franchisee networks used in this paper. This section also describes the financial variables related to franchised outlets and the fees established in the franchise agreement.

The franchisor and franchisee networks: Data sample

The sector analyzed in this study is the Spanish beauty industry. A franchisor in this sector was chosen for three reasons. First, the franchisor uses both formal governance mechanisms (i.e., a contract) and a combination of formal and relational (i.e., trust) governance mechanisms because of the variety of franchisee networks within the franchise. Second, availability of financial data was good, with financial data available for 51.60% of the franchisees in the network. This constitutes a good sample size considering that the availability of financial data is one of the main limitations when the unit of analysis is the franchisee. Third, the chosen franchisor runs a major national and international franchise in the beauty sector. No+Vello is the world leader in intense pulsed light (IPL) treatments. The brand started in Spain in 2007 and registered as a franchise in 2008. No+Vello is now present in 13 countries and has more than 1,000 outlets. Spain has more outlets than any other country (219).

At the time of the study, the franchise had the following franchisee networks: an SUF network with 154 franchisees who ran only one outlet; an MUF network with 60 franchisees who ran more than one outlet each, 2 of whom ran outlets for other brands from the fashion and sport sector; a cross-franchising network with 5 No+Vello franchisees who concurrently ran other franchised outlets for other brands from the fashion, hospitality, sport, and beauty sectors; and, finally, 1 franchisee who handed over the running of his or her 3 outlets to another No+Vello franchisee. According to the CEO of the brand, the latter case was exceptional. The situation arose because of the trust between the franchisees in question. The franchisee who handed over the running of his or her outlets was a franchisee-investor who lacked the time to run the outlets. This franchisee therefore requested assistance from another No+Vello franchisee, whom the franchisee trusted, to run the three outlets. The franchisee-investor payed a monthly fee to the franchisee in charge of running the outlets. The franchisor had no company-owned outlets, so we were unable to analyze the effectiveness of the dual distribution.

The franchisor applies only formal governance mechanisms to the SUF network, whereas both formal and relational governance mechanisms are applied to the MUF, cross-franchising, and franchisee-investor networks. The sample comprised 113 franchisees belonging to the aforementioned franchisee networks. The sample was chosen based on the availability of financial and contractual data for the franchised outlets. The SABI database provided the financial data, while the franchisor provided the contractual data. All 113 outlets were operating in Spain under formal and relational governance mechanisms. The franchise had franchised outlets in other countries, but no such outlets were included in the sample. Therefore, in addition to applying formal governance mechanisms, the franchise may also use relational mechanisms. This is because the specific know-how of the franchisor is tacit, so the franchise contract is incomplete, forcing the franchisor to delegate decision rights to the franchisee on account of the intangibility of the franchisor's know-how.

Description of financial and contractual variables

The literature offers different methods of calculating performance (Kacker, Dant, Ermerson, & Couglan, 2016). In this study, seven financial ratios were calculated using the data available for 113 franchisees between 2008 and 2015. Although the database identification numbers were available for other No+Vello franchisees, the financial data were not. Many franchisees are self-employed, so they are not obliged to file their financial statements with the regulatory authorities. Table 1 gives a description of the most common ratios used in the literature to profile a company's finances and predict bankruptcies.

In addition to the financial data obtained from the SABI database, contractual data regarding franchisees was gathered from the franchisor (see Table 2). The additional data consisted of the following variables: initial investment, franchise fee, royalties, advertising fees, franchised outlet age, and province.

Half of the initial investment may be financed by the franchisor. The franchisee must return the amount within three years. The royalties for use of the brand, technical assistance, marketing, and training is a fixed amount that does not vary with sales. This amount has been updated regularly since 2014. Because the franchisor demands a fixed amount in royalties, he or she does not seem to safeguard against potential opportunistic behavior by franchisees. This feature suggests

Table 1. Financial Variables of Franchisees

Variable	Description
Earnings before interest and tax (EBIT) / financial expenses	Measures the franchisee's ability to make a profit. High ratios indicate greater solvency, taking into account the franchisee's debt structure.
Financial expenses / total assets	Measures the franchisee's level of debt. High values indicate high debt levels or high financing costs.
Equity / total assets	Measures the franchisee's leverage. High values indicate that most assets belong to the franchisee, not the creditors.
Cash and liquid assets / total assets	Measures the franchisee's ability to make short-term payment commitments.
Sales / current assets	Measures the franchisee's ability to generate sales revenues.
Return on total assets (%) (ROA).	Measures the ability of the assets of the franchisee's business to generate income for themselves.
Return on equity (%) (ROE).	Measures the return on the franchisee's own funds or the ability of the franchisee's business to repay the franchisee for any investment made.

Table 2. Contractual Variables of No+Vello's Franchisees

Variable	Definition
Initial investment	Initial amount paid by the franchisee to the franchisor to open a franchised outlet.
Franchise fee	The fixed up-front fee paid by the franchisee to the franchisor.
Royalties	The revenues paid in royalties by the franchisee to the franchisor.
Advertising fees	% paid for advertising campaigns led by the franchisor.
Franchised outlet age	Difference between the year of the financial statements and the date the outlet was opened.
Province	The Spanish province where the franchisee operates.

that the franchisor has general trust in the franchisees and that the contract is in some sense inflexible. The year that each outlet opened provides an indication of how old the outlet is and how well established in the marketplace it is. Table 3 presents the results of a preliminary descriptive analysis of the financial ratios for the sample to identify any anomalies in the data.

Discussion of results

Figure 2 shows the SOM and the clusters resulting from the K-means cluster analysis. As per the values for the Davies-Bouldin index, the optimal number of franchisee groups was three. These groups were labelled from 1 to 3 according to the financial profile of the franchisees in each group. Group 1 comprised the

Table 3. Descriptive Analysis

Financial Ratio	Mean	Std. Dev.	Min.	Max.	5th Pctl.	Lower Qtl.	Median	Upper Qtl.	95th Pctl.
EBIT / Financial expenses	-7.94	20.07	-109.82	25.01	-52.91	-8.46	-0.78	1.54	9.28
Financial expenses / Total assets	0.02	0.02	0.00	0.17	0.00	0.00	0.01	0.02	0.05
Equity / Total assets	-0.55	2.77	-18.14	0.96	-2.34	-0.30	0.05	0.27	0.54
Cash and liquid assets / Total assets	0.18	0.19	0.00	0.86	0.01	0.05	0.10	0.26	0.59
Sales / Current assets	8.33	9.17	0.26	55.75	0.62	3.15	4.63	10.45	28.08
Return on total assets (%) (ROA)	-0.27	102	-7.92	1.73	-1.05	-0.20	-0.02	0.02	0.15
Return on equity (ROE) (%)	-6.27	15.49	-109.90	8.89	-40.03	-5.32	-0.07	0.15	2.08

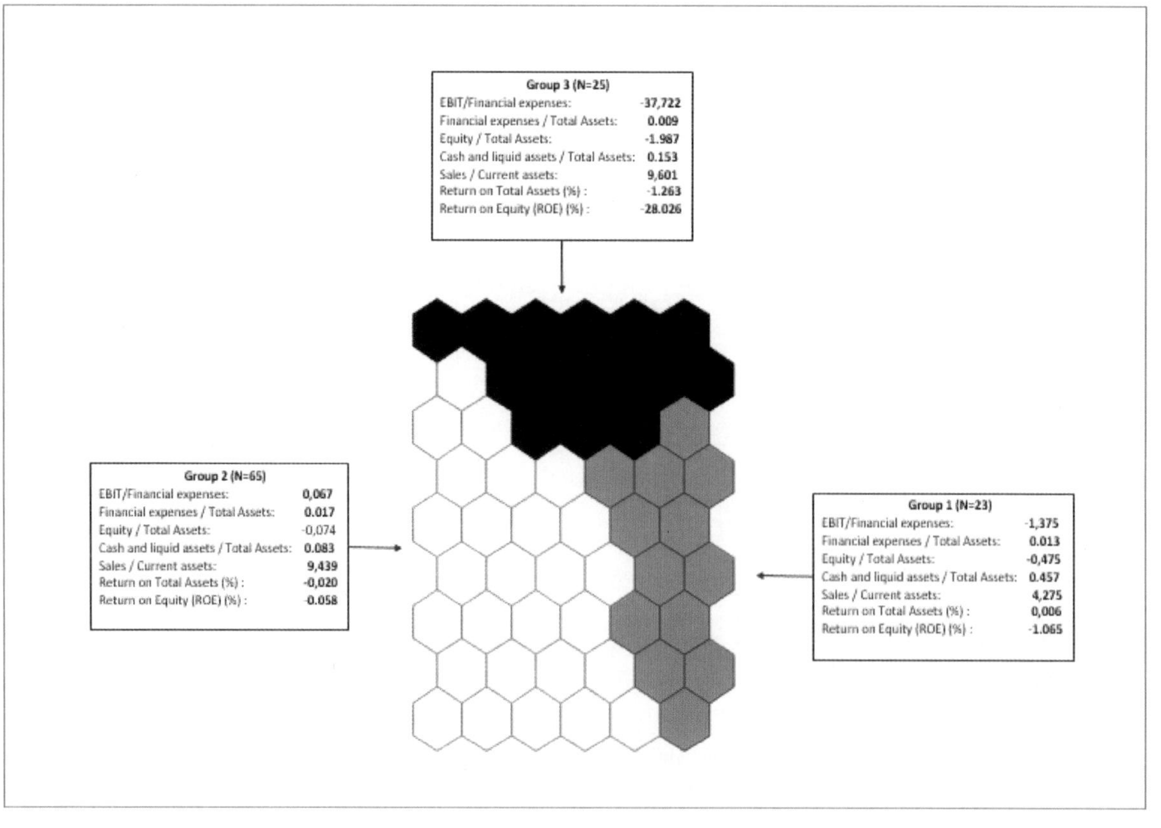

Figure 2. Franchisor SOM

Table 4. Average Values in Ratios and ANOVA Analysis by Group

Variables	Group 1	Group 2	Group 3	F-Stat	P-value
EBIT / Financial expenses	-1.38	0.07	-37.72	72.52	0.00
Financial expenses / Total assets	0.01	0.02	0.01	1.25	0.29
Equity / Total assets	-0.48	-0.07	-1.99	4.30	0.02
Cash + liquid assets / Total assets	0.46	0.08	0.15	99.33	0.00
Sales / Current assets	4.28	9.44	9.60	3.27	0.04
Return on total assets (%) (ROA)	0.01	-0.02	-1.26	17.88	0.00
Return on equity (%) (ROE)	-1.07	-0.58	-28.03	56.89	0.00

most solvent franchisees, whereas Group 3 comprised the franchisees in the weakest economic situation. This classification was based on the average values of the ratios for the franchisees in each group.

Table 4 shows the same mean values as in Figure 2. Table 4 also presents the results of the ANOVA, which was conducted to identify differences between clusters in terms of the mean values of the financial ratios. All ratios, except financial expenses/total assets (p-value > 0.05), were significantly different across groups for alpha = 0.05.

To better describe the characteristics of each group, Figure 3 shows the component planes (or heat maps). These maps show the values of one variable in each map unit. Blue colors represent low values, and red colors represent high values of the ratios. These maps visually represent the main characteristics of the groups. Moreover, by comparing the pattern of shaded map cells in each map, it is possible to analyze the relationships between variables.

Comparing the cells representing Group 1 in Figure 2 (i.e., the right-hand cells of the map) with the cells in the component planes yielded information regarding the characteristics of franchisees in Group 1. For instance, franchisees in Group 1 had high values for the ratios EBIT to financial expenses, equity to total assets, ROA, and ROE. This group of franchisees had the most profitable businesses. This group of franchisees also had good liquidity in terms of the ratio of cash and liquid assets to total assets. This group comprised 22.13% of the franchisees in the sample.

The cells representing Group 2 (i.e., the left-hand cells of the map) had lower values than the cells representing Group 1 for the aforementioned ratios in Table 4. One of the main differences among the three groups in Table 4 can be found in the financial expenses to total assets ratio. Franchisees in Group 2 had high levels of debt, which consumes a considerable amount of their businesses' total revenue. This group comprised 57.52% of the sample.

Finally, the franchisees in Group 3 had solvency problems. Some franchisees in Group 3 had negative net profits, high levels of debt, and poor liquidity. Despite these problems, franchisees in Group 3 had high sales to current assets ratios. This ratio measures the efficiency with which the franchisees use their assets to generate sales revenue. Businesses with low profit margins often have high values for this ratio usually because of strong price competition. This group comprised 20.35% of the sample.

As it can be seen, SOM provides a useful tool for a franchisor in order to assess in the solvency or the performance of its franchisees in a visual way. After analyzing the financial behavior of the franchisees, we analyzed whether the patterns we observed were linked to any one of the franchise networks described in the method section. Table 5 shows that most SUF franchisees were in Group 2. High debt was the main characteristic of these franchisees. Franchisees in the MUF network, however, were in the worst financial situation (Group 3). Franchisees in the cross-franchising network had the best financial profile (Group 1).

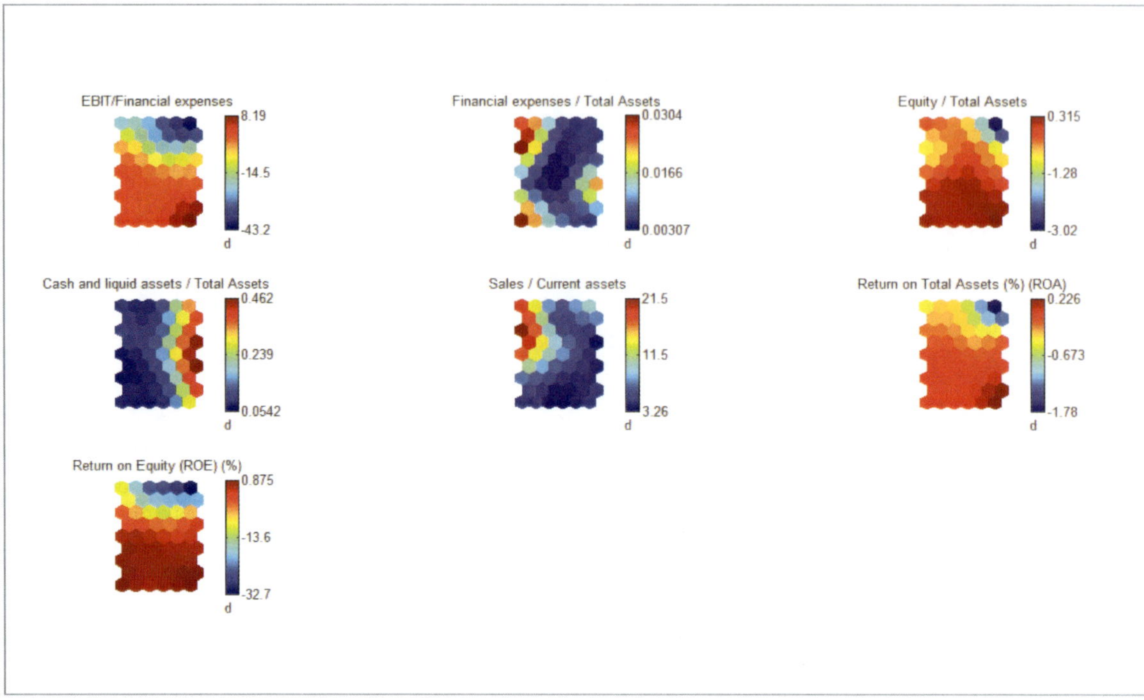

Figure 3. SOM by Variables

To analyze the effect of governance mechanisms on franchisees' financial performance, we calculated the means of each contractual variable for each group of franchisees (see Table 6) and for each type of network (see Table 7). According to the data in Table 6, the age of the franchised outlet seems to determine which group each franchisee belongs to. The longer franchisees had been operating franchised outlets, the healthier their financial profile.

Table 7 shows that the age of the franchised outlet also determines which network the franchisee belongs to. Franchisees in the SUF network had the franchised outlets that had been operating for longest. The SUF network is the most traditional and most common type of franchise network. The franchisor started with this franchisee network before building other franchisee networks governed by relational governance mechanisms. SUF franchisees had, on average, made the greatest initial investment and paid the highest advertising fees. The contractual differences between the SUF and MUF networks were small, the only difference being in terms of royalties, which were higher in the MUF network.

The greatest differences were observed for the cross-franchising network. The franchisor seems to impose less rigorous contract demands than those imposed upon franchisees in the other two franchisee networks. The fixed up-front fee was omitted from Table 7 because, unlike the other fees, it did not change between 2008 and 2015.

The time frame of the study (2008–2015) spanned the period during which the effects of the global economic downturn were causing widespread uncertainty in markets around the world (see Tables 8 and 9). Between 2008 and 2009, most franchisees fell into Group 2. Franchisees in Group 2 (SUF) had large debt levels. At that time, these franchisees had not yet been able to recover the large investments demanded by the franchisor because the franchise had only just been established. Only 14.29% of the franchisees were in the weakest group. Over the next four years, however, the effects of the economic crisis in Spain saw many franchisees move from Group 1 (mainly cross franchising) to Group 2 in 2010 and 2011. The economic situation for the franchisees worsened in 2012 and 2013, with the proportion of franchisees in Group 3 reaching its

Table 5. Franchisees' Financial Profile by Franchise Network

Network	Group 1	Group 2	Group 3
SUF	19.12%	70.59%	10.29%
MUF	22.86%	34.29%	42.86%
CROSS-FRANCHISING	40.00%	50.00%	10.00%

Table 6. Contractual Variables by Franchisee Group

Group	Initial investment (€)	Royalties (€)	Franchise fee (€)	Franchisee outlet age (years)
1	12715.38	330.00	1907.32	5.40
2	9600.00	343.86	1931.84	3.20
3	10304.35	342.16	2208.17	2.52

Table 7. Contractual Data by Type of Franchise Network

Network	Initial Investment (€)	Royalties (€)	Advertising fee (€)	Franchisee outlet age (years)
SUF	12617.65	330.67	2013.76	5.28
MUF	10757.14	346.13	2001.26	3.00
CROSS-FRANCHISING	6900.00	331.58	1608.00	2.50

Table 8. Evolution of Franchisees' Financial Profile (2008–2015)

Group/Period	2008–2009	2010–2011	2012–2013	2014–2015
Group 1	35.71%	17.24%	18.92%	26.67%
Group 2	50.00%	72.41%	54.05%	46.67%
Group 3	14.29%	10.34%	27.03%	26.67%

Table 9. Matrix of Migration between Groups

Group T \ Group T+1	Group 1	Group 2	Group 3
Group 1	73.68%	21.05%	5.26%
Group 2	2.04%	89.80%	8.16%
Group 3	12.50%	25.00%	62.50%

Table 10. Geographical Distribution of Franchisees by Group

Province	Group 1	Group 2	Group 3
Almeria	4	0	0
Badajoz	0	4	1
Barcelona	5	0	5
Cadiz	0	1	5
Ciudad Real	0	6	0
Girona	3	10	1
Gipuzkoa	3	0	0
Huelva	0	2	1
Balearic Islands	0	12	0
Las Palmas	0	0	1
Madrid	3	16	7
Malaga	0	0	2
Tenerife	5	0	0
Seville	2	9	0
Zaragoza	0	5	0
Total	25	65	23

peak (27.03%). Between 2014 and 2015, the economic situation improved, and the number of franchisees in Groups 1 and 2 rose accordingly. At this time, the franchisor updated some of the financial clauses applicable to the franchisees.

Table 9 shows the results of a complementary analysis. The table provides a matrix of migration among groups. This table indicates one-year group migration probabilities based upon available data. For example, a franchisee in Group 1 had a 21.05% chance of moving to Group 2 after one year, whereas 73.69% of the franchisees in Group 1 remained in the same group the next year. Group 2 was the most stable group, with 89.80% of franchisees remaining in that group. The percentage of franchisees remaining in Group 3 was 62.50%.

We also analyzed whether competition between franchisees located in the same province could have affected the franchisees' financial profile (see Table 10).

Madrid accounted for almost a quarter of No+Vello's franchised outlets. The next most populous provinces in terms of number of No+Vello franchised outlets were Gerona, the Balearic Islands, Seville, and Barcelona, although all of these provinces had considerably fewer outlets than Madrid. Girona had the highest proportion of profitable outlets, and Madrid had the lowest. In some provinces such as Almeria, Gipuzkoa, and Tenerife, all outlets were profitable. In contrast, all outlets were financially weak in Malaga, Cadiz, and Las Palmas. Nevertheless, the location of the franchisees did not appear to determine their financial profile.

Each of the sampled franchisees had one of three financial profiles, summarized below.

1. The franchisees with greatest solvency, profitability, and liquidity mostly belonged to the cross-franchising network, although some belonged to the SUF network. The analysis revealed that these

franchisees were efficient because they had the lowest employee cost as a percentage of operating revenues. Franchisees from the cross-franchising network were the newest members of the franchise and those who paid the smallest initial investment, royalties, and advertising fees. Although the small number of franchisees in Group 1 with just one outlet (SUF) paid more in initial investment, royalties, and advertising fees, by the time the study took place, they had had enough time to recover their investment and thus establish their businesses in the marketplace. They were located mainly in coastal provinces.

2. The franchisees with the highest debt levels were mostly in the SUF network. These franchise holders had been with the franchise less time than the other franchisees and had been required to pay the highest amounts in initial investment and advertising fees without recovering the investment. Franchisees in Group 2 were located in both inland and coastal provinces. This profile became more prevalent between 2010 and 2011 among franchisees who had previously run profitable operations. Franchisees in this group were the least likely to improve or worsen financially.
3. The franchisees with the lowest levels of solvency, profitability, and liquidity belonged to the MUF network. Large provinces had a high proportion of outlets in such a situation. The main differentiating characteristic of the franchisees with this profile was a high degree of efficiency in the use of assets to generate sales revenues. This efficiency is common among retail businesses because of heavy price competition, which leads to high volume and low margins. These were the most likely franchisees to improve their financial situation.

Conclusions, practical implications, and limitations of the study

The right application of contract-based governance mechanisms and/or trust-based governance mechanisms affects franchisee performance and consequently franchisor performance. A self-organizing map (SOM) visually classified franchisees into three groups. This classification is potentially highly useful for franchisors. Having many franchisees in the financially weakest group may damage the franchisor's solvency and future profitability. The franchisor can use this information to establish a governance policy with each franchisee to guarantee steady growth for both franchisor and franchisee.

The main conclusions are as follows. Franchisees in the MUF network were the least profitable. The financial behavior of these franchise holders negatively affected franchisor performance. Opening a second outlet soon after the first gave the franchisee insufficient time to become familiar with the brand and market, acquire experience, and establish the business. The franchisor had an excess of knowledge-based trust in MUF franchisees. When deciding whether to let a franchisee open a new outlet, the franchisor based his or her decision on knowledge acquired at the time the franchisee was originally selected. The franchisor failed to continue gathering knowledge about the franchisee as the relationship developed. Consistent with Gillis et al.'s (2011) findings, franchisees' reputations provide basic information to help franchisors assign new outlets to franchisees. These findings may counteract franchisors' tendency toward MUF based solely on the positive influence of knowledge-based trust in franchisees (Griessmair et al., 2014).

Franchise holders in the cross-franchising network had the best financial behavior, exerting a positive influence on franchisor performance. The franchisor's trust as an informal governance mechanism led to this financial behavior by franchise holders in the cross-franchising network. These franchisees were the least controlled by formal mechanisms (i.e., contracts) because the franchise agreement demanded a smaller investment than that required of other franchisees. Among these franchisees, general trust had a greater weight than knowledge-based trust because they had been operating franchised outlets for the shortest time, yet they had been allowed to open outlets with another brand despite the moral hazard involved.

Finally, most SUF franchisees ran financially inefficient outlets, thereby negatively affecting franchisor performance. The use of a contract as the only mechanism of formal governance applied by the franchisor to govern the relationship led to this financial behavior by SUF franchisees. The franchisor failed to make the financial clauses of the SUF agreement flexible enough and did not update the clauses when the economic context changed. The franchisor seems not to have modified the contract in accordance with the franchisees' environment despite the recent period of economic uncertainty in Spain. Using the contract as the only governance mechanism does not positively affect the franchisees' performance—and consequently franchisor performance—unless the contract is tailored to each franchisee's situation. Hence, a contract alone is insufficient to make franchised outlets in an SUF network profitable. An SUF network would be profitable, however, if some relational governance mechanism were applied to foster the relationship and were tailored to the situation of each franchisee. Finally, environmental uncertainty affected the financial behavior of the franchisees and thus of the franchisor; the location of the outlets, their size, and the local weather did not.

These conclusions have general implications for franchisors with franchisees spread across several franchisee networks. The SOM method trained a model that allows the franchisor to predict the financial behavior of potential franchisees based on the profiles described in this paper, thereby minimizing the scope for error when selecting franchisees. Franchisors can visually analyze the financial status of their franchisees and make the contract more flexible, modifying clauses to adapt to each franchisee's situation. Franchisors can thus choose whether to use contracts or trust (or a combination) as the governance mechanism depending on any potential franchisee's profile. The main practical implications of the study are as follows. The franchisor should prevent franchisees in the MUF network from opening new outlets in the same city and competing for the existing outlet's customers. Because the same franchisee operates both outlets, he or she has no incentive to act aggressively and gain market share. In addition, the franchisor should not let MUF franchisees open new outlets simply because their existing outlets are profitable. It is also advisable to have a good knowledge of other personal characteristics of the franchisee.

This study has limitations. The first limitation concerns the data source used to gather the financial data on the franchisees, who are organized into several different franchisee networks. For instance, we encountered difficulties in gathering financial data for franchisee-investors who do not operate their own outlets. Furthermore, many franchisees were self-employed, so they were not required to file their financial statements with the regulatory authorities. Second, the study examined only one franchisor's relationship with franchisees. The study could be enriched by considering another franchisor-franchisee relationship in a different sector. This limitation nonetheless presents an opportunity for further research.

References

Adler, P. (2001). Market, hierarchy, and trust: The knowledge economy and the future of capitalism. *Organization Science, 12*(2), 214–234.

Baesens, B., Gestel, T. V., Stepanova, M., Van den Poel, D., & Vanthienen, J. (2005). Neural network survival analysis for personal loan data. *Journal of the Operational Research Society, 56*(9), 1089–1098.

Becerra-Fernandez, I., Zanakis, S. H., & Walczak, S. (2002). Knowledge discovery techniques for predicting country investment risk. *Computers and Industrial Engineering, 43*(4), 787–800.

Bradach, J., & Eccles, R. (1989). Price, authority, and trust: From ideal types to plural forms. *Annual Review of Sociology, 15*, 97–118.

Cavusgil, S. T., Deligonul, S., & Zhang, C. (2004). Curbing foreign distributor opportunism: An examination of trust, contracts, and the legal environment in international channel relationships. *Journal of International Marketing, 12*(2), 7–27.

Davies, D. L., & Bouldin, D. W. (1979). A cluster separation measure. Proceding from IEEE transactions on pattern analysis and machine intelligence PAMI, *1*(2), 224–227.

Dyer, J. H., & Singh, H. (1998). The relational view: Cooperative strategy and sources of inter-organizational competitive advantage. *Academy of Management Review, 23*(4), 660–679.

Falavigna, G., (2012). Financial ratings with scarce information: a neural network approach. *Expert Systems with Applications 39*(2), 1784–1792

Geringer, J. M., & Hebert, L. (1989). Control and performance of international joint ventures. *Journal International Business Studies, 20*(2), 235–254.

Geysken, I., Steenkamp, J., & Kumar, N. (1998). Generalizations about Trust in Marketing Channel Relationships Using Meta-Analysis. *International Journal of Research in Marketing, 15*(3), 223–248.

Ghoshal, S., & Moran, P. (1996). Bad for practice: A critique of the transaction cost theory. *Academy of Management Review, 21*(1), 13–47.

Gillis, W. E., McEwan, E., Crook, T. R., & Michael, S. C. (2011). Using tournaments to reduce agency problems: The case of franchising. *Entrepreneurship Theory and Practice, 35*(3), 427–447.

Gorovaia, N., & Windsperger, J. (2013). Determinants of knowledge transfer strategy in franchising: Integrating knowledge-based and relational governance perspectives. *Service Industries Journal, 33*(12), 1117¬1134.

Grace, A. R., Frazer, L., Weaven, S., & Dant, P. (2016). Building franchisee trust in their franchisor: Insights from the franchise sector. *Qualitative Market Research: An International Journal, 19*(1), 65-83.

Granovetter, M. (1985). Economic action and social structure: The problem of embeddedness. *American Journal of Sociology, 91*(3), 481–510.

Griessmair, M., Hussain, D., & Windsperger, J. (2014). Trust and the tendency towards multi-unit franchising: A relational governance view. *Journal of Business Research, 67*, 2337–2345.

Grünhagen, M., & Mittelstaedt, R. A. (2005). Entrepreneurs or investors: Do multi-unit franchisees have different philosophical orientations? *Journal of Small Business Management, 43*(3), 207-225.

Gulati, R. (1995). Does familiarity breed trust? The implications of repeated ties for contractual choice in alliances. *Academy of Management Journal, 38*(1), 85–112.

Hendrikse, G., Hippmann, P., & Windsperger, J. (2015). Trust, transaction costs and contractual incompleteness in franchising. *Small Business Economics, 44*(4), 867¬888.

Herz, M., Hutzinger, C. L., Seferagic, H., & Windsperger, J. (2016). Trust, decision rights delegation, and performance: The case of franchising. *Journal of Small Business Management, 54*(3), 973¬991.

Huang, W., Nakamori, Y., & Wang, S. Y. (2005). Forecasting stock market movement direction with support vector machine. *Computers and Operations Research, 32*(10), 2513–2522.

Hussain, D., & Windsperger, J. (2013). A property rights view of multi-unit franchising. *European Journal of Law and Economics, 35*(2), 1–17.

Jap, S. D., & Ganesan, S. (2000). Control mechanisms and the relationship life cycle: Implications for safeguarding specific investments and developing commitment. *Journal of Marketing Research 37*(2), 227–245.

Jindal, R. (2011). Reducing the size of internal hierarchy: The case of multi-unit franchising. *Journal of Retailing, 87*(4), 549-562.

Kacker, M., Dant, R., Ermerson, J., & Couglan, A. T. (2016). How firm strategies impact size of partner-based retail networks: Evidence from franchising. *Journal of Small Business Management, 54*(2), 506-531.

Kohonen, T. (1990). The self-organizing map. In: Proceedings of the Institute of Electrical and Electronics Engineers (IEEE) *Knowledge and Data Engineering Exchange, 78*, 1464–1480.

Laaksonen, T., Jarimo, T., & Kulmala, H. I. (2009). Cooperative strategies in customer– supplier relationships: The role of interfirm trust. *International Journal of Production Economics, 120*(1), 79–87.

Liu, Y., Luo, Y., & Liu, T. (2009). Governing buyer–supplier relationships through transactional and relational mechanisms: Evidence from China. *Journal of Operations Management, 27*(4), 294–309.

Lo, Z., Yu, Y., & Bavarian, B. (1993). Analysis of convergence properties of topology preserving neural networks. In: Proceedings of the Institute of Electrical and Electronics Engineers (IEEE) T*ransactions on Neural Networks, 4*(2), 207–220.

Luo, Y. (2002). Contract, cooperation, and performance in international joint ventures. *Strategic Management Journal, 23*(10), 903–919.

Lusch, R. F., & Brown, J. R. (1996). Interdependency, contracting, and relational behavior in marketing channels. *Journal of Marketing, 60*(4): 19–38.

Macaulay, S. (1963). Non-contractual relations in business: A preliminary study. *American Sociological Review, 28*(1), 55–67.

Moreno, D., & Olmeda, I. (2007). Is the predictability of emerging and developed stock markets really exploitable? *European Journal of Operational Research, 182*(1), 436–454.

Mumdziev, N., & Windsperger, J. (2011). The structure of decision rights in franchising networks: A property rights perspective. *Entrepreneurship Theory and Practice, 35*(3), 449-465.

Nooteboom, B., J. Berger, & Noorderhaven, N. G. (1997). Effects of trust and governance on relational risk. *Academy of Management Journal, 40*(2), 308–338.

Poppo, L., & Zenger, T. (2002). Do formal contracts and relational governance function as substitutes or complements? *Strategic Management Journal, 23*(8), 707–725.

Pyle, D. (1999). *Data preparation for data mining*. San Francisco, CA: Morgan Kaufman.

Quinn, B., & Doherty, A. M. (2000). Power and control in international retail franchising: Evidence from theory and practice. *International Marketing Review, 17*, 354–372.

Rajab, T., Kraus, F., & Wieseke, J. (2013). Resolving conflict over salespeople's brand adoption in franchised channels of distribution. *Review Management Science, 7*, 443-473.

Ring, P. S., & Van de Ven, A. H. (1994). Developmental processes of cooperative interorganizational relationships. *Academy of Management Review, 19*, 90–118.

Shane, S. A. (1996). Hybrid organizational arrangements and their implications for firm growth and survival: A study of new franchisors. *Academy of Management, 39*(1), 216–234.

Tikoo, S. (2002). Franchiser influence strategy use and franchisee experience and dependence. *Journal Retailing, 78*, 183–192.

Tikoo, S. (2005). Franchisor use of influence and conflict in a business format franchise system. *International Journal Retail Distribution Management, 33*, 329–342.

Uzzi, B. (1997). Social structure and competition in interfirm networks: The paradox of embeddedness. *Administrative Science Quarterly, 42*, 35–67.

Vesanto, J., Himberg, J., Alhoniemi, E., & Parhankangas, J. (2000, April 20). SOM toolbox for Matlab 5. Helsinki: Helsinki University of Technology. Retrieved from http://www.cis.hut.fi/somtoolbox/package/papers/techrep.pdf

Wang, L., Yeung, J. H. Y., & Zhang, M. (2011). The impact of trust and contract on innovation performance: The moderating role of environmental uncertainty. *International Journal Production Economics, 134*, 114–122.

Weick, K. E., Sutcliffe, K. M., & Obstfeld, D. (2005). Organizing and the process of sensemaking. *Organization Science, 16*, 409–421

Windsperger, J. (2004). Centralization of franchising networks: Evidence from the Austrian franchise sector. *Journal of Business Research, 57*(12), 1361¬1369.

Williamson, O. E., (1991). Comparative economic organization: The analysis of discrete structural alternatives. *Administrative Science Quarterly, 36*(2), 269–296.

Yamagishi, T., & Yamagishi, M. (1994). Trust and commitment in the United States and Japan. *Motivation and Emotion, 18*, 129–166.

5

Assessing Outsourced Distribution Channels

Jan Vlachý[1]

ABSTRACT

We respond to recent failed initiatives of the Czech banking market to develop business models for the sale of retail deposit products, based on third-party distribution channels. We argue that the issue is the application of inappropriate capital budgeting methods. While static cost-benefit analysis seems to be generally appropriate for conventional banking projects based on branching or internet, they provide grossly misleading estimates of commissioning expenses, which can lead to completely unrealistic project assessments and poorly designed commission schedules. Alternatively, we derive a dynamic model based on statistical simulation (Monte Carlo) and using a real-life case study to illustrate the impacts of particular value drivers on commissioning costs. Our analysis shows that conventional and simulation-based budgeting generates inverse cost functions over time, and the difference becomes operationally tangible in the second and third year of the project, which is commensurate with the apparent timing of the bank's business strategy revisions. To fulfill the goal of this paper, we demonstrate that statistical simulation is an expedient tool for managerial support and capital budgeting in cases where value drivers are impacted by non-linear dynamic processes.

KEY WORDS: Consumer Banking, Capital Budgeting, Distribution Networks, Sales Outsourcing, Statistical Simulation

---

[1] Czech Technical University in Prague - Masaryk Institute of Advanced Studies, Czech Republic

Introduction

In recent years, a number of banks in the Czech Republic have considered opportunities to distribute their retail deposit products, in particular, popular interest-bearing saving accounts, primarily by means of independent sales force channels (Plhoň, 2010). Several new entrants to this segment of the market, namely, ING, mBank (a Commerzbank group unit) and AXA Bank, have actually chosen to set up their consumer banking businesses utilizing this approach. Such an approach is sometimes used in combination with existing tied insurance agents (ING, AXA), supplemented with internet sales and banking facilities (ING), or rudimentary branch and kiosk coverage (mBank).

Various arguments have been used to substantiate such proposals, commensurate with trends seen in other countries (Deloitte, 2014; Mas & Sladek, 2008; McDonald & Keasey, 2002; Omarini, 2015) and industries (Rogers, 2009). Sales forces ranging from large nationwide organized networks to local outfits and individual operators do exist and have been successfully

Correspondence concerning this article should be addressed to: **Jan Vlachý**, Czech Technical University in Prague - Masaryk Institute of Advanced Studies, Kolejní 2637/2a, Praha 6 160 00, Czech Republic. E-mail: jan.vlachy@cvut.cz

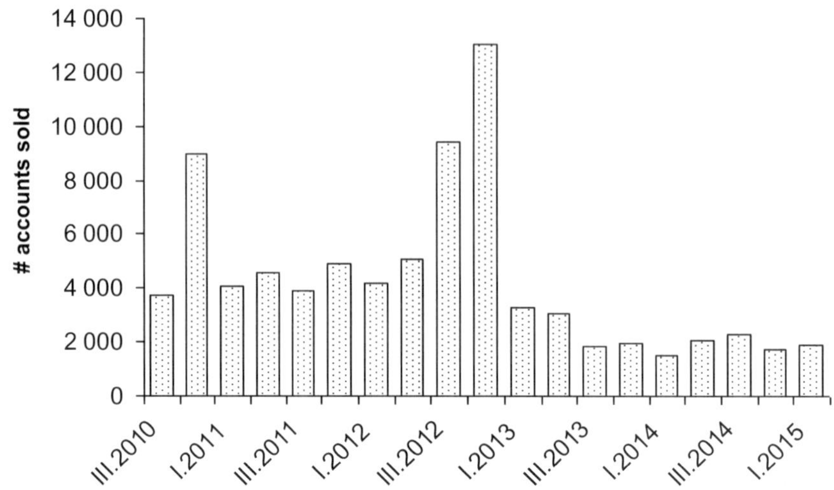

Figure 1. Development of saving account sales by third-party distributors
Source: Adapted from "Finančně poradenský trh [Market in financial consultancy]" by USF (2015). Retrieved from http://www.usfcr.cz/financne-poradensky-trh/

selling financial services and products in the country, thereby acting as an essential distribution vehicle primarily for insurance and pension fund policies as well as construction savings & loans and residential mortgages. The two existing industry associations, namely, Association of Financial Intermediaries and Financial Advisers of Czech Republic [AFIZ] and USF, which jointly represent 26 non-tied networks as well as cca 1,000 individual members, have published aggregate sales figures for 2014, showing that their combined memberships have negotiated 868 thousand contracts in a population of 10.5 million (AFIZ, 2015; Czech Statistical Office [CZSO], 2015; Union of Financial Mediation and Consulting Firms [USF], 2015).

A historically high level of concentration (Řepková, 2012; Schoenmaker & Peek, 2014) in Czech retail banking has also obliged late entrants and aspiring competitors to consider particular innovation strategies, such as specialization, cross-selling or co-branding (CNB, 2012).

Last but not least, outsourcing distribution may be thought to reduce operating leverage of a business project (Anderson & Trinkle, 2005; Helfert, 2001). The substantial fixed costs of branching or establishing dedicated in-house sales forces could thus be avoided, thereby mitigating aggregate business risk.

The present research has been motivated by the fact that regardless of its initial attractiveness, third-party distribution has not made the proven break-through its proponents anticipated. The bank that based its business solely on this model (AXA) wound up closing in December 2013, just three years after its inception, due to gross underperformance (Skalková, 2013). Overall, country-wide sales figures for savings accounts by non-tied distributors had essentially collapsed by mid-2013, as illustrated by Figure 1, reaching a meager 7,586 accounts in 2014, compared to 31,759 in the peak year of 2012 (AFIZ, 2015; USF, 2015); however, total household deposits grew during that same period (CNB, 2015).

The goal of this paper is to design a model suitable for the assessment of a capital budgeting project comprising third-party distribution, consider its practical viability and ease of use; furthermore, the goal is to use an actual business case to test the performance of such a model. Initially, the case will be parametrized and analyzed using conventional budgeting methods, which will show their weaknesses. Consequently, a stochastic model will be developed and applied to properly grasps the dynamics of the problem and provide more realistic results. The quantities and parameters used will be fundamentally based on components of the AXA business case as developed in 2009, making results relevant for further conclusions.

To design the model, we shall use statistical simulation, sometimes called the Monte Carlo method because of its purported inspiration from the casino game, roulette (Metropolis, 1987; Eckhardt, 1987). This particular technique of numerical mathematics has been initially developed by researchers on the Manhattan Project during World War II (Metropolis & Ulam, 1949) and has since become common for applications in a number of scientific and engineering disciplines (Halton, 1970; Mordechai, 2011; Richey, 2010), including, more recently, finance (McLeish, 2005).

From the theoretical point of view, the approach proposed in this paper is innovative because it directly addresses the dynamics of actual processes rather than just variations in banks' balance sheets, which have been analyzed in various contexts by scholars, including Rangarajan (1966), Gambs (1975), Hester and Pierce (1975), Gilkeson, List and Ruff (1999) and Kalkbrener and Willing (2004). The approach bears more resemblance to engineering-based applications such as quality control, which may also result in assessments of value drivers but is usually not used for financial services management (Chen, 2014; Hao, Zhao, Xu & Zheng, 2013; Ivy & Nembhard, 2005; Lesage & Dehombreux, 2015); this approach is also similar to evolutionary population algorithms (Mannion, Ruskin & Pandey, 2000; Mortier, Rossi, Guillot, Gourlet-Fleury & Picard, 2012).

Conventional Project Description and Analysis

The following situation will be examined: a commercial bank considers initiation of a retail saving account business as an independent stand-alone capital budgeting project. Market research indicates that the bank has potential to gradually attract up to 200 thousand accounts with the average initial balance amounting to 50 thousand crowns (CZK).

Financial projections have to be made over several years, and thus, it is necessary to define the number of accounts A_t and their average balance B_t as functions of time. One may reasonably (Falta & Willett, 2013) choose the exponential function (1)

$$(1) \quad A_t = A\,(1 - e^{-\alpha t}),$$

converging towards the target number of accounts A at the rate α, with the initial average balance B_0 growing at the rate β according to (2)

$$(2) \quad B_t = B_0\, e^{\beta t}.$$

A quarterly breakdown of the bank's business plan over eight years, based on assumptions of A = 200,000, B_0 = CZK 50,000, α = 0.4, and β = 8% would then imply a development of total deposits as indicated in Table 1.

A pro forma budget of such a business can then be set up using customary cost-volume-profit analysis, with some elements of the activity-based costing approach (Drury, 2004; Soin and Scheytt, 2008).

We estimate (all estimates have been based on calibrated Delphi panel evaluations and budgetary assumptions) a constant annual interest margin of μ = 1.25% p.a., fixed overheads of CZK 50 mil./yr., and annual direct costs χ = 0.50% of total deposits, requiring an initial investment of CZK 30 mil. for the conventional (branching) strategy. Assuming a discount rate of 10%, the project has a net present value NPV = CZK 87.7 mil. over the eight-year horizon, assuming a null terminal value. It will be expected to achieve operating profitability in 2.1 years and (non-discounted) break even in 4.8 years.

$$(3) \quad F + C_B \geq R - P.$$

Using total deposits as the key value driver, numerical simulation suggests a linear relationship between percentage changes in NPV and D with sensitivity $\Delta NPV / \Delta D$ = 4.4 (i.e., a 1% decrease in D results in a 4.4% decrease in NPV). Break-even would thus be reached upon a comprehensive 22.5% drop in projected D.

Table 1. Total deposits projection (conventional budgeting)

i	**0**	**1**	**2**	**3**	**4**	**5**	**6**
t [yrs]	0.00	0.25	0.50	0.75	1.00	1.25	1.50
D_i [CZK mil.]	0	971	1,887	2,752	3,571	4,349	5,087
i	**7**	**8**	**9**	**10**	**11**	**12**	**13**
t [yrs]	1.75	2.00	2.25	2.50	2.75	3.00	3.25
D_i [CZK mil.]	5,791	6,462	7,105	7,721	8,313	8,884	9,435
i	**14**	**15**	**16**	**17**	**18**	**19**	**20**
t [yrs]	3.50	3.75	4.00	4.25	4.50	4.75	5.00
D_i [CZK mil.]	9,969	10,487	10,991	11,483	11,964	12,436	12,899
i	**21**	**22**	**23**	**24**	**25**	**26**	**27**
t [yrs]	5.25	5.50	5.75	6.00	6.25	6.50	6.75
D_i [CZK mil.]	13,356	13,807	14,253	14,695	15,134	15,571	16,007
i	**28**	**29**	**30**	**31**	**32**		
t [yrs]	7.00	7.25	7.50	7.75	8.00		
D_i [CZK mil.]	16,442	16,878	17,314	17,752	18,192		

The conclusions from such an analysis are straightforward. The project is deemed to be acceptable based on the positive *NPV* criterion, provided sales targets are met. Admittedly, there does exist a residual interest margin risk (with the break-even interest margin being 1.08% p.a.), requiring caution in terms of pricing strategy and competition benchmarking, but this can serve as further argument for a sales-driven business approach.

Third-Party Distribution Project Analysis

Distribution utilizing third parties (agents) diminishes the project's leverage and thus its financial risk by reducing the required initial investment and overheads. Instead, commissions are paid based on actual sales performance, and part of the business risk is thus borne by the third parties.

Ideally, the bank's and agent's commercial interests would be coupled by deriving the commissioning schedule from the product's main value driver, i.e., the balance of current deposits. Thus, at the end of every year, the average balance on an account would be calculated, and the bank would pay the agent a fixed percentage therefrom. Commission expenses would become the prevailing direct costs of conducting business.

Let us assume that using third-party distribution, overheads would drop by 80% to just CZK 10 mil./yr., the remaining assumptions/parameters remaining unchanged. Retaining the *NPV* of the branching strategy allows for total annual direct costs of 0.77%, which means that the bank would be in a position to offer its agents' commissions up to 0.27% of current deposits. Thus, the bank would still project *NPV* = CZK 87.7 mil. but with substantially less risk, as indicated by the sales sensitivity ΔNPV / ΔD = 2.5 and its break-even point at -40.1% of sales.

Unfortunately, such a commissioning schedule is not viable. One reason is legal issues; due to banking secrecy, a third party cannot possibly obtain unmiti-

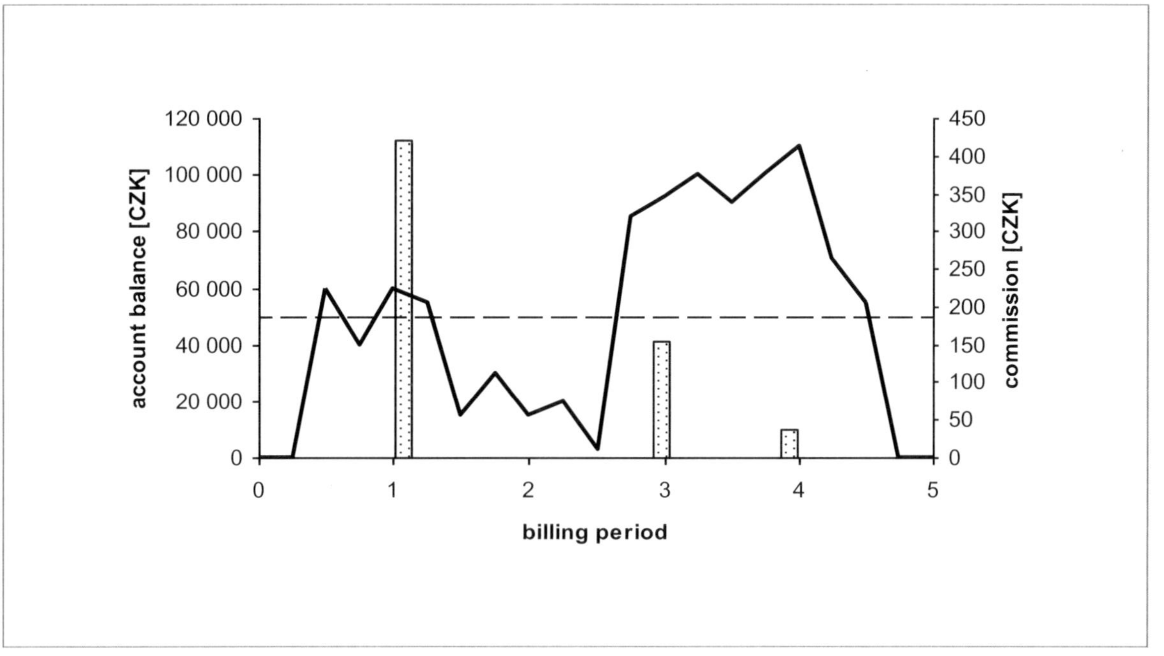

Figure 2. Impact of account volatility on commission cost

gated access to clients' account balances, which are necessary to properly reconcile the commissions claim. Another reason is that such a commissioning schedule goes against generally accepted industry practice, derived primarily from insurance sales, which represent most agents' primary source of income and conform to their rather myopic mode of operation, as well as to the needs of the multilevel structures characteristic for major networks.

It would simply not be worth the effort for most agents to acquire a banking client; for example, if the average account balance reached CZK 50,000, the agent would receive CZK 135 (just €4.90) in a year's time, even if there were an upside potential over the long term. In practice, the bank is only in a position to negotiate schedules comprising a flat commission (i.e., a finder's fee paid to the agent upon the opening of an account), a volume-based commission (i.e., a performance fee based on the deposit increment), or some combination of the two.

A major inconvenience of such an arrangement, however, stems from the fact that neither of these cost drivers translates directly into the total deposit value driver. It is therefore grossly misleading to use conventional-style budgeting for its analysis. To illustrate this point, the bank might conclude that under a flat-fee only system, it would pay total quarterly commissions amounting to the projected increase in the number of accounts multiplied by the flat fee rate (i.e., budget its total commission costs) as in (4)

$$(4)\quad \Gamma_i = (A_i - A_{i-1})\,\Pi.$$

This finding suggests a capacity to pay commissions of up to Π = CZK 1,400 per account, again using the *NPV* = CZK 87.7 mil. branch network-based benchmark. Such a figure actually seems competitive even when compared to commissions on products, which are generally much more profitable from the financial institutions' point of view. However, such reasoning is fundamentally flawed.

In particular, the net increment in the number of accounts includes account closings. Thus, more accounts have to be opened and paid for, which is a factor that becomes more significant in later years of the project. Making the same point from a different perspective, it seems unrealistic to run a sustainable business that would spend CZK 27 mil. on commissions in the first quarter, CZK 4 mil. in the 20th quarter and just over CZK 1 mil. in 8 years' time.

Similarly, if the bank were to choose a schedule based purely on net incremental deposits, its calculation could be based on (5)

(5) $\Gamma_i = (D_i - D_{i-1})\,\pi,$

allowing for performance fee rates up to π. = 1.66%. Again, such an intuitive approach would be incorrect, due to the volatility of saving accounts. Sooner or later, the balance on any account is due to decrease, and it is unrealistic to assume that most agents would be readily prepared to refund the bank based on its claim of realized "negative balance increments."

Let us further illustrate the issue by using a combined schedule of Π = CZK 300 and $\pi = 0.2\%$ and the average anticipated balance of CZK 50,000 deposited with the bank over the account's life. A naïve calculation would assume total commissioning costs on that account of CZK 400, consisting of a CZK 300 flat fee and a CZK 100 acquisition fee (CZK 50,000 × 0.2%). However, the actual account balance might develop e.g., as in Figure 2 (thick line, rather than the dashed line). Even though the average balance (i.e., source of revenue for the bank) remains unchanged, actual commission payments (graph columns) would total CZK 610 when all the pertaining billing periods (e.g., quarterly) are summed.

The essential weakness of the conventional budgeting approach thus stems from the fact that saving accounts tend to behave erratically, which strongly understates the budget whenever conventional, i.e., static analytical methods are used.

Statistical Modeling of Distribution Costs

Accordingly, an alternative mode to study and quantify the impacts of commissioning schedules on costs and performance, has been designed, using statistical simulation.

The model has been set up to perform a number of simulation runs, commensurate with the target number of accounts A or its multiples (i.e., $n = \mu A$ runs with μ set as a natural number). In the present case, we use $\mu = 1$, which, with $n = A = 200{,}000$, assures reasonable accuracy of the *NPV* estimate (mean error CZK 0.25 mil.), as well as processing times, when using specialized simulation software (Mun, 2006; Charnes, 2012).

Each simulation run represents the dynamics of a single account maintained with the bank over 32 quarterly periods (for the sake of process optimization, the same account can technically be used by different clients upon former clients' account closings, without loss of generality). Under this model framework, any client's modeled behavior is defined by three random processes characterizing the initial account balance (deposit), development of that balance over time, and the account-closing event.

Accounts are modeled so that their total number at the end of each period t fits the function $A_t = A\,(1 - e^{-\alpha t})$. This value thus grows asymptotically, in accordance with the business plan assumption, which facilitates calibration.

The initial deposit is characterized as a random value with mean B_t and standard deviation σ_B following a log-normal distribution, ensuring positive initial deposits. Again, there is an assumption of $B_t = B_0\,e^{-\beta t}$, calibrated against the business plan.

Intertemporal balance changes (until termination) on any given account db_i are described as a geometric diffusion process, defined by a stochastic differential function, where dw is generated as Gaussian random variable (testing the model on several alternative distribution functions, it has been shown not to be distribution-sensitive when calibrated on low-order moments). Therefore, the current balance always depends on the previous balance, a trend parameter β, and volatility σ according to the function (6)

(6) $db_i / b_i = \beta\,dt + \sigma\,dw.$

Ultimately, account closings are characterized as a Poisson process event, where the probability of closing an account within a period ΔT from its opening equals (7)

(7) $P(z) = \omega\,e^{-\omega\Delta T}.$

The point of time in which any particular account will be closed can then be determined using a standardized, uniformly distributed random number U using the inverted function (8)

Table 2. Functional and stochastic parameters of the simulation

A	200,000	B_0	CZK 50,000
α	0.4	β	8%
σ	50%	σ_B	CZK 30,000
ω	0.4		

Table 3. Project assessment variants

Distribution	Calculation	*NPV*	Oper. Break-even
Branches	Conventional	CZK 87.7 mil.	2.1 yrs
Third-party	Conventional	CZK 232.5 mil.	1.2 yrs
	Simulation (σ = 50%, ω = 0.4)	CZK 9.5 mil.	2.7 yrs
	Simulation (σ = 10%, ω = 0.4)	CZK 10.6 mil.	2.7 yrs
	Simulation (σ = 50%, ω = 0.2)	CZK 13.1 mil.	2.7 yrs

(8) $T = -\ln U / \omega.$

The impact of the account volatility factors, using parameters summarily listed in Table 2, can now be clearly illustrated and compared to the results of the static budgeting approach, assuming a commissioning schedule that combines Π = CZK 300 and π = 0,2%.

Conventional budgeting, as applied earlier, suggests an *NPV* = CZK 232.5 million, operating profitability in 1.2 years and break-even in just 3 years, which is clearly superior to the branching strategy. However, the use of simulation dramatically changes this result. With a projected *NPV** = CZK 9.5 million, it not only diminishes the project's perceived value substantially but also makes it even less valuable than branching.

These results and further simulations shown in the latter rows of Table 3 demonstrate that this fundamental conclusion is not particularly sensitive in terms of the model's stochastic parameters' estimation. Even extreme parameter adjustments result in simulated *NPV* ranging from CZK to 9.5 million to CZK 13.1 million, any of which would lead to reconsideration of the business plan in practice.

To illustrate the essential difference between the two analytical approaches used for assessing third-party distribution, Figure 3 compares the temporal development of total commission payments; the dashed line representing conventional budgeting and the full line representing smoothed simulation. While the former assumes that costs would decline, simulation correctly captures their growth in time.

Finally, even though the *NPV* calculations seem to suggest an inferior, but still positive result for third-party distribution, it should be emphasized that this business model induces an agency situation (Eisenhardt, 1989; Krafft, Albers, & Lal, 2004), which may lead to further deterioration due to perverse incentives of agents, a factor not specifically dealt with in this paper. Nevertheless, certain abuses, including openings of underperforming accounts and proselytizing of customers between different product providers, seem to thrive in insurance and mortgage sales (Mašek, 2015; Pokorný, 2014).

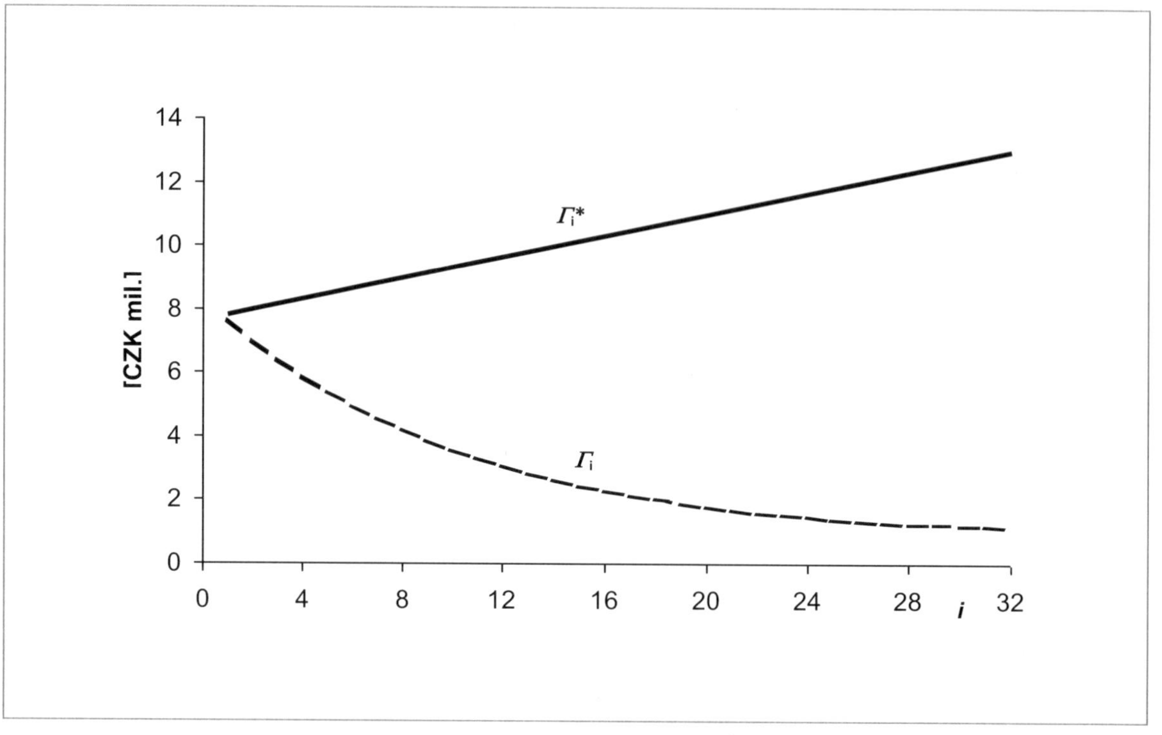

Figure 3. Commissioning costs projections

Conclusion

We have developed a model to solve a capital budgeting problem encountered by a bank intent on outsourcing its deposit-sales business. The resulting figures and, in particular, contradictory decision-making outcomes, clearly illustrate the inadequacy of conventional costing approaches and suggest the necessity of innovative solutions. More generally, we have shown statistical simulation to be a viable and comprehensive tool for managerial support and improved business projections wherever value drivers are impacted by non-linear dynamic processes. In contrast to conventional budgeting, simulation captures actual process dynamics, which provides much more realistic results.

In the context of actual market developments, where banks have not succeeded in meeting their commercial objectives, it is striking that conventional and simulation-based budgeting generate inverse cost functions in time. This discrepancy becomes manifest in the second and third year of the project, which is commensurate with apparent revisions of bank's business strategies in the Czech Republic.

Several contentious issues may arise with using the statistical simulation model, merited primarily by parametrization assumptions and lack of feedback, which may ignore potential agency problems. Additionally, quantitative methods tend to disregard sundry strategic considerations that are not explicitly embraced by the model, such as global positioning, brand development or cross-selling potential. However, statistical simulation does clearly outperform any form of conventional static analysis, due to its addressing the dynamics of the underlying processes.

In practical application, developing simulation models in the present context may serve several distinct purposes. In addition to improving financial projections used for capital budgeting, as shown in this paper, they may facilitate quantitative comparisons using various commission schedules and their sensitivities towards particular behavioral assumptions, as well as analyzing and quantifying the impacts of potentially effective and negotiable commercial measures such as counterparty segmentation, account-pool based commissioning or variants of deferred remuneration. Further development can possibly expand their role from that of an alternative to conventional capital budgeting to a comprehensive instrument of strategic decision-making in the area of distribution-channel management.

References:

Anderson, E., & Trinkle, B. (2005). *Outsourcing the sales function: The real costs of field sales*. Mason, OH: South-Western.

AFIZ. (2015). *Asociace finančních zprostředkovatelů a finančních poradců České republiky* [Association of financial intermediaries and financial advisors of the Czech Republic]. Retrieved from http://www.afiz.cz/data/pdf/VZ_2014.pdf

Charnes, J. M. (2012). Financial modeling with Oracle Crystal Ball and Excel (2nd ed.). Hoboken, NJ: John Wiley.

Chen, H. L. (2014). The application of statistical process control in the simulation experiment of distribution process capability analysis. *International Journal of Information Processing and Management*, 5(4), 106-113.

CNB. (2012, May 30). CNB opinion and answers to questions asked on the European Commission consultation material 'Green Paper on Shadow Banking'. Retrieved from http://ec.europa.eu/finance/consultations/2012/shadow/docs/contributions/public-authorities/czech-republic-national-bank_en.pdf

CNB. (2015). Zprávy o finanční stabilitě [Financial stability reports]. Available at http://www.cnb.cz/en/index.html

CZSO. (2015, May 1). Statistical Yearbook of the Czech Republic – 2015. Available at https://www.czso.cz/csu/czso/statisticka-rocenka-ceske-republiky

Deloitte (2014, March). Competition in retail banking. Sydney: Australian Bankers' Association. Retrieved from https://www2.deloitte.com/content/dam/Deloitte/au/Documents/Economics/deloitte-au-economics-retail-banking-competition-010314.pdf

Drury, C. (2004). *Management and Cost Accounting* (6th ed.). London, UK: Thomson.

Eckhardt, R. (1987). Stan Ulam, John von Neumann, and the Monte Carlo Method. *Los Alamos Science, 15*, 131-137.

Eisenhardt, K. M. (1989). Agency theory: An assessment and review, *Academy of Management Review*, 14(1), 57-74.

Falta, M., & Willett, R. J. (2013). The impact of exponential growth variables on regression models of the market-accounting relation. *Journal of Accounting, Auditing and Finance*, 28(3), 243-272.

Gambs. C. M. (1975). Interest-bearing demand deposits and bank portfolio behavior. *Southern Economic Journal*, 42(1), 79-82.

Gilkeson, J. H., List, J. A., & Ruff, C. K. (1999). Evidence of early withdrawals in time deposit portfolios. *Journal of Financial Services Research*, 15(2), 103-122.

Halton, J. H. (1970). A retrospective and prospective survey of the Monte Carlo Method. *SIAM Review*, 12(1), 1-63.

Hao, X., Zhao, H., Xu, Z., & Zheng, C. (2013). Population balance: Monte Carlo simulation for gas-to-particle synthesis of nanoparticles. *Aerosol Science and Technology*, 47(10), 1125-1133.

Helfert, E.A. (2001). Financial analysis: Tools and techniques. A guide for managers. New York, NY: McGraw-Hill.

Hester, D. D., & Pierce, J. L. (1975). Bank management and portfolio behavior. New Haven, CT: Yale University Press.

Ivy, J. S., & Nembhard, H. B. (2005). A modeling approach to maintenance decisions using statistical quality control and optimization. *Quality and Reliability Engineering International*, 21(4), 355-366.

Kalkbrener, P., & Willing, J. (2004). Risk management of non-maturing liabilities. *Journal of Banking and Finance*, 28(7), 1547-1568.

Krafft, M., Albers, S., & Lal, R. (2004). Relative explanatory power of agency theory and transaction cost analysis in German salesforces. *International Journal of Research in Marketing*, 21(3), 265-283.

Lesage, A., & Dehombreux, P. (2015). Simulation of manufacturing processes subject to maintenance and quality control. Sensitivity analysis and numerical example. *International Journal of Mechanical Engineering and Automation*, 2(3), 119-126.

Mannion, R., Ruskin, H. J., & Pandey, R. B. (2000). A Monte Carlo approach to population dynamics of cells in a HIV immune response model. *Theory in Biosciences*, 119(2), 145-155.

Mas, I., & Sladek, H. (2008, May). Banking through networks of retail agents (*Focus Notes* No. 47). Washington, DC: The Consultative Group to Assist the Poor. Retrieved from http://www.cgap.org/sites/default/files/CGAP-Focus-Note-Banking-Through-Networks-of-Retail-Agents-May-2008.pdf

Mašek, F. (2015, April 14). Výměna životních pojistek vynáší prodejcům miliardy [Switching life policies earns agents billions]. Hospodářské noviny, p. 7.

McDonald, O., & Keasey, K. (2002). The future of retail banking in Europe. Chichester, UK: John Wiley.

McLeish, D. L. (2005). Monte Carlo simulation and finance. Hoboken, NJ: John Wiley.

Metropolis, N. (1987). The beginning of the Monte Carlo method. *Los Alamos Science, 15*, 125-130.

Metropolis, N., & Ulam, S. (1949). The Monte Carlo method. *Journal of the American Statistical Association*, 44(247), 335-341.

Mordechai, S. (Ed.). (2011). *Applications of Monte Carlo in Science and Engineering*. The Hague: InTech.

Mortier, F., Rossi, V., Guillot, G., Gourlet-Fleury, S., & Picard, N. (2012). Population dynamics of species-rich ecosystems: the mixture of matrix population models approach. *Methods in Ecology and Evolution*, 4(4), 316-326.

Mun, J. (2006). Modeling risk: Applying Monte Carlo simulation, real options analysis, forecasting, and optimization techniques. Hoboken, NJ: John Wiley.

Omarini, A. (2015). Retail banking: Business transformation and competitive strategies for the future. London, UK: Palgrave Macmillan.

Plhoň, T. (2010, August 4). Češi mají spořící účty v oblibě i přes pokles úroků [Czechs like savings accounts regardless of declining interest rates]. *Ekonom*. Available at https://ekonom.ihned.cz/c1-45441220-ekonom-cesi-maji-sporici-ucty-v-oblibe-i-pres-pokles-uroku

Pokorný, F. (2014). *Praktiky finančních poradců* [Practices of financial advisors]. Praha: e-bohém.

Rangarajan, C. (1966). Deposit variability in individual banks. *National Banking Review*, 4(1), 61-71.

Řepková, I. (2012). Market power in the Czech banking sector. *Journal of Competitiveness*, 4(1), 143-155.

Richey, M. (2010). The evolution of Markov chain Monte Carlo methods. *The American Mathematical Monthly*, 117(5), 383-413.

Rogers, B. (2009). An exploratory study of the make-or-buy decision in pharmaceutical sales. *Journal of Medical Marketing*, 9(1), 11-20.

Schoenmaker, D., & Peek, T. (2014, January 27). *The State of the Banking Sector in Europe*. OECD: Economics Department (Working Paper No. 1102). OECD. Economic Department. Available at https://ssrn.com/abstract=2390645

Skalková O. (2013, May 23). Axa v Česku končí s bankou [Axa discontinues its bank in Czech]. *Hospodářské noviny*, p. 6.

Soin, K., & Scheytt, T. (2008). Management accounting in financial services. In C.S. Chapman, A. G. Hopwood, & M. D. Shields (Eds.), *Handbook of Management Accounting Research* (Vol. 3, pp. 1385-1395). Oxford, UK: Elsevier.

USF. (2015). Unie společností finančního zprostředkování a poradenství [Union of financial mediation and consulting firms]. Available at http://www.usfcr.cz/financne-poradensky-trh/

6

Director Training and Financial Disclosure: Asian Insights

Qaiser Rafique Yasser[1], Abdullah Al Mamun[2], Marcus Rodrigs[2]

ABSTRACT We provide evidence regarding the relationship between director training programs and improved financial reporting. Director Training Programs (DTP) help directors better understand the specific context in which a firm operates, including its operations and environment; awareness of business norms and values; standards of probity and accountability; and their fiduciary duties as an agent of investors. This study explores a recent requirement for director training and its effect on the quality of financial reporting for publicly listed companies in three eastern countries. This study examines the relationship between DTP and the quality of financial reporting of Australian, Malaysian and Pakistani publicly listed companies by using a sample of data from 2011 to 2013. We determined that Australian companies that incur additional DTP expenditures and have a flexible training schedule (Online DTP)improve their financial reporting quality and that a well-established DTP positively affects financial reporting quality in Malaysia. In addition, the results indicate that firm size negatively affects financial reporting quality in the Asia Pacific and older companies (firm age) suffer from low-quality financial reporting.

KEY WORDS: Director training, financial reporting quality

[1] University Malaysia Sarawak, Malaysia; [2]University of Newcastle - Newcastle Business School, Australia

Introduction

Recent accounting scandals in the international financial community have raised many concerns regarding the quality of periodical financial disclosures (Agrawal & Chadha, 2005; Bowen, Call, & Rajgopal, 2010). Several prominent companies have suffered from accounting fraud and incompetent management, including Enron, WorldCom, HIH Insurance, and Parmalat, which has weakened principals' (investors) confidence in Agents (directors)and the eminence of financial reports (Beekes & Brown, 2006; Brown & Caylor, 2006; Firth, Fung, & Rui, 2007; Karamanou & Vafeas, 2005; Petra, 2007). Now, more than ever before, directors must understand their fiduciary, legal and ethical responsibilities because the bar has been raised. Investors' confidence in corporations has reached an all-time low, and the role of directors has become even more challenging and demanding (Bowen et al., 2010; Easley & O'Hara, 2004; Grossman & Haskisson, 1998; Peasnell, Pope, & Young, 2005;). According to Sloan (2001), financial information is the first source of independent and factual communication regarding the

Correspondence concerning this article should be addressed to: **Qaiser Rafique Yasser,** University Malaysia Sarawak, Malaysia - FEB Kota Samarahan , Kuching 94300, Malaysia E-mail: qaiser_rafique1@hotmail.com

performance of a company and its directors, which makes financial reporting a primary indicator of management's control and proficiency.

Doh (2003) suggests that individuals can be taught how to engage in effective board leadership and systematic training programs affect organizations' leadership strategies (Barling, Weber, & Kelloway, 1996; Dvir, Eden, Avolio, & Shamir, 2002). Parry and Sinha (2005) investigate the effects of training and report a significant increase in leadership strategies and a significant effect on performance through the enhancement of transformational strategies (Dvir et al., 2002). In addition, leadership training significantly affects self-reported employee variables such as employee commitment (Barling et al., 1996) follower development (Dvir et al., 2002), satisfaction with leadership (Hassan, Fuwad, & Rauf, 2010) extra follower effort (Parry & Sinha, 2005) and certain objective performance measures (Barling et al., 1996). However, the impact of director training programs on the financial reporting quality is not well understood. Recently, the association between leadership characteristics and financial reporting quality has been discussed in developed countries. Emphasis was placed on specific governance mechanisms including insider domination of shareholding (Yeo, Tan, Ho, & Chen, 2002;), board independence (Beekes, Pope, & Young, 2004; Bradbury, Mak, & Tan, 2006; Petra, 2007), director shareholding (Sánchez-Ballesta & García-Meca, 2007) and the reputation of the auditing firm (Agrawal & Chadha, 2005). Recent studies have analyzed board attributes and financial reporting quality in rapidly growing emerging economies that have distinctive features of corporate control, capital allocation and regulations (Bradbury et al., 2006; Dimitropoulos & Asteriou, 2010; Firth et al., 2007).

Countries around the world are characterized by their corporate governance systems and scholars debate the efficiency, superiority and effectiveness of these systems. We use a dataset that includes large Australian, Malaysian and Pakistani firms; these three Anglo-Saxon countries have common characteristics in terms of their basic governance systems (La Porta, Lopez-de-Silanes, Shleifer, & Vishny, 1998). Prowse (1992) suggests that judgments are inherently subjective because of sparse evidence regarding the relative performance of different corporate governance systems. Existing studies have generally examined the effects of corporate governance characteristics of firms that operate in only one country on earnings management (Armstrong, Barth, Jagolinzer, & Riedl, 2010; Larcker, Richardson, & Tuna 2007; Yasser & Mamun, 2015). In this study, we seek to fill this gap in the extant literature.

This study seeks to analyze the following question: *Do the director training programs of publically listed companies affect the quality of their financial reporting?* To address this question, we built a dataset by collecting data from the Australian Stock Exchange, the Kuala Lumpur Stock Exchange and the Pakistan Stock Exchange. We empirically analyzed the effect of director training programs on earnings management by examining a sample of matched industrial companies that are listed on the stock exchanges of the sample countries. Data were collected from annual reports and when necessary, these data were complemented and crosschecked with the corporate websites of the sample companies. First, we provide a review of prior empirical studies, which is followed by our hypotheses, the method, the study results, a discussion, and the conclusion.

Review of Prior Studies and Hypotheses

Mole (2000) distinguishes between training, education and development and proposes that training focuses on the present job, education focuses on a future job, and development focuses on the organization. Although some of the more traditional modes of provision, particularly for formal management programs, seek to enhance skills and knowledge and adopt a training approach, the current trend focuses more on education and development as indicated by the following statement: "Development programs prepare individuals to move in the new directions that organizational change may require" (Mole, 2000, p. 22).

Professional development is an important topic that is related to the characteristics of top management because it is related to distinct patterns of decision makers' cognitive processes, attention and final decisions (Wiersema & Bantel, 1992). In addition, Hambrick and Fukutomi (1991) suggest that managers are generally engaged in complicated, ambiguous and information overloaded situations. This implies that managers operate within a finite model or paradigm despite making use of all of the available information. Long-tenured managers are fixated on this paradigm, which makes it difficult for them to pay a great deal of attention to outside sources of information.

Hambrick and Mason (1984) argue that the demographic characteristics of top management including experience, age, gender and tenure affect their values and cognitive bases, which subsequently affect their decision-making and choices, particularly in complex situations and ultimately result in different organizational outcomes. Bertrand and Schoar (2003) developed an innovative design to determine that managers' personal characteristics influence their investment or financial decisions after controlling for firm and time fixed effects. This methodology has been applied by other studies, including Bamber, Jiang, and Wang (2010), which demonstrated that executives' disclosure styles are related to their personal backgrounds. These scholars argue that older executives use a conservative disclosure style and finance and accounting managers use a more precise disclosure style.

Although numerous studies have examined whether financial reporting quality is influenced by various governance mechanisms, generally, the empirical evidence has been mixed (Armstrong et al., 2010). In addition, prior studies that examine managerial compensation and its impact on financial reporting have failed to produce consistent results. Furthermore, certain studies have determined that a negative relationship exists between directors' equity incentives and the quality of financial reporting (Bergstresser & Philippon, 2006; Cheng & Warfield, 2005; Efendi, Srivastava, & Swanson, 2007); however, certain studies were unable to confirm that a relationship exists between directors' equity incentives and the quality of financial reporting (Baber, Liang, & Zhu, 2012; Erickson, Hanlon, & Maydew, 2006) and other studies reported that a positive relationship exists (Armstrong et al., 2010).

Studies that have examined the effects of various features of boards of directors on financial reporting have determined that more independent boards are associated with higher quality reporting (Efendi et al., 2007; Klein, 2002); however, other studies provided little evidence that board independence has a significant impact on financial reporting quality (Agarawal & Chadha, 2005; Kim & Qi, 2010; Larcker et al., 2007). Although numerous factors may contribute to the mixed results that are reported by extant literature, the joint endogeneity of corporate governance and financial reporting represents perhaps the greatest challenge (Armstrong et al., 2010). In addition, a companies' selection of a particular governance mechanism is endogenously determined by numerous factors, including firm fundamental characteristics, information environments, other governance mechanisms, and managerial attributes.

Most prior studies regarding the quality of financial reporting have focused on firm characteristics and other environmental factors (Dechow & Dichev, 2002; Dechow, Ge, & Schrand, 2010). However, agency theory suggests that decision makers are affected by contractual incentives and an organization's monitoring mechanisms and growth (Decker & Calo, 2007; Hermalin & Weisbach, 1998;). Conversely, the upper echelons theory suggests that directors' demographic characteristics and skills are associated with their unique cognitive styles and values and affect the managerial decision-making processes (Hambrick & Mason, 1984; Hermalin & Weisbach, 2003). Bertrand and Schoar (2003) documented that executive's demographic characteristics affect their decision-making capacity and accounting policies. In addition, Bamber et al. (2010) and Dyreng, Hanlon, and Maydew (2010) suggest that executive-specific fixed effects reflect systematic differences in executives' disclosure styles and tax avoidance strategies.

Prior studies propose that executive training can be used to develop needed competencies and help companies' strategic personnel to succeed in their specific organizational contexts (Burke & Hutchins, 2007). The effectiveness of director training has been studied from three different perspectives: the effects of training on attitudinal outcomes of trainees (Howell & Frost, 1989), the effects of training on subordinates' task performance (Kirkpatrick & Locke, 1996) and the impact of training on financial outcomes (Barling et al., 1996).

Studies regarding the impact of training on skill development have demonstrated that this effect is stronger for technical training than more complex types of managerial training programs and the effects of training are more significant for skills that can be segmented into step-by-step routines than for soft skills (Hunt & Baruch, 2003). Training could amplify the benefits of learning routines if regular reviews of performance trends are conducted through performance analysis, problem solving, and oral communication skills. In addition, training may better leverage discretion by increasing management's capacity to diagnose and redesign processes or by facilitating the appropriate use of targets and incentives to motivate employees (Kim & Qi, 2010).

Executive training conveys basic information regarding reform and its requirements; simply knowing more about a reform may encourage employees to implement the reform. This type of declarative knowledge (information about something) is generally perceived as inferior to procedural or tacit knowledge (information about how or which, when, and why) (Aguinis & Kraiger, 2009). However, providing information regarding important reform concepts, changes to central processes and routines, and expectations and rewards appear to be related to fundamental lower-order conditions for behavioral change. Prior studies have examined the effects of various features of boards of directors on financial reporting quality, but the results are mixed. For example, certain studies determined that directors' financial expertise is associated with higher quality reporting (e.g., Klein, 2002; Efendi et al., 2007), but other studies were unable to confirm that directors' financial expertise had a significant impact on the quality of financial reporting (e.g., Agarawal and Chadha, 2005; Larcker et al., 2007). Therefore, we propose the following hypothesis:

Hypothesis: *Director training programs have a positive impact on financial reporting quality.*

Regulatory Framework for Director Training

A code of corporate governance is the primary regulatory framework for a company according to statutes that have been enacted to improve the governance practices of firms that operate in each of the sample countries. Guidelines for developing code of corporate governance for promoting Director Training Programs (DTP) for each of the sample countries are as follows:

- Malaysia
  The Malaysian revised code of corporate governance (2012) recommends that the board of directors ensures that its members have access to appropriate continuing education programs. In addition, the code of corporate governance should include the following:

  "In a dynamic and complex business environment, it is imperative that directors devote sufficient time to update their knowledge and strengthen their skills through appropriate continuing education programs and life-long learning. This will enable directors to sustain their active participation in board deliberations. Director(s) should notify the chairman of the board of the planned and estimated time that will be spent on the training and development of new directorship appointments before accepting any new directorship. The nominating committee is responsible for reviewing the director's training program" (Section 4.2).

- Australia
  The Codes of corporate governance that were issued in 2014 focus on DTP and require that each listed entity have a program for inducting new directors and providing appropriate professional development opportunities for directors to develop and maintain the skills and knowledge that directors need to effectively perform their roles.

  "The board or nomination committee of a listed entity should regularly review whether the directors as a group have the skills, knowledge and familiarity with the entity and its operating environment required to effectively fulfill their role on the board and on board committees and, where any gaps are identified, consider what training or development could be undertaken to fill those gaps. Where necessary, the entity should provide resources to help develop and maintain its directors' skills and knowledge. This includes, in the case of a director who does not have specialist accounting skills or knowledge, ensuring that he or she has a sufficient understanding of accounting matters to fulfill his or her responsibilities in relation to the entity's financial statements. It also ensures that all directors receive ongoing briefings on developments in accounting standards" (Section 2.6).

- Pakistan
  The revised Codes of corporate governance that were issued in 2012 specify the requirements for

Table 1. Selection of Variables

Country	Index	Companies	Percentage
Australia	Australia Stock Exchange	90	33.33%
Malaysia	Kuala Lumpur Stock Exchange	90	33.33%
Pakistan	Pakistan Stock Exchange	90	33.33%
Total Sample Companies (Three Years: 2011 to 2013)		270	100.0%

director training programs of locally listed companies by stating the following:

"All listed companies shall make appropriate arrangements to provide orientation courses for their directors to acquaint them with this code, applicable laws, their duties and responsibilities to enable them to effectively manage the affairs of the listed companies for and on behalf of shareholders. It shall be mandatory for all the directors of listed companies to be certified by any directors' training program offered by institutions—local or foreign—that meets the criteria as specified by the SECP. From June 30, 2012 to June 30, 2016, every year, a minimum of one director on the board shall obtain the said certification under this program each year and thereafter, all directors shall obtain it. Furthermore, individuals with a minimum of 14 years of education and 15 years of experience on the board of a listed company local and/or foreign shall be exempted from the directors' training program" (Section xi).

Research Methodology

The dataset includes a large sample of firms that operate in multiple sectors (manufacturing, services, agriculture, and construction). We describe our sample selection procedure in Table 1. The primary constraint on our sample size is the availability of data from 2011 to 2013 for companies that operate in Australia, Malaysia and Pakistan. The top indexed companies used in this study were obtained from the Australian Stock Exchange (AXS), the Kuala Lumpur Stock Exchange (KLSE) and the Pakistan Stock Exchange (PSE); 33.3% of the firms in the sample were obtained from each stock exchange.

Multivariate Regression Models

In the multivariate analysis, we used the absolute value of the residue of the regression models to measure the quality of the accruals. Dechow and Dichev (2002) and Francis, LaFond, Olsson, and Schipper (2005) used the standard deviation of errors in the estimation of accruals to measure the quality of the accruals; however, we use the absolute value of this residue. Multivariate regression models were used to analyze the relationship between DTP and financial reporting quality as follows:

$$\textit{Financial Reporting Quality} = \\ = AR + PAaccr + TCaccr + AGGRE \quad (1)$$

$$\text{Financial Reporting Quality} = \\ = \alpha + \beta_1 \text{ DTP} + \beta_2 \text{ Control} + \epsilon \quad (2)$$

Dependent, Explanatory and Control Variables

The variables that are used in our equations are described in Table 2.

Independent Variables

DTP starts (DTPY) refer to the number of year(s), beginning in 2011, that sample companies offered director training programs. However, the variable 'DTP expense' (DTPX) represents the amount of money (in USD millions) that the company spent for the development of the board of directors during the sample year. Because members of the board members generally have busy schedules, most companies use online DTP. The variable 'Online DTP' (Online) represents the status of DTP delivery and is a dummy variable that is set as "1" as if the DTP is offline/physical and "0" otherwise. Specific AC is a variable that indicates the scope of DTP regarding the needs of audit committee members. For this dummy variable, "1" used if the specific audit committee needs DTP and "0" otherwise.

Table 2. Definition of Variables

Sr. #	Variables		Description
Independent Variable			
(A)	DTPY	DTP Start (Year)	Number of year(s) since DTP was launched for the first time.
(B)	DTPX	DTP Expenses	The amount of DTP expenditures.
(C)	SPAC	Specific Audit Committee Training	Dummy variable and is '1' if there is a specific DTP for Audit Committee members and '0' otherwise.
(D)	Online	Training Status	Dummy variable and is '1' if the DTP is offline and '0' otherwise.
Dependent Variables			
(E)	PAaccr	Performance Adjusted Discretionary Accrual	Total accruals are measured as the change in non-cash current assets minus the change in current non-interest bearing liabilities, minus depreciation and amortization expense, scaled by lagged total assets.
(F)	AR	Discretionary Revenue	The annual change in revenues and scaled by lagged total assets.
(G)	TCaccr	Total Current Accruals	Total current accruals are measured as the change in non-cash current assets minus the change in current non-interest bearing liabilities, scaled by lagged total assets.
(H)	Aggre.	Aggregate Accruals	An average of PAaccr, AR and TCaccr.
Control Variables			
(I)	FSIZE	Firm Size	The log of total assets
(J)	FL	Financial Leverage	Total Debt/Total Equity
(K)	BI	Board Independence	Percentage of non-executive director in board
(L)	FAGE	Firm Age	Number of years from the incorporation.

Control Variables

Motivated by prior empirical studies, we include firm size, board independence, financial leverage and firm age as control variables (Owolabi, Obiakor, & Okwu, 2011; Raheman & Nasr, 2007). To control for firm size, we included a variable for the natural logarithm of total assets (FSIZE). Firm age was calculated as the natural logarithm of the number of years since the incorporation of the firm, which helped to control for the organization's maturity (Arthurs, Hoskisson, Busentiz, & Johnson 2008; Matta & Beamish, 2008). The logarithmic form of analysis was applied to reduce heteroscedasticity (Finkelstein & D'Aveni, 1994). Hutchinson and Gul (2004) argued that a firm's leverage may lead to increased external control because creditors would monitor its capital structure more intensively to protect their interests. In alignment with Chen and Jaggi (2000), the debt-to-equity ratio (FL) was used to measure firm leverage.

Dependent Variables (Proxies for Financial Reporting Quality)

A solitary universally recognized measure for financial reporting quality has not been developed (Dechow et al. 2010). This study employs three measures that have been used in prior studies and an aggregate measure is included for the following reasons. First, this study focuses on financial reporting quality, which is multi-dimensional. Therefore, a single proxy may not include all of the facets of financial reporting quality. Second, the use of multiple proxies increases the adequacy of our results. Third, using alternative measures mitigates the possibility that results using one particular proxy capture a factor other than financial reporting quality.

The first measure is performance-adjusted discretionary accruals as proposed by Ashbaugh, LaFond, and Mayhew (2003), Kothari,

Leone, & Wasley (2005) and Chen, Harford, and Li (2007).

$$PAaccr_{i,t} = \alpha_0 + \alpha_1\left(\frac{1}{Assets_{i,t-1}}\right) + \alpha_2 \Delta Rev_{i,t} +$$
$$+ \alpha_3 PPE_{i,t} + \alpha_4 ROA_{i,t} + \epsilon_{i,t} \quad (1)$$

where, $PAaccr_{i,t}$ total accruals is measured as the change in non-cash current assets minus the change in current non-interest bearing liabilities, minus depreciation and amortization expenses for firm *i* at year *t*, scaled by lagged total assets ($Assets_{i,t}$); $\Delta Rev_{i,t}$ represents the annual change in revenues scaled by lagged total assets; $PPE_{i,t}$ represents property, plant, and equipment for firm *i* at year *t*, scaled by lagged total assets; and $ROA_{i,t}$ represents return on assets for firm *i* at year *t*. The residuals from the regression model are discretionary accruals. In our tests, we use the absolute values of discretionary accruals as a proxy for financial reporting quality. We multiply the absolute values of discretionary accruals by -1. Therefore, higher values of PAaccr represent higher financial reporting quality.

To calculate the second proxy, we align with Chen et al. (2007), McNichols and Stubben (2008) and use the following regression:

$$\Delta AR_{i,t} = \alpha_0 + \alpha_1 \Delta Rev_{i,t} + \epsilon_{i,t} \quad (2)$$

where, $\Delta AR_{i,t}$ represents the annual change in accounts receivable and $\Delta Rev_{i,t}$ represents the annual change in revenues, scaled by lagged total assets. Discretionary revenues are the residuals from Equation (2) that are estimated separately for each industry-country group. Our third proxy is based on the cross-sectional Dechow and Dichev (2002) and Tucker and Zarowin (2006) model, as modified by McNichols (2002), Francis et al. (2005) and Chen et al. (2007).

$$TCaccr_{i,t} = \alpha_0 + \alpha_1 OCF_{i,t-1} + \alpha_2 OCF_{i,t} + \alpha_3 OCF_{i,t+1} +$$
$$+ \alpha_4 \Delta Rev_{i,t} + \alpha_5 PPE_{i,t} + \epsilon_{i,t} \quad (3)$$

where, TCaccr represents total current accruals, which are measured as the change in non-cash current assets minus the change in current non-interest bearing liabilities, scaled by lagged total assets; OCF represents cash flow from operations, which is measured as the sum of net income, depreciation and amortization, and changes in current liabilities, minus changes in current assets, scaled by lagged total assets; $\Delta Rev_{i,t}$ represents the annual change in revenues scaled by lagged total assets; and $PPE_{i,t}$ represents property, plant, and equipment, scaled by lagged total assets.

The residuals from Equation (3) represent the estimation errors in the current accruals that are not associated with operating cash flows and cannot be explained by changes in revenue and levels of property, plant and equipment. Because of the short longitudinal time frame that is used in our study, we align with Srinidhi and Gul (2007) and Chen et al. (2007) and use the absolute value of this residual as a proxy for financial reporting quality. Therefore, higher values of TCaccr represent higher financial reporting quality. To reduce the measurement errors of the financial reporting quality mechanism and to present evidence based on general financial reporting metrics, we aggregate these proxies into one score. In alignment with Biddle, Hilary, and Verdi (2009), we normalize all proxies and then calculate the average of the three measures as our summary financial reporting quality statistic (AGGRE).

Empirical Results

Descriptive Statistics

Table 3 provides the descriptive statistics for the variables that are used in our primary tests. The number of observations varies with data availability and selection for each dependent variable because we utilize all available observations for each measure of financial reporting quality.

The results indicate that the mean value of 'DTP Start' is lowest in Pakistan at 6 years and is 12 years in Malaysia and 24 years in Australia. However, DTP expenditures are highest in Malaysia with a mean value of 29.61 million and are 21.23 million in Pakistan and 29 million in Australia, with a minimum expense of 0.20, 2.8 and 10 million in Pakistan, Malaysia and Australia, respectively.

Table 3. Descriptive Statistics

	Australia				Malaysia				Pakistan			
	Min.	Max.	Mean	SD	Min.	Max.	Mean	SD	Min.	Max.	Mean	SD
DTP Start	9.0	36.0	23.85	8.15	3.0	24.0	12.23	4.13	1.0	15.0	5.87	3.71
DTP Expense	10.0	43.0	28.87	6.81	2.8	58.0	29.61	12.11	0.20	170.8	21.23	81.9
Specific AC	0.0	1.0	0.87	0.34	0.0	1.0	0.87	0.34	0.0	1.0	0.66	0.48
Online DTP	0.0	1.0	0.89	0.32	0.0	1.0	0.88	0.33	0.0	1.0	0.83	0.37
Firm Age	11	196	89.64	50.14	3	72	34.13	14.88	1.0	106	40	25.81
Firm Size	3.70	5.91	4.81	0.59	3.14	5.72	4.55	0.63	3.77	6.23	5.03	0.59
BI	0.10	1.00	0.62	0.48	0.00	1.00	0.49	0.59	0.00	1.00	0.39	0.38
FL	0.00	1.21	0.13	0.22	0.01	1.50	0.19	0.34	0.00	2.12	0.32	0.48
AR	0.71	1.10	0.87	0.11	0.86	1.47	1.14	0.15	0.84	1.38	1.07	0.12
Paaccr	1.29	2.31	1.79	0.31	1.37	2.75	1.94	0.32	1.48	2.52	2.02	0.24
Tcaccr	1.46	2.77	2.19	0.37	1.73	2.86	2.35	0.28	1.83	3.47	2.54	0.29
AGGRE	3.65	6.12	4.87	0.76	4.58	6.40	5.43	0.44	4.48	6.76	5.63	0.42

Table 4. Correlation Coefficient Analysis

	Variables	1	2	3	4	5	6	7	8
1.	DTP Start	1							
2.	DTP Expense	0.015	1						
3.	Specific Audit Committee	0.117	0.225**	1					
4.	Online DTP	-0.070	0.123	0.357**	1				
5.	AR	-0.202	-0.088	-0.080	-0.038	1			
6.	Paaccr	0.216**	0.091	0.069	-0.019	-0.879**	1		
7.	Tcaccr	0.318**	0.128	0.094	-0.034	-0.680**	0.780**	1	
8.	AGGRE	0.290**	0.120	0.083	-0.046	-0.715**	0.895**	0.963**	1

Table 3 indicates that the number of firms that have specific audit committee training and development is lowest in Pakistan with a mean value of 0.66; in addition, the trend for online DTP is lowest in Pakistan with a mean value of 0.83. The firm age is 196 years for the Australian sample, which is the highest of all three countries, and the maximum firm age in Malaysia is 72 years.

The correction coefficient analysis results of the variables are presented in Table 4 below. The results indicate that starting director training programs (DTP Start) early is positively correlated with financial reporting quality. However, 'Specific AC' was not correlated to any of the financial reporting measures. In addition, the other DTP variables were not correlated to any of the financial reporting measures.

Regression Results

Tables 5 through 8 report the impact of DTP on the financial reporting quality of firms that operate in Australia, Malaysia and Pakistan.

Table 5 indicates that the dependent variable AR is positively associated with starting DTP early in Pakistan and Australia and DTP expenditures in Austra-

Table 5. AR as the Dependent Variable

	Australia	Malaysia	Pakistan
DTP Start	3.70**	-1.72	2.11**
DTP Expenses	3.93**	-0.65	-0.29
Specific DTP for Audit Committee	-0.54	-0.23	-0.49
Online DTP	2.34**	-0.28	0.78
Firm Age	-1.13	-3.59**	-1.57
Firm Size	-7.08**	-7.66**	-6.63**
Financial Leverage	5.02	6.56	5.98
Board Independence	0.56	0.55	0.75
R^2	65.9%	56.7%	38.7%
Adj. R^2	62.0%	53.0%	34.3%
F-Statistics	17.03	15.34	8.75
Prob.	0.000	0.000	0.000

Table 6. PAaccr as the Dependent Variable

	Australia	Malaysia	Pakistan
DTP Start	1.92	1.79	-1.23
DTP Expenses	2.79**	0.83	1.08
Specific DTP for Audit Committee	-1.78	0.27	1.68
Online DTP	3.27**	-0.24	1.97**
Firm Age	1.167	-2.44	0.53
Firm Size	-6.43**	-8.25**	-8.91**
Financial Leverage	5.88	5.74	6.59
Board Independence	0.59	0.85	0.66
R^2	61.5%	57.1%	51.7%
Adj. R^2	57.2%	53.4%	48.2%
F-Statistics	14.13	15.57	14.78
Prob.	0.000	0.000	0.000

lia are positively associated with AR. The results of the coefficient analysis indicate that the model used in this study is statistically significant at a level of 5% ($p<0.05$).In this study, the R^2 when AR was the dependent variable was 65.9%, 56.7% and 38.7%, which was adjusted to better fit the model in the population and the final adjusted R^2 was 62%, 53% and 34.3%, respectively, for Australia, Malaysia and Pakistan.

In addition, the results indicate that firm size is significantly negatively correlated with the financial reporting measure "AR" in Australia, Malaysia and Pakistan. However, Firm age is negatively associated

Table 7. TCaccr as the Dependent Variable

	Australia	Malaysia	Pakistan
DTP Start	1.09	3.05**	-0.34
DTP Expenses	1.89	0.82	0.12
Specific DTP for Audit Committee	-1.02	0.48	1.71
Online DTP	3.46**	-0.38	0.21
Firm Age	0.99	-4.19**	-0.78
Firm Size	-3.24**	-3.88**	-6.83**
Financial Leverage	4.59	5.15	5.25
Board Independence	0.84	0.67	0.88
R^2	46.3%	42.3%	40.6%
Adj. R^2	40.2%	37.4%	36.3%
F-Statistics	7.624	8.597	9.450
Prob.	0.000	0.000	0.000

Table 8. AGGRE as the Dependent Variable

	Australia	Malaysia	Pakistan
DTP Start	1.82	2.66**	-0.25
DTP Expenses	2.56**	0.88	0.58
Specific DTP for Audit Committee	-1.35	0.42	1.96
Online DTP	3.47**	-0.49	1.45
Firm Age	0.89	-3.27**	-0.75
Firm Size	-5.20**	-5.57**	-7.58**
Financial Leverage	5.26	5.88	5.65
Board Independence	0.78	1.06	0.89
R^2	57.1%	47.1%	45.6%
Adj. R^2	52.3%	42.6%	41.6%
F-Statistics	11.76	10.42	11.57
Prob.	0.000	0.000	0.000

with financial reporting quality in Malaysia and the trend of using online DTP is positively associated with "AR" in Australia.

Table 6 indicates that the dependent variable PAaccr is positively associated with DTP expenditures and Online DTP in Australia. Online DTP is also positively associated with the quality of financial reporting in Pakistan, and firm size (FSIZE) is negatively associated with the quality of financial reporting for all three countries. The results of the coefficient analysis indicate that the model is statistically significant at a level of 5% ($p<0.05$). In this study, the R^2 when

AR was the dependent variable was 61.5%, 57.1% and 51.7%, which was adjusted to better fit the model in the population, and the final adjusted R^2 was 57.2%, 53.4% and 48.2%, respectively, for Australia, Malaysia and Pakistan.

Table 7 indicates that the dependent variable TCaccr is positively associated with starting DTP early in Malaysia and online DTP is positively associated with financial reporting quality in Australia. In this study, the R^2 for the TCaccr dependent variable was 46.3%, 42.3% and 40.6%, which was adjusted to better fit the model for the population, and the final adjusted R^2 was 40.2%, 37.4% and 36.3%, respectively, for Australia, Malaysia and Pakistan.

In addition, the results indicate that firm size is negatively associated with the financial reporting measure "TCaccr" in Australia, Malaysia and Pakistan. However, Firm age is negatively associated with financial reporting quality in Malaysia.

Table 8 indicates that the dependent variable AGGRE is positively associated with starting DTP early in Malaysia and DTP expenditures are positively associated with financial reporting quality (AGGRE) in Australia. The results of the coefficient analysis indicate that the model of this study is statistically significant at a level of 5% ($p<0.05$). In this study, the R^2 when AR was the dependent variable was 57.1%, 47.1% and 45.6%, which was adjusted to better fit the model in the population, and the final adjusted R^2 was 52.3%, 42.6% and 41.6%, respectively, for Australia, Malaysia and Pakistan.

In addition, the results indicate that firm size is negatively associated with the financial reporting measure "AGGRE" in Australia, Malaysia and Pakistan. However, firm age is negatively associated with financial reporting quality in Malaysia.

Surprisingly, firm size has a negative significant impact of on the quality of financial reporting. However, these results align with Yasser and Mamun (2015).

Vijayakumar and Tamizhselvan (2010) document that firm size is related to transparency and firm value in the neoclassical view of a firm; this concept is referred to as economies of scale. Economies of scale may occur for various reasons, including financial reasons (a large firm has more resources to hire top professionals and consultants with the most advanced expertise); organizational reasons (specialization and division of labor); technical reasons (high fixed costs can be distributed across a large number of units). In alignment with this concept, we expect that positive relationships exist between firm size and firm age and financial reporting quality. Conversely, a conceptual framework that advocates a negative relationship between firm size and transparency is noted in alternative theories regarding firms and suggests that large firms are controlled by managers who pursuing self-interested goals and therefore, profit maximization as the firm's primary function may be replaced by a managerial utility maximization function (Foss, Lando, & Thomsen, 2000).

Summary and Conclusion

To our knowledge, this study provides the first documented evidence of an association between directors training programs and measures of accounting quality that explicitly recognizes that a firm's investment in accounting and auditing is not independent from one period to the next. Prior studies have provided conflicting results regarding the extent to which audit fees are associated with accounting quality (i.e., whether fees are consistently high or consistently low) and we can reliably identify instances where a conscious investment was made in more (or less) auditing; however, a director's impact on the financial reporting quality was ignored. We argue that the relationship between measures of accounting quality and measures of unexpected audit fees based on a single period are interpreted by relying on one dimension of agency theory.

The results of this study indicate that companies that operate in Australia that incur additional expenditures for DTP and offer flexible training schedules (Online DTP) report improved financial reporting quality. However, a long-term director training program positively affects financial reporting quality. These results are relevant because of the increased attention that regulators and other market participants have placed on the importance of director training programs and development in firm governance. The results may be of particular interest to regulators, capital market participants and academics. Regulators may be interested because the results have policy implications when considering the quality of financial reporting and director development. Investors and creditors may find the results useful for evaluating investment decisions.

Finally, academics who seek to broaden their experiences by serving on corporate boards may find the information useful in making decisions regarding their personal development.

The results of the analysis demonstrate that firm size and firm age negatively affect the quality of financial reporting. There are several possible reasons for this influence. Because of their market power, larger and older firms are able to charge higher prices and subsequently earn higher profits. In addition, higher profits could result from economies of scale and stronger negotiating power that provides larger firms with more favorable financing conditions. In addition to inflexible organization structures and technology, a change in the strategic logic that is used by firms (it became more important to survive during a global economic crisis than to increase profitability) may explain the weak relationships between firm size and firm age and reporting quality.

This study contributes to the extant literature in three dimensions: first, this study combines market-based and standard accounting financial indicators as measures of financial reporting to test the predictions of agency theory. Second, this study provides new empirical evidence regarding the effects of director training programs on a firm's financial reporting quality in all sectors of the Asia Pacific stock markets. Finally, this study provides additional evidence regarding the effect of director training on financial reporting in developed and developing countries by using the same variables and analysis techniques.

References:

Agrawal, A., & Chadha, S. (2005). Corporate governance and accounting scandals. *The Journal of Law and Economics, 48*(2), 371-406.

Aguinis, H., & Kraiger, K. (2009). Benefits of training and development for individuals and teams, organizations and society. *Annual Review of Psychology, 60*, 451–474.

Armstrong, C. S., Barth, M. E., Jagolinzer, A. D., & Riedl, E. J. (2010). Market reaction to the adoption of IFRS in Europe. *The Accounting Review, 85*(1), 31-61.

Arthurs, J. D., Hoskisson, R. E., Busentiz, L. W., & Johnson, R. A. (2008). Managerial agents watching other agents: Multiple agency conflicts regarding underpricing in IPO firms. *Academy of Management Journal, 51*(2): 277-294.

Ashbaugh, H., LaFond, R., & Mayhew, B. W. (2003). Do nonaudit services compromise auditor independence? Further evidence. *The Accounting Review, 78*(3), 611-693.

Baber, W., Liang, L., & Zhu Z. (2012). Associations between internal and external corporate governance characteristics: Implications for investigating financial accounting restatements. *Accounting Horizons, 26*(2), 219-237.

Bamber, L. S., Jiang, J., & Wang, I. Y. (2010). What's my style? The influence of top managers on voluntary corporate financial disclosure. *The Accounting Review, 85*(4), 1131-1162.

Barling, J. B., Weber, T., & Kelloway, E. K. (1996). Effects of transformational leadership training on attitudinal and financial outcomes: A field experiment. *Journal of Applied Psychology, 81*(6), 827-832.

Beekes, W., & Brown, P. (2006). Do better-governed Australian firms make more informative disclosures. *Journal of Business Finance & Accounting, 33*(3-4), 422-450.

Beekes, W., Pope, P., & Young, S. (2004). The link between earnings and timeliness, earnings conservatism and board composition: Evidence from the UK. *Corporate Governance: An International Review, 12*(1), 47-59.

Bergstresser, D., & Philippon, T. (2006). CEO Incentives and Earnings Management. *Journal of Financial Economics, 80*(3), 511–529.

Bertrand, M., & Schoar, A. (2003). Managing with style: The effects of managers on firm policies. *The Quarterly Journal of Economics, 118*(4),1169-1208.

Biddle, G. C., Hilary, G., & Verdi, R. S. (2009). How does financial reporting quality relate to investments efficiency? *Journal of Accounting and Economics, 48*(2-3), 112-131.

Bradbury, M., Mak, Y. T., & Tan, S. M. (2006). Board characteristics, audit committee characteristics and abnormal accruals. *Pacific Accounting Review, 18*(2), 47-68.

Bowen, R. M., Call, A. C., & Rajgopal, S. (2010). Whistle-blowing: Target firm characteristics and economic consequences. *The Accounting Review, 85*(4), 1239-1271.

Brown, L., & Caylor, M. (2006). Corporate governance and firm valuation. *Journal of Accounting and Public Policy, 25*(4), 409-434.

Burke, L. A., & Hutchins, H. M. (2007). Training transfer: An integrative literature review. *Human Resource Development Review, 6*(3), 263–296.

Chen, X., Harford, J., & Li, K. (2007). Monitoring: Which institutions matter? *Journal of Financial Economics, 86*(2), 279–305.

Chen, C. J. P., & Jaggi, B. (2000). Association between independent non-executive directors, family control and financial disclosures in Hong Kong. *Journal of Accounting and Public Policy, 19*(4-5), 285-310.

Cheng, Q., & Warfield, T. D. (2005). Equity incentives and earnings management. *The Accounting Review, 80*(2), 441-476.

Dechow, P. M., & Dichev, I. D. (2002). The quality of Accruals and Earnings: The role of Accrual Estimation Errors. *The Accounting Review, 77*, 35-59.

Dechow, P., Ge, W., & Schrand, C. (2010). Understanding earnings quality: A review of the proxies their determinants and their consequences. *Journal of Accounting and Economics, 50*(2-3), 344-401.

Decker, W. H., & Calo, T. J. (2007). Observers' impressions of unethical persons and whistleblowers. *Journal of Business Ethics, 76*(3), 309-318.

Dimitropoulos, P. E., & Asteriou, D. (2010). The effect of board composition on the informativeness and quality of annual earnings: Empirical evidence from Greece. *Research in International Business and Finance, 24*(2), 190-205.

Doh, J. P. (2003). Can leadership be taught? Perspectives from management educators. *Academy of Management Learning & Education, 2*(1), 54-67.

Dvir, T., Eden, D., Avolio, B. J., & Shamir, B. (2002). Impact of transformational leadership on follower development and performance: A field experiment. *The Academy of Management Journal, 45*(4), 735-744.

Dyreng, S. D., Hanlon, M., & Maydew, E. L. (2010). The effects of managers on corporate tax avoidance. *The Accounting Review, 85*(4), 1163-1190.

Easley, D., & O'Hara, M. (2004). Information and the cost of capital. *The Journal of Finance, 59*(4) 1553-1583.

Efendi, J., Srivastava, A., & Swanson, E. P. (2007). Why do corporate managers misstate financial statements? The role of option compensation and other factors. *Journal of Financial Economics, 85*(3), 667-708.

Erickson, M., Hanlon, M., & Maydew, E. L. (2006). Is there a link between executive equity incentives and accounting fraud? *Journal of Accounting Research, 44*(1), 113-143.

Finkelstein, S., & D'Aveni, R. A. (1994). CEO duality as a double-edged sword: How boards of directors balance entrenchment avoidance and unity of command. *The Academy of Management Journal, 37*(5), 1079-1108.

Firth, M., Fung, P., & Rui, O. (2007). Ownership, two-tier board structure, and the informativeness of earnings: Evidence from China. *Journal of Accounting and Public Policy, 26*(4), 463-496.

Foss, N. J., Lando, H., & Thomsen, S. (2000). The Theory of the firm. In B. Bouckaert & G. De Geest (Eds.), *Encyclopedia of Law and Economics, Volume III. The Regulation of Contracts* (pp. 631-658). Cheltenham, UK: Edward Elgar.

Francis, J., LaFond, R., Olsson, P., & Schipper, K. (2005). The market pricing of accruals quality. *Journal of Accounting and Economics, 39*(2), 295–327.

Grossman, W., & Haskisson, R. E. (1998). CEO pay at the crossroads of Wall Street and Main: Toward the strategic design of executive compensation. *Academy of Management Executive, 12*(1), 43-57.

Hambrick, D. C., & Mason, P. A. (1984). Upper echelons: The organization as a reflection of its top managers. *The Academy of Management Review, 9*(2), 193–206.

Hambrick, D. C., & Fukutomi, G. D. S. (1991). The seasons of a CEO's tenure. *The Academy of Management Review, 16*(4), 719-742.

Hassan, R. A., Fuwad, B. A., & Rauf, A. I. (2010). Pre-training motivation and the effectiveness of transformational leadership training: An experiment. *Academy of Strategic Management Journal, 9*(2), 123-131.

Hermalin, B. E., & Weisbach, M. S. (1998). Endogenously chosen boards of directors and their monitoring of the CEO. *The American Economic Review, 88*(1), 96-118.

Hermalin, B. E., & Weisbach, M. S. (2003). Boards of directors as an endogenously determined Institution: A survey of the economic Literature. *Federal Reserve Bank of New York Economic Policy Review, 9*(1), 7-26.

Howell, J. M., & Frost, P. J. (1989). A laboratory study of charismatic leadership. *Organizational Behavior and Human Decision Processes, 43*(2), 243-269.

Hunt, J. W., & Baruch, Y. (2003). Developing top managers: The impact of interpersonal skills training. *Journal of Management Development, 22*(8), 729-752.

Hutchinson, M., & Gul, F. A. (2004). Investment opportunity set, corporate governance practices and firm performance. *Journal of Corporate Finance, 10*(4), 595-614.

Karamanou, I., & Vafeas, N. (2005). The association between corporate boards, audit committees, and management earnings forecasts: An empirical analysis. *Journal of Accounting Research, 43*(3), 453- 486.

Kim, D., & Qi, Y. (2010). Accruals quality, stock returns, and macroeconomic conditions. *The Accounting Review, 85*(3), 937-978.

Kirkpatrick, S. A., & Locke, E. A. (1996). Direct and indirect effects of three core charismatic leadership components on performance and attitudes. *Journal of Applied Psychology, 81*(1), 36-51.

Klein, A. (2002). Audit committee, board of director characteristics, and earnings management. *Journal of Accounting and Economics, 33*(3), 375-400.

Kothari, S. P., Leone, A. J., & Wasley, C. E. (2005). Performance matched discretionary accrual measures. *Journal of Accounting and Economics, 39*(1), 163-197.

La Porta, R., Lopez-de-Silanes, F., Shleifer, A., & Vishny, R. W. (1998). Law and finance. *The Journal of Political Economy, 106*(6), 1113-1155.

Larcker, D. F., Richardson, S. A., & Tuna, I. (2007). Corporate governance, accounting outcomes and organizational performance. *The Accounting Review, 82*(4), 963-1008.

Matta, E., & Beamish, P. W. (2008). The accentuated CEO career horizon problem: Evidence from international acquisitions. *Strategic Management Journal, 29*(7), 683–700.

McNichols, M. F. (2002). Discussion of the quality of accruals and earnings: The role of accrual estimation errors. *The Accounting Review, 77*, 61-69.

McNichols, M. F., & Stubben, S. R. (2008). Does earnings management affect firms' investment decisions? *The Accounting Review, 83*(6), 1571-1603.

Mole, G. (2000). *Managing management development.* Buckingham, UK: Open University Press.

Owolabi, S. A., Obiakor, R. T., & Okwu, A. T. (2011). Investigating Liquidity - Profitability Relationship in Business Organization: A Study of Selected Quoted Companies in Nigeria. *British Journal of Economics, Finance and Management Sciences, 1*(2), 17-25.

Parry, K. W., & Sinha, P. N. (2005). Researching the trainability of transformational organizational leadership. *Human Resource Development International, 8*(2), 165-183.

Peasnell, K. V., Pope, P. F., & Young, S. (2005). Board monitoring and earnings management: Do outside directors' influence abnormal accruals? *Journal of Business Finance and Accounting, 32*(7-8), 1311-1346.

Petra, S. T. (2007). The effects of corporate governance on the informativeness of earnings. *Economics of Governance, 8*(2), 129-152.

Prowse, S. D. (1992). The structure of corporate ownership in Japan. *Journal of Finance, 47*(3), 1121-1140.

Raheman, A., & Nasr, M. (2007). Working capital management and profitability: Case of Pakistani firms. *International Review of Business Research Papers, 3*(1), 279- 300.

Sánchez-Ballesta, J. P., & García-Meca, E. (2007). A meta-analytic vision of the effect of ownership structure on firm performance. *Corporate Governance: An International Review, 15*(5), 879–893.

Sloan, R. G. (2001). Financial accounting and corporate governance: A discussion. *Journal of Accounting and Economics, 32*(1-3), 335–347.

Srinidhi, B. N., & Gul, F. A. (2007). The differential effects of auditors' nonaudit and audit fees on accrual quality. *Contemporary Accounting Research, 24*(2), 595-629.

Tucker, J. W., & Zarowin, P. A. (2006). Does income smoothing improve earnings informativeness? *The Accounting Review, 81*(1), 251-270.

Vijayakumar, A., & Tamizhselvan, P. (2010). Corporate size and profitability: An empirical analysis. *Journal for Bloomers of Research, 3*(1), 44-53.

Wiersema, M. F., & Bantel, K.A. (1992). Top management team demography and corporate strategic change. *The Academy of Management Journal, 35*(1), 91-121.

Yasser, Q. R., & Mamun, A.A. (2015). The impact of CEO duality attributes on earnings management in the East. *Corporate Governance, 15*(5), 706-718.

Yeo, G. H. H., Tan, P. M. S., Ho, K. W., & Chen, S. (2002). Corporate ownership structure and the informativeness of earnings. *Journal of Business Finance and Accounting, 29*(7-8), 1023-1046.

7

Corporate Internet Reporting and Firm Performance: Evidence from Malaysia

Chai J Sia[1], Rayenda Brahmana[1], Gesti Memarista[2]

ABSTRACT

Anecdotal evidence showed that the portion of internet users to the population in Malaysia is relatively higher among developing economies. However, there are not many Malaysian listed companies that use the internet as a platform for financial information disclosure. Perhaps, the managers do not believe that there is positive association between internet reporting and firm performance. Therefore, this study aims to examine the impact of corporate internet reporting (CIR) on firm performance for a sample of 583 non-financial listed companies in Malaysia over the year of 2013. We use content analysis to retrieve the internet reporting items and test its validity and reliability before running the regression model. The findings showed that CIR has a significant effect on firm value. This means that more related information that is regularly disclosed on the company's websites can contribute more value to the firms. Meanwhile, company size does not significantly influence firm value. The firm's leverage is negative and statistically significant, and the growth brings a positive significant effect to the firm's value. In addition, in this study, the results support the resource-based view theory and the signaling theory between corporate internet reporting and firm value. The findings of the research suggest that companies should disclose more information through the internet in order to ensure the accessibility of financial information for stakeholders, and this will present a better image and reputation of the company's best practices in financial performance. CIR will help them to have meaningful investment decisions and persuade them to invest in the company.

KEY WORDS: Corporate internet reporting (CIR), firm performance, size, leverage, growth

[1] Universiti Malaysia Sarawak - Faculty of Economics and Business, Malaysia; [2] Universitas Kristen Petra - Faculty of Economics, Indonesia

Introduction

Firms' stakeholders need fast and reliable financial information to satisfy their requirements for timely decision making. Hence, information technology provided by the internet can meet that expectation through internet reporting. According to Willis, Tesnie're, and Jones (2003), internet reporting can be used as a new information communication tool to provide information quicker and timelier in better and more effective ways. By using internet financial reporting, the information will be disseminated worldwide and facilitate broader stakeholders.

This is in line with the growth of internet users around the world. The number of worldwide internet consumers have increased more than seven-fold in ten years from 394 million in 2000 to 2,923 million users in 2014 (Statista, 2014). This implies that there

Correspondence concerning this article should be addressed to: **Gesti Memarista**, Universitas Kristen Petra - Faculty of Economics, Siwalankerto 121-131, Surabaya 60236, Indonesia. E-mail: gesti@petra.ac.id

is a growth in the population of corporate internet reporting (hereafter CIR) users. Therefore, internet reporting is essential in the current information technology era (Adhikari & Tondkar, 1992; Jones & Xiao, 2003; Khan & Ismail, 2011).

The demands of voluntary disclosure via internet reporting increase the curiosity among investors at the present time (Aly, Simon, & Hussainey, 2010). As shown by Shehata's (2014) study, more available information would help investors' decision making reach the optimum level. Even though internet reporting provides fast information, it does not definitely mean better earnings results (i.e., Bakos, 1991; Brynjolfsson & Hitt, 1996). Bharadwaj, Bharadwaj, and Konsynki (1999) also documented that businesses are curious about the impact of internet reporting on their company's performance. Note that establishing CIR about both the costs of instituting a system and revealing the current and latest performance of the company. Hence, the company will consider what will be the benefits for the company after investing in that technology (Chao, Hsu, & Yeh, 2010).

Firms will reduce information asymmetry when there is more disclosure information through the internet (Diamond & Verrecchia, 1991). This information can lead to better performance because it improves the company's image, reputation, and trustworthiness. This is well explained by the resource-based view theory, whereby information is important for a company. This resource is allocated heterogeneously (unequally) within an industry, meaning that each firm has similar information, yet each firm disseminates information differently in the internet.

Peteraf (1993) and Daft (1983) stated that the resource-based view theory defines resources as the firm's assets, capabilities, organizational processes, attributes, information, and knowledge about the components controlled by the firm that enable it to conceive and implement strategies that enhance its efficiency and effectiveness. Prior research has tested how different types of resources may have different impacts on firm performance. For example, Williamson (1975) focuses on more physical capital resources and Tomer (1987) focuses more on organizational resources. Meanwhile, Becker (1967) and Porter (1985) focus more on financial statements and information.

The case incorporates the resources and capabilities of the firm's fundamental features into its long-term strategy. It primarily includes the internal resources and capabilities that give the basic direction of the strategy of the firm, and second, it establishes resources as the primary source of profits for the firm (Grant, 1991). The ability of a firm to generate profit margins exceeding its costs of capital depends upon the attractiveness of the industry in which it is located and its establishment of a competitive advantage over its rivals. In this research study, the information available on the internet can add great resource contributions to the organization for cheaper costs of capital since it has lower information asymmetry.

Additionally, information on the internet can give signals to stakeholders regarding the performance of the firm. According to Hanafi, Kasim, Ibrahim, and Hancock (2009), the voluntary disclosure will give a signal to investors as the reaction to the asymmetric information in the market. Thus, asymmetries will be reduced if there is a part with more information signals to others. Spence (1973) stated that signaling theory can also help to explain voluntary disclosures. Craven and Marston (1999) stated that the use of the internet itself might be a signal of the high quality of the company. It shows that the company is up-to-date and modern when using the latest technology rather than conservative and old-fashioned methods. The company tends to adopt the same level of disclosure through the internet (Craven & Marston, 1999).

This phenomenon indicates that the CIR will affect firm performance. Through the CIR, the firm has a modern indicator to measure the performance through the concept of creating firm value (Beaver, 1968). The good company will disclose more information to enable the stockholders to be able to differentiate between the good firm and the bad ones. According to Lai, Lin, Li, and Wu (2010), internet reporting will minimize the shareholder shocks due to negative news, which will be reflected in the company's stock price. Consequently, shareholders find it easier to assess the company's performance from the firm value. Chao et al. (2010) and Lazarides, Drimpetas, Argyropoulou, and Motwani (2009) stated that CIR with an accurate and more timely disclosure mechanism will facilitate deterrence, detect manipulation and fraud, improve the stock market's efficiency, reduce the underpricing of IPOs, lead to a higher firm value, and improve organizational performance.

Since there was a growth in use of internet reporting, there is no more ignorance in society about the current situations of firms (Heye, 2009). Therefore, administrators of the firm's website possess the authority to cover or to hide the real facts from disclosure (Heye, 2009). Even major news corporation are no longer able to cover it, and internet reporting manages to generate more credible and accurate information about a firm's value than the mass media.

There are many global papers that have studied the extent of CIR in the last decade (Craven & Marston, 1999 for the UK context; Bharadwaj et al, 1999 for the US context; Chao et al, 2010 for the Taiwanese context; Aly et al, 2010 for the Egyptian context; and Khan & Ismail, 2011 for certain industries in Malaysia). It shows that many countries have started focusing on the employment of CIR. However, within Malaysia, there are only a few findings that use the firm's value as the dependent variable and study whether it is positively or negatively influenced by CIR. Therefore, this research aims to examine the relationship between CIR and firm value.

Web-based reporting overcomes the major weaknesses of paper-based reporting, such as more readers, greater efficiency, and easier access. However, according to Hussey and Sowinska (1999), one of its drawbacks would be the probability of lower effectiveness in the methods of implementation and compliance and the value of the whole reporting. Hussey and Sowinska (1999) also stated that the security and the integrity of internet reporting may be compromised either intentionally or unintentionally, and thus the companies have the responsibility to ensure the security and the integrity of information in the internet. There is unauthorized-access risk when internet reporting is not properly managed and leads to others to insert errors into data files that can cause security problems. For instance, the hacker might spoil the data with the aim to disrupt business operations (Hansen, 2001). Thus, the quality of the internet disclosure information is one of the issues that needed to be emphasized in this study.

Apart from unauthorized-access risk, there are also equipment failure risks (Hansen, 2001). The research explained that "transmissions between senders and receivers can be disrupted, destroyed, or corrupted by equipment failures in the communication system" (p. 1159). Moreover, equipment failure will cause the stored programs and databases to be lost on the network server (Hansen, 2001). The information may be transmitted inefficiently and ineffectively when there are poor or interrupted network connections.

In summation, this study investigates the role of CIR on firm performance. Furthermore, we use the indexation approach of Aly et al. (2010) to measure the CIR. In addition, we have extended the estimation model to a new empirical context in terms of some measures and some definitions. We also follow previous research by controlling the firm's characteristics to ensure the model's robustness.

This research's contributions are threefold. First, this study adds to the management information literature through the understanding of this research area of Malaysia, which is less developed country. Second, we also document the empirical findings of internet disclosure's impacts on the firm performance of Malaysian listed companies. Third, we provide the items of internet reporting that can be the benchmarks for the developing countries' context. Additionally, unlike prior research in this area, we take all listed companies in Malaysia as our sample. This means that we do not perform industrial-based research. Instead, we conduct it for the whole of publicly listed companies.

The rest of this research is organized as follows. Section 2 provides the theoretical background and the literature review. Section 3 describes the research methodology used in testing the estimation models. Section 4 reports the research's empirical findings. Lastly, section 5 concludes the research.

Literature review

Corporate internet reporting (CIR) refers to the financial disclosure through the internet of historical and financial data and the exposition of the current situation and future plans. It provides the financial information to the principals and stakeholders in regards to the investment decision-making and market efficiency (Check, Mohamad, Yunus, & Norwami, 2013). Aly et al. (2010) state that CIR provides the financial performance and the company's branding and market position.

This CIR has been through three phases of implementation. First, the rise of information systems allows firms to use the internet as the platform to disclose their existing written financial reports. Then, companies will change their information dissemination strategy from printed reports to the internet. The last phase is when companies prepare their financial information and disclose it wide and fast beyond the standard information given in a printed report. Having more information disclosed may lead to the increase of awareness about their companies to the stakeholders.

In general, the users of CIR could be divided into two groups, such as internal users and external users. The internal users consist of the workforces and shareholders. The workforces are concerned about the company's future prospects since it directly affects their income, whereas shareholders refer to the reporting for their decision making. Meanwhile, the external users are banks and creditors. The CIR is important for them as it is the fastest source in establishing credit ratings or solvency analysis. On the other hand, competitors also refer to the reports to better understand the positions of their rivals and learn how to improve their operational skills and methods.

Hence, this shows the importance of CIR since systematic and informative corporate disclosures can improve the understanding of firm performance. Firms are encouraged to keep information updated and to govern the security of information where it disclosed through the networks so that the company's objective will be achieved.

Several researchers in the era of the introduction of internet, such Bakos (1991) and Brynjolfsson and Hitt (1996), show that internet has also lowered entry barriers, maintained monopoly power, and intensified market competition, thereby creating losses for firms. It was confirmed by Li and McConomy (1999) who showed that the firms might be unwilling to follow new standards of accounting disclosure. This is because the firms aimed to protect their business value, maintain their credibility, and minimize litigation risk.

However, research after the internet boom, such Krishnan and Sriram (2000) and Marston and Polei (2004), argue that internet reporting gives better performance for companies. As shown by Hunter and Smith (2009), listed stocks on developing market stock exchanges were performing well after conducting online financial disclosures. It showed that using internet reporting has a positive relationship with stock market prices. In the study of Brown, Gatian, and Hicks (1995), they showed that the use of information technology is positively related with the financial performance in the company. The stock market reacted to the firms' announcements. It showed that when the companies were investing in *Strategic Information Systems* (SISs), the firms would tend to have increased production and profits. Those conditions will be better than in their respective industries. According to Krishnan and Sriram's (2000) study, it stated that the performance of firms is improved when there is an increase in information technology investments. Meanwhile, Barua, Knebel, and Mukhopadhyay (1995) also agreed that information technology contributed positively to firm performance.

Hence, this research hypothesizes the following: *There is a positive relationship between corporate internet reporting and firm performance.*

Methodology

Baseline Model

This study uses the regression to analyze the relation between firm value and the other three independent variables, which are size, leverage, and growth. Thus, the function of the equation model is formulated as follows:

$$Q = f\,(Size, Leverage, Growth)$$

The estimation model is as follows:

$$Q_i = \beta_0 + \beta_1 SIZE_i + \beta_2 LEVERAGE_i + \beta_3 GROWTH_i + \varepsilon_i \quad (1)$$

where Q is the company's performance that measured by Tobin's q, Size is the company's size, Leverage is the company's total debt divided by total assets, and Growth is capital expenditures divided by total sales.

Estimation Model

Furthermore, in this estimation model, the CIR is added into the equation to investigate the effect of CIR on the firm's value. Therefore, the function of the second equation model is formulated as follows:

$$Q = f\,(Size, Leverage, Growth, Internet\_Reporting)$$

Table 1. Operational Variables

Variables	Types	Variable Definition	Type of Scale	Hypothesis Direction
Firm performance	Dependent	$\frac{MVE + PS + DEBT}{TA}$	Ratio	-
CIR	Independent	$Ij = \frac{\sum_{i=1}^{nj} Xij}{njj}$	Ratio	positive
Size	Independent	Log (total assets)	Ratio	positive
Leverage	Independent	$\frac{\text{Book value of debt}}{\text{Total assets}}$	Ratio	positive
Growth	Independent	$\frac{\text{Relative capital expenditure}}{\text{Sales}}$	Ratio	positive

The estimation model is:

$$Q_i = \beta_0 + \beta_1 SIZE_i + \beta_2 LEVERAGE_i + \beta_3 GROWTH_i + \\ + \beta_3 CIR_i + \varepsilon_i \quad (2)$$

This model is formed under a cross sectional regression. However, it has to pass the classical assumptions, such as normality, autocorrelation, heteroscedasticity, and multicollinearity.

Firm performance

The study of Bharadwaj et al. (1999) used the Tobin's Q that is adapted from the Chung and Pruitt (1994) for measuring firm performance. According to Chung and Pruit (1994) and Wolfe and Sauaia (2003), Tobin's Q is the statistic can proxy from firm value. It is also a standardized performance measure (Chung & Pruit, 1994). Moreover, Fauzi and Locke (2012) mentioned that "Tobin's Q value from zero to one is considered as a low performance, and it may indicate that the stock is undervalued" (p. 55). The formula of Tobin's Q based on Bharadwaj et al.'s (1999) paper is shown as follows:

$$\text{Tobin's Q} = \frac{MVE + PS + DEBT}{TA} \quad (3)$$

MVE (market value of equity) shows the closing price of a stock at the end of a period multiplied by the number of outstanding common stocks. PS shows the liquidating value of the company's outstanding preferred stocks. DEBT shows the difference between current liabilities and current assets, plus the book value of inventories and long term debt (LTD). TA shows the book value of total assets.

The construction of internet financial reporting index

This research uses the content analysis approach to measure the CIR. It follows the study from Aly et al. (2010) in calculating the disclosure information for each non-financial Malaysian listed company. We use the same method from Aly et al. (2010) because it is comprehensible and provides an evaluation result that is consistent with previous studies. The index consists of 36 items: 12 items of the disclosure format, and 24 of the content items. The disclosure index calculation for every company is done by dividing the actual scores with the maximum possible scores that are appropriate for the company.

$$I_j = \frac{\sum_{i=1}^{nj} Xij}{njj} \quad (4)$$

where njj $= n_j$ is number of relative items applicable to company *j*. $X_{ij} = 1$ if the item is disclosed and 0 if the item is not disclosed.

Table 2. Descriptive Statistics of All Variables

Variables	N	Min	Mean	Max	Median	Sd	Skewness	Kurtosis
Firm value	583	.000	.199	.690	.183	.159	.550	-.456
Size	583	.000	.380	.640	.389	.119	-.340	.201
CIR	583	4.35	5.633	7.680	5.575	.598	.640	.306
Leverage	583	-.380	.155	.630	.139	.149	.388	1.358
Growth	583	-6.910	-3.441	.570	-3.381	1.405	-.194	.000

Findings

Descriptive results

Table 2 shows the descriptive statistics for all variables in this study, such as the firm's value, size, CIR, leverage, and growth. This research sample covers 583 non-financial listed firms at Bursa Malaysia in the year 2013. All variables are presented in their ratio form. The average of the dependent variable, firm value, is 0.199 and its median is 0.183. The mean (median) of the independent variables of size, CIR, leverage, and growth are 0.380 (0.389), 5.633 (5.575), 0.155 (0.139), and -3.441 (-3.381), respectively.

The descriptive statistics display that both the skewness and kurtosis indicate that all variables in this study are normally distributed. According to Haniffa and Hudaib's (2006) study, the data are statistically considered to be normally distributed when the skewness value is within ±1.96 and the kurtosis value is within ±3. Based on Table 2, the skewness and the kurtosis of all variables are between ±1.96 and ±3 respectively, and thus all variables are normally distributed.

Table 3 reports the baseline model results of firm value and the control variables. Its results display that size is positive statistically significant associated with firm value at the 1% level. This implies that if a firm's size increases, it would add more value to the firm. For example, the firm value would increase by 19% if the firm's size grew by 1%. Moreover, the leverage has a negative statistically significant relationship with firm value at the 1% level. It indicates that when the liability increases, more firm values would be reduced. For instance, the firm's value would decrease by 18.4% if the leverage increased by 1%. In addition, growth presents a positive statistically significant association with firm value at the 5% level. This denotes that the firms that have higher growth rates would tend to contribute more value to its firm. It could be explained that the 1.4% increase of a firm's value would be the result of an increase in the growth rate by 1%.

Referring to Table 3, it shows that the R-Squared is 15.3% with the adjusted R-Squared of 14.6%. This means that the independent variables explain 15.3% of the control variable. According to Gujarati and Porter (2009), an R-Squared in a cross-sectional study is good if it is within 10% to 90%. Thus, this result has a good R-Squared. The F-value is 8.068 and is significant at the 1% level. This also indicates the model is robust enough and has a good fit.

Table 4 reports the CIR model's results that show the effect of CIR on firm value. Again, this second model's result produces a positive relationship between firm size and firm value, which has the coefficient value of 0.083. However, its result is statistically insignificant. Next, the CIR has a positive statistically significant relationship with firm value at the 1% level. It implies that if the companies disclose more information of their reporting through the internet, the values of their firms would be increased. For instance, a CIR increase of 1% would cause the firm's value to increase by 8.7%. Other than that, the leverage shows a negative statistically significant relationship with firm value at the 1% level. This represents that a 1% increase in the debt of firms would cause the firm value to decrease by 23.3%. In contrast, there is a positive statistically significant relationship between firm growth and firm value in this CIR model at the 10% level. This denotes that the

Table 3. Baseline Model Results

In this study, the baseline model and corporate internet reporting model are run separately. The regression is performed using the GLS regression to analyze the association between firm value and the control variables. The stated figures are the coefficient values with the standard error in parentheses. The dependent variable is the firm value (Q). The control variables are the Size (Siz), Leverage (Lev), and Growth (Growth).

The baseline model is as follows: $Q_i = \beta_0 + \beta_1 Siz_i + \beta_2 Lev_i + \beta_3 Growth_i + \varepsilon_i$

Constant	0.215***
	(0.032)
Size	0.190***
	(0.055)
Leverage	-0.184***
	(0.047)
Growth	0.014**
	(0.005)
R-Squared	0.153
Adjusted R-Squared	0.146
F Test	8.068***

Note: *, **, and *** denote statistical significance at the 10%, 5%, and 1% levels, respectively.

Table 4. Corporate internet reporting (CIR) Model Results

At this phase, the CIR model is run again with the dependent variable as Tobin's Q (Q), the main independent variable is CIR (IR), and the control variables are Size (Siz), Leverage (Lev), and Growth (Growth).

CIR model is as follows: $Q_i = \beta_0 + \beta_1 Siz_i + \beta_2 Lev_i + \beta_3 Growth_i + \beta_4 IR_i + \varepsilon_i$

Constant	0.240***
	(0.066)
Size	0.083
	(0.054)
CIR	0.087***
	(0.011)
Leverage	-0.233***
	(0.045)
Growth	0.008*
	(0.005)
R-Squared	0.143
Adjusted R-Squared	0.136
F Test	19.257***

Note: *, **, and *** denote statistical significance at the 10%, 5%, and 1% levels, respectively.

Table 5. Hypotheses Results

Hypothesis	Results	Significance level	Supported by
H1: There is a positive relationship between corporate internet reporting (CIR) and firm value.	Accepted	1%	Brown et al. (1995), Krishnan and Sriram (2000), and Hunter and Smith (2009).
H2: There is a positive relationship between size and firm value.	Rejected	-	Errunza and Senbet (1984) and Naceur and Goaied (2002).
H3: There is a positive relationship between leverage and firm value.	Rejected	1%	Miller and Rock (1985), Brush, et al. (2000), and Denis, et al. (2002).
H4: There is a positive relationship between growth and firm value	Accepted	10%	Brush et al. (2000), Fauver, et al. (2004), and Cho and Pucik's (2005).

firms that expand or develop by 1% would increase their firm's value by 8%.

It shows that the R-Squared is 14.3% with the adjusted R-Squared of 13.6%. This means that the independent variables (size, CIR, leverage, and growth) explain the dependent variable (firm value) at the level of 14.3%. Note that a good R-Squared in a cross-sectional study is if it is within 10% to 90% (Gujarati & Porter, 2009). The F-value is 19.257 and is significant at the 1% level. This also indicates that the model is robust enough and has a good fit.

This research finds that CIR has a positive and significant relationship with firm value at the 1% significance level. This outcome is the same as the findings from Hunter and Smith (2009) in which the increase in practicing internet reporting would improve the firm's performance. In addition, it also agrees with the research findings of Brown et al. (1995) in which the productivity of firms would be improved when strategic information systems are implemented. Moreover, it has a similar assumption with the findings of Krishnan and Sriram (2000) in which the high tendency of using information technology in investments can lead to a competitive advantage and thus improve the firm's performance.

Conclusion

This study investigates the relationship between firm performance and corporate internet reporting (CIR). The scope of this research is non-financial Malaysian public listed companies in the year 2013. Furthermore, this study contains a number of control variables that consist of firm size, leverage, and growth for developing a better estimation model. In addition, the general theoretical literature on this topic and specifically in the context of Malaysia is scant.

The estimation model refers to previous literatures such as Kelton and Yang (2008) and Aly et al. (2010). Moreover, this estimation model has to pass through the normality, multicollinearity, autocorrelation, and heteroscedasticity test before the linear regression model. The standard error is controlled by the model since it violates the heteroscedasticity assumption. In short, this study has ensured that the model is robust enough to answer the research questions.

The outcomes of this study found that CIR has a significant effect on firm value at the 1% level. This research finding is consistent with prior studies, such as Brown et al. (1995), Krishnan and Sriram (2000), and Hunter and Smith (2009). This implies that the outcome of the first research question is that there is a significant association between CIR and firm value. Furthermore, for the second research question, the answer is that there is a positive but insignificant association between firm size and firm value. This result is similar to the findings from Errunza and Senbet (1984) and Naceur and Goaied (2002). It may depend on the specific type of corporate disclosure. Ho and

Wong (2001) stated that CIR may be complementary or substitutive disclosures. No matter the size of the company, the disclosure should not rely solely on the market mechanism (Hermalin & Weisbach, 2012). The manager also should take all the necessary measures to ensure all information in the disclosure items is adequately disclosed in order to avoid penalties.

Moreover, the answer for third research question is that leverage has a negative statistically significant effect on firm value at the 1% level. This can be supported by the findings from Miller and Rock (1985), Brush, Bromiley, and Hendrickx (2000), and Denis, Denis, and Yost (2002). For the last research question, growth has a positive statistically significant effect on firm value. This result is consistent with the outcomes of the previous studies of Cho and Pucik (2005), Fauver, Houston, and Naranjo (2004) and Brush et al. (2000). In short, this study reveals that CIR significantly affects firm value. It means that more related information that is regularly disclosed on companies' websites can contribute more value to the firms.

This study contributes to the resource base view theory in two ways. First, it confirms Porter (1985) that information is a part of the resources that are needed by a firm to enhance their company's performance. Available information represents the good image and reputation of a company. It also enables fast decision making for related parties. Hence, it boosts the firm's performance through the channel of a better collection period, higher demand, or even lower capital costs. This is in line with prior studies, such as Mata, Fuerst, and Barney (1995), Bharadwaj et al. (1999), Barney and Ray (2015), and Mithas and Rust (2016).

In addition, this research also contributes to signaling theory. It further explores the principle that signaling theory is associated with the relation between the CIR and firm value. This theory indicates that the information effect that can be given by company as a signal to the investors (Craven & Marston, 1999; Myers, 1984). In this study, it uses voluntary disclosures as a mean of signaling. Therefore, if a firm can disclose additional information above the mandatory requirement, it tends to signal good business performance (Craven & Marston, 1999). Hence, this study is to give extra proof that the signaling theory can increase firm value.

This study contributes useful findings on the impact of CIR towards firm value. This is because those regulators can rely on it to establish suitable policies to improve the quality of internet disclosures. It is crucial to raise awareness of the limitations of mandatory disclosures among policy makers so that they can increase the level of mandatory disclosures to meet the investors' needs in decision making.

Conversely, this research also investigates the other factors that could influence firm value. In this study, firm size, profitability, leverage, growth, and ownership structure are examined to assess their impacts on the development of firm value. Thus, regulators could refer to the findings of this study to enforce and implement appropriate rules and regulations to ensure that the value of the firm is protected.

For future work, we suggest several developments, as follows. First, future study can explore the differences in the information in format items and content items for a disclosure index that can impact the firm's performance. Thus, the CIR index can be measured using a questionnaire addressed to the manager(s) of the firm to assess the details about the disclosure methods and the different types of information, such as financial and non-financial. Second, future study may elaborate on the rationale behind internet reporting such as earnings management, managerial entrenchment, and other agency cost issues. Future study may also relate the internet reporting as the media for the director to establish their "curriculum vitae" and relate it to their compensation. Furthermore, further research can use financial listed firms for the sample since they have special financial policies and characteristics that are different from non-financial firms.

References

Adhikari, A. & Tondkar, R. H. (1992). Environmental factors influencing accounting disclosure requirements of global stock exchanges. *Journal of International Financial Management and Accounting*, 4(2), 75-105.

Aly, D., Simon, J,. & Hussainey, K. (2010). Determinants of corporate internet reporting: Evidence from Egypt. *Managerial Auditing Journal*, 25(2), 182-202.

Bakos, J. Y. (1991). A strategic analysis of electronic marketplaces. *MIS Quarterly*, 15(3), 295-310.

Barney, J., & Ray, G. A. U. T. A. M. (2015). How information technology sources can provide a competitive advantage in customer service. *Planning for Information Systems*, 3(2), 444-460.

Barua, A., Kriebel, C. H., & Mukhopadhyay, T. (1995). Information technologies and business value: An analytic and empirical investigation. *Information Systems Research*, 6(1), 3-23.

Beaver, W. H. (1968). The information content of annual earnings announcements. *Journal of Accounting Research*, 6, 67-92.

Becker, G. S. (1967). Human capital and the personal distribution of income: An analytical approach. An Arbor, MI: Institute of Public Administration.

Bharadwaj, A. S., Bharadwaj, S. G., & Konsynski, B. R. (1999). Information technology effects on firm performance as measured by Tobin's q. *Management Science*, 45(7), 1008-1024.

Brown, R. M., Gatian, A. W., & Hicks, Jr. J. O. (1995). Strategic information systems and financial performance. *Journal of Management Information Systems*, 11(4), 215-248.

Brush, T. H., Bromiley, P., & Hendrickx, M. (2000). The free cash flow hypothesis for sales growth and firm performance. *Strategic Management Journal*, 21(4), 455-472.

Brynjolfsson, E. & Hitt, L. (1996). Paradox lost? Firm-level evidence on the returns to information systems spending. *Management Science*, 42(4), 541-558.

Chao, C. F., Hsu, C. C., & Yeh, H. S. (2010). The relationship between information transparency and firm value: Evidence from Taiwan. *International Journal Business Excellence*, 3(2), 125-141.

Check, I. T., Mohamad, Z. Z. B., Yunus, J. N. & Norwami, N. M. (2013). Corporate social responsibility (CSR) disclosure in consumer products and plantation industry in Malaysia. *American International Journal of Contemporary Research*, 3(5), 118-125.

Cho, H. J., & Pucik, V. (2005). Relationship between innovativeness, quality, growth, profitability, and market value. *Strategic Management Journal*, 26(6), 555-575.

Chung, K. H., & Pruitt, S. W. (1994). A simple approximation of Tobin's q. *Financial Management*, 23(3), 70-74.

Craven, B. M. & Marston, C. L. (1999). Financial reporting on the internet by leading UK companies. *The European Accounting Review*, 8(2), 321-333.

Daft, R. L. (1983). *Organization theory and design*. St. Paul, MN: West Publishing Company.

Denis, D. J., Denis, D. K., & Yost, K. (2002). Global diversification, industrial diversification, and firm value. *The Journal of Finance*, 57(5), 1951-1979.

Diamond, D. W. & Verrecchia, R. E. (1991). Disclosure, liquidity and the cost of capital. *The Journal of Finance*, 46(4), 1325 - 1359.

Errunza, V. R., & Senbet, L. W. (1984). International corporate diversification, market valuation, and size-adjusted evidence. *The Journal of Finance*, 39(3), 727-743.

Fauver, L., Houston, J. F., & Naranjo, A. (2004). Cross-country evidence on the value of corporate industrial and international diversification. *Journal of Corporate Finance*, 10(5), 729-752.

Fauzi, F., & Locke, S. (2012). Board structure, ownership structure and firm performance: A study of New Zealand listed-firms. *Asian Academy of Management Journal of Accounting and Finance*, 8(2), 43-67.

Gujarati, D. N., & Porter, D. C. (2009). *Basic econometrics (5th ed.)*. Boston, MA: McGraw-Hill.

Grant, R. M. (1991). The resource-based theory of competitive advantage: Implications for strategy formulation. *Knowledge and Strategy*, 33(3), 114-135.

Hanafi, S. R. B. M., Kasim, M. A. B., Ibrahim, M. K. B., & Hancock, D. R. (2009). Business reporting on the internet: Development of a disclosure quality index. *International Journal of Business and Economics*, 8(1), 455-479.

Haniffa, R., & Hudaib, M. (2006). Corporate governance structure and performance of Malaysian listed companies. *Journal of Business Finance and Accounting*, 33(7-8), 1034-1062.

Hansen, J. V. (2001). Internet commerce security: Issues and models for control checking. *The Journal of the Operational Research Society*, 52(10), 1159-1164.

Hermalin, B. E., & Weisbach, M. S. (2012). Information disclosure and corporate governance. *The Journal of Finance*, 67(1), 195-233.

Heye, D. (2009, September 28). *ACORN Story shows how internet reporting is beating The New York Times*. Retrieved from http://www.usnews.com/opinion/blogs/doug-heye/2009/09/28/acorn-story-shows-how-internet-reporting-is-beating-the-new-york-times

Ho, S. S. M., & Wong. K. S. (2001). A study of the relationship between corporate governance structures and the extent of voluntary disclosure. *Journal of International Accounting, Auditing and Taxation*, 10(2), 139-156.

Hunter, S. A., & Smith, L. M. (2009). Impact of internet financial reporting on emerging markets. *Journal of International Business Research*, 8(2), 21-40.

Hussey, R. & Sowinska, M. (1999). The risks of financial reports on the internet. *Accounting and Business*, 3, 18–19.

Jones, M. J. & Xiao, J. Z. (2003). Internet reporting: current trends and trends by 2010. *Accounting Forum*, 27(2), 132-165.

Kelton, A. S., & Yang, Y. W. (2008). The impact of corporate governance on internet financial reporting. *Journal of Accounting and Public Policy*, 27(1), 62-87.

Khan, M. N. A. A. & Ismail, N. A. (2011). The level of internet financial reporting of Malaysian companies. *Asian Journal of Accounting and Governance*, 2, 27-39.

Krishnan, G. V., & Sriram, R. S. (2000). An examination of the effect of it investments on firm value: The case of Y2K-compliance costs. *Journal of Information Systems*, 14(2), 95-108.

Lai, S. C., Lin, C., Li, H. C., & Wu, F. H. (2010). An empirical study of the impact of internet financial reporting on stock prices. *The International Journal of Digital Accounting Research*, 10, 1-26.

Lazarides, T., Drimpetas, E., Argyropoulou, M. & Motwani, J. (2009), Corporate governance and the information systems excellence factor. *International Journal of Business Excellence*, 2(1), 16–29.

Li, Y., & McConomy, B. J. (1999). An empirical examination of factors affecting the timing of environmental accounting standard adoption and the impact on corporate valuation. *Journal of Accounting, Auditing and Finance*, 14(3), 279-313.

Marston, C., & Polei, A. (2004). Corporate reporting on the internet by German companies. *International Journal of Accounting Information Systems*, 5(3), 285-311.

Mata, F. J., Fuerst, W. L., & Barney, J. B. (1995). Information technology and sustained competitive advantage: A resource-based analysis. *MIS Quarterly*, 19(4), 487-505.

Miller, M. H., & Rock, K. (1985). Dividend policy under asymmetric information. *The Journal of Finance*, 40(4), 1031-1051.

Mithas, S. & Rust, R. T. (2016). How information technology strategy and investments influence firm performance: Conjectures and empirical evidence. *MIS Quarterly*, 40(1), 223-245.

Myers, S. C. (1984). The capital structure puzzle. *The Journal of Finance*, 39(3), 575- 592.

Naceur, S. B., & Goaied, M. (2002). The relationship between dividend policy, financial structure, profitability and firm value. *Applied Financial Economics*, 12(12), 843-849.

Peteraf, M. A. (1993). The cornerstones of competitive advantage: A resource-based view. *Strategic Management Journal*, 14(3), 179-191.

Porter, M. (1985). *Competitive strategy*. New York, NY: Free Press.

Shehata, N. F. (2014). Theories and determinants of voluntary disclosure. *Accounting and Finance Research*, 3(1), 18-26.

Spence, M. (1973). Job market signaling. *The Quarterly Journal of Economics*, 87(3), 355-374.

Statista. (2014). *Number of worldwide internet users from 2000 to 2015 (in millions)*. Available at http://www.statista.com/statistics/273018/number-of-internet-users-worldwide/

Tomer, J. F. (1987). *Organizational capital: The path to higher productivity and well-being*. New York, NY: Praeger.

Williamson, O. E. (1975). *Markets and hierarchies*. New York, NY: Free Press.

Willis, M., Tesnie're, B. & Jones, A. (2003). Corporate communications for the 21st century. A white paper discussing the impact of internet technologies on business reporting. New York, NY: PricewaterhouseCoopers.

Wolfe, J., & Sauaia, A. C. A. (2003). The Tobin q as a business game performance indicator. *Developments in Business Simulation and Experiential Learning*, 36(2), 238-249.

Appendix

Disclosure items

FORMAT

1. Annual report in multiple file formats
2. Financial data in processable format
3. Hyperlinked table of contents
4. Drop-down navigational menu
5. Hyperlinks inside the annual report
6. Hyperlinks to data on a third-party's website
7. Audio files
8. Video files
9. Email alerts
10. Direct e-mail to investor relations
11. Dynamic graphic images
12. Internal search engines

CONTENT

13. Current year's annual report
14. Last year's annual report
15. Recent quarterly report
16. Other filings
17. Link to EDGAR or 10-K Wizard
18. Charters for the audit committee
19. Code of conduct and ethics for directors, officers and employees
20. Members of the Board of Directors
21. Recent monthly financial data
22. Performance overview (e.g., highlights, fact-sheet, and 'FAQ')
23. Earnings estimates
24. Calendar of events of interests to investors
25. Recent financial news releases
26. Listing of analysts following the firm
27. Analyst ratings
28. Text of speeches and presentations
29. Same-day stock prices
30. Historical stock prices
31. Information about the firm's stock transfer agent
32. The advantages of holding the firm's stock
33. Information regarding a dividend reinvestment plans
34. Dividend history
35. Corporate governance principles/guidelines
36. Charters for other committees

Source: Kelton, A. S. and Yang, Y. (2008, p. 71)

8

Financial Sustainability Criteria and their testing in the conditions of the Slovak Non-Profit Sector

Denisa Gajdová[1], Helena Majdúchová[1]

ABSTRACT

Socio-economic and political changes after November 1989 have strongly influenced Slovak society, with impacts being observed on almost all areas of economic, political, social and public life. Highly intensive development of the so-called "third sector" has been among these factors. A new legislation framework has been created. Non-profit organizations have become the state's partners in the area of providing social services not secured by the state, and these organizations have strong economic and social power, influencing the development of the whole society. Today, financial sustainability is one of the fundamental problems in the non-profit sector. This problem has become more important due to foreign capital withdrawal by donors to non-profit organizations, primarily during the 1990s. National support from public sources is limited and is not sufficient for the functioning of non-profit organizations. In non-profit organizations, we emphasize the necessity of the diversity of financial resource structures, ensuring their independence, financial stability and sustainability from both short-term and long-term perspectives. The aim of this article is to establish key criteria for non-profit organizations' financial sustainability, subsequently investigating these criteria's dependence and the level of financial source acquisition in a selected sample of Slovak non-profit organizations. We assume that owing to these criteria, non-profit organisations (NPOs) could better formulate their financial strategies, diversify and stabilize their financial sources and transform this strategy into a long-term strategic plan to maintain and develop their entrepreneurial missions.

KEY WORDS: non-profit organization, financial sustainability, criteria of financial sustainability, stability

[1] University of Economics in Bratislava, Slovakia

Introduction

Non-profit organizations play a relevant role in society by attempting to satisfy human needs in different ways or as a complement to lucrative firms and governmental activity (Soriano & Galindo, 2010; Svidroňová Vaceková, & Valentinov, 2016). The non-profit sector in Slovakia, as in other countries, has been the subject of important modifications since 1989 in the area of legislative organization, as well as in the fields of personal, material and financial resource achievement. One difficult problem that is common to non-profit organizations in all post-communist countries is their need for financing. This problem has been mentioned in the

Correspondence concerning this article should be addressed to: **Denisa Gajdová**, University of Economics in Bratislava, Dolnozemská cesta 1/b, 852 35 Bratislava 5, Slovak Republic, E-mail: denisa.gajdova@euba.sk

works of many authors. The crisis has increased the interest in 'ethics' in the business world, at least in certain of its circles. Dembinski (2011) emphasized that the 'profit motive' is an incomplete and even dangerously reductive description of the true purpose of business.

In recent years, one of the more frequently mentioned topics concerning the non-profit sector has been the effort to achieve financial stability and the sustainability of organizations. To be able to achieve its determined aims and to fulfill the requests of receivers of its services has been discussed in the works of various authors (Bienzle et al., 2007; Bryson, Crosby & Stone, 2006; Davis & Etchart, 1999; Kotler & Lee, 2005; Kuvíková, 2009; Reider, 2001; Selsky & Parker, 2005; Svidroňová & Vaceková 2012; Valentinov, 2012; Valentinov, Hielscher & Pies, 2015). This topic is also associated with so-called donor fatigue (the authors understand this concept to be sequential restriction or cutting off of donations or benefits from donors to non-governmental organizations), which emerges in highly developed states. The literature has more frequently mentioned that non-governmental organizations (NGOs) could take more control over their finances and be financially sustainable. In reality, we can find this concept discussed regarding various types of organizations, e.g., NGOs, non-profit organizations (NPOs), and voluntary organizations (VO). These concepts could be considered synonyms because there is only one specific aspect emphasized, e.g., independence from government (non-governmental), establishment without a profit motive (non-profit), and a high percentage of voluntary work (voluntary).

The term *financial sustainability of non-profit organizations* has become a common phrase in the non-profit sector in recent years. Various authors have focused on this topic (Atkinson, 2003; Boukal & Vávrová, 2007; Boris & Steuerle, 2006; Weerawardena, McDonald & Mort 2010; Valentinov & Vaceková, 2015). In this case, foreign resources use the term financial sustainability, which has occurred more frequently, although we can also observe the idea of financial stability mentioned there. Organizations are financially stable if the core of their activity does not decrease when external donor resources decrease (The Management Accounting for Non-Governmental Organisations [Mango], 2013a).

Financial stability is, according to us, the position in which non-profit organizations ensure stable financial resources well and continuously pursue their own functions, and financial stability is sufficiently resistant to unfavorable financial conditions. Maintaining stability does not indicate rigidity or efforts not to change anything; in contrast, it supposes flexibility and the ability of NGOs to react flexibly to economic changes surrounding NPOs and themselves. The framework for flexible decision-making is broader if the NPO has some financial resources. Financial stability is the one of basic conditions of the total sustainability of NGOs. According to Canarella, Nouray, and Sullivan (2014), together with these points, it is very important to maintain an optimal capital structure.

The financial sustainability of non-governmental organization is the situation in which the organization has reasonable expectations about its cost coverage in the foreseeable future through financing from donors. If the number of donors decreases, organizations can work on returning to financial sustainability with the help of cost decreases and income generation (according to the United States Agency for International Development [USAID], 2008). Another definition says that financial sustainability is considered the long-term financial security of an organization, based on strong relations with a number of participants, various resources, incomes, specifically unlimited resources and general reserves (Mango, 2013b). The key to financial sustainability is varying compositions of resources of difference types, at least some of which are guaranteed over the long term (Etchart, Davis, Messing, & Guštafík, 2003). It is necessary to measure the profitability of achieved results, which could cause difficulties in the conditions of non-profit organizations. (Majdúchová, 2012).

According to us, a financially sustainable organization has more than sufficient financing. It should be able to ensure long-term and various income with the aim of provide activity according to its mission, being transparent and trustworthy and fulfilling criteria established for the achievement of the financial sustainability of NPOs. In this context, we examined the index of non-profit organization sustainability.

The index of non-profit organization sustainability (INPOS) is the key analytic tool that measures the development of NGOs in the regions of Central and Eastern Europe and Eurasia. Over fifteen years, the index has shown the development of NGOs in 29 countries.

The index examines the total favorable environment influencing the NGO, and it focuses on the legal environment, organizational capacity, financial vitality, defense of interests, provision of services, infrastructure and the perception of NPOs by the public. Every area is evaluated using a seven point scale, in which 1 indicates a very advanced level and 7 indicates a low level of development. The index was created by the United States Agency for International Development (USAID) with the cooperation of local organizations from all countries. According to information from USAID (2013), the index found 8 characteristics and 4 indicators marked by decreasing tendencies (see Table 1 in the Appendix).

The next figure (see Figure 1 in the Appendix) compares the index of sustainability from the subsequent three years in these countries.

Development of the sustainability index did not show a positive tendency in the V4 countries during 2013-2015, except for Poland. The results for Slovakia were extremely negative, showing decreased development and concerns about financial sustainability, as well. In addition, these indicators demonstrated the increased importance of this topic for non-profit organizations.

Financing of non-profit organizations in Slovakia

The financial situation of the non-profit sector in Slovakia has been influenced by enormous foreign support since 1989. Later, a reduction in the foreign public resources connected to integration into the EU and NATO occurred, including the achievement of a specific level of NGO maturity in Slovakia. Finally, development is characterized by a higher level of dependency on new methods of financing and national resource involvement.

Requirements of high professionalism also increase with the quality demanded of offered services, and non-profit organizations use criteria that are more serious. These criteria for completion are based on the financial and social performance of the organization and its ability to satisfy the needs of donors. This movement requires the following.

- An essential change in the attitude of non-profit organizations toward accepting financial resources and ongoing transfer in seeking new sponsors and donors through the creation of relationships with a stable donor base
- The stimulation of organizations themselves to create financial resources
- A permanent increase in the effectiveness of used resources (Majdúchová, 2009)

Now, we can identify the following structure of financial resources in non-profit organizations in Slovakia (see Table 2 in the Appendix).

Non-profit organizations in Slovakia receive support from individual budget chapters of individual ministries of the Slovak government. The level of these resources is not possible to set accurately. One of the important public resources consists of assignations of 2 % from the income tax levied on natural and legal entities. The total amount was 52 million euros. These sources were applied to more than 11,800 organizations in 2015. There exists a disproportion of success among individual organizations (Boehnke, Rippl & Fuss, 2015; Hagedorn, 2014).

Only foundations established as highly profitable enterprises with the possibility of sending them two percent have long-term profits from this assignation. Enterprises have sent on average to the third sector €4 200, while the remainder have sent only €443.

Charitable activity covered by paid taxes could be used for the promotion of one's own enterprise.

The percentage mechanism is the one important tool of indirect public support of non-governmental organizations, and it is also very popular for receiving organizations and legal entities.

Financing of non-profit organizations in Slovakia from national private resources could be divided into resources from the entrepreneurial sector and resources from individual donors. In this regard, it is necessary to mention that there are no official statistics at this time that can provide information about the level of provided resources from the entrepreneurial sector or from individual donors.

Support from the entrepreneurial sector very often has the following form.

Enterprise donorship (corporate philanthropy) – indicating the willingness of the enterprise to offer a degree of value for beneficial public purposes without a request for counter-value. Now, there are no legal tools that motivate entrepreneurs and enterprises to financially support the activities of the non-profit sector (in the past, there was the possibility of depreciating the value of gifts from the tax base). Voluntary contributions of NPs (natural persons) and LPs (legal persons) as sources of income for NPOs do not have long-term histories. Therefore, this resource is often unexpected and uncertain for the future. Enterprises usually create foundation funds, to which entrepreneurial subjects give their own resources or sends 2 % from taxes. The scale of the most important enterprise contributors every year creates forums of donors (so-called Top Enterprise Philanthropy), a unique index in the Slovak Republic, which since 2005 provides information about enterprise donorship. Additionally, it is very important that NGOs do not ask only for financial support because, for local entrepreneurs or enterprises, it is often more acceptable to provide one's own services free, for example, copying of documents, cheaper rentals, or one's own products, such as computing technology or furniture. Important company donors often enter into long-term cooperation with selected NPOs, with programs or activities supported for various years. Thus, Dubcová (2014) found that a large task is the strengthening of socially responsible behavior, mainly "the existence of relevance of the functional strategy for corporate responsibility" (p. 69). We can speak about the following types of activities.

- *Sponsorship*
- *Campaign leadership*
- *Philanthropic marketing* (cause related)
- *Strategic partnerships with the community*

Individual resources for financing are the smallest part of NPO financing, but in no case are these resources less important. They are created by the resources of individuals, and we can say that the methods of achievement of such resources are among the most stable and difficult. It is important to have many small donors, which is very difficult; in contrast, the loss of donors does not influence the stability of organization. According to Rugman and Verbeke (2004), we live in a world of semi-globalization. However, in Slovakia, individual donors (taxpayers, families who freely decide to support NGOs according to their work results) focused on relatively few NPOs because they expect much personnel, material, time and financial capacity. In such cases, the organization is able to achieve the confidence of a great number of individuals, and such resources could be very important and sustainable for the future (Brozmanová et al., 2009).

In 2011, the Coalition for Support of Individual Donorship was created, which signed a document between members' non-governmental organizations. The reason for its creation was the acute need for the improvement of the donor environment in Slovakia.

Now, non-profit organizations in Slovakia use some basic forms of individual donor address, such as wage deductions, public philanthropy activities, direct contact, member contributions, and donor SMS and permanent charge orders. An important source of NPO financing is self-financing, which is the acquisition of financial sources by one's own activities, e.g., sale of products, provision of services, use of tangible and intangible assets, and investment in securities (Vaceková & Svidroňova, 2014).

Financial sustainability of non-profit organizations

Non-profit organizations face an increasing expectation to be more business-like (Sanders & McClellan, 2012). Business is very often associated with financial sustainability. Determination of the idea of financial sustainability is slightly connected with the identification of key criteria, which are significant for its achievement. We obtained their determination from information published in the USA (the Nature Conservancy Organization) and the UK (Mango, 2013a). The concept of sustainability is often unclear and confusing. It has many definitions and forms: environmental, economic, social and political (Svidroňová, 2013). The sustainability of NPOs remains importance in today's quickly changing business environment of multidisciplinary studies. This is the outcome of NPO activity in a complex environment that has many contradictory effects; e.g., the commercialization of NPO activities increases together with requests to cooperate with public institutions and other NPOs. We are speaking about analyzing methods created in the UK and the USA. Statements of criteria, which are suitable for financial sustainability, are the work of the Mango non-profit organization registered in the UK. Its aim was to strengthen the financial management and financial responsibility of non-profit organizations and their partners. In 2010, this non-profit organization created a methodology that address the financial management of non-profit organizations and that could help NPOs to use their own resources effectively.

American skills were taken from the Nature Conservancy Organization, which cooperates with various non-profit organizations worldwide and which decided to share its experiences obtained in previous years. It prepared a document that could help to non-profit organizations solve daily issues. One part of the document in the cycle "Resources for Success" is a manual about the financial sustainability of non-profit organizations, entitled "Four pillars of financial sustainability" by Patricia León. It is a unique source that summarizes information about financial sustainability very comprehensively.

The analysis and subsequent synthesis created a list of the most important things that non-profit organizations can do for the maintenance of financial sustainability in practice. The criteria mentioned are not obligatory for every NPO because each of them differs and solves individual problems. It is suitable to consider this methodology a guideline and to adapt it to one's own organization. Some criteria could be modified or eliminated, and new ones could be added.

Objectives and Methods

The objective of this article is to provide more information about the financial sustainability of non-profit organizations in Slovakia through the examination of the dependency of the financial sustainability criteria of NPOs and the extent of financial resource achievement in NPOs. According to the data from USAID, this decreased in the long term, and if they achieved an index of financial vitality of 3.0 in 1997, in 2013, it was only 3.6. We evaluate the fulfillment of such objectives through research questions based on mathematic-statistical methods. The research questions were closely related to the criteria for financial sustainability, which we synthetize using the aforementioned methods.

The number of research questions is in slight interaction with the criteria for financial sustainability evaluation according to the methodology of the Nature Conservancy and Mango organization. Their testing in the area of non-profit organizations in Slovakia focused on the determination of criteria with decisive impacts on financial sustainability.

Research question 1: Are there any dependencies between private financial resources achievement and the NPO's subject of activity?

Research question 2: Are there any dependencies between the achievement of private financial resources and the character of the cooperation of the NPO with the entrepreneurial sector?

Research question 3: Are there any dependencies between the achievement of private financial resources and the number of donors to the NPO?

Research question 4: Are there any dependencies between the achievement of private financial resources and the use of fundraising by the NPO?

Research question 5: Are there any dependencies between the achievement of private financial resources and the relationship between the NPO and donors?

Research question 6: Are there any dependencies between the achievement of private financial resources and the activity of the management of an NPO itself?

Research question 7: Are there any dependencies between the achievement of private financial resources and the strategic planning of an NPO?

Research question 8: Are there any dependencies between the achievement of private financial resources and the financial planning of an NPO?

Research question 9: Are there any dependencies between the achievement of private financial resources and the existence of financial information and the records of an NPO?

The need to evaluate the existence of dependency between the level of achievement of private financial resources and the criteria for financial sustainability have required using knowledge from the area of econometrics. Data were analyzed statistically using the selected statistical software program SPSS (Statistical Package for the Social Sciences, IBM 2009, NY, US), and we examined the data for common characteristics and links. This analysis was performed through two size induction statistics, which have been applied using the Kruskal-Wallis H test and analysis of variance (ANOVA).

The Kruskal-Wallis H test is an extended Mann-Whitney test with three or more samples (in case of two samples, they are equivalent), and it represents a non-parametric alternative to one factor analysis of variance. The aim of the test is to determine whether, in the sample of determined differences of individual groups, meridians (according to the factor level) are statistically significant (between those examined with any relationship) or whether it is only coincidence (there is no relationship between them). The zero statistics hypothesis was tested regarding the equality of all meridians (Rimarčík, 2007). During testing, the rule that at least one of the examined pairs is ordinary was met. We established the order of solutions from the best to the worst with the evaluation of individual questions, and we established a point range from 5 (max) to 1 point (min). Because the examined variables are not cardinal variables in ordinary division, **we believe that** application **of the Kruskal-Wallis test (also after consultation with professionals in statistics) is appropriate.**

For the evaluation of research questions, we also used **one factor analysis of dispersion**, which is a form of ANOVA. One factor (simple) ANOVA examines the relationship between the dependent variable and the nominal variable (factor). The aim of analysis of dispersion is to examine whether, in the observed sample, differences in the averages of individual groups (according to the factor level) are statistically significant (between variables is the relation) or it is only coincidence (there is no relationship between them). In the process of testing, the total variability (sum of square dispersion of the variable value from its average) is divided into intragroup (coincidence fail) and intergroup (set by the difference of groups average). The F-statistics denote the relationship of intragroup and intergroup variability, and it is used for the zero statistics hypothesis test regarding the equality of averages.

We also verified the results of testing with **multifactorial analysis of dispersion (multifactor ANOVA)**, which divides selected files in two groups according to the individual modifications of factors and tests whether there could be discovered differences among the averages of the groups as a mere coincidence or whether they are statistically significant. If the averages of these groups differ significantly, this factor is statistically important, indicating that there is a relationship between the dependent variance and the factor. An advantage of multifactorial analysis of dispersion compared with one factor is the higher power (there is need of fewer observations for capture of an important effect).

As a research tool, we used a questionnaire in which we asked 1015 non-profit organizations about the existence of dependences between the level (extent) of obtained private financial resources and each of the following:

- Subject of activity of non-profit organizations;
- Character of the common cooperation of NPOs with the entrepreneurial sector;
- Diversification (number) of donors of non-profit organizations;
- Use of fundraising in NPOs;
- Relations of NPOs with donors;
- Activity of the management of NPOs themselves;
- Strategic planning of NPOs;
- Financial planning of NPOs; and
- Existence of financial reports and statements of NPOs.

Of 1015 contacted organizations, 105 organizations participated in the research. Their structures reflect the statistical example according to the following criteria: legal format; number of employees; area of activity; age; and regional structure.

We verified the normal division using the Shapiro-Wilk W test, which has in most cases the highest power of all normality tests. Considering calculations and statistics, we can say that in the case of a variable – level of private financial resource achievement -- we refute the null hypothesis about the normality of the distribution. **The normality test results show that, in the case of hypothesis testing about the dependency of the level of achievement of private financial resources, some criteria are suitable for the use of nonparametric tests (see Table 3 in the Appendix).**

A nonparametric alternative to one factor analysis of dispersion is the Kruskal-Wallis H test, which we use for verification of the dependency.

The aim of the test is to determine whether differences in the meridians of individual groups (according to the factor level), which are shown in the observed sample, are statistically significant (there are relations among variables) or whether they are coincidences (among variables there is no relationship). The null statistic hypotheses about the equality of all medians are tested.

If the p-value is less than the chosen level of significance (traditionally 5 % = 0.05), the null hypothesis is refuted, indicating that the difference is too greater.

This difference is among one of the medians counted from the sample. It could be the outcome of the statistically significant chance selection. There is a relationship among the variables.

If the p-value equals or exceeds the selected value of importance, the null hypothesis cannot be refuted, indicating that the differences between every pair of medians from the sample are the only outcomes of the incident selection, which means that it is not statistically significant, i.e., there is no relationship between variables.

Research Outcomes

In this part of our article, we focus on the evaluation of financial sustainability criteria in non-profit organizations according to methodology created by the Nature Conservancy (USA) and Mango (UK) organizations. We evaluate the dependency of selected criteria on the achievement of private financial resources by non-profit organizations. During testing, the respondents did not answer some questions; **therefore, the number of responses can differ.**

1. ***Dependency between private financial resource achievement and the NPO's subject of activity?***
   As we have already mentioned, the majority of examined NGOs are active in the area of education (18 %), culture (18 %), social services (18 %) and sports (12 %). Seven percent of NGOs have the subject of activity another mentioned possibility, such as social and legislative protection, development and humanitarian help, problems of Roma, defense of citizens' rights and interest activities, spiritual development, work with youths, or environmentalism, or the NGOs are cultural activities organization involved in philanthropy and free time organizing. We checked the dependency between the subject of activity and the existence of private financial resources by the Kruskal-Wallis test (see Table 4 in the Appendix).
   The outcome indicates that there are differences between the achievement of private financial resources **under the conditions of the area of activity,** which means that the area of NGO activity is very important if it asks for the entrepreneurial subjects' support and wishes to increase the number of private financial resources **among total incomes**. The entrepreneurial subject financially supports organizations acting in the social services in particular, affirming the research question.

2. ***Dependency between the achievement of private financial resources and the character of cooperation of NPOs with the entrepreneurial sector***
   Research outcomes confirm that 66 % cooperate with some entrepreneurial subjects. We asked respondents about the character of this cooperation: whether it is regular (47 %), occasional (38 %) or ad hoc cooperation (15 %). The research confirmed a low percentage of individual incomes, compared with regular or occasional incomes. The verification of the characteristics of cooperation influences the level of gained financial resources from private/individual resources. We used the Kruskal-Wallis test again (see Table 5 in the Appendix). In cases of private financial resource achievement, regard the dependency and character of cooperation, statistical dependency was not confirmed.

3. ***Dependency between the achievement of private financial resources and numbers of donors of NPOs***
   Burger (2015) observed that foreign donors increasingly transfer aid resources directly to NGOs and not to governments. According to León (2001), a minimum of 60 % of the total budget of an organization can come from five difference sources. This condition, according to the research, is the case in 42 % of organizations. One source of financing (donors) represents more than 80 % of organization incomes according to 13 % of respondents, and 18 % of respondents represent more than one source for 60 % of organization incomes. Any other modification in decisions of these donors can lead to a crisis or instability in an organization (see Table 6 in the Appendix).

4. ***Dependency between the achievement of private financial resources and usage of fundraising in NPOs***
   Answers to this question confirmed the dependency between the number of donors and the level of private financial resource achievement.
   The Kruskal-Wallis test at the level of significance of 0.05 showed (see Table 7 in the Appendix) that forms and methods of fundraising influence the level and extent of private financial resource

achievement. Organizations that systematize activities of source generation and that contact donors (71 %) achieve private financial resources from various areas at higher levels. In contrast, in organizations where there are no systematic activities leading to source generation, the volume of private financial resource achievement is very low (29 %).

5. ***Dependency between the achievement of private financial resources and relations between NPOs and donors***
   This research question addresses the preconditions for whether non-profit organizations build their images and publicity or, stated in other words, whether credibility and transparency in the form of annual reports impact private financial resource achievement (see Table 8 in the Appendix).
   In the case of dependency of the quality of relations and the level of private financial resource achievement, there is strong statistical dependency. An organization that attempts to maintain mutually beneficial and better than standard relations is more successful in achieving private financial sources. In contrast, an organization that does not have good long-term relations is usually not very successful in private financial resource achievement. The results of the research confirm that 76 % of non-governmental organizations have long and better than standard relations with their donors. If an NGO attracts a donor, communicates effectively, provides information about the obtained results regularly and shows transparency in handling financial resources, it achieves the most stable source of support (Plenipotentiary of the SR Government for the Development of NGO [RNNO], 2014).

6. ***Dependency between the achievement of private financial resources and activity of the management of the NPO itself***
   Fifty-two percent of non-governmental organizations mentioned an active member of the board who manages the organization effectively and ensures its long-term institutional and financial stability. There committees were established with the task of solving specific problems, such as investment financial stability/sustainability and fundraising. Inactive members of the board were mentioned by 5 % of organizations, and the remaining 44 % mentioned only partial support from the management (see Table 9 in the Appendix).
   In case of testing dependency, the activity of management and the level of private financial resources there acknowledged no dependency.

7. ***Dependency between the achievement of private financial resources and strategic planning of the NPO***
   It follows from the results (see Table 10 in the Appendix) that approximately 65 % of respondents had a long-term plan (organization strategy) that they update regularly and use in the decision-making processes of the organization. In contrast, there was a large number of organizations that did not consider a long-term plan as inevitable (32 %). The plan prepared by 13 % of respondents and by many non-profit organizations was considered out of date.
   No dependency was acknowledged between the form and level of utilization of the strategic plan of an enterprise and the volume of private financial resource achievement.

8. ***Dependency between the achievement of private financial resources and financial planning of the NPO***
   The Kruskal-Wallis test confirmed strong statistical importance in cases of financial planning dependency along with the identification of the financial needs and objectives of NGO and the level of private financial resources achievement (see Table 11 in the Appendix). Approximately 40 % of respondents are not interested in financial planning and do not identify minimum financial needs inevitable to the administrative or program objectives for the next 3-5 years. This group was created by approximately 90 % of NGOs associated with 0-5 employees.

9. ***Dependency between the achievement of private financial resources and the existence of financial information and the records of the NPO***
   According to Ellis (2014), "Typically, most companies only publish full financial accounts once a year, although interim updates on sales and profitability are common. To undertake a detailed assessment of the strength of an individual debtor's

balance sheet, it is therefore necessary to wait for these accounts published, often with a significant lag to the reporting period. Break-even maturity as a guide to financial distress" (p. 389).

For NGOs, it is very important to be, in the area of economics, transparent for the long term, mainly in cooperation with entrepreneurial subjects and for the confidence of members, the public or clients, without which no organization can survive (see Table 12 in the Appendix).

The results of the research confirm that 71 % of respondents regularly inform receivers and donors through financial reports about the economics of the NGO. Twenty-nine percent prepare financial reports and statements that cannot be created due to the unwillingness of NGOs to publicize how the organization is managed or send annual reports, and in this way, they show the legitimacy of requested subsidies. The research shows that 62 % of requested NGOs and other legal forms of respondents show effectiveness in financial management (financial reports for external users), indicating that we consider publishing this information to be the most important, together with statements and supplements and comments from the organization's management. Only complex statements suitably explained and amended by comments from the organization's management can provide to users a clear picture of the organization's situation. It is useful to mention the comparison of reality and planning, as well as future expectations.

The strong statistic importance has been acknowledged between the form of financial statement preparation and the extent of private financial resource achievement.

In this chapter, we analyze whether the selected criteria have any impact on the extent of private financial resource achievement in non-governmental organizations. We present the summary of the analysis (see Table 13 in the Appendix).

Confirming the majority of research questions (Řezáková, 2007), we consider the objective confirmed in case of 6 attested research questions out of 9. We can say that there are criteria that influence the volume of private sources of financing in NGO achievement. The research results show strong statistical dependency, as confirmed in the criteria sustaining mutually useful relations with donors, financial planning and the existence and transparency of financial statements of NGO to donors (with bold letters). Additionally, in the last year, the economic forum in Davos, a barometer of confidence, showed expressly that non-governmental organizations have higher confidence than the governments of individual countries or financial institutions, which are responsible for the global crisis. Calls for non-governmental organizations could sustain this confidence and develop it in the current period of economic instability. For NGOs, it is very important to have a sense of long-term transparency in the economy, mainly in cooperation with entrepreneurial subjects and the confidence of members, the public or clients, without which no organization can survive for long.

Plenty of internal and external factors influence the long-term sustainability of non-profit organizations. The most important criterion for the existence of a non-profit organization is to provide financial resources optimally.

Prerequisites that are inevitable for the sustainability of NPOs are the following.

- Diversification of financial resources -- which means decreasing the dependency of one source of financing
- Generation of purposeless financial sources -- which means freedom in financial resource utilization in accordance with the missions of non-profit organizations and purposes, which are important from the point of view of strategy development

The highest level of independency comes from self-financing as the internal resource of financing and financing from 2 % income tax. Organizations could use these obtained resources in accordance with the requests of donors. We can observe that higher levels of such financial resource achievement not only provide advanced financial sustainability but also increase the independence of organizations. We can see also synergy in the long-term sustainability.

Strategic management application is another precondition of NGO financial sustainability. Strategic management, according to (Hanzelková, Keřkovský, Odehnalová, & Vykypěl, 2009), can possibly be divided into functional strategies following individual functions. Financial or personal marketing is ranked among functional strategies. Well-known authors (Sakál & Podskľan 2004) have mentioned other functional strategies applied mainly in the non-profit sector, such as products (production) and environmental, innovative, political-legal, and information. NPOs increasingly use the practices of the entrepreneurial sector. According to our research, NPOs reached a total financial sustainability level of 55 % in Slovakia. Following from the results of research conducted by the Delft method, we chose the following functional strategies important for the long-term sustainability of NGOs (see Table 14 in the Appendix).

The most important criterion in reaching financial sustainability for NGOs is considered *strategic and financial planning and the effectiveness of the organization,* specifically active management of organizations. NPOs coincide with the financial planning of NPOs being very low.

According to research audits and accounting, Slovak NGOs are NPOs of the highest level from all criteria.

Proposals for increasing private financial resources as financial sustainability criteria

Private financial sources (incomes from enterprises/individuals, grants and 2 % from income tax) represent 61 % of all sources and constitute the major part of NPO incomes. The cooperation of enterprises with NPOs is very important in the financing of their activity. Based on this research, we identified criteria that influence private sources of NGO financing achievement. Strong statistical dependency confirms criteria for financial planning, the existence of financial statements and the maintaining of mutually beneficial relations with donors. With research question 1, we analyzed the impact of activity on private financial source achievement, and the analysis confirmed dependency. In NGO examination, we can observe mutual differences mainly in the subject of the activity of the organization. According to the analysis, enterprises support NGOs acting in social services. We were not able to verify this statement. According to the outcomes of research in companies, mainly activities for children and youths are supported. Low participation of enterprises in research does not enable us to comment on the obtained data for all entrepreneurial groups. If NGOs are transparent, reliable, and active in attracting enterprises, and they are able to meet criteria for financial sustainability, they will be successful in the creation of cooperation and the benefits derived from it. We recommend realizing surveys on the current situation in NGOs and speaking mainly to enterprises (and concentrating mainly on enterprises) disclosing their interest in cooperation with NGOs to the public. An important precondition from the financial sustainability point of view has been important, slight interaction and a coincidence between the strategy and objectives of an entrepreneurial subject as a donor and the NPO as a beneficiary of financial sources in the concrete area of its interest. Therefore, we recommend that organizations be more active in achieving financial resources by searching for partners with philanthropy incentives included directly in their entrepreneurial strategies.

Statistical dependency was not confirmed in research question 2 from the characteristic of cooperation. NGOs had to evaluate individually the form of cooperation: regular, occasional or ad hoc. We recommend to young NPOs or organizations with individual incomes from enterprises to address more experienced organizations through networking. Forming networks with these organizations can lead to benefits on both sides: the starting NGO can attain new, innovative ideas, and the NGO already acting in the market for longer can provide professional advice and consultation, including new ideas and know-how acquired from entrepreneurial subjects.

Research question 3 confirmed dependency among the number of donors and the level of private financial resource achievement. NPOs have established a wide range of financial sources. In one third of organizations, one source of financing represents more than 60 % of organization income. It should be useful to such an extent that no one resource participates in more than 25 % of NPO total incomes. *Research question 4* was confirmed, and fundraising influences the level of private financial resource achievement. Fundraising itself is active in NGOs (71 % of respondents contact donors), and maintaining stable relations with donors was evaluated very positively. We recommend that NPOs take the position of a fundraiser that can, apart from searching for new external sources, look for new opportunities on the market where non-governmental organizations with self-financing activities could enter.

The results from the non-profit sector showed that ¾ of examined NPOs sustaining longer and more standard relations with donors. *Research question 5* confirmed the strong statistical dependency of this criterion in the achievement of resources from enterprises. We recommend maintaining the level of activities that we mention at the end of this subchapter and continuously attempting to improve it.

NPOs could be professional not only from the development and education of employees' points of view but also from independence, eventually with the individuality of the management point of view. We examined this criterion in *research question 6*, for which analysis did not confirm dependency in resource achievement from enterprises. Management of organizations connects NPOs with their surroundings, and their task is to ensure appropriate support of organizations and to ensure the effective and responsible utilization of obtained resources. Members of boards who are not active were mentioned by only 5 % of organizations, and 44 % respondents support NPOs only partially. According to experts, active management is just one of the most important criteria for the financial sustainability of organizations. The importance of NPO administration and the role of administrative bodies as guarantors of transparency and responsibility in NPOs should be closely evaluated, and the idea of fair, transparent and socially responsible behavior of organizations could be supported.

Despite the instant benefits of strategic planning, a disadvantage lies in it being very demanding concerning time, finances and people. *Research question 7* did not confirm the statistical dependency of private financial resource achievement on strategic planning. According to experts, e.g., Burger, Dasgupta, and Owens (2015), strategic planning is one of the important criteria of NPOs attaining financial sustainability. Approximately 65 % of NPOs have prepared strategies of organization, and we propose continuing with its regular updating and using strategic plans in the decision-making processes of organizations. The activation, realization and maintenance of strategic planning are costly and require some level of risk from the viewpoint of the management of organizations; therefore, management of all of the functions of strategic planning in some non-governmental organizations can require years, which is why some NGOs can propose a simplified strategy (donor strategy or financial, marketing, personal strategy) and not the whole plan.

Through analysis, a precondition was confirmed of *research question 8* regarding the dependency of private financial resource acquisition on the financial planning of NPOs. Alarming is the determination that 40 % of respondents do not perform financial planning and do not identify financial objectives for the next 3-5 years. Financial planning was mentioned as one of the three most important criteria in the Delft method (together with strategic planning and active management of organizations) of NGO financial sustainability achievement. The present situation of third sector organizations is not ideal; there is an enormous space for improvement. NPOs can first count the financial needs of projects or the organization itself or plan a budget and fundraising for the achievement of financial resources needed for the plan of activity realization. Cooperation with the entrepreneurial sector creates not only financial sufficiency but also the possibility for the experience of exchange and achievement of information and knowledge in financial planning.

In case of financial reports, the existence of dependency in NPOs is acknowledged in *research question 9*. Administration is closely related to transparency, responsibility and credibility. Confidence relationships are inevitable, mainly for donors and sponsors who provide organizations with financial resources. Forming partnerships, as well as resource acquisition from internal and external sources, is important for NGOs with the aim of creating an image of a trustful and transparent organization with great impact on the support of non-governmental organizations from the public. Several times in the past, speculative incentives were detected for the establishment of NGOs that abused acquired financial resources, which is why NPOs have a mainly negative image to the public (Austin, 2000; Bútora, Mesežnikov, & Kollár, 2011; Sičáková-Beblavá & Baťová, 2009).

Annual reports should include financial parts, which should be comprehensible mainly to those with economic-financial relations with NPOs. With transparency, the public (donors) could have the possibility of seeing how it is manipulated financially and whether an organization uses its resources for the purpose for which it was established. Transparency could be mainly in the annual report presentation, which should be automatic. We recommend to NPOs to continue strengthening the credibility and good reputations of organization through the following activities:

- Communication with important partners and local community – involvement of public with the activities of NPOs in the form of volunteering or financial support. To promote actively the activities of NPOs that creates the preconditions for long-term cooperation, we recommend organizing, apart from leaflet distribution or sending newsletters, the following activities:
  - Open door days; and
  - Activities for partners who support NPOs.
- Creation of communication culture – application of ethical codes, which support the credibility of NPOs, presentation of NPOs' visions and missions, creation of logos, establishment of internal relations and communication standards.
- Creating, updating and maintaining Web pages – publication of one's own donors.
- Relationship with the media – establishing partnership with publishing houses and magazines, with the of focusing on NPOs and publishing constant press releases about ongoing events.
- To establish a self-regulation mechanism in which an NGO determines its own standards of good practice and transparency, for example, in the area of public information about the financial activities of NGOs. To create schemas for accounting statements comprehensible to the public, this mechanism should engage every organization and member of the public in its annual report. The status of public utility, which should set basic standards for NGO transparency, is connected to taxes or other financial advantages.
- Using transparency and good reputations in resource acquisition from enterprises/individuals and being charged with acquired financial resources.
- Training of employees in the area of management (managerial practice for non-profit sector) and fundraising in the area of personal strategy.
- To run performance audits, so-called value audits for obtaining invested resources (value-for-money audits), in which the money audited is expressed in value creation activities. It is suitable tool for the control of economics, effective and efficient financial resource disposal and economic transparency.

As the research results show, we have provided criteria for financial sustainability (see Table 15 in the Appendix), with strong statistical dependency granting the achievement of private financial sources (enterprises/individuals, grants, 2 % from income tax).

The results (from the table) show that NPOs should pay more attention to financial planning, which is, according to Delft method experts, one of the most important criteria for then achievement of financial sustainability of NPOs, but its level is very low in NPOs. Of all of the previously proposed forms of mutual partnership of NPOs with enterprises, the creation of long-term cooperation is demanding of the abilities of organizations, which should be able to react to market needs with managerial practices and plans and with the aforementioned functional strategies. Hence (Shenkar, 2001). Control (and, in extension, entry mode) is not the only product of cultural "distance"; it is also a potential trigger of cultural friction. The most important aim is to attract long-term donors and not only one-time support. This reality asks for the permanent confidence of such organizations and instructive forms of supporter attraction.

Discussion

As indicated by our research and the analyzed scientific articles and research of many authors, the financial sustainability of NPOs in Slovakia is becoming worse systematically. This situation is influenced by many factors. Organizations realize many projects and activities to show their vitality. In contrast, it requires the capacity for the diversification of their financial sources. The situation of organizations that depend on 2 % assignation of taxes because the conditions for legal persons in providing this support has begun to worsen. In Slovakia, there is no legislation concerning donor support as a tax advantage. The severity of the administration has increased the management of NPOs. The number of grants from public sources is decreasing, which could have impacts mainly on organizations focusing on culture and human rights. Concerning European Union sources, the majority of organizations have no impact on this support because of bureaucracy and the extremely high demand for co-financing.

Our research has provided us with information that serves as criteria for financial sustainability (which we have proposed) and confirms strong statistical dependency on private financial sources (enterprise/individuals, grants, 2 % from income tax). The criteria are the following:

- Precise financial planning
- Creation of long-term relations with donors
- Transparent financial statements and audits

The outcomes of our research concerning NPOs showed the need for attention to be paid to financial planning as the one of most important criteria for the financial sustainability of NPOs, which is in these organizations very low. (Browman, 2011; Vaceková & Svidroňova, 2014). This result is the outcome that the majority of organizations operate with very low budgets; their incomes are irregular, influenced by a number of factors, such as modifications by legislation, consideration of donors and their economic situations, policy, etc. What must be evident in every organization is the total budget, which consists of costs and budget sources. The cost budget include all items that an organization plans to use during the year, including wages, operation costs, insurance, and the cost of new project achievement. Cost budgets must be added to source budgets, in which sources and items covering costs are included. The total financial plan must reflect the strategic plans of organizations. In this context, the question of an organization's financial sources is highlighted. The useful combination of financial sources, e.g., resources created by one's own activities, grants, and donations, can possibly ensure solid financial planning and long-term financial sustainability, as well.

As the outcome of another part of our research, the creation of long-term partnerships of NPO with enterprises is another precondition of long-term financial sustainability. (Kuvíková, Vaceková 2009, Maier & Meyer, 2014). The creation of long-term cooperation emphasizes an organization's own abilities, which must be able to react to market needs, use managerial practices and plan the aforementioned functional strategies. The most important thing is to attract long-term donors, not only individual (ad hoc) supporters. This long-term cooperation expects the long-term confidence of an organization and creative forms of donor attraction. We recommend that organizations establish their own self-regulation mechanisms, in which organizations define their own standards as good experiences from practice and transparency, e.g., in the area of information for the public about financial operations and statements, develop relations with the mass media, and create their own codes of ethics. Powerful tools are also performance audits and audits of value for spending resources, which are audits with money expressed as value created activities. These are suitable tools for economic, effective and useful control of financial source usage and transparent economics.

The aforementioned precondition of financial sustainability is closely connected to the last criterion of financial sustainability emphasized in our research, which is the importance of transparent and publicly understandable financial statements. This criterion also enables organizations to establish and measure their performance. Productivity is the basic test of every institution. Pressure on non-profit organizations as providers of frequently used or mutually used services to measure their productivity or performance in general comes from various interested sides: founders, donors, volunteers, employees, and clients and mainly from public authorities that provide sources for their activities. Requests of non-profit organizations to be commercial providers of services expects from them complex measurement of productivity.

The dynamism of present economic development has forced NPOs to integrate into their strategies the preconditions and outcomes of entrepreneurial strategies focused on long-term sustainability (Vaceková & Svidroňová 2014; Renz, 2016).

It is important to note that the indicators of financial sustainability mentioned in the literature, such as cooperation with the community and a good name for organizations, have not been confirmed in Slovakia (Bray 2013; Renz 2016). Reasons for this lack of confirmation could be found in the less developed non-profit sector in Slovakia.

Financial sustainability continues in the interest of NPOs that face numerous problems in their creation. Our article showed many challenges and recommendations for NPOs to create and maintain long-term financial sustainability. This concept must also be understood as a long-term, dynamic and continuing process. Creation of clear strategic plans, which define the society's mission and integrates the impact of interest groups with the missions of organizations, could overcome long- and short-term problems of financial sustainability. This article could help NPOs with their definitions of key indicator of their financial sustainability.

Conclusions

Non-profit organizations realize that their long-term financial stability and sustainability are the elementary preconditions for their existence and their ability to fulfill their missions. The basic problem is the recognition and establishment of the key criteria that influence the ability of an organization to ensure sufficient financial resources for its activity. NPOs operate according to a specific paradox – compared with the profit sector, their financial management is much more complicated because the benefits of non-profit products are divided between two groups: the real recipient (beneficent); and the payer (donor). Satisfaction of both groups' interests obliges NPOs to seek ways to increase their effectiveness and performance. The outcomes of our research bring new challenges to the area of the non-profit Sector, mainly due to the proposals of new concrete recommendations for the achievement of increased levels of private financial resources. Their application can contribute to the increase in NPOs' quality of work, as well as to the increased possibility of fulfilling their missions, not only in the Slovak entrepreneurial area but also in the remaining transition economies.

Non-profit organizations are in the market environment, and they require material, human and financial sources for their activities. The question of their long-term financial sustainability is increasingly important today. It combines with the exhaustion or loss of present, mainly foreign financial sources. Organizations are forced to search for ways and forms of long-term and stable incomes to be able to realize their missions. Our investigation showed that the most important criteria for non-profit organization sustainability are solid financial planning, the maintaining of long-term and stable relations with donors and joint diversification of sources and financial transparency oriented toward the establishment and measurement of performance and capacity.

In our research, we noted the most important criterion for financial sustainability shown by non-profit organizations in our research, and we provided possible recommendations, the realization of which could lead to increased independency of organizations and their financial stability and long-term subsistence security.

References

Atkinson, R. (2003). Planning for NGO Sustainability – Self-financing Strategies. NGO FAIR – 3rd Forum of the Civil Society in Macedonia. Available at http://www.civicworld.org.mk/index855d.html?ItemID=E593518372C55843A6150450D6F3EB27

Austin, J. E. (2000). The Collaboration Challenge: How Non-profits and Business Succeed through Strategic Alliances. San Francisco, CA: Jossey-Bass.

Bienzle, H., Gelabert, E., Jütte, W., Kolywa, K., Meyer, N., & Tilkin, G. (2007). The Art of Networking. European Networks in Education. Wien: die Berater - Unternehmensberatungs GmbH.

Boehnke, K., Rippl, S., & Fuss, D. (2015). Sustainable Civil-Society Engagement: Potentials of a Transnational Civil Society in French-German, Polish-German, and Czech-German Border Regions. *Sustainability*, 7(4), 4078–4099.

Boris, T. E., & Steuerle, C.E. (2006). Non-profits and Government. (2nd ed.). Washington, DC: Urban Institute Press.

Boukal, P., & Vávrová, H. (2007). Ekonomika a financování neziskových organizací [Economics and financing of nonprofit organisation]. Praha: Oeconomica.

Bowman, W. (2011). Financial capacity and sustainability of ordinary nonprofits. *Nonprofit Management & Leadership, 22*(1), 37–51.

Bray, I. (2013). Effective Fundraising for Nonprofits: Real-World Strategies that Work (4th ed.). Berkeley, Ca: Nolo.

Brozmanová, A., Adolfova, I., Hirt, B., Kunická, J., Pirošík, V., Štulrajterová, A., Vrbický, L. (2009). Tretí sektor a mimovládne organizácie [Third sector and non-governmental organisations]. Banská Bystrica: Pedagogická fakulta, UMB.

Bryson, J. M., Crosby, B. C., Stone, M. M. (2006). The Design and Implementation of Cross-Sector Collaborations: Propositions from the Literature. *Public Administration Review*, 66 (1), 44-55.

Burger, R., Dasgupta, I., Owens, T. (2015). A Model of Nongovernmental Organization Regulation with an Application to Uganda. *Economic Development and Cultural Change*, 64(1), 71-111.

Bútora, M., Mesežnikov, G., & Kollár, M. (2011). Slovakia 2009. Trends in Quality of Democracy. Bratislava: Institute for Public Affairs.

Canarella, G., Nourayi, M., & Sullivan M. J. (2014). An alternative test of the trade-off theory of capital structure. *Contemporary Economics*, 8(4), 365-386.

Davis, L., Etchart, N. (1999) Profits for Nonprofits. Santiago: NESsT. Retrieved from

Dembinski, P. H. (2011). The Incompleteness of the Economy and Business: A Forceful Reminder. Journal of Business Ethics, 100, 29-40.

Dubcová, G. (2014). Relevantnosť existencie funkčnej stratégie zodpovedného podnikania. Aktuálne problémy podnikovej sféry [Relevance of the functional strategy of responsible entrepreneurship. Current problems of entrepreneurial sphere]. Bratislava: Ekonóm.

Ellis, C. (2014). Break-even maturity as a guide to financial distress. *Contemporary Economics*, 8 (4), 387-396.

Etchart, N., Davis, L., Messing, J., Guštafík, P. (2003). Príručka podnikania neziskových organizácií: ako vytriediť podnikateľské nápady [The handbook of nonprofit organisations entrepreneurship: how to sort out entrepreneurial ideas]. Bratislava: Centre for prevention and conflict solution.

Hagedorn, K. (2014). Post-socialist farmers' cooperatives in Central and Eastern Europe. *Annals of Public and Cooperative Economics*, *85*(4), 555–577.

Hanzelková, A., Keřkovský, M., Odehnalová, D., Vykypěl, O. (2009). Strategický marketing pro teorii a praxi [Strategic marketing for theory and practice]. Praha: C. H. Beck.

Kotler, P., Lee, N. (2005). Corporate social responsibility: Doing the Most Good for Your Company and Your Cause. New Jersey, NJ: John Wiley & Sons.

Kuvíková H., Vaceková G. (2009). Diversification of financial sources in nonprofit organisations. *E+M Ekonomie* a management/ *Economics and Management, 12*(4), 84-96.

León, P. (2001). Four Pillars of Financial Sustainability. Arlington, VA: The Nature Conservancy.

Maier, F., Meyer, M., & Steinbereintner, M. (2014). Nonprofit Organizations Becoming Business-Like. A Systematic Review, 45(1), 64-86.

Majdúchová, H. (2009). Neziskové organizácie [Nonprofit organisations]. Bratislava: Sprint dva.

Majdúchová, H. (2012). Stanovenie hodnoty neziskovej organizácie. Aktuálne problémy podnikovej sféry [Current problems of corporate sector [Determining the value of a nonprofit organization. Current issues in the business sphere]. Bratislava: Ekonóm.

MANGO. (2013a). Global Sustainable Development Report 2013. Retrieved from http://www.classtoolkit.org/sites/default/files/documents/Mango%20FME%20handbook%20%5Bmain%20text%5D%20%20March%202013.pdf

MANGO. (2013b). Financial sustainability – Risk assessment. Retrieved from http://www.mango.org.uk/Guide/RiskAssessment.

Plenipotentiary of the SR Government for the Development of Civil Societies. (2014). Zhodnocení koncepce podpory neziskového sektoru [Evaluation of the nonprofit sector concept support] [PowerPoint slides]. Available at http://www.rokovanie.sk/File.aspx/ViewDocumentHtml/Mater-Dokum-207009?prefixFile=m_

Reider, R. (2001). Improving the Economy, Efficiency, and Effectiveness of Not-for-Profits: Conducting Operational Reviews. New Jersey, NJ: John Wiley & Sons.

Renz, D. O. (Ed.). (2010). Nonprofit leadership and management. Jossey-Bass Hand Book of Nonprofit Leadership and Management (3rd ed.). San Francisco, CA: John Willey & Sons Inc.

Řezáková, H. (2007). Analýza dát z dotazníkových šetření [Data analysis from questionaire research]. Praha: Professional Publishing.

Rimarčík, M. (2007). Štatistika pre prax [Statistics for practice]. Bratislava: Marián Rimarčík.

Rugman, A. M., Verbeke, A. (2004). A perspective on regional and global strategies of multinational enterprises. *Journal of International Business Studies*, 35(1), 3-18.

Sanders, M. L., McClellan, J. G. (2012). Being business-like while pursuing a social mission: Acknowledging the Inherent Tensions in US Nonprofit Organizing. *Organization*, 21(1), 68–89.

Sakál, P., Podskľan, A. (2004). Strategický manažment [Strategic Management]. Bratislava: STU.

Selsky, J. W., Parker, B. (2005). Cross-sector partnerships to address social issues: challenges to theory and practice. *Journal of Management*, 31(6), 849 - 873.

Shenkar, O. (2001). Cultural distance revisited: Towards a more rigorous conceptualization and measurement of cultural differences. *Journal of International Business Studies*, 32(3), 519-535.

Sičáková–Beblavá, E., Baťová, D. (2009). Pridaná hodnota transparentnosti II [Added value of transparency]. Bratislava: Transparency International Slovensko.

Soriano, D. R., Galindo, M. Á. (2010). An overview of entrepreneurial activity in non-profit organizations in the international context. *Small Business Economics*, 38 (3), 265-269.

Svidroňova, M. (2013). Sustainability strategy of non-government organisations in Slovakia. *Ekonomie a Management/ Ekonomics and Management*, 16(3), 85-100.

Svidroňová, M. Vaceková, G., Valentinov, V. (2016). The theories of Non-profits: A Reality Check from Slovakia. Lex Localis - Journal of Local Self-Government, 14(3), 399-418.

Svidroňová, M., Vaceková, G. (2012). Current state of self-financing of private non-profit organizations in the conditions of the Slovak Republic. *TEDE, 18*(3), 438–451.

USAID. (2008, August). Financial Capacity Building for NGO Sustainability. Program Brief No. 12. Retrieved from http://pdf.usaid.gov/pdf_docs/Pnadn555.pdf

USAID. (2013, June). The 2012 CSO Sustainability Index for Central and Eastern Europe and Eurasia (16th ed.). Retrieved from https://www.usaid.gov/sites/default/files/documents/1863/2012CSOSI_0.pdf

Vaceková, G., Svidroňová, M. (2014). Benefits and Risks of Self-Financing of NGOs—Empirical Evidence from the Czech Republic, Slovakia and Austria. *Ekonomie a Management/ Ekonomics and Management, 17*(2), 120-129.

Valentinov, V., Vacekova, G. (2015). Sustainability of Rural Nonprofit Organizations:

Czech Republic and Beyond. *Sustainability* 2015, *7*, 9890-9906.

Valentinov, V., Hielscher, S., & Pies, I. (2015). Nonprofit organizations, institutional economics, and systems thinking. *Economics Systems, 39*(3), 491-501.

Valentinov, V. (2012). Toward a critical systems perspective on the nonprofit sector. *Systematic Practise and Action Research, 25*(4), 355–364.

Weerawardena, J., McDonald, R. E., Mort, G. S. (2010). Sustainability of nonprofit organizations: An empirical investigation. Journal of World Business, 45(4), 346–356.

Appendix

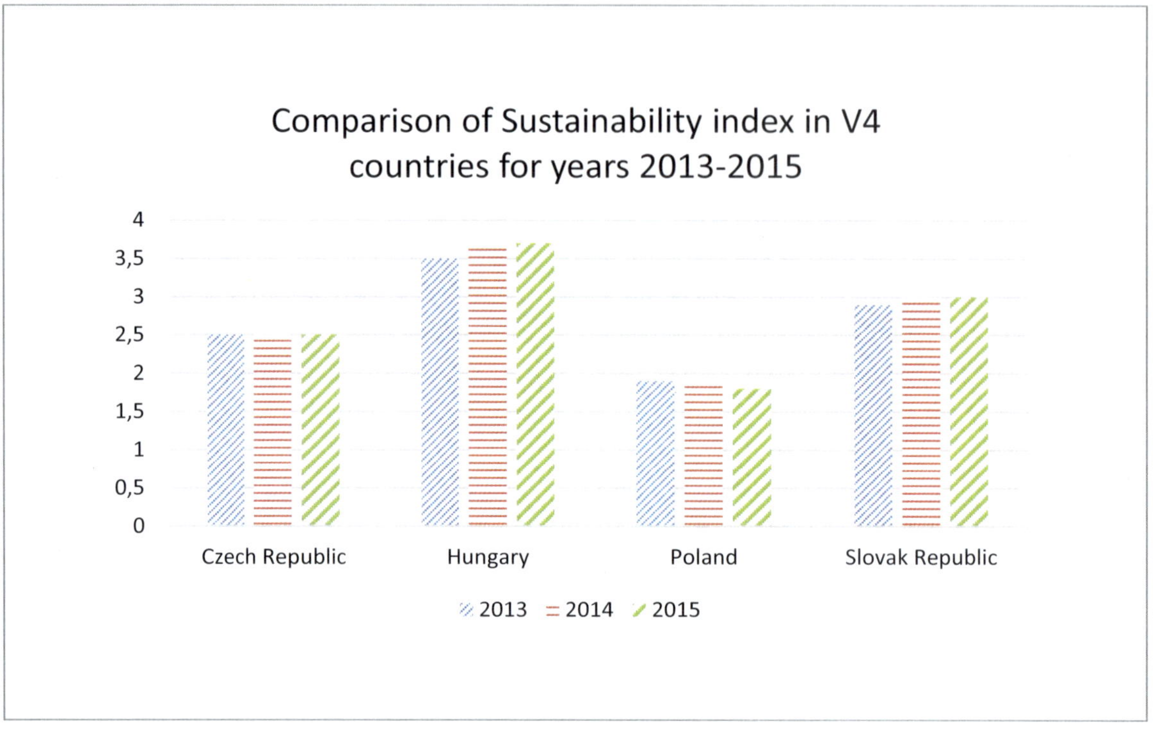

Figure 1. Comparison of sustainability indices in V4 countries for 2013-2015
Source: Adapted from "*Financial Capacity Building for NGO Sustainability*" by USAID (2008, August). Retrieved from http://pdf.usaid.gov/pdf_docs/Pnadn555.pdf

Table 1. Index of Non-profit Organizations' sustainability in Slovakia (2015)

Legal Environment	Change	Organizational capacity	Change	Financial Viability	Change	Advocacy	Change	Service Provision	Change	Infrastructure	Change	Public Image	Change	CSO Sustainability	Change
3,0	=	3,1	↓	3,7	↓	2,6	=	2,6	=	2,9	↓	2,5	=	2,9	↓

Source: Adapted from "*The 2012 CSO Sustainability Index for Central and Eastern Europe and Eurasia (16th ed.).*" by USAID (2013, June). Retrieved from https://www.usaid.gov/sites/default/files/documents/1863/2012CSOSI_0.pdf

Table 2. Forms of non-profit organizations' financing in conditions of SR

External resources -- fundraising	Public resources (governmental and local administration)	**Direct support** • subsidies (contribution, grants) from state budget • subsidies (contribution, grants) from municipality budgets, cities (further mentioned as district units (DUs)) • payments and contributions for services based on contracts and agreements • public orders **Indirect support** • assignation of the percentage share of tax from the income of private entities and income taxes of legal entities • customs and tax exemptions
	National private resources	• sponsorships • grants from foundations • gifts from natural and legal entities • financing from individual resources
	Foreign resources	**Public** • funding and programs of the European Union, • other international grant programs of foreign public institutions **Private** • private foreign foundations • company donors • individual donors
Internal resources – self-financing	Resources created by own activity	• memberships and other charges • sale of products or services • sales or rentals of tangible or intangible property • advertising activity

Table 3. Normality test

Variable	Normality tests					
	N	max D	K-S p	Lilliefors p	W	p
Obtained private finance	104	0.192659	**p<.01**	**p<.01**	**0.898454**	**0.000**

Table 4. Test of dependency achievement of private financial resources from the area of activity of NPO

Dependent: Private finance achievement	Kruskal-Wallis ANOVA; private finance achievement Independent (grouping) variable: area of activity Kruskal-Wallis test: H (5, N= 104) = 14.19714 **p=0.0275**		Confirmation of examined question
	Number of effective	Sum of orders	
Other	26	1565.000	
Culture	20	888.000	
Education, Training	20	1064.000	✓
Social services	19	1214.500	
Sport	12	352.000	
Healthcare services	7	376.500	

Table 5. Test of dependency achievement from character of cooperation of NPO with enterprise

Dependent: Private finance achievement	Kruskal-Wallis ANOVA; private financial profit Independent (grouping) variable: character of cooperation Kruskal-Wallis test: H (2, N= 90) = 1.363174 **p=0.5058**		Confirmation of examined question
	Number of valid responses	Total orders	
Ad hoc	14	588.500	
Occasional	34	1456.500	X
Regular	42	2050.000	

Table 6. Test of dependency achievement of private financial resources from number of donors of NPO

Dependent: Private finance achievement.	Kruskal-Wallis ANOVA: private financial profit Independent (grouping) variable: diversification of sources Kruskal-Wallis test: H (4, N= 102) = 12.63848, **p=0.0132**		Confirmation of examined question
	Number of valid responses	Total order	
5 – organization has broad base of donors of at least 8 different sources; no source contributes more than 25 % on total annual costs	26	1362.500	
4 – at least 5 financial sources represent 60 % of total budget	17	906.500	
3 – one source of financing represents more than 40 % of incomes, and at least 4 other sources create the remaining 40 %	28	1757.500	✓
2 – one source represents more than 60 % of organization incomes	18	843.500	
1 – one source represents more than 80 % of organization incomes	13	383.000	

Table 7. Test of dependency achievement of private financial resources from fundraising achievement in NPO

Dependent: Private finance achievement	Kruskal-Wallis ANOVA: private financial profit. Independent (grouping) variable: fundraising Kruskal-Wallis test: H (4, N= 104) = 10.29287 **p=0.0358**		Confirmation of examined question
	Number of valid responses	Total order	
5 – fundraising is integrated into administration and financial system	7	444.500	
4 – fundraising objectives are clearly defined, and financial plan is created	14	945.000	
3 – organization began to systematize activities that generate sources and starts applying fundraising	26	1531.000	✓
2 – one person is responsible for source generation	27	1236.500	
1 – no systematic activities are applied for source generation	30	1303.000	

Table 8. Test of dependency achievement of private financial resources from sustaining mutually beneficial relations of NPO with donors

Dependent: Private finance achievement	Kruskal-Wallis ANOVA: private financial profit. Independent (grouping) variable: quality of relations Kruskal-Wallis test: H (4, N= 104) = 18.52651 **p=0.0010**		Confirmation of examined question
	Number of valid responses	Total order	
5 – organization has created donorship strategy, with donors maintained relations above standard, and they are part of annual report	32	2011.000	
4 – organization informs donors about its activities in annual reports without personal contact	37	1819.500	✓
3 – communication with donors is only occasional and ad hoc	10	670.000	
2 – organization only learns communication with donors, and their portfolios are created	15	745.500	
1 – organization does not maintain any relations with donors	10	214.000	

Table 9. Test of dependency achievement of private financial resources from activity of management

Dependent: Private finance achievement	Kruskal-Wallis ANOVA: private financial profit. Independent (grouping) variable: activity of management Kruskal-Wallis test: H (4, N= 104) = 7.642676 **p=0.1056**		Confirmation of examined question
	Number of valid responses	Total order	
5 – members of management actively and effectively manage organization and ensure its long-term financial stability; there are specific committees for investment, and financial sustainability established	11	632.000	
4 – majority of management members participate in regular meetings, helping in source achievement	43	2579.000	X
3 – some members of management are active, and they help, but other members are passive	5	281.000	
2 – only a few members of management contribute their time, effort and money	41	1821.000	
1 – members of management are inactive and formal	4	145000	

Table 10. Test of dependency achievement of private financial resources from use of the strategic plan

Dependent: Private finance achievement	Kruskal-Wallis ANOVA: private financial profit. Independent (grouping) variable: strategic plan Kruskal-Wallis test: H (4, N= 102) = 5.754475 **p=0.2183**		Confirmation of examined question
	Number of valid responses	Total order	
5 – strategic plan is regularly updated, it contains long-term financial planning, and it is created as a result of employee participation, leadership and external consulting	13	799.500	
4 – employees use present strategic plan, which includes financial plan	16	950.500	X
3 – strategic plan exists, and employees are informed about it	27	1388.500	
2 – strategic plan is old and is not revised	13	694.000	
1 – strategic plan does not exist	33	142.500	

Table 11. Test of dependency achievement of private financial resources from use of financial plan

Dependent: Private finance achievement	Kruskal-Wallis ANOVA: private financial profit. Independent (grouping) variable: financial plan Kruskal-Wallis test: H (4, N= 104) = 17.85883 **p=0.0013**		Confirmation of examined question
	Number of valid responses	Total order	
5 – plan of financial sustainability was implemented and is monitored, and objectives are updated	14	776.000	
4 – organization has been tested and analyzed for various incomes and has integrated such strategies that achieve sets of financial objectives	11	904.500	
3 – organization has begun to develop fundraising and works with short financial plans	13	618.500	✓
2 – organization knows and quantifies financial needs and creates program development	24	1384.000	
1 – organization does not identify financial needs minimum	42	1777.000	

Table 12. Test of dependency achievement of private financial sources from existence of financial statements of non-governmental organization

Dependent: Private finance achievement.	Kruskal-Wallis ANOVA: private financial profit. Independent (grouping) variable: financial reports Kruskal-Wallis test: H (4, N= 104) = 14.10833 **p=0.0070**		Confirmation of examined question
	Number of valid responses	Total order	
5 – financial reports for external evaluation are used for decision process, are part of the annual report and are published	29	1949.500	
4 – financial reports are used only sometimes for decision making and are published	23	1228.500	✓
3 – financial reports are created	22	1026.000	
2 – financial reports are very short and incomplete and are published with delay	2	137.000	
1 – financial reports are available only for internal purposes	28	1119.000	

Table 13. Examination of the dependency between private financial resources achievement and selected factors

Determinant	**Dependency**	**Confirmation of examined question**	**P**
Object of activity	dependent	✓	0.0275
Character of cooperation	independent	x	0.5058
Number of donors	dependent	✓	0.0132
Fundraising utilization	dependent	✓	0.0358
Keeping mutually useful relations with donors	dependent	✓	0.0010
Active management of organization	independent	x	0.1056
Strategic planning	independent	x	0.2183
Financial planning	dependent	✓	0.0013
Existence of financial statements	dependent	✓	0.0070

Table 14. Preconditions of the long-term sustainability of non-profit organizations

Financial strategy	Marketing strategy	Personal strategy
Diversification of financial sources	PR, image and publicity	Activation of organization management
Fundraising	Good relations with donors and maintenance	Education and training
Generation of purposeless financial sources	Transparency and credibility	
Financial plan		

Table 15. Criteria influencing acquisition of private financial sources

Criteria influencing acquisition of private financial sources	NPO 2014 Situation in Slovakia	Delft method 2014 Situation in Slovakia	Importance of NPO financial sustainability criteria according to experts
1. Relations of NPO with donors	60 %	40 %	70 %
2. Financial planning	20 %	40 %	80 %
3. Existence of financial statements	60 %	40 %	60 %

9

Scientific research activity and GDP: An analysis of causality based on 144 countries from around the world

Wiesław Dębski[1], Bartosz Świderski[2], Jarosław Kurek[2]

ABSTRACT

Using the Granger methodology, this paper presents the causal relationship between scientific research activity, expressed as the number of significant publications, and gross domestic product (GDP). With causality tests, this relationship is investigated from two points of view: for each individual country (144 were selected) and for each specific academic field (28 were selected). Considering annual data from 1996 to 2012, two hypotheses are tested. The first suggests that scientific research activity in a given country has a significant effect on GDP; the second verifies how much each specific field of scientific research activity affects this growth. Our research confirmed the existence of this relationship for a relatively large number of countries, especially highly developed countries and those with a high potential both in the fields of scientific research activity and in GDP. Moreover, this study identifies the most significant fields of this activity that affect GDP. Additionally, the article includes an empirical study regarding how information related to the number of significant scientific publications influenced the quality of Polish GDP forecasts for 2011-2012.

KEY WORDS: Granger causality, weighted least squares method, number of significant publications, GDP, forecast quality

[1] University of Finance and Management in Warsaw - Management and Finance, Poland; [2] Warsaw University of Life Sciences - Faculty of Applied Informatics and Mathematics, Department of Applied Informatics, Poland

Introduction

GDP (gross domestic product) has been used in economic research for centuries and for various types of analyses, e.g., at the GDP level in economic development analysis in order to analyze the quality of life or wealth of society, at the GDP per capita level, and at the GDP growth rate level in economic cycle analysis. In macroeconomic analyses, especially in economic growth models or econometric models of national economies, the GDP level is used most frequently. Researchers have always been interested in the cause-effect relationship between economic growth and the factors from which it results. The factors most commonly used in models describing how a country's economic growth is determined include 1) capital, which is usually measured as the value of fixed assets or the value of productive fixed assets, 2) employment, which is measured as the number of employed people or the amount of time worked, and 3) technological—or more generally, technological and organizational—progress. The problems of specifying and measuring

Correspondence concerning this article should be addressed to: **Wiesław Dębski**, University of Finance and Management in Warsaw - Management and Finance, 55 Pawia Str., Warsaw 01-030, Poland. E-mail: wdebski@vizja.pl

these relationships have been considered in detail when developing and estimating econometric models of national economies (econometric macro-models). An extensive overview of these issues can be found in (Ashley, 1988; Bodkin, Klein, & Marwah, 1991; Welfe, 2013). The last factor, i.e., taking into account technological developments in research showing the development of GDP or production, was first considered by Solow (1957; 1962) in detail. In econometric models of national economies, the most difficult issue regarding this factor was always choosing the appropriate measure of technological development. In the most basic method, this development was expressed by the symptomatic variable t (e.g., the simple Cobb-Douglas function in which the set of exogenous variables was enlarged by the time variable t), the value of the newest machines or devices, or the expenditure incurred to acquire them. In a somewhat later period (the 1980s and 1990s) this factor was also expressed as expenditure on research and development (R&D). Examples of such work include (Coe & Helpman, 1995; Eckstein, 1984). After the year 2000, this topic generated widespread discussion; participants included (Engelbrecht, 2002; Keller, 2004; Saggi, 2002; Welfe, 2004). There were also attempts to decompose this factor into tangible development (resulting from using the newest machines and devices) and intangible development (resulting from raising the qualifications of the employed, measured as the number of graduates from technical universities, the number of patents and licenses granted, expenditure on research and higher education, for example). Works by (Lee, 2005; Welfe, 2006; Xu & Wang, 1999; 2000) can be cited as examples of such attempts. Subsequently, intellectual—or even more widely, human—capital was taken into account when determining GDP. Nonetheless, the greatest problem encountered was selecting the appropriate measure of this intellectual capital. Real or cumulated expenditure on academic research activity was often used in empirical studies (Borensztein, De Gregorio, & Lee, 1998; Cincera & Van Pottelsberghe de la Potterie, 2001; Van Pottelsberghe de la Potterie & Lichtenberg, 2001; Welfe, 2006; 2009). Thus, as time passed, explaining the cause-effect relationship between the economic growth and scientific research activity of a given country, which illustrates human capital, became increasingly important in economic models, especially econometric models of national economies describing the development of economic growth.

This fact is connected with the primary aim of the following article, which is focused on researching the degree of causality of academic research activity in a country to determine its economic growth, a phenomenon of interest to many economists. As mentioned above, the issue of defining the influence of scientific research activity on economic growth has been the subject of much investigation; however, no study has included as wide a range of countries as this paper. The main issue that arises here is to find a "good" measure of scientific R&D activity. Because our research includes cross-sectional time data and covers 144 countries, an important issue to be addressed was the wide availability of data (a statistical database for all the countries covered) and its comparability. Taking into account these two criteria, we decided to use the number of documents or the number of citable documents referring to a given country as a measure, which can be considered a symptomatic variable of human capital or technical-organizational development in a narrower sense, or possibly non-material technological development, which influences economic growth. The main aim of the article is not to elaborate a specific econometric model describing a given country's GDP but to verify if scientific research activity significantly, in the Granger sense (Engle & Granger, 1987), results in a country's economic growth. Another aim of this paper is to perform a comparative study, which results from the cross-sectional and temporal nature of the research. This study compares the significance of causality of individual research fields and for individual countries. Therefore, this paper verifies the main empirical hypothesis, which states that the scientific research activity of a given country, expressed by the number of published or cited academic papers, contributes significantly to determining the GDP of this country. In the second hypothesis, the degree to which chosen academic fields contribute to GDP growth in the given countries is tested.

Due to the availability of statistical data during our investigation, the following two measures have been adopted as the indicator of a given country's scientific research activity ("IoSA"):

1) Documents – the number of documents published during the selected year, usually called the country's scientific output.

Table 1. The result of correlation coefficients (Pearson's, Spearman's, Kendall's)

rho (lag(PKB,-1), lag(IoSA,1))			
	Pearson	**Spearman**	**Kendall**
Documents	0.9345	0.8759	0.7096
Citable documents	0.9348	0.8766	0.7105

2) Citable documents – the number of citable documents for the selected year. Only articles, reviews and conference papers are considered.

Because two alternative indicators of academic research activity were adopted, their cause-effect relationship with GDP in the Granger sense was investigated. The tests were carried out for various orders of lag between these indicators and GDP. Statistical data (in an annual framework) related to the indicators for academic research activity were drawn from www.scimagojr.com. The data concern various fields of publication and cover the 1996-2012 period. The information obtained includes the number of documents and citable documents by country and by academic field (28 different fields). Additionally, the data provide information on publications for each given country spanning all academic fields in the form of a summary "all" field.

Information regarding GDP in current prices originates from the World Bank service (data.worldbank.org). These data were recalculated to 2011 prices in order to ensure comparability (the 2011 was taken as the base year). Because such data were incomplete, the research takes into consideration only those countries that had complete indicator numbers for scientific research activity, as well as GDP spanning the years 1996-2012. This sample was the longest possible sample that could be achieved, and 144 countries fulfilled the above conditions.

To begin, we decided to check the degree of general correlation between scientific research activity and GDP in the countries being investigated by combining two vectors [lag(PKB,-1),lag(IoSA)] in one matrix with two columns, where lag(PKB,-1) indicates the GDP observation vector for a given country from the second to the last observation, and lag (IoSA,1) indicates the IoSA observation vector from the first to the penultimate observation. These vectors were then placed into consecutive two-column matrices—one for each country–resulting in a matrix with the dimensions of 144 x (2012-1996) = 2304 x 2). The correlation coefficients (Pearson's, Spearman's, Kendall's) between the first and second columns were then calculated. These coefficients are presented in table 1.

The values presented in the above table clearly show a high degree of correlation between the adopted scientific research activity indicators and GDP in the countries covered by the investigation. An analysis of the signs of the obtained correlation coefficients between lag(PKB,-1) and lag(IoSA,1) for each country individually shows that the correlations according to Pearson, Spearman and Kendall are positive in over 80% of these cases.

1. Granger causality test

As shown in the article, the study analyzes causality in the Granger sense, where the cause is defined as scientific research activity (expressed as two indicators that signify the number of publications) in a given country, and the effect is defined as that country's GDP. The usefulness of this activity is also investigated in terms of its influence on the quality of Polish GDP forecasts complied using a linear model for the years 2011-2012.

In the primary view of examining causality, the validity of following equation is considered

$$x_t = c_1 + \alpha_1 x_{t-1} + \alpha_2 x_{t-2} + \ldots + \alpha_p x_{t-p} + \beta_1 y_{t-1} + \beta_2 y_{t-2} + \\ + \ldots + \beta_p y_{t-p} + \mu_t \tag{1}$$

against its alternative formulation

$$x_t = c_0 + \gamma_1 x_{t-1} + \gamma_2 x_{t-2} + \ldots + \gamma_p x_{t-p} + e_t \tag{2}$$

estimated using the ordinary least squares (OLS) method.

Table 2. The rejection frequency for tests (1) and (2) in relation to the lag order p

p	RF			
	Test 1		Test 2	
	Documents	Citable documents	Documents	Citable documents
1	29.86%	29.86%	34.03%	34.72%
2	34.72%	34.03%	51.39%	52.08%
3	42.36%	43.75%	71.53%	69.44%
4	46.53%	47.22%	84.72%	84.72%
5	81.94%	83.33%	97.92%	97.22%

Examining causality is based on the general statement that variable *y* is the cause in relation to variable *x* if past values of *x* help explain future values *y* more accurately (Granger, 1969). Therefore, the following hypothesis is tested:

$$H_0 : \beta_1 = \beta_2 = \ldots = \beta_p = 0 \tag{3}$$

There are many varieties of Granger causality tests (Ashley, Granger, & Schmalensee, 1980; Amblard, 2012; Berndt, 1991; Can-Zhong & Qing-Wen, 2017; Ding, Chen, & Bressler, 2006; Geweke, 1982; Geweke, Meese, & Dent, 1983; Sims, 1972; Zhou & Sornette, 2006). In this paper, two are applied, and both are considered to be among the most popular varieties (Hamilton, 1994; Sims 1980). The statistics S_1 for the first test and S_2 for the second test are as follows (the results from these tests are denoted as *test 1* and *test 2*, respectively):

$$S_1 \equiv \frac{\frac{RSS_0 - RSS_1}{p}}{\frac{RSS_1}{T-2p-1}} \tag{4}$$

$$S_2 \equiv \frac{T\left(RSS_0 - RSS_1\right)}{RSS_1} \tag{5}$$

where

$$RSS_1 = \sum_{t=1}^{T} \hat{u}_t^2 \tag{6}$$

$$RSS_0 = \sum_{t=1}^{T} \hat{e}_t^2 \tag{7}$$

It is assumed that statistics S_1 and S_2 have the corresponding distributions: $F(p, T\text{-}2p\text{-}1)$ and $x^2(p)$, respectively, where T is the number of observations. In this study, a 5% significance level is applied as standard.

The following part of the paper analyzes the hypothesis rejection frequency (RF) H_0 at a significance level of 0.05:

$$RF = \frac{1}{K}\sum_{i=1}^{K} h_i \tag{8}$$

where:

$$h_i = \begin{cases} 1 & \text{if } p\text{-}value_i < 0.05 \\ 0 & \text{if } p\text{-}value_i \geq 0.05 \end{cases}$$

$p\text{-}value_i$ – denotes the significance level of the Granger test for a given country,
k – number of countries (for all research areas = 144).

The table 2 shows the rejection frequency for tests (1) and (2) in relation to the lag order *p*.

The value of 42.36% (item [3,1]) indicates that for the lag order of 3 (years), out of 144 countries researched, the hypothesis was rejected in 42.36% of cases (at a significance level of 5%). It should be noted that assuming full (not asymptotic) congruity of tests, a rejection of hypothesis H_0 should be observed at a

Table 3. The differences between RF and *RF rand*

	RF-RFrandom			
Lag	Test 1		Test 2	
	Documents	Citable documents	Documents	Citable documents
1	23.92%	23.93%	22.99%	23.72%
2	26.03%	25.37%	28.86%	29.57%
3	27.89%	29.25%	28.76%	26.65%
4	19.85%	20.62%	14.37%	14.47%
5	13.30%	14.68%	2.23%	1.52%

level of approximately 5% of cases for random indicators of scientific research activity.

2. Comparing causality tests with the random permutation version

Keeping in mind the asymptotic properties of the test adopted for this study and the fact that both of the above statistics have a tendency for an easier rejection of hypothesis H_0 as the number of observations decreases or by increasing the order p, we decided to compare the test results with their alternative versions. Specifically, the results obtained from the statistics were compared with their versions for a random arrangement of the IoSA vector, i.e., the Granger test was repeated for every country analogically to the tests described above, with the one difference that instead of the original citation vector (IoSA), its random permutation was applied. The idea for this approach arises from the observation that if past scientific research activity remains unrelated to future values of GDP, one may expect a similar result for the Granger causality test for randomly selected values of the IoSA vector in the statistics of the applied test. However, to maintain the same IoSA distribution in the simulation, a permutated IoSA vector (in relation to the original) was applied.

This procedure was repeated 10,000 times. As a result, 10,000 different indicators of RF_rand_i rejection were obtained. The results were averaged to obtain one value of RF_rand for a given country. The differences between RF and RF_rand are presented in the table below. A positive difference between RF and RF_rand indicates a more frequent rejection of hypothesis H_0 for real IoSA values than for their random permutations (carried out independently for each of the countries studied).

For both of the above tests, higher values of $RF\text{-}RF_{random}$ in the table 3 are an indication in favor of hypothesis H_1 (the hypothesis of a lack of causality in comparison to randomly permutated IoSA values is more frequently rejected).

Interpreting the obtained results, one can state that the value of 27.89% (item [3.1]) suggests that if randomly permutated Documents values are applied, then the indicator for the rejection of hypothesis H_0 would nominally be 27.89 percentage points lower than the same indicator obtained from non-random (i.e., original) Documents values. The indicators shown in the above table imply that scientific research activity, measured as the amount of published articles, results in an economic effect after approximately 2-3 years (i.e., considering lag orders from 1 to 4, the relatively highest values are lag orders 2 and 3).

3. Causality in individual scientific fields

The research presented so far tested the causality of scientific research activity, measured as the general number of publications in all fields, in determining the GDP for all countries. Let us study this causality

Table 4. The results of rejection frequency of the zero hypothesis

	RF								RF - RFrandom								NoC
	Documents				Citable documents				Documents				Citable documents				
	Lag 2		Lag 3		Lag 2		Lag 3		Lag 2		Lag 3		Lag 2		Lag 3		
test	1	2	1	2	1	2	1	2	1	2	1	2	1	2	1	2	
all	0.35	0.51	0.42	0.72	0.34	0.52	0.44	0.69	0.26	0.29	0.28	0.29	0.25	0.30	0.29	0.27	144
Agricultural and Biological Sciences	0.28	0.43	0.31	0.60	0.26	0.44	0.32	0.59	0.19	0.20	0.16	0.17	0.17	0.22	0.18	0.16	124
Arts and Humanities	0.10	0.29	0.15	0.46	0.13	0.33	0.21	0.42	0.01	0.06	-0.01	0.03	0.03	0.10	0.06	-0.02	48
Biochemistry, Genetics and Molecular Biology	0.30	0.46	0.37	0.69	0.30	0.45	0.38	0.68	0.21	0.23	0.23	0.26	0.21	0.22	0.24	0.25	105
Business, Management and Accounting	0.32	0.47	0.43	0.70	0.30	0.45	0.42	0.66	0.23	0.24	0.29	0.27	0.21	0.22	0.27	0.23	53
Chemical Engineering	0.19	0.44	0.30	0.59	0.22	0.44	0.29	0.56	0.11	0.21	0.16	0.16	0.13	0.21	0.14	0.13	73
Chemistry	0.24	0.48	0.32	0.65	0.22	0.49	0.32	0.66	0.15	0.25	0.17	0.23	0.13	0.26	0.17	0.24	92
Computer Science	0.27	0.52	0.32	0.62	0.27	0.52	0.32	0.62	0.18	0.29	0.18	0.19	0.18	0.29	0.18	0.19	71
Decision Sciences	0.16	0.41	0.22	0.55	0.14	0.41	0.24	0.51	0.07	0.19	0.07	0.12	0.05	0.19	0.09	0.08	51
Dentistry	0.15	0.37	0.34	0.63	0.15	0.34	0.34	0.59	0.06	0.14	0.20	0.21	0.06	0.12	0.20	0.16	41
Earth and Planetary Sciences	0.29	0.44	0.30	0.58	0.26	0.45	0.30	0.57	0.20	0.21	0.16	0.15	0.18	0.22	0.16	0.15	103
Economics, Econometrics and Finance	0.35	0.41	0.29	0.63	0.35	0.41	0.31	0.59	0.26	0.18	0.15	0.20	0.26	0.18	0.17	0.16	51
Energy	0.16	0.38	0.28	0.55	0.17	0.38	0.28	0.55	0.07	0.15	0.13	0.12	0.09	0.15	0.13	0.12	69
Engineering	0.18	0.42	0.25	0.53	0.18	0.40	0.26	0.52	0.09	0.19	0.10	0.10	0.09	0.18	0.11	0.09	89
Environmental Science	0.25	0.51	0.35	0.63	0.25	0.48	0.34	0.63	0.16	0.28	0.20	0.21	0.16	0.26	0.19	0.20	104
Health Professions	0.19	0.38	0.21	0.57	0.14	0.38	0.19	0.60	0.10	0.15	0.07	0.14	0.06	0.15	0.05	0.17	42
Immunology and Microbiology	0.17	0.37	0.28	0.57	0.17	0.36	0.26	0.56	0.08	0.14	0.13	0.14	0.09	0.13	0.11	0.13	109
Materials Science	0.21	0.38	0.22	0.54	0.21	0.38	0.23	0.56	0.12	0.16	0.08	0.12	0.12	0.16	0.09	0.13	81
Mathematics	0.29	0.49	0.33	0.67	0.27	0.48	0.34	0.67	0.20	0.27	0.18	0.24	0.18	0.26	0.20	0.24	79
Medicine	0.23	0.38	0.39	0.62	0.23	0.38	0.37	0.67	0.15	0.15	0.25	0.19	0.14	0.15	0.22	0.24	128
Multidisciplinary	0.18	0.33	0.20	0.63	0.20	0.31	0.22	0.53	0.09	0.10	0.06	0.20	0.11	0.08	0.08	0.10	49
Neuroscience	0.21	0.43	0.27	0.46	0.23	0.48	0.25	0.52	0.13	0.20	0.12	0.04	0.15	0.26	0.10	0.09	56
Nursing	0.39	0.47	0.33	0.64	0.33	0.44	0.36	0.58	0.30	0.25	0.19	0.21	0.25	0.22	0.21	0.15	36
Pharmacology, Toxicology and Pharmaceutics	0.20	0.33	0.24	0.53	0.19	0.28	0.25	0.49	0.12	0.10	0.10	0.10	0.10	0.05	0.11	0.07	79
Physics and Astronomy	0.20	0.45	0.30	0.61	0.20	0.46	0.31	0.60	0.11	0.23	0.15	0.18	0.11	0.24	0.16	0.17	84
Psychology	0.26	0.47	0.25	0.45	0.28	0.47	0.23	0.47	0.17	0.24	0.09	0.03	0.19	0.25	0.08	0.05	53
Social Sciences	0.30	0.54	0.32	0.65	0.29	0.47	0.27	0.62	0.21	0.31	0.18	0.22	0.20	0.25	0.12	0.20	93
Veterinary	0.22	0.54	0.25	0.58	0.24	0.51	0.24	0.61	0.13	0.32	0.10	0.16	0.15	0.29	0.09	0.18	72

Table 5. Sum of ranks (in descending order)

1	All
2	Biochemistry, Genetics and Molecular Biology
3	*Business, Management and Accounting*
4	Mathematics

with respect to particular scientific fields. The table 4 shows the results (rejection frequency of the zero hypothesis) for these fields based on the previously mentioned tests, with the lag orders 2 and 3 for the original base data (RF). Differences compared to the results obtained for randomly permutated IoSA vectors (RF – RFrandom) are also listed.

Additionally, the table includes the indicator NoC (number of countries), defined as the number of countries for which combined data were available, i.e., both regarding GDP and the number of publications for each country for the 1996-2012 period. Thus, in further calculations, only those countries that had complete data were taken into account. Because some observations were missing from the database, different scientific fields of study had data from different numbers of countries. For example, data from the field of chemistry was available for only 92 countries (which could also be the result of natural inactivity of some countries in this field). A smaller number of countries results in a smaller number of observations used in the calculations. It also often leads to a change in the structure among the researched countries. Ultimately, it has a negative impact on the representativeness of the results. In the table below, where the number of countries used for calculations was less than half, i.e., 144 / 2 = 77 (144 is the number of countries with full data used to study the relationship between GDP and the number of publications in any and all fields – all), the results are shown in italics.

The interpretation of the results shown in the table above is the same as for the previous study, e.g., for item [5, 3] the value 0.43 indicates that for the lag order of 3 (years) in the field of business, management and accounting, for 53 countries studied, hypothesis H_0 was rejected in 43% of cases (at the significance level of 5% for test 1, testing Documents). In turn, item [5, 11] with a value of 0.29 means that if, in the same test, randomly permutated IoSA values are used, the result would be 29 percentage points lower; therefore, the rejection frequency for hypothesis H_0 would equal 43% - 29% = 14%. It should be emphasized that the above results are aggregate estimates, and the real effect of scientific research activity on economic growth may vary depending on the specifics of a given country.

If the sum of ranks (in descending order, meaning that the largest value would be given the rank of 1) is calculated for each column (except the last, which lists the indicators of the number of countries) and subsequently sorted in descending order, the following fields appear in positions 1 to 4:

The above scientific fields (shown in the table 5) can be seen (from the point of view of the approach applied above) as the areas that are most conducive to economic growth.

4. Testing Granger causality for specific countries

The table 6 lists significance levels (p-value) for hypothesis H_0, verified for the total number of publications (divided into Documents and Citable documents) in all areas of scientific research activity (all) with reference to specific countries with lag orders 2 and 3. Lower values reflect easier rejection of hypothesis H_0 in favor of an alternative hypothesis, and they are associated with a more significant causal relationship between the past number of publications in a given country and its subsequent GDP, i.e., that the number of publications from two years earlier influences the current level of GDP to a greater degree.

The rejection frequencies (RF) for hypothesis H_0 (lack of causality) for particular groups of countries

Table 6. Significance levels (p-value) for hypothesis *H0*

Test	p-value							
	Documents				Citable documents			
	Lag 2		Lag 3		Lag 2		Lag 3	
	Test 1	Test 2	Test 1	Test 2	Test 1	Test 2	Test 1	Test 2
Albania	0.4815	0.3325	0.0158	0.0000	0.4529	0.3013	0.0205	0.0000
Algeria	0.4543	0.3028	0.0087	0.0000	0.4502	0.2984	0.0075	0.0000
Angola	0.4725	0.3226	0.0012	0.0000	0.5051	0.3589	0.0021	0.0000
Armenia	0.2154	0.0839	0.2662	0.0501	0.2486	0.1087	0.3399	0.0926
Australia	0.0010	0.0000	0.0057	0.0000	0.0007	0.0000	0.0047	0.0000
Austria	0.4351	0.2824	0.4448	0.1758	0.4061	0.2523	0.4319	0.1642
Azerbaijan	0.0063	0.0000	0.1093	0.0040	0.0077	0.0000	0.1239	0.0059
Bahamas	0.8299	0.7647	0.2392	0.0379	0.8853	0.8400	0.0836	0.0017
Bangladesh	0.0029	0.0000	0.0100	0.0000	0.0030	0.0000	0.0057	0.0000
Belarus	0.1455	0.0400	0.3553	0.1032	0.0998	0.0187	0.5857	0.3269
Belgium	0.4937	0.3460	0.5059	0.2361	0.4691	0.3189	0.5193	0.2503
Benin	0.9876	0.9825	0.1333	0.0073	0.9955	0.9936	0.1476	0.0099
Bhutan	0.0264	0.0008	0.1539	0.0112	0.0263	0.0008	0.1371	0.0080
Bolivia	0.0173	0.0003	0.0065	0.0000	0.0169	0.0003	0.0069	0.0000
Bosnia and Herzegovina	0.6256	0.5011	0.0291	0.0000	0.6334	0.5106	0.0297	0.0000
Botswana	0.5645	0.4274	0.8419	0.7045	0.5484	0.4086	0.8172	0.6627
Brazil	0.0868	0.0139	0.0016	0.0000	0.0879	0.0143	0.0020	0.0000
Brunei Darussalam	0.2576	0.1158	0.9196	0.8434	0.3771	0.2230	0.5940	0.3372
Bulgaria	0.2153	0.0838	0.5342	0.2667	0.1986	0.0722	0.5057	0.2359
Burkina Faso	0.8408	0.7793	0.6144	0.3628	0.9048	0.8668	0.4923	0.2219
Burundi	0.6766	0.5645	0.7845	0.6091	0.7108	0.6080	0.7852	0.6102
Cambodia	0.0051	0.0000	0.2228	0.0314	0.0041	0.0000	0.2450	0.0404
Cameroon	0.0821	0.0124	0.0101	0.0000	0.0748	0.0101	0.0142	0.0000
Canada	0.0018	0.0000	0.0028	0.0000	0.0031	0.0000	0.0036	0.0000
Central African Republic	0.9607	0.9446	0.9231	0.8498	0.9861	0.9804	0.7952	0.6265
Chad	0.1446	0.0395	0.0211	0.0000	0.1368	0.0354	0.0205	0.0000
Chile	0.0061	0.0000	0.0244	0.0000	0.0063	0.0000	0.0236	0.0000
China	0.0105	0.0001	0.0217	0.0000	0.0096	0.0000	0.0212	0.0000
Colombia	0.0045	0.0000	0.0170	0.0000	0.0042	0.0000	0.0132	0.0000

Table 6. Significance levels (p-value) for hypothesis *H0* (Continued)

Test	p-value							
	Documents				Citable documents			
	Lag 2		Lag 3		Lag 2		Lag 3	
	Test 1	Test 2	Test 1	Test 2	Test 1	Test 2	Test 1	Test 2
Congo	0.6914	0.5832	0.6277	0.3801	0.5045	0.3582	0.6860	0.4597
Costa Rica	0.0240	0.0007	0.0087	0.0000	0.0339	0.0016	0.0099	0.0000
Croatia	0.9053	0.8676	0.9617	0.9236	0.8985	0.8581	0.9599	0.9200
Cyprus	0.5936	0.4621	0.0517	0.0003	0.5695	0.4334	0.0552	0.0004
Czech Republic	0.3704	0.2165	0.1049	0.0035	0.2802	0.1343	0.1043	0.0035
Denmark	0.6608	0.5446	0.5248	0.2564	0.5983	0.4678	0.3370	0.0907
Dominican Republic	0.6528	0.5346	0.6470	0.4057	0.5904	0.4583	0.6082	0.3549
Ecuador	0.7544	0.6645	0.6149	0.3635	0.6831	0.5727	0.5200	0.2511
Egypt	0.6333	0.5104	0.8447	0.7093	0.6271	0.5029	0.8468	0.7129
El Salvador	0.1801	0.0601	0.6813	0.4530	0.1701	0.0540	0.6521	0.4125
Eritrea	0.4264	0.2732	0.1156	0.0048	0.3892	0.2351	0.0838	0.0017
Estonia	0.1343	0.0341	0.3525	0.1012	0.1055	0.0210	0.3598	0.1064
Ethiopia	0.0048	0.0000	0.0190	0.0000	0.0043	0.0000	0.0154	0.0000
Fiji	0.0032	0.0000	0.0483	0.0003	0.0037	0.0000	0.0499	0.0003
Finland	0.2119	0.0814	0.2310	0.0346	0.1932	0.0686	0.2218	0.0310
France	0.2810	0.1350	0.1441	0.0092	0.2249	0.0907	0.1453	0.0095
Gabon	0.1139	0.0245	0.0329	0.0001	0.1466	0.0405	0.0845	0.0018
Gambia	0.9943	0.9919	0.6282	0.3807	0.8893	0.8454	0.2251	0.0322
Georgia	0.0032	0.0000	0.0035	0.0000	0.0031	0.0000	0.0031	0.0000
Germany	0.1397	0.0369	0.2031	0.0244	0.1418	0.0380	0.2139	0.0281
Ghana	0.9575	0.9401	0.7421	0.5426	0.9212	0.8896	0.7445	0.5462
Greece	0.2443	0.1054	0.0017	0.0000	0.1844	0.0629	0.0015	0.0000
Grenada	0.1612	0.0487	0.1875	0.0196	0.1238	0.0290	0.1831	0.0183
Guatemala	0.0074	0.0000	0.0147	0.0000	0.0101	0.0001	0.0200	0.0000
Guinea	0.4739	0.3241	0.6871	0.4613	0.4749	0.3252	0.6949	0.4724
Guinea-Bissau	0.8152	0.7449	0.8653	0.7452	0.9208	0.8889	0.8760	0.7641
Guyana	0.1445	0.0394	0.0957	0.0026	0.0844	0.0131	0.0481	0.0002
Honduras	0.0958	0.0171	0.0067	0.0000	0.1229	0.0286	0.0071	0.0000
Hong Kong	0.0042	0.0000	0.0020	0.0000	0.0057	0.0000	0.0027	0.0000

Table 6. Significance levels (p-value) for hypothesis *H0* (Continued)

Test	p-value							
	Documents				Citable documents			
	Lag 2		Lag 3		Lag 2		Lag 3	
	Test 1	Test 2	Test 1	Test 2	Test 1	Test 2	Test 1	Test 2
Hungary	0.3506	0.1974	0.5126	0.2432	0.4107	0.2569	0.5622	0.2988
Iceland	0.7437	0.6506	0.3235	0.0820	0.7495	0.6581	0.3851	0.1253
India	0.8963	0.8551	0.1707	0.0151	0.7895	0.7108	0.0980	0.0028
Indonesia	0.0000	0.0000	0.3494	0.0991	0.0000	0.0000	0.3443	0.0956
Italy	0.1411	0.0376	0.0024	0.0000	0.1062	0.0213	0.0025	0.0000
Japan	0.2131	0.0822	0.7568	0.5653	0.2110	0.0807	0.7876	0.6141
Jordan	0.7967	0.7203	0.2561	0.0453	0.8206	0.7522	0.3858	0.1259
Kazakhstan	0.0276	0.0009	0.0368	0.0001	0.0281	0.0010	0.0313	0.0000
Kenya	0.3866	0.2325	0.0926	0.0024	0.4045	0.2506	0.1929	0.0212
Kyrgyzstan	0.1264	0.0302	0.0094	0.0000	0.1171	0.0259	0.0091	0.0000
Laos	0.0000	0.0000	0.0004	0.0000	0.0000	0.0000	0.0003	0.0000
Latvia	0.1141	0.0246	0.1299	0.0068	0.1315	0.0327	0.1364	0.0078
Lebanon	0.0162	0.0002	0.0064	0.0000	0.0160	0.0002	0.0023	0.0000
Lesotho	0.0657	0.0076	0.1967	0.0224	0.0872	0.0140	0.2161	0.0289
Lithuania	0.0616	0.0066	0.0077	0.0000	0.0621	0.0067	0.0083	0.0000
Luxembourg	0.8931	0.8507	0.0535	0.0004	0.8873	0.8427	0.0678	0.0008
Macedonia	0.0334	0.0015	0.0141	0.0000	0.0415	0.0026	0.0195	0.0000
Madagascar	0.7443	0.6513	0.6766	0.4465	0.7991	0.7235	0.7522	0.5582
Malawi	0.6713	0.5578	0.6068	0.3532	0.6428	0.5222	0.7835	0.6076
Malaysia	0.1652	0.0510	0.0198	0.0000	0.1572	0.0464	0.0256	0.0000
Mali	0.4313	0.2783	0.0071	0.0000	0.5002	0.3533	0.0047	0.0000
Malta	0.8098	0.7378	0.0787	0.0014	0.8162	0.7463	0.0615	0.0006
Mauritania	0.0205	0.0004	0.2158	0.0288	0.0189	0.0003	0.2190	0.0299
Mauritius	0.0333	0.0015	0.0503	0.0003	0.0206	0.0004	0.0357	0.0001
Mexico	0.1487	0.0417	0.0224	0.0000	0.1592	0.0476	0.0189	0.0000
Moldova	0.0585	0.0058	0.0005	0.0000	0.0562	0.0053	0.0004	0.0000
Mongolia	0.0396	0.0023	0.0003	0.0000	0.0495	0.0040	0.0004	0.0000
Morocco	0.0157	0.0002	0.0070	0.0000	0.0082	0.0000	0.0030	0.0000
Mozambique	0.1345	0.0342	0.1283	0.0065	0.1537	0.0445	0.1281	0.0065

Table 6. Significance levels (p-value) for hypothesis *H0* (Continued)

Test	p-value							
	Documents				Citable documents			
	Lag 2		Lag 3		Lag 2		Lag 3	
	Test 1	Test 2	Test 1	Test 2	Test 1	Test 2	Test 1	Test 2
Namibia	0.0477	0.0037	0.0938	0.0025	0.0515	0.0044	0.1096	0.0040
Nepal	0.0001	0.0000	0.0002	0.0000	0.0002	0.0000	0.0004	0.0000
Netherlands	0.2472	0.1076	0.1353	0.0077	0.2068	0.0778	0.1361	0.0078
Nicaragua	0.6506	0.5319	0.0341	0.0001	0.6130	0.4857	0.0550	0.0004
Niger	0.9509	0.9308	0.0850	0.0018	0.9349	0.9085	0.0837	0.0017
Nigeria	0.0019	0.0000	0.0021	0.0000	0.0017	0.0000	0.0018	0.0000
Norway	0.0045	0.0000	0.0050	0.0000	0.0090	0.0000	0.0075	0.0000
Pakistan	0.1993	0.0727	0.0226	0.0000	0.2100	0.0801	0.0220	0.0000
Panama	0.6655	0.5505	0.0993	0.0030	0.7233	0.6241	0.1004	0.0031
Papua New Guinea	0.5914	0.4594	0.8085	0.6483	0.6533	0.5352	0.8529	0.7236
Paraguay	0.0335	0.0015	0.1024	0.0033	0.0230	0.0006	0.0691	0.0009
Peru	0.0000	0.0000	0.0002	0.0000	0.0001	0.0000	0.0002	0.0000
Philippines	0.0000	0.0000	0.0066	0.0000	0.0000	0.0000	0.0067	0.0000
Poland	0.0021	0.0000	0.0000	0.0000	0.0017	0.0000	0.0000	0.0000
Portugal	0.9835	0.9766	0.4365	0.1683	0.9937	0.9910	0.3862	0.1262
Puerto Rico	0.0400	0.0024	0.1999	0.0234	0.0371	0.0020	0.1867	0.0193
Romania	0.5174	0.3728	0.9791	0.9578	0.5161	0.3714	0.9787	0.9570
Russian Federation	0.0357	0.0018	0.0001	0.0000	0.0435	0.0029	0.0001	0.0000
Rwanda	0.0119	0.0001	0.0293	0.0000	0.0268	0.0009	0.0548	0.0004
Saint Kitts and Nevis	0.3914	0.2373	0.4761	0.2057	0.4459	0.2938	0.3443	0.0956
Samoa	0.0702	0.0088	0.0232	0.0000	0.0835	0.0128	0.0324	0.0001
Senegal	0.4988	0.3518	0.5000	0.2299	0.4321	0.2792	0.4210	0.1547
Seychelles	0.0007	0.0000	0.0092	0.0000	0.0005	0.0000	0.0064	0.0000
Sierra Leone	0.0290	0.0011	0.0508	0.0003	0.0378	0.0021	0.0423	0.0002
Singapore	0.0009	0.0000	0.0029	0.0000	0.0010	0.0000	0.0035	0.0000
Slovakia	0.7077	0.6040	0.1328	0.0072	0.6673	0.5528	0.2027	0.0243
Slovenia	0.4949	0.3474	0.6142	0.3626	0.4830	0.3342	0.5976	0.3416
Solomon Islands	0.0114	0.0001	0.0112	0.0000	0.0235	0.0006	0.0053	0.0000
South Africa	0.0372	0.0020	0.0001	0.0000	0.0290	0.0011	0.0001	0.0000

Table 6. Significance levels (p-value) for hypothesis *H0* (Continued)

Test	p-value							
	Documents				Citable documents			
	Lag 2		Lag 3		Lag 2		Lag 3	
	Test 1	Test 2	Test 1	Test 2	Test 1	Test 2	Test 1	Test 2
South Korea	0.0137	0.0001	0.0128	0.0000	0.0132	0.0001	0.0195	0.0000
Spain	0.5469	0.4068	0.0728	0.0011	0.4641	0.3135	0.0266	0.0000
Sri Lanka	0.0996	0.0186	0.1342	0.0075	0.0952	0.0169	0.1263	0.0062
Sudan	0.4591	0.3080	0.3332	0.0882	0.4594	0.3083	0.3501	0.0996
Suriname	0.8657	0.8132	0.0321	0.0001	0.8491	0.7906	0.0527	0.0003
Swaziland	0.2651	0.1218	0.2927	0.0638	0.2648	0.1216	0.3397	0.0925
Sweden	0.0065	0.0000	0.0521	0.0003	0.0042	0.0000	0.0341	0.0001
Switzerland	0.0503	0.0041	0.0204	0.0000	0.0720	0.0093	0.0279	0.0000
Tajikistan	0.4754	0.3258	0.4768	0.2063	0.4781	0.3288	0.4816	0.2111
Tanzania	0.0321	0.0014	0.0277	0.0000	0.0311	0.0013	0.0265	0.0000
Thailand	0.0001	0.0000	0.0009	0.0000	0.0001	0.0000	0.0012	0.0000
Togo	0.6341	0.5114	0.0609	0.0006	0.4985	0.3514	0.0699	0.0009
Trinidad and Tobago	0.0265	0.0009	0.0133	0.0000	0.0249	0.0007	0.0246	0.0000
Tunisia	0.9833	0.9764	0.0475	0.0002	0.6559	0.5385	0.0099	0.0000
Turkey	0.0012	0.0000	0.0069	0.0000	0.0014	0.0000	0.0075	0.0000
Turkmenistan	0.4661	0.3157	0.0701	0.0009	0.4233	0.2700	0.0477	0.0002
Uganda	0.0322	0.0014	0.0665	0.0008	0.0461	0.0034	0.0655	0.0007
Ukraine	0.4539	0.3024	0.4993	0.2292	0.4920	0.3442	0.5767	0.3160
United Kingdom	0.0168	0.0003	0.0081	0.0000	0.0325	0.0014	0.0121	0.0000
United States	0.0181	0.0003	0.0048	0.0000	0.0315	0.0013	0.0104	0.0000
Uruguay	0.6434	0.5229	0.2647	0.0494	0.6357	0.5134	0.3187	0.0790
Uzbekistan	0.4317	0.2787	0.4330	0.1652	0.4196	0.2661	0.4206	0.1543
Vanuatu	0.4848	0.3362	0.7913	0.6202	0.5873	0.4545	0.8273	0.6796
Venezuela	0.7894	0.7106	0.9794	0.9584	0.7805	0.6988	0.9800	0.9595
Vietnam	0.1779	0.0587	0.2655	0.0498	0.1792	0.0596	0.2668	0.0504
Yemen	0.1335	0.0337	0.2521	0.0435	0.1136	0.0244	0.1964	0.0223
Zambia	0.0921	0.0158	0.2276	0.0332	0.1037	0.0202	0.3733	0.1163
Zimbabwe	0.1035	0.0201	0.1250	0.0060	0.1343	0.0341	0.1609	0.0127

Table 7. The rejection frequencies (RF) for hypothesis *H0* (lack of causality) for particular groups of countries and significance level 0.01

	RF (p-value = 0.01)								
	Documents				Citable documents				
	Lag 2		Lag 3		Lag 2		Lag 3		
Group	**Test 1**	**Test 2**	**Test 1**	**Test 2**	**Test 1**	**Test 2**	**Test 1**	**Test 2**	**Number of countries**
All	0.174	0.382	0.236	0.611	0.181	0.368	0.243	0.611	144
G20	0.308	0.692	0.538	0.769	0.385	0.692	0.462	0.846	13
European Union	0.080	0.160	0.200	0.600	0.080	0.160	0.160	0.560	25
Very high human development	0.237	0.368	0.316	0.658	0.237	0.368	0.263	0.632	38
High human development	0.156	0.375	0.250	0.656	0.156	0.375	0.281	0.688	32
Medium human development	0.194	0.472	0.278	0.583	0.222	0.444	0.278	0.639	36
Low human development	0.108	0.297	0.108	0.568	0.108	0.270	0.162	0.514	37
Asia	0.333	0.545	0.333	0.636	0.364	0.545	0.364	0.697	33
Africa	0.070	0.302	0.163	0.581	0.093	0.279	0.186	0.535	43
North America	0.133	0.400	0.267	0.600	0.067	0.400	0.200	0.667	15
South America	0.250	0.500	0.250	0.750	0.250	0.500	0.250	0.750	12
Europe	0.146	0.317	0.244	0.634	0.146	0.317	0.220	0.610	41
Australia and Oceania	0.286	0.571	0.286	0.714	0.286	0.429	0.429	0.714	7

and significance levels 0.01 and 0.05 are listed in Tables 7 and 8, respectively.

Generally, higher values are seen than may have been expected to result from the respective significance levels (1% and 5%). The presence of relatively low values for the European Union is striking (except for two cases in test 2). This situation may be explained by a longer period of relative economic stagnation in which the development of scientific research activity has a lesser impact on GDP. The situation is different in the remaining G20 countries, where this relationship is most visible among the researched countries. When comparing continents, a relatively strong relationship between scientific research and GDP exists in Asia and South and North America. The cause-effect relationship between scientific research activity and GDP is visibly weaker in Europe than in Australia and Oceania. This relation is especially evident in the USA, United Kingdom, Canada, Australia, and Sweden, as well as Far Eastern countries such as China (including Hong Kong), South Korea, the Philippines, Thailand, Singapore, Russia, Turkey and Poland. The table also shows the weakest relationship in the 37 countries that constitute the "low human development" group. Generally, it seems that the scientific activity is not a (significant) driver of economic development in all countries. For example, there are countries where the economy is based mainly on the mining industry or tourism, where science plays a secondary role.

Table 8. The rejection frequencies (RF) for hypothesis *H0* (lack of causality) for particular groups of countries and significance level 0.05

	RF (p-value = 0.05)								
	Documents				Citable documents				
	Lag 2		Lag 3		Lag 2		Lag 3		
Group	Test 1	Test 2	Test 1	Test 2	Test 1	Test 2	Test 1	Test 2	Number of countries
All	0.347	0.514	0.424	0.715	0.340	0.521	0.438	0.694	144
G20	0.692	0.846	0.769	0.846	0.692	0.846	0.769	0.846	13
European Union	0.120	0.280	0.200	0.680	0.120	0.280	0.280	0.680	25
Very high human development	0.316	0.474	0.395	0.711	0.316	0.474	0.447	0.711	38
High human development	0.375	0.531	0.531	0.750	0.375	0.563	0.563	0.719	32
Medium human development	0.417	0.583	0.472	0.722	0.389	0.583	0.444	0.667	36
Low human development	0.270	0.459	0.324	0.676	0.270	0.459	0.324	0.676	37
Asia	0.545	0.636	0.515	0.818	0.545	0.667	0.545	0.758	33
Africa	0.279	0.442	0.326	0.651	0.256	0.442	0.326	0.651	43
North America	0.400	0.600	0.533	0.800	0.400	0.600	0.467	0.800	15
South America	0.500	0.667	0.583	0.833	0.500	0.667	0.583	0.750	12
Europe	0.244	0.439	0.366	0.683	0.244	0.439	0.415	0.683	41
Australia and Oceania	0.429	0.571	0.714	0.714	0.429	0.571	0.714	0.714	7

5. Testing the influence of IoSA on GDP forecasts using the example of Poland

This chapter first examines, based on the previous two tests, the level of Granger causality between the number of publications in given fields of scientific research and GDP for Poland. We chose Poland (our home country) as an example for a detailed analysis. Additionally, we chose one country due to the volume of the article. The study was carried out for lag orders 2 and 3. The table 9 lists the p-values resulting from this testing. Next, the direct influence of information contained in the IoSA vector on the quality of Polish GDP forecasts for 2011-2012 is tested using the adopted linear model (described later in this chapter).

It is clear from the results presented in the above table that the total number of publications (all) resulting from scientific research activity in Poland has a significant effect (p-value less than 0.01) in the Granger sense on Polish GDP growth. This conclusion is drawn based on both scientific research activity indicators used in the tests, as well as both tested lag orders. The same conclusions can be formulated in relation to the following fields of scientific research activities in Poland: biochemistry, genetics and molecular biology, chemistry, immunology and microbiology, medicine, and physics and astronomy. Moreover, test 2 shows that the same conclusion can be drawn for other fields of scientific research. Generalizing these results, it can be claimed that publications related to scientific research associated with highly innovative

Table 9. The result of p-values for lag orders 2 and 3

Area	p-value							
	Documents				Citable documents			
	Lag 2		Lag 3		Lag 2		Lag 3	
	Test 1	Test 2	Test 1	Test 2	Test 1	Test 2	Test 1	Test 2
All	0.0021	0	0	0	0.0017	0	0	0
Agricultural and Biological Sciences	0.5423	0.4014	0.7037	0.4853	0.5517	0.4124	0.7117	0.4969
Arts and Humanities	0.9384	0.9134	0.7852	0.6102	0.9288	0.9	0.7231	0.5139
Biochemistry, Genetics and Molecular Biology	0.0051	0	0.0002	0	0.0042	0	0.0001	0
Business, Management and Accounting	0.9409	0.9169	0.9428	0.8871	0.954	0.9352	0.9694	0.9386
Chemical Engineering	0.0558	0.0052	0.1147	0.0047	0.0499	0.004	0.1048	0.0035
Chemistry	0.0011	0	0.0004	0	0.0011	0	0.0005	0
Computer Science	0.0848	0.0132	0.2136	0.028	0.0687	0.0084	0.1822	0.0181
Decision Sciences	0.0587	0.0059	0.0435	0.0002	0.0508	0.0042	0.0371	0.0001
Dentistry	0.83	0.7648	0.058	0.0005	0.825	0.7581	0.0845	0.0018
Earth and Planetary Sciences	0.0085	0	0.028	0	0.0111	0.0001	0.0357	0.0001
Economics, Econometrics and Finance	0.7108	0.608	0.114	0.0046	0.725	0.6263	0.162	0.013
Energy	0.5472	0.4071	0.4486	0.1794	0.5147	0.3698	0.4646	0.1945
Engineering	0.1031	0.02	0.1633	0.0133	0.0879	0.0143	0.1523	0.0109
Environmental Science	0.2178	0.0856	0.0102	0	0.2203	0.0874	0.0126	0
Health Professions	0.0125	0.0001	0.0554	0.0004	0.0157	0.0002	0.0656	0.0008
Immunology and Microbiology	0.0006	0	0.0005	0	0.0004	0	0.0005	0
Materials Science	0.0463	0.0034	0.1078	0.0038	0.0498	0.004	0.1114	0.0043
Mathematics	0.2078	0.0785	0.4117	0.1468	0.2034	0.0755	0.4108	0.1461
Medicine	0.0006	0	0.0006	0	0.0004	0	0.0005	0
Multidisciplinary	0.6011	0.4712	0.3312	0.0869	0.4434	0.2911	0.4998	0.2297
Neuroscience	0.0896	0.0149	0.2501	0.0426	0.1021	0.0196	0.28	0.057
Nursing	0.0489	0.0039	0.1423	0.0089	0.096	0.0172	0.2313	0.0346
Pharmacology, Toxicology and Pharmaceutics	0.7455	0.6529	0.8929	0.7944	0.7583	0.6696	0.935	0.8723
Physics and Astronomy	0.002	0	0.0071	0	0.0019	0	0.0067	0
Psychology	0.0197	0.0004	0.019	0	0.0114	0.0001	0.0138	0
Social Sciences	0.3404	0.1878	0.1178	0.005	0.3073	0.1576	0.1089	0.004
Veterinary	0.0875	0.0141	0.0589	0.0005	0.0859	0.0136	0.0582	0.0005

Note: Scientific fields characterized by all p-values below 0.01 are emphasized in bold.

technological development have the largest impact on GDP growth in Poland (with a lag of 2 and 3 years).

The second part of the study, as stated earlier, comprises an analysis of the influence of information contained in the IoSA vector on the forecast quality of Polish GDP. In other words, an attempt is made to examine how past knowledge contained in publications (Documents, Citable documents) influences the forecast quality of future GDP. A test was carried out for the GDP forecasts for 2011-2012. Such forecasts of Polish GDP were made for these years based the model described below and subsequently checked for quality by calculating the errors, expressed as root mean square error (RMSE) and mean absolute percentage error (MAPE). The forecasts were created by first estimating the model parameters based on data from the IoSA vector for the years 1996-2010, then calculating the GDP forecast for 2011 using the estimated model parameters, and, finally, repeating the procedure for 2012 but with the model estimated based on data for 1996-2011. For both forecast years, the average forecast error was calculated as RMSA and MAPE.

An additional phenomenon was analyzed during the above test. When forecasting Polish GDP for a given year, it is possible to apply a model estimated from data pertaining solely to Poland or one estimated from data pertaining solely to other countries. One may imagine suitably formulated time series in both cases to estimate, e.g., the parameters of an autoregressive model with the appropriate lag order. It is also possible to use data pertaining to all countries except Poland to estimate the model. The first approach (estimating the model parameters using only data pertaining to Poland) corresponds to the case where all the observations are used; however, a non-zero weight (in the weighted OLS method) equal to a certain positive constant is assigned only to observations for Poland, while the remaining observations have weights equal to zero. The other approach, where a GDP model for Poland is estimated using data from 1996-2010/2011 for other countries, matches the case where all the observations are used (pertaining to Poland and other countries); however, the observation weight for Poland would assume the value of zero, and all observations relating to other countries would have a certain non-negative weight. An interesting situation arises if these weights are defined as variables. Such a case is examined below.

It is assumed that observation weights pertaining to Poland in proportion to other countries are related as Θ to (1- Θ), where Θ denotes a number in the range [0,1]. Therefore, if Θ is equal to 1, only observations pertaining to Poland are used to estimate the parameters of the regression equation. On the other hand, if Θ is equal to zero, only observations from other countries are used to estimate the model. If, in turn, Θ is equal to 0.5, all the observations have the same weight, and if $\Theta = 0.75$, the weight of observations for Poland is 3 times (0.75/ (1-0.75) = 3) greater (this corresponds to the situation in which observations pertaining to Poland would be repeated 3 times).

Two alternative model descriptions were used in this test:

$$GDP_t = c_1 + \alpha_1 GDP_{t-1} + \alpha_2 GDP_{t-2} + \ldots + \alpha_p GDP_{t-p} + \\ + \beta_1 A_{t-1} + \beta_2 A_{t-2} + \ldots + \beta_p A_{t-p} + \mu_t \tag{9}$$

and

$$GDP_t = c_0 + \gamma_1 GDP_{t-1} + \gamma_2 GDP_{t-2} + \ldots + \gamma_p GDP_{t-p} + e_t \tag{10}$$

where A denotes Documents or Citable documents and p denotes the lag order.

The quality of the GDP forecasts for 2011 and 2012 was tested by applying random terms μ_{2012}, μ_{2011}, e_{2012}, and e_{2011} in the following models:

$$GDP_{2012} = c^1_{2012} + \alpha'_{2011} GDP_{2011} + \ldots + \alpha'_{1996} GDP_{1996} + \\ + \beta'_{2011} A_{2011} + \ldots + \beta'_{1996} A_{1996} + \mu_{2012} \tag{11}$$

$$GDP_{2011} = c^1_{2011} + \alpha''_{2010} GDP_{2010} + \ldots + \alpha''_{1996} GDP_{1996} + \\ + \beta'_{2010} A_{2010} + \ldots + \beta'_{1996} A_{1996} + \mu_{2011} \tag{12}$$

$$GDP_{2012} = c^0_{2012} + \gamma'_{2011} GDP_{2011} + \ldots + \gamma'_{2010} GDP_{2010} + \\ + \ldots + \gamma'_{1996} GDP_{1996} + e_{2012} \tag{13}$$

$$GDP_{2011} = c^0_{2011} + \gamma'_{2010} GDP_{2010} + \ldots + \gamma'_{2009} GDP_{2009} + \\ + \ldots + \gamma'_{1996} GDP_{1996} + e_{2011} \tag{14}$$

From a technical estimation point of view, information used to prepare the forecast based on the above equations can be divided into the following two types:

a) Information obtained from past relationships between past GDP and future GDP (optionally taking into account IoSA) only for observations pertaining to Poland,

b) Information obtained from past relationships between past GDP and future GDP (optionally taking into account IoSA) only for observations pertaining to countries other than Poland (i.e., for 144 - 1= 143 countries).

To eliminate the natural difference in the countries' size, GDP and IoSA data were divided by their average values for the period 1996-2010, calculated for each country. This information can be used to estimate the parameters of the tested equations with different weights, as mentioned earlier. A more accurate specification is made below on the example of estimating the error in μ_{2012}, i.e., for 2012. In the case of estimating the remaining errors (i.e., μ_{2011}, e_{2011}, e_{2012}), the procedure is analogical. Assuming

$$
X_1 = \begin{bmatrix}
GDP_{2010\_Poland} & \cdots & GDP_{2011\text{-}p\_Poland} \\
GDP_{2009\_Poland} & \cdots & GDP_{20110\text{-}p\_Poland} \\
\vdots & \vdots & \vdots \\
GDP_{1996+p\text{-}1\_Poland} & \cdots & GDP_{1996\_Poland} \\
GDP_{2010\_Country1} & \cdots & GDP_{2011\text{-}p\_Country1} \\
GDP_{2009\_Country1} & \vdots & GDP_{2010\text{-}p\_Country1} \\
\vdots & \vdots & \vdots \\
GDP_{1996+p\text{-}1\_Country1} & \cdots & GDP_{1996\_Country1} \\
GDP_{2010\_Country2} & \cdots & GDP_{2011\text{-}p\_Country2} \\
GDP_{2009\_Country2} & \vdots & GDP_{2010\text{-}p\_Country2} \\
\vdots & \vdots & \vdots \\
GDP_{1996+p\text{-}1\_Country2} & \cdots & GDP_{1996\_Country2} \\
 & \vdots & \\
GDP_{2010\_CountryN} & \cdots & GDP_{2011\text{-}p\_CountryN} \\
GDP_{2009\_CountryN} & \cdots & GDP_{2010\text{-}p\_CountryN} \\
\vdots & \vdots & \vdots \\
GDP_{1996+p\text{-}1\_CountryN} & \cdots & GDP_{1996\_CountryN}
\end{bmatrix}
$$

$$
X_2 = \begin{bmatrix}
A_{2011\text{-}p\_Poland} & \cdots & A_{2011\text{-}p\_Poland} \\
A_{2009\_Poland} & \cdots & A_{2010\text{-}p\_Poland} \\
\vdots & \vdots & \vdots \\
A_{1996+p\text{-}1\_Poland} & \cdots & A_{1996\_Poland} \\
A_{2010\_Country1} & \cdots & A_{2011\text{-}p\_Country1} \\
A_{2009\_Country1} & \vdots & A_{2010\text{-}p\_Country1} \\
\vdots & \vdots & \vdots \\
A_{1996+p\text{-}1\_Country1} & \cdots & A_{1996\_Country1} \\
A_{2010\_Country2} & \cdots & A_{2011\text{-}p\_Country2} \\
A_{2009\_Country2} & \vdots & A_{2010\text{-}p\_Country2} \\
\vdots & \vdots & \vdots \\
A_{1996+p\text{-}1\_Country2} & \cdots & A_{1996\_Country2} \\
 & \vdots & \\
A_{2010\_CountryN} & \cdots & A_{2011\text{-}p\_CountryN} \\
A_{2009\_CountryN} & \cdots & A_{2010\text{-}p\_CountryN} \\
\vdots & \vdots & \vdots \\
A_{1996+p\text{-}1\_CountryN} & \cdots & A_{1996\_CountryN}
\end{bmatrix} \tag{15}
$$

where $country_i$ denotes the i-th country out of the researched countries other than Poland, N=143, m=16 (for 2012; however, m=15 in the forecast for 2011).

$$
\mathbf{\Theta} = \begin{bmatrix}
\Theta \\ \Theta \\ \vdots \\ \Theta \\ 1-\Theta \\ 1-\Theta \\ \vdots \\ 1-\Theta \\ 1-\Theta \\ 1-\Theta \\ \vdots \\ 1-\Theta \\ \vdots \\ 1-\Theta \\ 1-\Theta \\ \vdots \\ 1-\Theta
\end{bmatrix} \tag{16}
$$

May **W** denote the matrix with diagonal elements $\mathbf{\Theta}$ on the main diagonal. For the discussed case, this matrix will constitute the weighting matrix, where observations pertaining to Poland are weighted with respect to observations pertaining to the remaining countries.

To shorten the notation, let us assume

$$\mathbf{X}=[\mathbf{1}, \mathbf{X}_1, \mathbf{X}_2] \tag{17}$$

where **1** denotes the vector of ones related to the free term, $\mathbf{X}_1$ represents GDP, and $\mathbf{X}_2$ represents the IoSA vector (in the case of the model with a random term denoted as e, $\mathbf{X}_2$ is an empty vector). Consequently, the WOLS (weighted OLS) estimator may be used; thus,

$$
\begin{bmatrix} \tilde{c} \\ \alpha \\ \beta \end{bmatrix} = \left[\boldsymbol{X}^T \boldsymbol{W} \boldsymbol{X} \right]^{-1} \boldsymbol{X}^T \boldsymbol{W} \boldsymbol{y} \tag{18}
$$

For the model parameters estimated in this way, the forecast errors $\widetilde{PKB}_{2011}$ and $\widetilde{PKB}_{2012}$ can be calculated (in other words, the realizations of random terms: μ_{2012}, μ_{2011}, e_{2012}, and e_{2011}). RMSE and MAPE

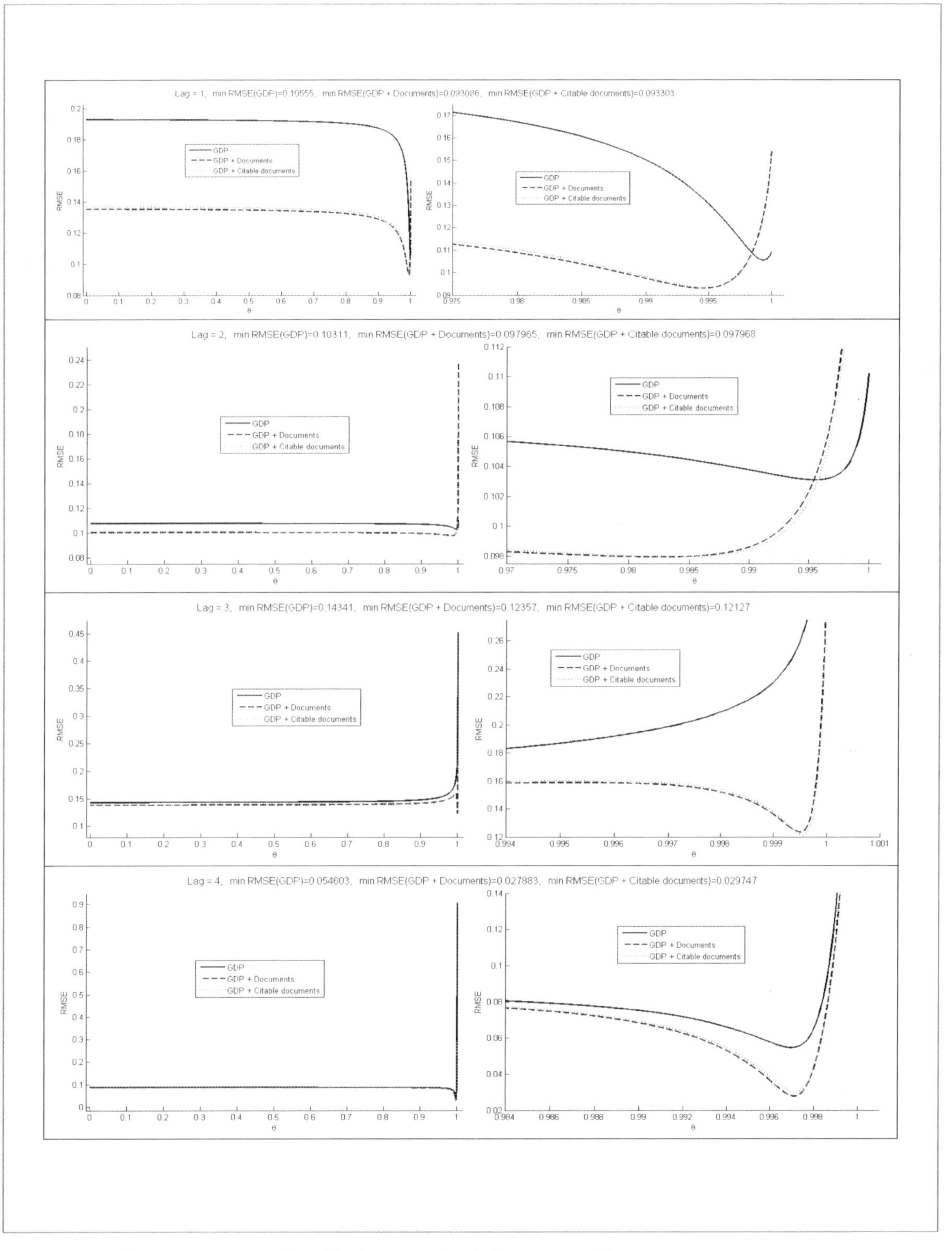

Figure 1. RMSE for "Documents" and "Citable documents" with function _ and lag=1,2,3,4

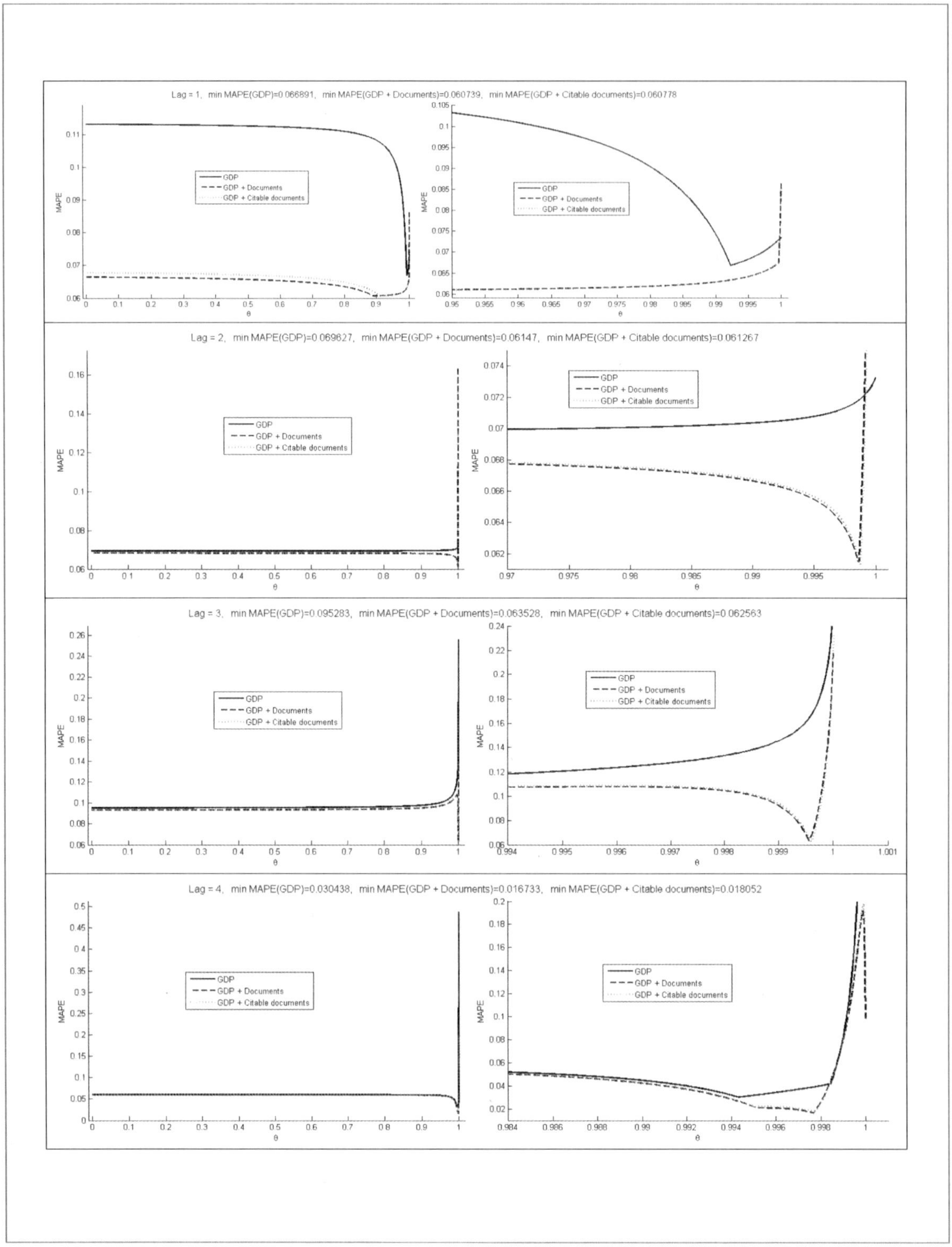

Figure 2. MAPE for "Documents" and "Citable documents" with function _ and lag=1,2,3,4

shall be used as measures of error. These are defined as follows:

$$RMSE = \sqrt{\frac{\left(\left(\widetilde{GDP}_{2012} - GDP_{2012}\right)^2 + \left(\widetilde{GDP}_{2011} - GDP_{2011}\right)^2\right)}{2}} \quad (19)$$

$$MAPE = \frac{1}{2}\left(\left|\frac{\widetilde{GDP}_{2012} - GDP_{2012}}{GDP_{2012}}\right| + \left|\frac{\widetilde{GDP}_{2011} - GDP_{2011}}{GDP_{2011}}\right|\right) \quad (20)$$

As explained earlier, parameter $\boldsymbol{\Theta}$ reflects the relationship between the share of observations for Poland and observations for other countries. Therefore, both types of errors are functions of $\boldsymbol{\Theta}$. The model error figure with and without indicators of scientific research activity (number of publications) are presented in figure 1 for various lag orders. RMSE graphs for "Documents" and "Citable documents" as a function $\boldsymbol{\Theta}$ are shown for two forecast variants, i.e., with and without the adopted indicators of scientific research activity. For most cases, an interesting phenomenon is visible near the value $\boldsymbol{\Theta} = 0.99$. The error curve falls to a certain minimum value, after which it rises again. Thus, information from other countries (or, more precisely, using observations pertaining to other countries in the process of estimating the parameters for the equation applied to forecast Polish GDP) improves the forecast of Polish GDP. However, this information should be balanced by an appropriately small weight. The graphs on the right side show an enlargement of the same error graph for the upper range of $\boldsymbol{\Theta}$.

Graphs representing MAPE for "Documents" and "Citable documents" with function $\boldsymbol{\Theta}$ are presented in figure 2, analogically to RMSE above. The graphs on the right show an enlargement of the left error graph for the upper range of $\boldsymbol{\Theta}$.

It is worth noting that for all of the above graphs, the lowest forecast error is observed for the predictive equation variant taking into account the characteristics of scientific research activity (i.e., GDP + Documents or GDP + Citable documents). For each lag in the range of 1-4, the lowest RMSE and MAPE appear when applying a non-zero weight for countries other than Poland. In both cases, i.e., Documents and Citable documents, the lowest RMSE appears in the model with a lag order equal to 4). In all cases, it is evident that scientific research activity indicators help better explain GDP.

Conclusions

The subject of research described in this paper was the causality, in the Granger sense, between scientific research activity and GDP. The research was carried out using annual data pertaining to 144 countries around the world and 28 distinct areas of scientific research activity. Generally, the study confirmed the main proposed hypothesis, which claims that in many countries and fields of study, a causal relationship exists between scientific research activity, measured as the number of significant publications, and GDP. This relationship is very pronounced in many countries, including the USA, United Kingdom, Canada, Australia, Russia, and China. Generally, this relationship is most visible in the G20 group of countries (which have a large potential for both scientific research activity and GDP), with the exclusion of European Union countries. The relatively less visible relationship between scientific research activity and GDP in the European Union is striking, especially in countries such as Germany, France and Italy (which may be caused by an extended period of economic stagnation). Conversely, this relationship is clearly visible on the Asian and American continents. The weakest relationship is found in countries belonging to the low human development group.

The second hypothesis, which claims a varied influence of distinct scientific research activities on GDP, proved that fields of study such as (1) biochemistry, genetics and molecular biology; (2) business, management and accounting; and (3) mathematics are most conducive to fostering economic growth.

References

Amblard, P.O., & Michel, O. J. J. (2012). The Relation between Granger Causality and Directed Information Theory: A Review. *Entropy, 15(1)*, 113-143. https://doi.org/10.3390/e15010113

Ashley, R. (1988). On the Relative Worth of Recent Macroeconomic Forecasts. *International Journal of Forecasting, 4(3)*, 363-376.

Ashley, R., Granger, C. W. J., & Schmalensee, R. (1980). Advertising and Aggregate Consumption: An Analysis of Causality. *Econometrica, 48(5)*, 1149-1168.

Bodkin, R. G., Klein, L. R., & Marwah K. (1991). A History of Macroeconometric Model-Building. Northampton, UK: Edward Elgar Publishing.

Berndt, E. (1991). The Practice of Econometrics: Classic and Contemporary. New York, NY: Addison-Wesley.

Borensztein, E., De Gregorio, J., & Lee, J. W. (1998). How does foreign direct investment affect economic growth. *Journal of International Economics, 45(1)*, 115-135.

Can-Zhong, Y., & Qing-Wen, L. (2017). The mutual causality analysis between the stock and futures markets. *Physica A: Statistical Mechanics and its Applications, 478,* 188-204. https://doi.org/10.1016/j.physa.2017.02.071

Cincera, M., & Van Pottelsberghe de la Potterie, B. (2001). International R&D spillovers: A survey. *Cahiers Economiques de Bruxelles, 169*(1), 1-20.

Coe, D.T., Helpman, E. (1995). International R&D spillovers. *European Economic Review, 39(5)*, 859-887. https://doi.org/10.1016/0014-2921(94)00100-E

Ding, M., Chen, Y., & Bressler, S. (2006). Granger causality: Basic theory and application to Neuroscience. In S. Schelter, M. Winterhalder, & Timmer J. (Eds.), Handbook of Time Series Analysis (pp. 437-460). Wienheim: Wiley. https://doi.org/10.1002/9783527609970.ch17

Eckstein, O. (1984). The Dri Model of the U.S. Manufacturing Industries. New York, NY: Mcgraw-Hill.

Engelbrecht, H. J. (2002). Human capital and international knowledge spillovers in TFP growth of a sample of developing countries: an exploration of alternative approaches. *Applied Economics, 34(7)*, 832-841. https://doi.org/10.1080/00036840110061947

Engle, R. F., & Granger, C. N. J. (1987). Co-integration and error correction: representation, estimation and testing. *Econometrica, 55(2)*, 251-276.

Geweke, J. (1982). Measurement of linear dependence and feedback between multiple time series. *Journal of the American Statistical Association, 77(378)*, 304-313.

Geweke, J., Meese R., & Dent, W. (1983). Comparing Alternative Tests of Causality in Temporal Systems: Analytic Results and Experimental Evidence. *Journal of Econometrics, 21(2),* 161-194. https://doi.org/10.1016/0304-4076(83)90012-X

Granger, C. W. J. (1969). Investigating Causal Relations by Econometric Models and Cross-spectral Methods. *Econometrica, 37*(3), 424-438.

Hamilton, J. D. (1994). Time Series Analysis. 1-1. New Jersey, NJ: Princeton University Press.

Keller, W. (2004). International technology diffusion. *Journal of Economic Literature, 42(3)*, 752-782.

Lee, G. (2005). Direct versus indirect international R&D spillovers. *Information Economics and Policy, 17(3)*, 334-348.

Saggi, K. (2002). Trade, Foreign direct investment and international technology transfer: a survey. *The World Bank Observer, 17*(2), 191-235. Retrieved from https://openknowledge.worldbank.org/handle/10986/19843

Sims, C. (1972). Money, income and causality. *American Economic Review, 62(4)*, 540-552.

Sims, C. (1980). Macroeconomics and reality. *Econometrica, 48(1)*, 1-48.

Solow, R. (1957). Technical change and aggregate production function. *Review of Economics and Statistics, 39(3)*, 312-320.

Solow, R. (1962). Technical progress, capital formation and economic growth. *American Economic Review, 52(2)*, 76-86.

Van Pottelsberghe de la Potterie, B., & Lichtenberg, F. R. (2001). Does foreign direct investment transfer technology across borders? *Review of Economics and Statistics, 83(3)*, 490-497. https://doi.org/10.1162/00346530152480135

Welfe, W. (Ed.). (2004). Długookresowy, makroekonometryczny model W8D gospodarki polskiej [Long-term macroeconometric model W8D of the Polish economy]. Lódź: Wydawnictwo Uniwersytetu Łódzkiego.

Welfe, W. (2006, July). Towards modelling knowledge-based economies. Paper presented at Second international symposium in management, engineering and informatics, Orlando, FL.

Welfe, W. (Ed.). (2009). Knowledge-based economies. Models and methods. Frankfurt/Main: Peter Lang.

Welfe, W. (2013). Macroeconometric models. Berlin: Springer Verlag.

Xu, B., & Wang, J. (1999). Capital goods trade and R&D spillovers in OECD. *Canadian Journal of Economics, 32*(5), 1258-1274.

Xu, B., & Wang, J. (2000). Trade, FDI and international technology diffusion. *Journal of Economic Integration, 15(1)*, 585-601.

Zhou, W. X., & Sornette, D. (2006). Non-parametric determinants of real-time lag structure between two time series: The optimal thermal causal path method. *Journal of Macroeconomics, 28(1)*, 195-224. https://doi.org/10.1080/14697680500383763

10

Quantitative and Qualitative Analysis of X-efficiency in the Croatian Market

Ozren Rafajac[1], Marinko Skare[2]

ABSTRACT This article aims to explain the idea of X-efficiency, which indicates the difference between potential and actual output. If any business subject produces below its own potentials, it can be considered X-inefficient. To determine whether X-inefficiency in Croatian companies exists, how large it is in its volume and why it appears, in 2014, empirical research was conducted. Since only 22% of interviewed companies use all their available resources and given that the mean capacity utilization rate is only 70% and the mean resource utilization rate is 68%, our study results suggest that among business subjects in the Republic of Croatia, X-inefficiency exists to a large extent. Qualitative analysis shows that X-inefficiency appears mostly because of the competitive pressure. Other reasons include legal and administrative problems, the existence of inertness and a lack of motivation, the decision to work "less for more", inadequate demand, economic crisis, the decision to save resources for future use, seasonal demand, incompetence of the government, corruption, and the risk of debt collection as well as local organizational problems.

KEY WORDS: X-efficiency, social efficiency, market failures, transitional economies

---

[1] Polytechnic of Rijeka, Croatia; [2] Juraj Dobrila University of Pula, Croatia

Introduction

According to Leibenstein's theory of X-efficiency, if a business subject is producing the maximum size of output it can produce, then it can be considered X-efficient (Leibenstein, 1978). X-inefficiency occurs when X-efficiency is not accomplished. The theory of X-efficiency is based upon several elementary postulates such as imperfect markets, incomplete work contracts/production functions, an effort as a discretionary variable, selective rationality and inert areas (Leibenstein, 1978). Within neo-liberal theory, in a perfectly competitive market, X-inefficiency would not exist because if any company is less efficient than the rest of their competitors, it would not generate enough profit to stay in business in the long run. However, a perfectly competitive market is only an imaginary and unrealistic idea. In all other market forms in which we usually participate, such as oligopoly and monopoly, there is almost always some degree of X-inefficiency. This does not mean that optimal decisions cannot be made but only highlights the fact that sub-optimal decisions are possible. By accepting this possibility, the XE theory provides a theoretical background for discussion on some interesting questions: Do business subjects always minimize their costs, and do they always maximize their profits? How efficiently do they use their resources? How does the size of a company

Correspondence concerning this article should be addressed to: **Ozren Rafajac,** Polytechnic of Rijeka, Business Department, Vukovarska 58, 51000 Rijeka, Croatia. E-mail: ozren.rafajac@veleri.hr

affect its X-efficiency? What are the main causes of X-inefficiency? How does one become X-efficient? Although the problem of the efficient use of resources should be the focus of economists, in conventional economics, the phenomenon of X-efficiency has been unfairly neglected, understated and considered as less important. This is particularly true for transitional economies where, until now, despite its importance in the explanation of economic reality, very little research about X-efficiency has been conducted.

The main justification for the implementation of this research arises from the fact that in the Republic of Croatia, numerous resources (human and material) are still not optimally utilized. In the last 20 years, since a process of transition from public to private ownership began, many companies in transitional countries have been faced with a problem of non-allocative efficiency. Unfortunately, local scientists have shown little interest in this subject. Their unfamiliarity with the idea of X-efficiency is fairly evident from the related research studies and the literature that is mostly focused solely on themes of economic growth and competition that not even remotely consider the factors such as effort, inertia, interpersonal interactions and agent-principal relationship. Consequently, these theoretical and empirical studies are not able to provide a complete picture of the growth and development process in CEE economies. Selective rationality, principal-agent relations, effort choice, inert areas and effort entropy are all factors closely associated with the growth of businesses and thus with the national growth in general. In former socialist countries (now transitional such as Croatia), the capital–labor relationship was based on public and not on private ownership, which in turn dictated the individual, household and firm behavior. Without an understanding that motivation is a transitional variable that might depend on many specific factors (i.e., type of leadership, culture, legal framework) and might depend on whether an individual is an owner or only an employee of a company (because they do not necessarily share the same interests), the role of the firms and entrepreneurship in the economic development of CEE countries cannot be clearly defined. Consequently, the fact that some of the CEE countries have converged more rapidly with EU countries than with others also cannot be explained.

In conventional microeconomic theory, there is no distinction between individual agents (companies with one employee) and organized groups of agents (medium or large enterprises). Although many advocates of free markets suggest that small and medium enterprises are more efficient than large ones, these people usually do not have any supportive evidence for their claims. In addition, even if they do and their results are confirmed, a counter argument could be that bigger agents (large market players) have larger quantities of resources they can "keep and save" for investment and economic use in the future. By emphasizing that many of our resources are not optimally used and that motivation should not be a constant but a variable depending on many types of pressures that individuals feel during economics activities, Leibenstein's theoretical approach offers a far more realistic explanation of economic behavior than conventional microeconomic and growth theory. The purpose of our study is to show how the X-efficiency theory can be applied for better understanding of economic growth and development of transitional countries (such as Croatia) and to explain how a high degree of X-inefficiency can represent a main cause of slow economic convergence toward EU countries. Accordingly, we have set two main objectives:

(1) To measure the level of X-efficiency in the Croatian economy; and
(2) To identify X-inefficiency as the principal growth constraint factor in Croatia.

To accomplish these tasks, this paper compares the achieved level of overall growth and development with quantitative levels and with qualitative causes of X-inefficiency in Croatian firms. Fundamentally, this study responds to a call for a new economic approach for largely indebted transitional countries, such as Croatia, in the light of Leibenstein's theory, which has stressed the role of entrepreneurship in the development process. We expect that the findings presented in this paper will help policy makers and economists in transitional countries to expand their knowledge about the behavior and reasoning of economic subjects. However, the presented results are only preliminary findings that should be extended and confirmed by further studies on the role of entrepreneurship in the development of transitional economies. All this will in turn increase the awareness of policy makers and economic practitioners about the fact that transition is a process that is far more beyond price and trade liberalization, property protection, or a new fiscal and monetary system. Rather, it involves a switch in the mental behavior of all economic agents (individuals, households, firms and governments). Our results suggest that in the Croatian economy, such a transition has not yet occurred, which means that the transition to market economics is far from complete and that it has not ended with the official accession to the EU.

The paper comprises five parts. The first section represents the introduction that emphasizes an importance of the X-efficiency theory for the process of the economic growth and development. Section two offers a review of the relevant literature on economic transition for Croatia and Leibenstein's theory in general, whereas the research sample and methodology are presented in section three. Section four presents the empirical results of the investigation, while section five offers a conclusion about the implications and limitations of the conducted research as well as recommendations for future work in the field of X-efficiency theory in transitional economies.

Conceptual framework

According to Dean and Perlman (1998), Harvey Leibenstein can be considered a pioneer in experimental and behavioral economics. Although his theory of X-efficiency was established back in 1966, it went fairly unnoticed in mainstream economics. Within his XE theory, he assumed that markets are imperfect because of monopolistic power and asymmetric information. Although they can determine the number of work hours and assignments that must be completed, work contracts can never completely define the behavior of workers, just as different qualitative variations of the same draft or product are possible in production functions (Leibenstein, 1978). That implies that the worker's effort is a discretionary variable and not a constantly given value. In the X-efficiency approach, the term effort includes both physical and mental aspects, and thus, it is viewed as the outcome of an individual's response to motivations provided by his or her own psyche and/or by the external environment. Since the basic unit under analysis in this theory is an individual (not a household or a company as in neoliberal theory) and since it suggests that maximization is to be observed, but not assumed, XE theory is closer to the real-life circumstances than any other theory of economic behavior. In life practice, individuals choose how rational they want to be in different situations, which means that they demonstrate a selective rationality that is based on the concept of pressure. Leibenstein (1978) stated, "Individuals often make trade-offs between how they would like to behave without any constraints and how they should behave concerning constraints they are facing" (p. 22). Thus, the basic element of rational behavior is concern about the constraints we face.

The specific level of X-efficiency within an enterprise may be affected by many internal and external constraints. The boundary between external and internal is, admittedly, vague. External constraints are those that are part of the (external) environment within which a business subject operates and include the structure of regulations, the structure of the market, the structure of property rights, and the ownership form. Internal constraints include personality traits, work norms, (internal) motivational factors and transaction costs. Since it acknowledges the possibility of both maximizing and non-maximizing behavior and thus acknowledges the possibility that economic agents are not always equally persistent in the maximizing of their profit/utility or in the minimizing of their costs, which conventional neoclassical economics ignore, one would expect that Leibenstein's theory would have a significant impact on mainstream economic theory. Unfortunately, this was not the case.

It is important to stress that X-inefficiency is not the only type of inefficiency in economic practice. The X-efficiency considers only the outputs produced with the given inputs and disregards whether existing inputs that are being used are the best to use, which relates to the allocative efficiency. For example, a company that hires a surgeon to wash dishes can be X-efficient, although his relocation to the position of healing those who are ill would be far more efficient for the society in general (Leibenstein, 1978). Discussion on allocative and non-allocative efficiency was first begun by Leibenstein (1966) when he argued, "Microeconomic theory focuses itself on allocative efficiency to the exclusion of other types of efficiencies that, in fact, are much more significant in many instances than the allocative efficiency" (p. 392). Accordingly, Leibenstein (1966) observed non-allocative efficiency as an extremely important aspect in the growth process and suggested, "Minimizing of X-inefficiency can be accomplished by a higher level of competitive pressure and by specific motivational factors that improve the level of effort or motivated action" (p. 412). Still, his ideas did not pass without opposition. One of them was Stigler (1976), who said, "The increase of output which is the result of increased effort is not increase in efficiency, but a change in the input" (p. 213).

Although it has not received the attention it deserves in conventional economic circles, the theory of X-efficiency has not stopped being the subject of interesting discussions since it first appeared. The above statement is confirmed by the fact that since the late 1960s until the year 2002, more than 80 articles were published in which their authors tried to analyze X-efficiency (Frantz, 1982, 2004). According to Frantz (2007), the term X-efficiency is one of the most quoted according to The Social Science Citation Index, and it had its citation peak in the period between 1981 and 1985. The results of various conducted research were quite interesting. By analyzing the relationships between public monopolistic and public duopolistic enterprises in the field of electric power production in 49 cities in the USA, Primeaux and Nelson (1980) reached a conclusion that the degree of competition has no effect on the level of capacity utilization. Contrary to that, Sjöström and Weitzman (1996) have found that there exists a well-defined sense in which competition is a surprisingly powerful force for efficiency. An empirical study conducted by Altunbas, Evans and Molyneux (2001) have fund little evidence to suggest that privately owned banks are more efficient than their mutual and public-sector counterparts. Similar studies that tried to determine a connection between X-efficiency and the form of ownership are those done by Majumdar (1998) and Button and Weyman-Jones (1992). According to Fung (2006), initial differences in X-efficiency among bank holding companies can, between them, create permanent differences in steady-state productivity. Bogetoft, Färe and Obel (2006) discuss how to measure allocative efficiency without presuming technical efficiency, which is relevant when it is easier to introduce reallocations than improvements in technical efficiency. Moreover, X-efficiency was analyzed in relation to the level of wages or salary, and in that case, Altman (2006) has demonstrated how, contrary to standard theory, which claims that higher salaries decrease the search for work, implementing X-efficiency in a model leads to the state of things where higher salaries increase the search for work.

In the last decade, XE theory has been applied in several additional studies. After comparing the cost and profit efficiency level and the managerial behavior of banks in nine Central and Eastern European countries (the Czech Republic, Estonia, Hungary, Latvia, Lithuania, Poland, Romania, Slovakia and Slovenia), in the period 1995-2002, Rossi, Schwaiger and Winkler (2008) came to the conclusion that the low level of efficiency recorded in the CEEC banks could be partially ascribed to uncontrolled external factors that are beyond the control of management. Hai-bo and He-zhong (2009) discuss the main factors influencing Chinese port X-efficiency and propose that reforming the staff incentive system and company ownership system are the main factors that could improve the X-efficiency in Chinese ports. By analyzing technical efficiency in Nigerian farming Omonona, Egbetokun and Akanbi (2010) find that the farmers' average technical efficiency is 87% and suggest that farmers should be encouraged to join cooperative business models. By studying the impact of Information and Communication Technology (ICT) on labor productivity growth between 1995 and 2005, Ceccobelli, Gitto and Mancuso (2012) find that ICT technologies positively contribute to the generation of convergence clubs in the evolution of labor productivity. Fienhage (2014) applies XE theory in the Supply Chain Management and claims that XE theory can contribute to the sourcing strategy, the supplier strategy and the contracting decision of purchasers by giving practical suggestions to the purchasers.

While the literature about competitiveness and development issues in transitional economies is quite large, the issue of non-allocative efficiency has been almost completely forgotten. From Chikán (2008), who has tried to provide a framework for connecting macro and micro level research on competitiveness, to Lovrinčević, Mikulić and Rajh (2008), who have paid attention to the measuring of national competitiveness. Although researchers have paid attention to measuring the competitiveness of the manufacturing sector in relation to other Central, East and Southeast European economies (Gligorov & Vidovic, 2004), FDI and competiveness link (Sohinger & Horvatin, 2005), export competitiveness for manufacturing companies (Stojčić, Bečić, & Vojnić, 2012), innovation activities impact on competitiveness (Stojcic, Hashi, & Telhaj, 2011), external deficit and exchange rate influence on competitiveness (Vujčić & Presečan, 1999), corporate governance development importance for boosting competiveness (Ljubojević & Novičić, 2007), differences in foreign and domestic product competiveness (Leko-Šimić, 2001), major competitiveness element determinants (Tica, Cenan, & Bilas, 2004) and labor force competitiveness in Croatia (Bejaković and Lowther, 2004), very little research on X-efficiency in transitional countries has actually been conducted. As far as the authors know, in the last two decades, only two non-allocative efficiency research studies in the Republic of Croatia have been conducted. After measuring efficiency in the seventeen Croatian customs service houses, Benazić (2012) found that only five of them were working efficiently and that the main reason of inefficiency was in an inadequate organizational structure of the Croatian customs administration. Another attempt was measuring the efficiency and productivity of the Croatian banking sector in the period 2000-2004, and in that case, Primorac and Troskot (2005) found that many banks in that period operated with a negative profit. Given that most of the banks observed in that period changed considerably, the authors concluded that statistical analysis for a banking sector as turbulent as the Croatian is has proved useless.

Although all previously mentioned research studies have made contributions in proving the X-efficiency theory, it can be noted that these studies have not yet fully clarified why companies do not use all available resources X-efficiently. Analysis of the responses to the questions of why business subjects do not use all available resources and how to optimize capacity utilization rates should provide better insight into the qualitative dimension of X-inefficiency.

Methodology and data

To empirically ascertain whether X-inefficiency in Croatian companies exists, and if it exists, how large it is, and why it appears, we conducted an empirical survey between May and December 2014 on a randomly chosen sample of business subjects in Croatia. Research was conducted in the form of a web questionnaire, which has allowed managers to anonymously answer our questions. Such methodology was used in order to collect as many relevant answers as possible. The invitation to participate in the survey was sent to 5000 email addresses of business entities operating in the Republic of Croatia. All participants were asked to forward this invitation to their business partners. In addition, a call for participation in the research was set up on the Internet and on social networks.

Due to policy restrictions on the disclosure of business indicators, some managers did not participate in the survey, and of those who did, one segment did not want to disclose anything regarding their business performance. This led to a total of 375 business subjects who responded to the questionnaire (initial sample), while only 150 of them responded to all the questions. To achieve the highest possible level of statistical significance, the research sample is limited to those 150 (N) business subjects who fully completed our questionnaire.

Originally, the questionnaire comprised 22 questions divided into five different sections. This paper presents the results of the most significant questions from the first, second and fourth section. The first part describes the research sample and includes questions about industry, activity, ownership and the size of the companies. The second part addresses the capacity and resource utilization, along with the main reasons why some of the available resources were not engaged and with the main strategies that ensure optimal utilization of production/service capacities. The fourth section explored competitiveness through questions about the percentage of sales in different markets and the relevance of different factors that have provided business success to the examined business subjects. These answers were used to analyze X-inefficiency in the Croatian market.

With respect to their industry, the sample included 18% manufacturing companies, 14% in commerce and motor vehicles services, 12% in construction, 11.3% in diversified service activities, 8.7% in agriculture, fishing and forestry, 5.3% in transport and warehousing, 5.3% in information and communications, and 4.7% in accommodation and food service industry, while the shares of companies in other industries were allocated in lower percentages. The research sample comprised 18% production companies, 50.7% service companies and 31.3% who perform both, production and service activities. In the research sample, there were 74% companies that had hired up to 49 employees, 13.3% that had hired between 50 and 199 employees and 12.7% that had hired 200 or more employees. As far as the ownership was concerned, 92% were privately owned, 5.3% were publicly owned, and 2.7% had mixed or public-private ownership.

According to the data of the Croatian Financial Agency and the Croatian Chamber of Commerce in Croatia, in 2014, there were 104 116 micro, small and medium-sized enterprises (99.7% of total registered enterprises) operating, which had a share of 53% of total revenues, 68.4% of employment and 48.5% in Croatian exports (Alpeza et al., 2016). Given that this research sample includes 87.3% micro, small and medium-sized companies, it represents a relatively good (but not ideal) representation of the selected population.

Measuring of X-efficiency is not always a simple task. Given that the differences in estimates between actual and potential outputs (in both financial (market) and natural (physical) measuring units) can vary significantly, analysis is directed toward the closest possible measures, and these are the capacity utilization rate and the utilization rate of overall available resources, as both can be equally well used to indicate the level of X-inefficiency. As far as the interpretation of collected results is concerned, it must be noted that all collected answers are only subjective evaluations of the respondents, who often seek to present their business capabilities as better than they are to give a better impression about themselves or about their own company. Given the size of the sample and the scope of the analysis that followed, this investigation should be regarded as a preliminary attempt to recognize elementary tendencies that occur within socio-economic market relationships in Croatia. Finally, it is important that analysis of any socio-economic environment, because of the natural, climatic, social, political, formally legal and cultural differences, always represents a specific case that cannot instantly be projected onto other socio-economic environments.

Empirical results

The analysis of data concerning the utilization of production and service capacities (which indicates the difference between actual and potential output) showed that of 150 (N) collected answers, only 12.7% of examinees stated that their potential output is the same as their actual output, which means they were X-efficient. In answering the question about the utilization of all available resources, only 11.3% of examinees stated that they use all available resources, while in the next question, which was about qualitative aspects of X-efficiency, only 22% of respondents stated the same thing. With these three results on our mind, it is possible to conclude that in the Croatian market in 2014, at least 78% of companies were X-inefficient, which means they produced outputs that were lower than their potential outputs. This information directly confirms that in the Croatian market, X-inefficiency is present in a very large number of companies.

Since the start of the transition, the Croatian economy has experienced large issues with low economic competitiveness (see figure 1). Figure 1 shows the trend in global competitiveness for the Croatian Economy since year 2006. It can be observed that Croatian economy's global competitiveness performance on the competitiveness scale is moving about the mean value (1-7 best). A large drop in the economy's competitiveness was registered at the beginning of the global financial crisis in 2008, with the competitiveness index value significantly below values registered in 2006. The ethical behavior of firms and efficacy of corporate boards in Croatia during the 2006-2013 period is of interest to us since it is strongly connected with the X-efficiency theory explored in this study (see figure 2). The data in figure 2 show that the ethical behavior of the firms and corporate board efficacy are both significantly below the mean value for countries in the report (mean value for ethical behavior = 4.2; mean value for corporate board efficacy = 4.5).

Figure 3 exhibits transition indicator progress since 1989, with scale index = 1 meaning little or no change from planned economy to 4+ = standard market economy performance. During 1989-2012, significant progress (transition) on the macroeconomic environment in Croatia was achieved. Currently, the macroeconomic environment of the Croatian economy (price liberalization, trade and forex system, and

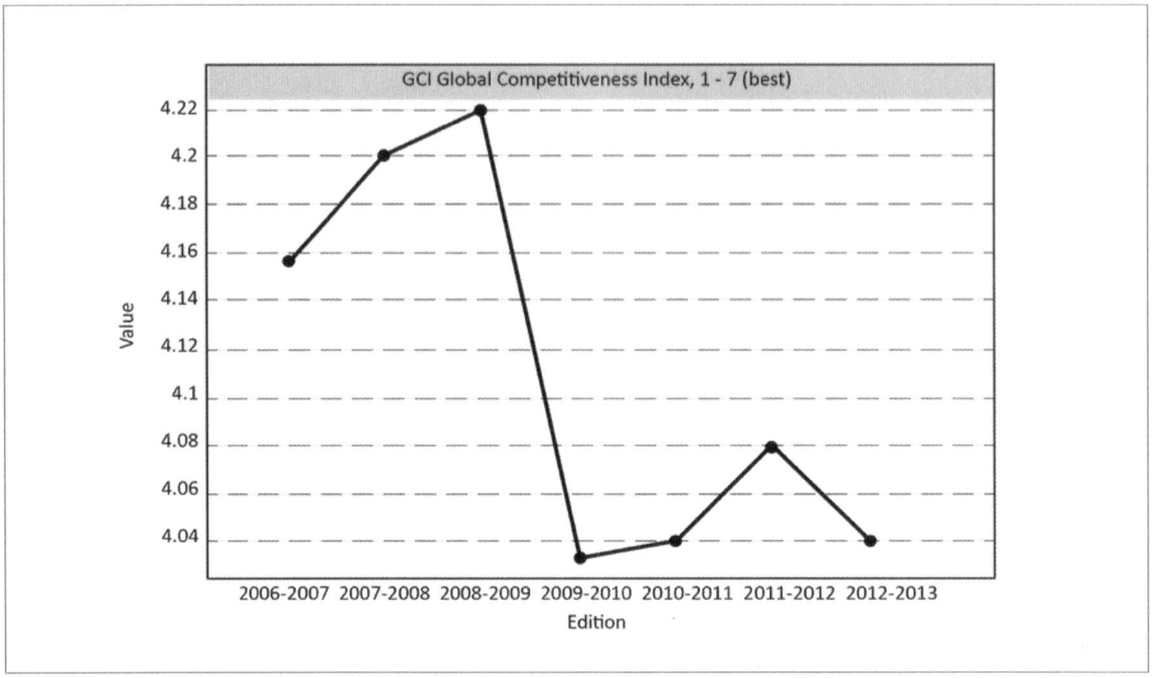

Figure 1. GCI Global Competitiveness Index Croatia, 2006-2013
Source: Adapted from "The Global Competitiveness Report 2013–2014.Full Data Edition" by K. Schwab (Ed.). (2013). Published by The World Economic Forum, Geneva Retrieved from http://www3.weforum.org/docs/WEF_GlobalCompetitivenessReport_2013-14.pdf

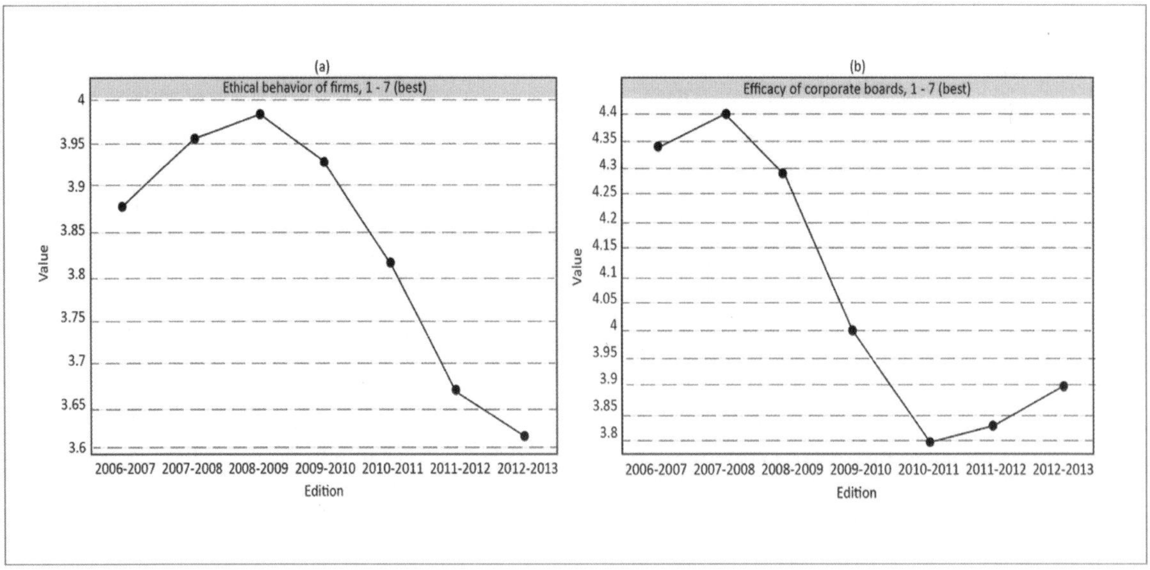

Figure 2. GCI Ethical behavior of firms (a) and corporate board efficacy (b) in Croatia, 2006- 2013
Source: Adapted from "The Global Competitiveness Report 2013–2014.Full Data Edition" by K. Schwab (Ed.). (2013). Published by The World Economic Forum, Geneva Retrieved from http://www3.weforum.org/docs/WEF_GlobalCompetitivenessReport_2013-14.pdf

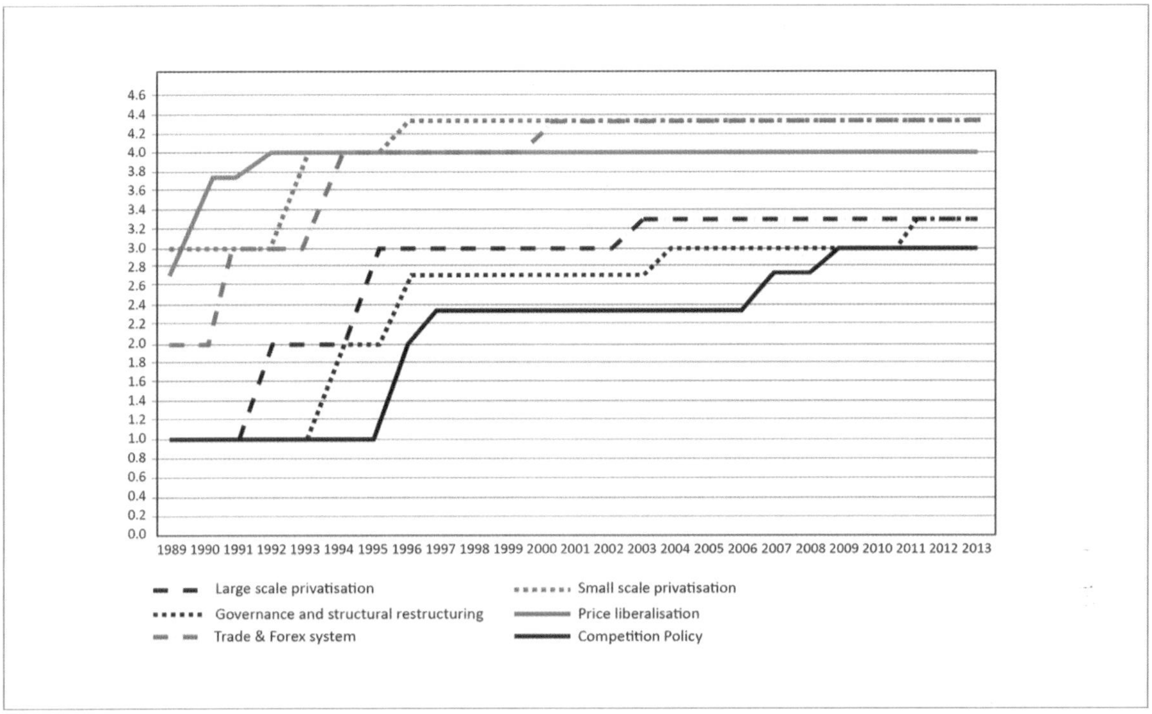

Figure 3. Transition progress (transition indicators) dynamics in Croatia, 2006-2013
Source: Adapted from "Transition Report 2012. Integration Across Borders" by European Bank for Reconstruction and Development. (2012). Retrieved from http://www.ebrd.com/downloads/research/transition/tr12.pdf

small-scale privatization) resembles the one present in western market economies. Steady but not quite strong progress (transition) has been achieved in governance and enterprise restructuring, large-scale privatization and competition policy. Looking at these indicators rather closely, one can find reasonable evidence of the X-inefficiency presence within the Croatian economy. In fact, both figures 2 and 3 clearly support such a hypothesis. However, the issue and level of X-inefficiency within the Croatian economy only in part shares a common denominator with the X-inefficiency phenomena in the western market economies. While in western market economies, X-inefficiency is a consequence of asymmetric information, incomplete production function and labor markets, discretionary efforts, rationality as a continuum and as psychological phenomenon and the existence of inert area (Hosseini, 2013), in a transitional economy such as Croatia, X-inefficiency appears as an explicit consequence of poor SME development policy fostered by the policy makers.

After the War of 1991-1995, entrepreneurs who were trying to start a business were forced to pay an average interest rate on domestic bank credits of approximately 18-23%. They could take out a foreign bank loan, but even in that case, they needed a domestic bank's guarantees that they were forced to pay approximately 12% plus LIBOR, which was the same as borrowing from a domestic bank. Since policy makers at that time (up until now) had no SMS development policy or any other constructive development plan, people started to rush into their businesses with the lowest starting business costs (travel agencies, groceries shops, consulting firms, apartments and room renting, small wellness firms, and small vine and oil production firms, etc.). Thus, a massive de-industrialization process occurred (see table 1). Consequently, enterprise reform suffered, allocative efficiency dropped and with inefficient al-

Table 1. Structural and Institutional Change Indicators for Croatia, 2004-2010

	2004	2005	2006	2007	2008	2009	2010
Enterprises							
Privatization revenues (cumulative, in percentage of GDP)	14.6	14.7	15.7	16.7	17.0	17.4	na
Private sector share in GDP (in percentage)	65.0	65.0	65.0	70.0	70.0	70.0	70.0
Private sector share in employment (in percentage)	66.0	68.0	68.0	70.0	70.0	70.0	na
Budgetary subsidies and current transfers (in percentage of GDP)	2.3	2.3	2291.7	2.4	2,376.2	2,424.5	na
Share of industry in total employment (in percentage)	21.7	20.5	21.0	21.6	21.7	18.8	na
Change in labor productivity in industry (in percentage)	2.5	8.8	-1.0	2.6	0.8	7.2	na
Investment/GDP (in percentage)	26.0	26.3	28.1	28.9	30.7	26.7	na
EBRD index of small-scale privatization	4.3	4.3	4.3	4.3	4.3	4.3	4.3
EBRD index of large-scale privatization	3.3	3.3	3.3	3.3	3.3	3.3	3.3
EBRD index of enterprise reform	3.0	3.0	3.0	3.0	3.0	3.0	3.0
Markets and trade							
Share of administered prices in CPI (in percentage)	0.0	0.0	0.0	0.0	0.0	na	na
Number of goods with administered prices in EBRD-15 basket	0.0	0.0	0.0	0.0	0.0	na	na
Share of trade with non-transition countries (in percentage)	71.3	68.5	68.3	65.2	64.7	na	na
Share of trade in GDP (in percentage)	60.9	61.5	64.6	64.9	59.6	50.1	69.2
Tariff revenues (in percentage of imports)	1.6	1.5	1.3	1.2	1.3	1.6	na
EBRD index of price liberalization	4.0	4.0	4.0	4.0	4.0	4.0	4.0
EBRD index of forex and trade liberalization	4.3	4.3	4.3	4.3	4.3	4.3	4.3
EBRD index of competition policy	2.3	2.3	2.3	2.7	2.7	3.0	3.0
Financial sector							
Number of banks (foreign-owned)	37(15)	34(13)	33(15)	33(16)	33(16)	32(15)	na
Asset share of state-owned banks (in percentage)	3.1	3.4	4.2	4.7	4.4	4.1	na
Asset share of foreign-owned banks (in percentage)	91.3	91.3	908.	90.4	90.8	91.0	na
Non-performing loans (in percentage of total loans)	7.5	6.2	5.2	4.8	4.8	7.8	na
Domestic credit to private sector (in percentage of GDP)	51.8	56.4	64.0	67.1	68.1	69.6	na
Domestic credit to households (in percentage of GDP)	30.4	34.0	38.2	41.4	37.1	36.9	na
Of which mortgage lending (in percentage of GDP)	10.1	12.0	14.7	16.4	15.3	15.9	na
Stock market capitalization (in percentage of GDP)	25.2	30.5	56.5	104.7	40.4	39.2	na
Stock trading volume (in percentage of market capitalization)	6.0	6.7	8.7	8.6	7.4	5.6	na
Eurobond issuance (in percentage of GDP)	3.8	0.0	0.8	1.3	0.0	4.9	na
EBRD index of banking sector reform	4.0	4.0	4.0	4.0	4.0	4.0	4.0
EBRD index of reform of non-bank financial institutions	2.7	2.7	3.0	3.0	3.0	3.0	3.0
Infrastructure							
Fixed-line (mobile) penetration rate (per 100 inhabitants)	42.4 (63.7)	42.4 (82.2)	41.3 (99.1)	41.7 (113.7)	41.9 (134.0)	na	na
Internet users (per 100 inhabitants)	30.9	33.1	38.0	44.8	50.8	na	na
Railway labor productivity (1989-100)	92.7	107.0	125.3	141.7	145.4	na	na
Residential electricity tariffs (USc kWh)	9.1	9.4	10.0	10.9	12.4	na	na
Average collection rate, electricity (in percentage)	69	98	100	100	100	100	na
GDP per unit of energy use (PPP in US dollars per kgoe)	6.2	6.6	na	na	na	na	na
EBRD index of infrastructure reform	3.0	3.0	3.0	3.0	3.0	3.0	3.0
Electric power	3.0	3.0	3.0	3.0	3.0	3.0	3.0
Railways	2.7	2.7	2.7	2.7	2.7	2.7	2.7
Roads	3.0	3.0	3.0	3.0	3.0	3.0	3.0
Telecommunication	3.3	3.3	3.7	3.7	4.0	4.0	4.0
Water and wastewater	3.3	3.3	3.3	3.3	3.3	3.3	3.3

Source: Adapted from "Transition Report 2012. Integration Across Borders" by European Bank for Reconstruction and Development. (2012). Retrieved from http://www.ebrd.com/downloads/research/transition/tr12.pdf

Table 2. The mean values in total sales of Croatian companies in selected countries

	N	Minimum	Maximum	Mean	Std. Deviation
Republic of Croatia	150	0	100	73.75	34.842
European Union	150	0	100	16.77	27.255
Former Yugoslavia countries (without Slovenia)	150	0	60	4.53	8.981
Middle East and Africa	150	0	40	0.54	3.531
North and South America	150	0	35	1.00	4.410
Far East and Asia	150	0	30	0.43	2.757
Other	150	0	20	0.97	3.472

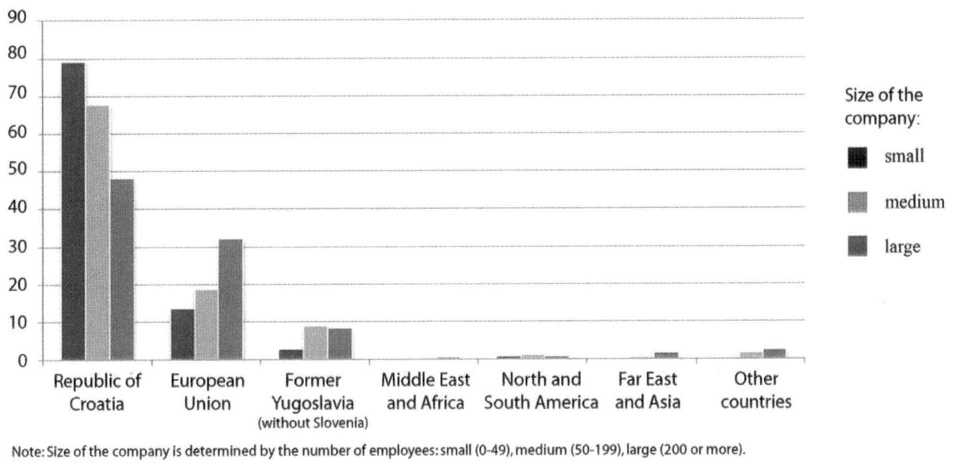

Figure 4. Percentage of sales in selected countries by the size of the company

location of resources within Croatian economy, inefficiency within Croatian firms surfaced. Therefore, X-inefficiency within Croatian firms represents a main obstacle to actual and future economic growth. Macroeconomic efficiency means nothing if X-inefficiency within firms is present.

The high X-inefficiency level within Croatian firms is an explicit cause of their low competitiveness in foreign markets, forcing firms to sell commodities on the domestic market, which is limited and has low consumption power (see table 2 and figure 4).

Given that all others are selling all their products and services only on the national market, only 32% of all interviewed businesses could be considered as exporters. Data analysis has shown that there is no significant correlation between the capacity utilization and exporting activities. With few exceptions, only medium-sized and large companies have enough strength to export their products and services (see figure 4). Further analysis shows that production oriented companies are exporting more to the European Union and to the former Yugoslavian countries (except Slovenia) than service and mixed oriented companies as well as that the general exporting power of Croatian companies is quite low for other markets other than the EU market (see figure 5).

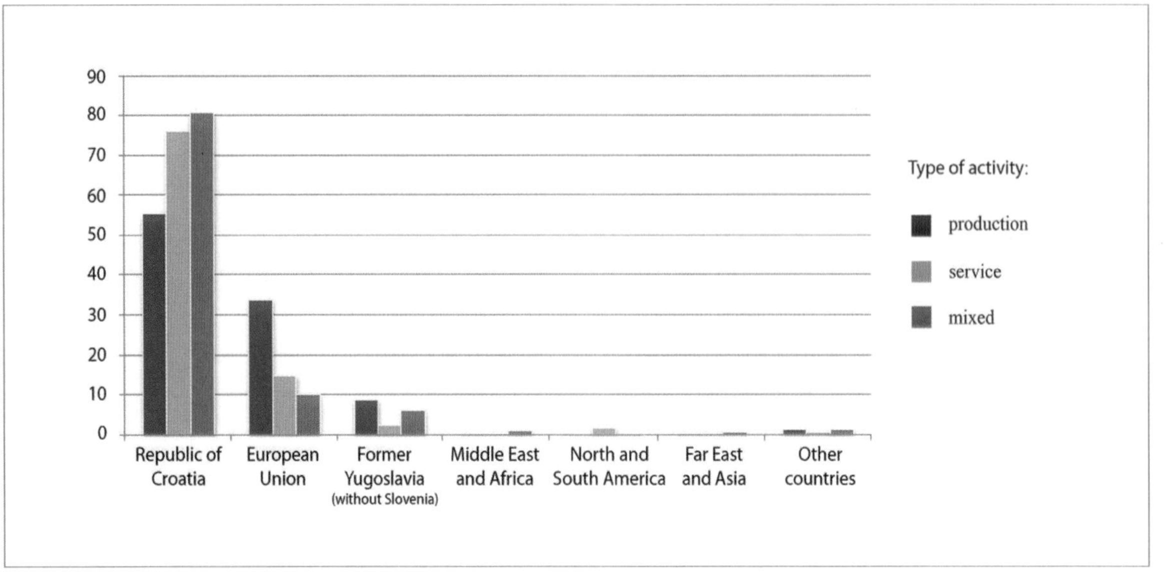

Figure 5. Percentage of sales in selected countries by the type of activity

Quantitative dimension of X-inefficiency in Croatian firms

The simplest way to observe the existence of X-inefficiency within a given company is to observe the utilization of production and service capacities (see table 3). Whereas some companies can have maximum utilization of manufacturing and/or service capacities and some resources will remain unused (i.e., intellectual capital, fields, buildings, financial capital, etc.), an additional measure that can be used in addressing problems of X-inefficiency is the one that observes the utilization of overall available resources. Within the research sample of 150 business subjects, the mean utilization of production and service capacities was 70%, while the mean utilization of overall available resources was 68.1%.

If X-efficiency is analyzed according to the size of the company, it is possible to conclude that among smaller companies (0-49 of employees), the utilization of available capacities and resources is lower than within larger companies (50 or more employees). In other words, there is a statistically significant difference in the utilization of productive/service capacities related to the size of the company (t=2.994, df=148, p=0.003). Organizations that employ up to 49 workers ($\bar{x}$ = 66.92, σ_X = 22.528) have smaller capacity utilization rates than those with 50 or more workers ($\bar{x}$ = 78.92, σ_X = 18.371). The same is true with the utilization of overall resources, where there can also be found a statistically significant difference in the utilization of all available resources, which is related to the size of the company (t=2.123, df=148, p=0.035). Organizations that employ up to 49 workers ($\bar{x}$ = 65.80, σ_X = 21.226) use a lower percentage of available resources than those with 50 or more workers ($\bar{x}$ = 74.51, σ_X = 24.244). The gathered data lead to an unexpected conclusion, i.e., X-inefficiency is more frequent in small companies than in large companies.

The mean capacity utilization rate in the production industry is 71.5%; in the service industry, it is 74.3%, while in companies that conduct business in both industries, the capacity utilization rate is only 62.3%. The situation is somewhat different in regard to the second question about the utilization of overall profitably exploitable resources. The mean utilization rate of all profitably exploitable resources in the production industry is 67.9%; in the service industry, it is 71.2%, while for the companies that are simultaneously performing both activities, the mean value of resource utilization is 63.2%. These data are shown in figures 6 and 7.

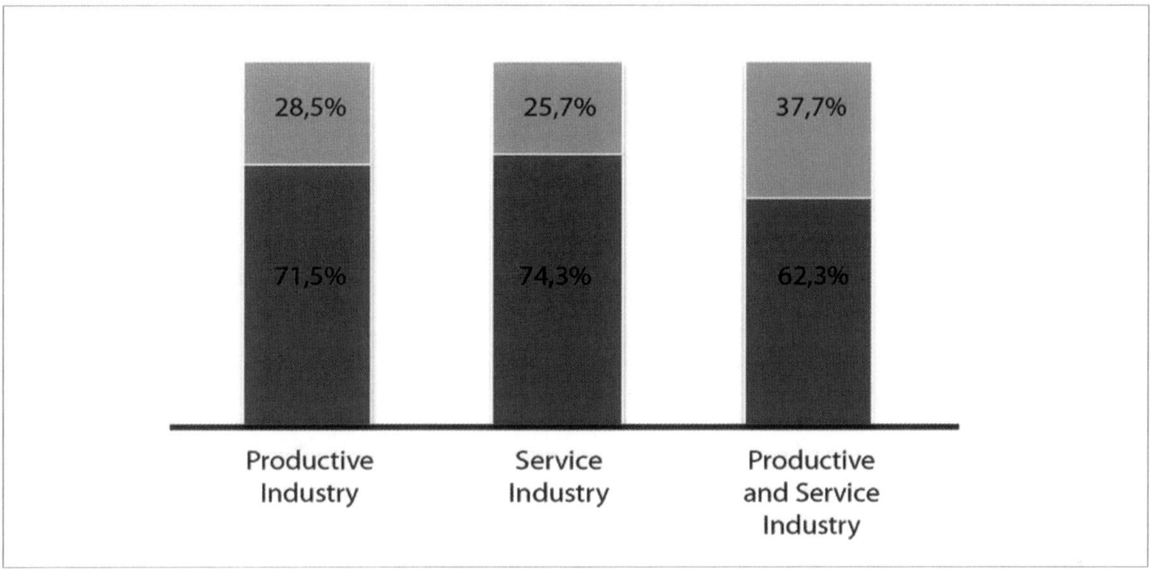

Figure 6. The mean utilization of production and service capacities by industry in percentage

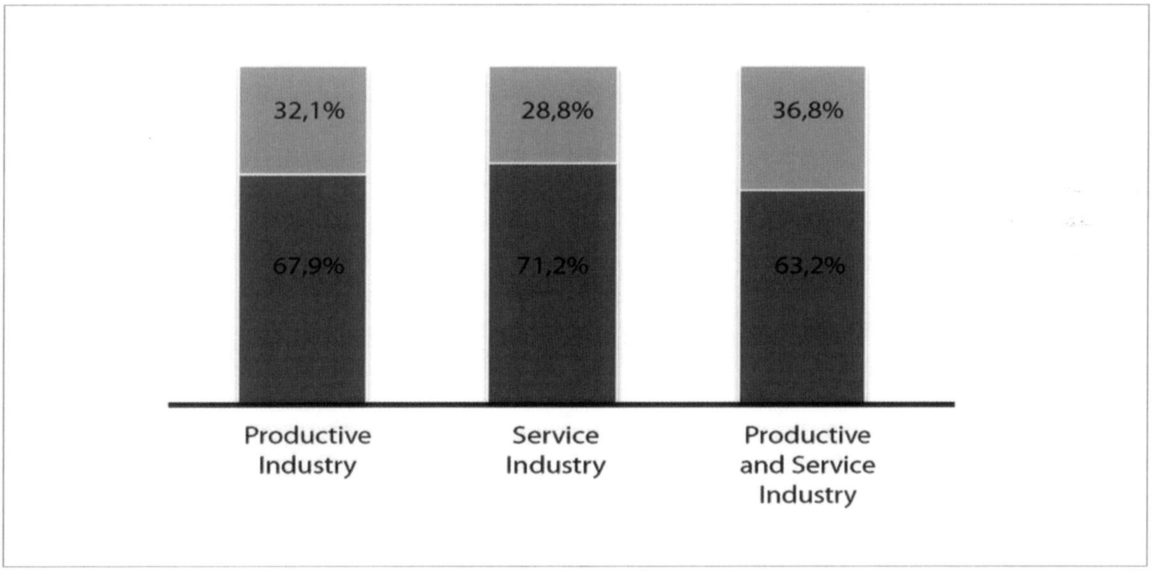

Figure 7. The mean utilization of overall profitable exploitable resources by industry in percentage

When actual and potential outputs are placed on the opposite sides of equation, the result is the social efficiency variable. The closer the relationship between actual and potential outputs is to the number 1, the higher the social efficiency of a given company becomes, and vice versa. Of course, the variable of social efficiency tells nothing about the activity that is being performed. It represents only a numerical value, while the qualitative value is determined within broader social discussions on desirability and undesirability of those activities (for example, a hospital or tobacco plant). According to the gathered data, the social efficiency of the service companies (0.74) is higher than social efficiency of the

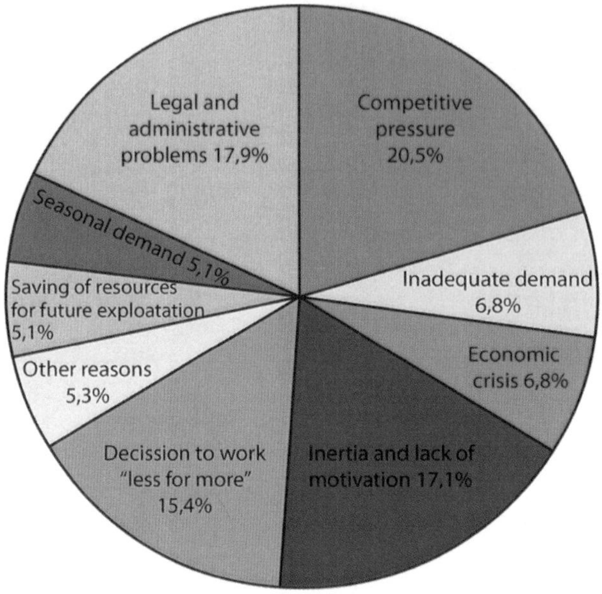

Figure 8. Specific reasons why companies do not use all of available resources

production (0.71) and mix-oriented (0.62) companies. Unfortunately, this study did not cover enough public and private-public companies to determine the differences in their social efficiency in relation to the privately owned companies. According to the empirical results, 17.3% of participants claim that there are no stronger competitors in their main market, while 74.7% of participants claim that there are only 5 or less competitors in their main market that are stronger than them. The conducted analysis suggests that there is no statistically significant correlation between capacity utilization and total number of competitors ($r = -0.066$, $p > 0.05$). However, there is a small but a statistically significant positive correlation between capacity utilization and market share ($r = 0.177$, $p < 0.05$). In addition, one-way variance analysis shows that there is a statistically significant difference in capacity utilization with respect to the type of activity ($F(2,147) = 4.62$, $p < 0.05$). Tukey's post hoc test shows that service ($\bar{x} = 74.33$) and mixed ($\bar{x} = 62.26$) activities differ.

Qualitative dimension of X-inefficiency in Croatian firms

The next part of the conducted research was aimed toward investigation of a qualitative dimension of the X-inefficiency. Examinees were offered six different answers and a free entry option to encompass all possible answers. While 33 respondents claimed that they use all available resources, 117 of them indicated the main reason why some of their resources were not fully engaged, and their answers are displayed in figure 8.

The most common reason that prevents business subjects from efficient use of their resources is the competitive pressure. In other words, 20.5% of respondents claim how excessive competition represents the main cause preventing them from full realization of their own potentials. Contrary to standard belief that competition makes us use and develop our capacities to the maximum, this research suggests that excessive competition disables us from maintaining our resource utilization at an optimal level. Although it may seem paradoxical in a short-term perspective, in a long-term perspective, it is obvious: if competitors cooperate, their rewards are even greater. Businesses that are successful in finding a common language with their surroundings (e.g., competitors, clients and customers) can reduce their costs and invest these saved resources in some other activity (e.g., research and development) that will bring them a long-term advantage in their market. If they want to accomplish a higher degree of utilization of their own resources, economic growth and development, companies should cooperate with others to a far greater extent than what they currently do. The same can be said for individuals, remarking that their own feeling of self-sufficiency can be sustained only inside strong socio-economic bonds. However, these claims should be considered carefully. First, cooperation and collaboration are not simple or cheap. Second, too much cooperation can also lead to monopoly, which causes X-inefficiency in some conditions. Another probable explanation is that the resource just cannot be purchased by the firms that can make full use of it and gain profit. Thus, under the pressure of competition, this resource just remains unexploited.

The second most important cause of X-inefficiency within Croatian firms can be found in legal and administrative problems. Approximately 17.9% of business subjects claim that legal and administrative issues are the main cause that preventing them from efficient engagement of their resources. According to the World Bank Group (2014), whose score shows how far on average an economy is at a point in time from the best performance achieved by any economy in the ease of doing business, for 2014, Croatia was ranked 85th, with a score of 64.44, which is just slightly better than Bosnia and Herzegovina (60.24) and Serbia (63.46) but worse than Italy (68.19), Slovenia (69.84) and Hungary (66.82), all being its immediate neighbors. An economy's distance to the frontier is reflected on a scale from 0 to 100, where 0 represents the lowest performance and 100 the frontier. Although the same study predicts an improvement of 0.71 points for the year 2015, this is still much worse than in the most developed western economies, whose scores for 2014 were Austria (77.10), Germany (80.02), the United Kingdom (80.75) and the United States (81.96).

The third reason why business subjects do not manage to utilize all available resources in their companies (documented in 17.1% of cases) is the personal inertia and lack of motivation. In the most general sense, the concept of inertia is used to indicate resistance or aversion to movement, change or action. Synonymous with inertia is inactivity. In psychology, sociology and economics, the term "inertia" is mainly used to describe a slow and inadequate adjustment of an individual to changes occurring in his or her own environment as well as the lack of desire to make a change or to respond to change. Socio-economic inertia becomes undesirable when the costs of changing are less than the benefits that can be achieved through it but when the change still is not occurring. Although cooperative behavior between economic agents can ensure significant mutual benefits (e.g., the reduction of costs), many contemporary companies and individuals do not cooperate to the extent they could. One of the main causes of such behavior lies in the fact that contemporary and mainstream economic science places a much greater emphasis on the benefits of competition than on the benefits of cooperation. Other reasons of such a state may include the lack of knowledge and personal inertia. We believe that through a wider discussion about the phenomenon of X-efficiency, this would probably change.

The fourth most important cause of X-inefficiency is deliberate decisions by businesses to work "less for more". Since 15.4% of examinees claim that they are deliberately creating an artificial scarcity (in order to obtain higher profits), these results are extremely indicative in the wider social sense. Companies that are intentionally producing below their own qualitative and/or quantitative potentials may not be considered as socially useful companies. In neoclassical theory, the producers are considered to behave in that way only if they are in a monopolistic position or if they have an oligopolistic agreement with other producers. However, practice shows that producers, regardless of their number, always choose one price that serves as the lowest wage they will work for. The best examples of such behavior are workers organized in unions who determine the minimal price of their work. It is perfectly normal to assume that investors will behave in the same way (when they determine the lowest return rate of their investments), which leads to the conclusion that almost all who are doing any type of business wish to work as little as possible to achieve as

Figure 9. The mean strategic value of activities that could contribute to the optimal utilization of production/service capacities (1-5)

much as possible. Although there is nothing wrong in such reasoning –"more for less" is the basic maxim of socio-economic development – to be done properly, it requires a significant amount of knowledge, effort and organizational skills. Although they work more, workers generally accept less than investors for the same amount of work, and that type of allocation leads to an increase in inequality.

Further reasons for the occurrence of X-inefficiency in Croatian firms has been inadequate demand (8.6%) and economic crisis (6.8%), which can both cause a portion of disposable resources to remain unused. Although inadequate demand can be caused by incorrect predictions about future trends, in this case, it is probably closely connected with an economic crisis that can arise from a much broader range of factors, such as an inadequate economic paradigm, incompetence of the government, or corruption. Before the global financial crisis of 2008-2009, the Croatian economy was growing at a healthy 4-5% annually, with incomes doubling, while economic and social opportunities dramatically improved. According to the World Bank Group (2014), the prolonged crisis and inadequate policy changes were the main causes that have resulted in the country now entering its sixth year of recession, having lost over 12% of its output from the start of the global financial crisis. Although there is some optimism about the prospect for growth in 2015, with exports projected to pick up in the Eurozone and private investments expected to increase, the structural reforms launched by the previous government have not yet stimulated job creation, productivity, and social cohesion. Whereas at the end of 2014, the unemployment rate was 17% with a youth unemployment rate of 40%, it is obvious that partial improvement measures cannot do much in the absence of a comprehensive development strategy. One of the main purposes of this study is to be helpful in that respect.

Another reason for the occurrence of X-inefficiency, documented in only 5.1% of cases, is the decision of business subjects to save their resources so that they can exploit them in the future. Such a small percentage of those who save their resources suggests that most companies that participated in the survey do not have the resources they could save.

Among other reasons for the X-inefficiency are seasonal demand (5.1%), incompetence of the government (1.7%), the risk of debt collection (1.7%) and local organizational problems (0.8%).

In the next question, respondents were asked to evaluate the importance of 10 different strategies that could contribute to the optimal utilization of production/service capacities in their firm. Within the observed sample of 150 answers and on a scale from 1

Figure 10. The mean strategic value of 10 factors that contribute to the success of a business organization (1-5)

(irrelevant) to 5 (highly important), the highest mean scores were given to the following strategies: reduction of the tax burden and other government levies (4.47), collaboration with clients/customers (4.31), investment in marketing (3.67), and simplification of administrative and legal procedures in hiring and firing (3.51). Middle-range scores were given to lowering of production costs with the same or higher quality of products/services (3.50), material motivation strategies (share of the profits, bonuses to salary, mobile, transportation) (3.49), and non-material motivation strategies (management by objectives, management style, organizational culture) (3.41). The lowest scores were given to automation of production and/or service processes (3.19), collaboration with competitors (2.79), and the lowering of profit margins due to entering a partnership (2.45).

Respondents in this survey think that reduction of the tax burden and other government levies represents the most important thing that could help them in the optimal utilization of their unused resources. While in the last two years the corporate tax has been reduced from 20% to 18%, the standard VAT in Croatia has been increased from 24% to 25% and is now among the highest rates in Europe. With such a big VAT that is significantly higher than those in its surrounding countries, Croatian products and services remain quite expensive for end-users. Despite the fact that competitive pressure has been scored as the most important reason for X-inefficiency, most respondents do not see collaboration with competitors as a strategy that could contribute to the optimal utilization of their resources. This fact can be interpreted in several ways. First, respondents probably feel that it is not possible to establish collaboration with their direct competitors. Second, people are inclined to see the causes of their own problems outside of themselves. Since the improvement in collaboration with competitors requires changes in their own behavior and additional efforts, the reduction of the tax burden by government seems like a much easier solution. Third, collaborating with others may involve disclosing strategic information, and this is something that most managers are reluctant to do. The good news is that many companies recognize collaboration with clients/customers as an important strategy for the optimization of their capacity utilization. The analysis has shown that there is a small but statistically significant positive correlation between capacity utilization and application of the following strategies: automation of production and service processes ($r = 0.239$, $p < 0.05$), material motivation strategies ($r = 0.240$, $p < 0.05$) and nonmaterial motivation strategies ($r = 0.235$, $p < 0.05$).

To emphasize how even the smallest difference between two (in all other aspects the same) businesses (such as a pleasant working atmosphere) can make a decisive advantage in optimizing non-allocative efficiency, Leibenstein (1978) added a prefix X to his revolutionary theoretical concept. By following the trace of this interesting idea about the factor X, in the last question, respondents were asked to indicate an importance of 10 different factors in relation to their usefulness for the business success of their organizations. On the scale form 1 (irrelevant) to 5 (highly important), the highest mean scores were given to these factors: quality of products/services (4.70), experienced and educated workers (4.37), and flexibility (4.20). Middle range scores were given to high-quality management (3.89), long-term guarantees on quality (3.85), and networking and contacts (3.83). Interestingly, the lowest evaluated factors that provide success to interviewed businesses were innovations (3.80), a high market share and business volume (3.19), geographical position/location (3.19), and lower prices compared to the competition (3.01).

The conducted analysis clearly shows how over simplification can be quite dangerous. Complex problems cannot be comprehended with linear logic, but only with holistic and a systemic way of thinking. In real life, multiple equilibria are both possible and desirable. The consequence is that there are different strategies for achieving business success and many different reasons why companies do not use all their available resources.

Conclusion

The way in which a certain society uses its resources directly affects the quality of life of its members, but it also relates to the question of its long-term sustainability and survival. If a business organization operates X-inefficiently, it means that there must be some unexploited and low-cost opportunities (for increasing its inner productivity and hence for reducing its total costs) that are still not, but could be used in its development. Although the low competitiveness of Croatian firms has long been considered the main obstacle for stronger economic growth and development, the conducted empirical research suggests a quite different direction. It seems that competition is not always the best strategy in addressing socio-economic problems and that ease of doing business, accompanied with cooperation and motivation, plays a much greater role in issues that relate to the economic development. Even in the most competitive environments, it is possible to identify business organizations that are producing outputs that are below their real potentials. Although these situations are an integral part of economic processes, they cannot be explained within the neo-liberal model of thinking. However, Leibenstein's theory offers a solid basis to explain such behavior.

The theory of X-efficiency provides a theoretical explanation of the fact that a conventional neoclassical economy ignores, which is that many available inputs are often not utilized as efficiently as they could be. This statement is confirmed by the results of empirical research conducted in the Croatian market where at least 78% of companies in 2014 were working below their full potential, which means they were doing their businesses with a certain degree of X-inefficiency. Since the mean utilization of production and service capacities within the observed sample is only 70% and the mean utilization of overall profitably exploitable resources is only 68.1%, the conducted analysis leads to the conclusion that X-inefficiency is a widespread phenomenon among companies in the Croatian market.

Empirical analysis suggests that the main reasons for X-inefficiency are competitive pressure (20.5%), legal and administrative problems (17.9%), inertia and lack of motivation (17.1%) and decision to work "less for more" (15.4%). Other reasons include inadequate demand (6.8%), economic crisis (6.8%), the decision to save resources for the future exploitation (5.1%), seasonal demand (5.1%), incompetence of the government (1.7%), corruption (1.7%), the risk of debt collection (1.7%) and local organizational problems (0.8%). If the empirical findings of this research are mapped to the entire society, it becomes clear that the Republic of Croatia needs a social policy in which the highest emphasis will be placed on quality, education and flexibility. If they want to achieve optimal utilization of available resources, our policy makers should create an efficient legal and practical framework that will motivate social individuals and companies to develop their full potentials. According to this research, automation of production and service activities and application of different (material and nonmaterial) motivation strategies are positively correlated with the high capacity utilization rate. Other important strategies that should enable optimal utilization of resources are the reduction of the tax burden and government levies in strategic industries, encouraging collaboration with clients and customers, and investing in marketing and the simplification of administrative and legal procedures in hiring and firing. Finally, the educational sector should put more emphasis on teaching about different reasons why X-inefficiency may appear.

The main drawback of the presented research comprises the fact that the collected answers represent only the subjective claims of respondents, who usually tend to describe their positions better than they actually are. Another deficiency is a relatively small research sample, which is particularly true for the state-owned and mix-owned companies. Although they should provide an additional level of responsibility toward government and the public, managers in state-owned companies showed no particular interest to participate in our survey. The presented results suggest that there is a need for further research in this area. Given that in the public sector, there exist a substantial amount of resources that are not optimally utilized, future analysis of X-efficiency in the Republic of Croatia should be directed toward public and civil organizations as well as toward ordinary individuals, who often do not possess adequate knowledge about the optimization of their own economic behavior.

References

Alpeza, M., Eterović, D., Novosel, M., Oberman-Peterka, S., Singer, S., & Šarlija, N. (2016). Izvješće o malim i srednjim poduzećima u Hrvatskoj – 2015. Uključujući rezultate GEM – Global Entrepreneurship Monitor istraživanja za Hrvatsku za 2014. godinu [Report on Small and Medium Enterprises in Croatia - 2015 including the results of GEM - Global Entrepreneurship Monitor for Croatia for 2014]. Zagreb, Croatia: CEPOR - Small and Medium Enterprises and Entrepreneurship Development Policy Center. Retrieved from http://www.cepor.hr/wp-content/uploads/2016/06/Cepor-izvjesce-2015-HR.pdf

Altman, M. (2006). What a difference an assumption makes: Effort discretion, economic theory, and public policy. In M. Altman (Ed.), *Handbook of Contemporary Behavioral Economics: Foundations and Developments* (pp. 125-164). New York, NY: Armonk.

Altunbas, Y., Evans, L., & Molyneux, P. (2001). Bank ownership and efficiency. *Journal of Money, Credit and Banking, 33*(4), 926-954. doi:10.2307/2673929

Bejaković, P., & Lowther, J. (Eds.). (2004). *The Competitiveness of Croatia's Human Resources.* Zagreb, Croatia: Institute of Public Finance.

Benazić, A. (2012). Measuring efficiency in the Croatian customs service: a data envelopment analysis approach *Financial Theory and Practice, 36*(2), 139-178. doi: 10.3326/fintp.36.2.2

Bogetoft, P., Färe, R., & Obel, B. (2006). Allocative efficiency of technically inefficient production units. *European Journal of Operational Research, 168*(2), 450-462. doi:10.1016/j.ejor.2004.05.010

Button, K. J., & Weyman-Jones, G. T. (1992). Ownership structure, institutional organization and measured x-efficiency. *The American Economic Review, 82*(2), 439-445.

Ceccobelli, M., Gitto, S., & Mancuso, P. (2012). ICT capital and labour productivity growth: A non-parametric analysis of 14 OECD countries. *Telecommunications Policy, 36*(4), 282-292. doi:10.1016/j.telpol.2011.12.012

Chikán, A. (2008). National and firm competitiveness: A general research model. *Competitiveness Review, 18*(1-2), 20-28. doi:10.1108/10595420810874583

Dean, J. W., & Perlman, M. (1998). Harvey Leibenstein as a pioneer of our time. *The Economic Journal, 108*(446), 132-152. doi:10.1111/1468-0297.00277

European Bank for Reconstruction and Development. (2012). *Transition Report 2012. Integration Across Borders.* Retrieved from http://www.ebrd.com/downloads/research/transition/tr12.pdf

Fienhage, L. (2014). Evaluation of the X-Efficiency Theory in the Supply Management Context (Bachelor Thesis). Retrieved from http://essay.utwente.nl/65251/1/Fienhage_BA_MB.pdf

Frantz, R. (2007). Empirical Evidence on X-Efficiency, 1967-2004. In R. Frantz (Ed.), Renaissance in Behavioral Economics: Essays in Honour of Harvey Leibenstein (pp. 211-228). London, UK: Routlege.

Frantz, R. (2004). The behavioral economics of George Akerloff and Harvey Leibenstein. *The Journal of Socio-Economics, 33*(1), 29-44. doi:10.1016/j.socec.2003.12.005

Frantz, R. S. (1982). Worker motivation and x-efficiency theory: A comment. *Journal of Economic Issues, 16*(3), 864-869.

Fung, M. K. (2006). Scale economies, X-efficiency, and convergence of productivity among bank holding companies. *Journal of Banking & Finance, 30*(10), 2857-2874. doi:10.1016/j.jbankfin.2005.11.004

Gligorov, V., & Vidovic, H. (2004). *Croatia's delayed transition: Competitiveness and economic policy challenges* (Research Report No. 304). The Vienna Institute for International Economic Studies. Retrieved from https://wiiw.ac.at/croatia-s-delayed-transition-competitiveness-and-economic-policy-challenges-dlp-274.pdf

Hai-Bo, K., & He-Zhong, L. (2009). Research on x-efficiency measure of Chinese ports. *Systems Engineering - Theory & Practice, 29*(2), 1-9. doi:10.1016/s1874-8651(10)60036-1

Hosseini, H. (2007). X-efficiency and underdevelopment : A Leibenstein's application of behavioral economics. In R. Frantz (Ed.), Renaissance in behavioral economics: essays in honor of Harvey Leibenstein (pp. 146-161). London, UK: Routlege.

Leibenstein, H. (1978). *General X-Efficiency Theory and Economic Development*. New York, NY: Oxford University Press.

Leibenstein, H. (1966). Allocative efficiency vs. "x-efficiency". *The American Economic Review, 56*(3), 392-415.

Leko-Šimić, M. (2001). Domestic vs. Foreign Product Competitiveness on Croatian Market: A Research of Croatian Buyer's Behaviour. *In* S. Goić (Ed.), *Enterprise in Transition: Fourth International Conference on Enterprise in Transition, Proceedings* (pp. 376-387). Split: Faculty of Economics, University of Split and the World Bank Group.

Lovrinčević, Ž., Mikulić, D., & Rajh, E. (2008). Comparison of methodologies for measuring national competitiveness - Competitive position of Croatian economy. *Ekonomski pregled [Economic Review], 59*(11), 603-645.

Ljubojević, G., & Novičić, M. (2007, September). Development of corporate governance in transition economies and achievement of competitiveness. Paper presented at the 4th International Conference "Global Challenges for Competitiveness: Business and Government Perspective" Pula, Croatia.

Majumdar, S. K. (1998). *Assessing comparative efficiency of the state-owned mixed and private sectors in Indian industry. Public Choice, 96*(1-2), 1–24. doi:10.1023/A:1004941023587

Omonona, B. T., Egbetokun, O. A., & Akanbi, A. T. (2010). Farmers resource - use and technical efficiency in cowpea production in Nigeria. *Economic Analysis and Policy, 40*(1), 87-95. doi:10.1016/s0313-5926(10)50006-7

Primeaux, W. J., & Nelson, R. A. (1980). An examination of price discrimination and internal subsidization by electric utilities. *Southern Economic Journal, 47*(1), 84-99. doi:10.2307/1057063

Primorac, M., & Troskot, Z. (2005). Measuring the efficiency and productivity of the Croatian banks with Malmquist's index of change of total factor productivity. *Financial Theory and Practice, 29*(4), 309-325.

Rossi, S. P., Schwaiger, M. S., & Winkler, G. (2008). Linking Managerial Behaviour to Cost and Profit Efficiency in the Banking Sectors of Central and Eastern European Countries. *Kredit und Kapital [Credit and Capital], 41*(4), 589-629. doi:10.3790/kuk.41.4.589

Schwab, K. (Ed.). (2013). *The Global Competitiveness Report 2013–2014.Full Data Edition*. Geneva: The World Economic Forum. Retrieved from
http://www3.weforum.org/docs/WEF_GlobalCompetitivenessReport_2013-14.pdf

Sjöström, T., & Weitzman, M. L. (1996). Competition and the evolution of efficiency. *Journal of Economic Behavior & Organization, 30*(1), 25-43.

Sohinger, J., & Horvatin, D. (2005). Foreign direct investment and competitiveness in transition economies: the case of Croatia. *International Journal of Entrepreneurship and Small Business, 2*(3), 266-282. doi:10.1504/ijesb.2005.006969

Stigler, J. G. (1976). The existence of x-efficiency. *The American Economic Review*, *66*(1), 213-216.

Stojčić, N., Bečić, M., & Vojinić, P. (2012). The competitiveness of exports from manufacturing industries in Croatia and Slovenia to the EU-15 market: A dynamic panel analysis. *Croatian Economic Survey, 14*(1), 69-105.

Stojcic, N., Hashi, I., & Telhaj, S. (2011). Innovation activities and competitiveness: Empirical evidence on the behaviour of firms in the New EU member states and candidate countries (*Network*

Studies and Analyses No. 424/2011). Center for Social and Economic Research. Retrieved from http://www.case-research.eu/upload/publikacja_plik/33632351_CNSA_2011_424.pdf

Tica, J., Cenan, D., & Bilas, V. (2004). The Competitiveness of Croatia and It's Strategy. In D. Kantarelis (Ed.), Global Business and Economics Review - Anthology 2004 (pp.466-478). Rhodos: Business & Economics Society International.

Vujčić, B., & Presečan, T. (1999). External Deficit, Exchange Rate, and Competitiveness in Croatia: Is There a Problem? In M. I. Blejer, M. Škreb (Eds.), *Balance of Payments, Exchange Rates, and Competitiveness in Transition Economies* (pp. 285-317). Boston MA: Kluwer Academic Publishers.

World Bank Group (2014). *Doing Business 2015: Going Beyond Efficiency* (12th ed.). Washington, DC: World Bank Group. doi: 10.1596/978-1-4648-0351-2. Retrieved from http://www.doingbusiness.org/~/media/WBG/DoingBusiness/Documents/Annual-Reports/English/DB15-Full-Report.pdf

11

Combining Equity Country Selection Strategies

Adam Zaremba[1]

ABSTRACT The recent increase in passive investment products has provided investors with easy access to international markets. The basic motivation of this paper is to offer new tools to investors who want to allocate assets across countries. This study investigates the performance of equity country selection strategies based on a combination of theoretically and empirically motivated variables. Thus, we create portfolios and assess their performance using asset pricing models. The empirical examination is based on data from 78 countries from 1999 to 2015. The strategies that are based on the earnings-to-price (EP) ratio, the turnover ratio, and skewness prove to be useful tools for international investors. Furthermore, portfolios from sorts on the blended rankings of skewness combined with the EP ratio or the turnover ratio are also characterized by an attractive risk-return ratio. However, joint strategies do not outperform strategies that are based on single metrics. Consequently, we argue that investors would be better off building a diversified portfolio rather than combining their options into one strategy because of the low correlation among returns on single-variable strategies.

KEY WORDS: country selection strategies, asset pricing, cross section of stock returns, value investing, momentum, skewness preference, liquidity premium, turnover ratio, international investments.

[1] Poznan University of Economics and Business, Poland

Introduction

The financial literature offers a growing number of equity country selection strategies for international investors. Most of these strategies are parallels of formerly discovered stock-level cross-sectional effects and anomalies. Balvers and Wu (2006), Bhojraj and Swaminathan (2006), and Asness, Moskowitz and Pedersen (2013) have found evidence for country-level momentum and reversal effects. Macedo (1995), Kim (2012), and Zaremba (2015a) have argued that stock markets with low fundamentals relative to price outperform those with high fundamentals relative to price. Keppler and Traub (1993) and Keppler and Encinosa (2011) have concluded that, regarding country equity selection, "small is beautiful". Zaremba (2015b; 2015c) has examined a number of inter-market anomalies related to various quality and risk metrics. Finally, Harvey (2000) and Zaremba and Nowak (2015) have suggested that the "skewness preference" phenomenon may be important for asset pricing not only at the stock level but also at the country level. The number of country-level anomalies discovered constantly increases, but it remains relatively modest in comparison with the abundant literature on stock-level effects. Only a few recent papers review dozens (Jacobs, 2015) or hundreds (Harvey, Liu, & Zhu, 2015) of stock-

Correspondence concerning this article should be addressed to: **Adam Zaremba,** Poznan University of Economics and Business, al. Niepodleglosci 10, 61-875 Poznan, Poland E-mail: adam.zaremba@ue.poznan.pl

level anomalies. It appears that the analogous development of country-level studies are in the future.

Many of the above-described stock market anomalies are commonly used by the fund management industry. These types of strategies are usually built into the quantitative trading strategies used by hedge funds, mutual funds, or smart-beta products (Pedersen, 2015). Nonetheless, it is not an easy task to find one's path through this zoo of stock market anomalies and to properly utilize them in portfolio management (Hsu & Kalesnik, 2014). In practice, stock-level portfolio managers take one of the two following approaches: they design a portfolio of independent strategies and achieve risk reduction through low correlation among them, or they blend strategies into one portfolio to benefit from the fact that certain strategies strengthen each other. The second approach is usually based on an average of the rankings or *z*-scores of a number of variables related to various cross-sectional strategies, and this is commonly examined in stock-level studies. A few papers can serve as examples of this. Novy-Marx (2013) has combined sorts on gross profitability with the book-to-market ratio, Piotroski (2000) has mixed a few financial ratios to form the well-known F-score, and Asness Frazzini and Pedersen (2014) has blended a large number of quality metrics to implement a quality-minus-junk strategy. Although the combinations of cross-sectional effects are commonly investigated in stock-level studies, they have not been examined from a country-level perspective. In other words, we still do not know whether it is beneficial for investors to blend country-selection strategies with each other or if it is better to build a portfolio of stand-alone strategies. The main objective of this paper is to fill this gap in the literature.

This study has two basic objectives. The first objective is to re-examine a number of cross-sectional equity country selection strategies that have been, thus far, best motivated, both theoretically and empirically, in the previous literature. The second objective is to investigate whether the combinations of these strategies provide returns that are superior to stand-alone strategies. In other words, we test whether it is rational to blend certain strategies in a portfolio or to leave them on a stand-alone basis. Thus, we build portfolios from sorts on single variables and on pairs of variables, and then we examine their performance using asset pricing models. Our tests are conducted with a sample of 78 countries using data from 1999–2015.

Our research is motivated by the profound changes that have occurred in the financial markets in recent years that have left investors without access to sufficient investment tools and strategies. Growing integration and openness to the global financial markets has increased the correlation between stock market returns across different countries (Bekaert & Harvey, 2000; Quinn & Voth, 2008), markedly reducing the diversification benefits for international investments (Goetzmann, Li, & Rouwenhorst, 2005). This change has accorded greater prominence to country selection strategies as a part of the investment process, and it has coincided with the wide proliferation of passive investment products that allow for easy access to international markets (e.g., futures, index funds, and exchange-traded funds [ETFs]) (Hester, 2013). Given both the wealth of opportunities and the considerable size of the global ETF market, the range of investment tools available to ETF investors continues to appear limited. The cross-sectional strategies largely await further development; we hope that this study will be a small step that helps to reduce this discrepancy.

The key findings of this study can be summarized as follows. Among the re-examined strategies from sorts on single variables, we found that three of these, those that are based on the EP ratio, the turnover ratio, and skewness, are useful tools for international investors. Moreover, strategies based on the combined ranking of the earnings-to-price (EP) ratio with skewness and the turnover ratio with skewness were also characterized by attractive alpha and Sharpe ratios. However, the blended strategies did not outperform portfolios based on single metrics. Consequently, we argue that, given the low correlation among the returns on single-variable strategies, investors would be better off building a diversified portfolio of strategies rather than blending them into one strategy. These observations are likely important for fund pickers and money managers who have a global investment mandate.

This paper is primarily related to the literature on country-level asset allocation strategies (e.g., Asness et al., 2013; Balvers & Wu, 2006; Bhojraj & Swaminathan, 2006; Harvey, 2000; 2004; Keppler & Encinosa, 2011; Keppler & Traub, 1993; Kim, 2012; Macedo, 1995; Zaremba, 2015a). Nonetheless, the cross-sectional patterns in the returns are usually due to inefficiencies that cannot be easily explained away due to cross-country capital flow constraints. Thus, this research is also related to studies on international asset pricing and the integration of capital markets (e.g., Adler & Dumas, 1983; Chaieb & Errunza, 2007; Errunza & Losq, 1985; Solnik & Zuo, 2012; Solnik, 1974; Stulz, 1981a, b) as well as the home bias effect, which explains the lack of full integration in international markets (cf., Cooper, Sercu and Vanpée (2013) for a comprehensive review).

The remainder of this paper is organized into three main sections. The next section presents research methods and data sources. It is followed by a section that presents our findings. The final section concludes the paper.

Data and Methods

This study tested the performance of country portfolios formed from combinations of various metrics. Thus, in practice, we tested three separate hypotheses. First, we re-examined whether the portfolios from sorts of four separate variables (the EP ratio, momentum, skewness, and the turnover ratio) revealed a cross-sectional pattern and delivered abnormal returns. Second, we investigated whether strategies based on combinations of these metrics were also useful for international investors. Finally, we examined whether blended strategies augmented the efficient frontier of the component strategies.

This section will present the data sources and procedures used in constructing the portfolios from sorts on single and double metrics, followed by the asset pricing tests and the model we used in this study. Finally, we outline the robustness checks that were undertaken.

Data Sources and Initial Preparation

This research was based on returns in international stock market indices from 78 countries: Argentina, Australia, Austria, Bahrain, Bangladesh, Belgium, Brazil, Bulgaria, Canada, Chile, China, Colombia, Croatia, Cyprus, Czech Republic, Denmark, Egypt, Estonia, Finland, France, Germany, Greece, Hong Kong, Hungary, Iceland, India, Indonesia, Ireland, Israel, Italy, Japan, Jordan, Kazakhstan, Kenya, Kuwait, Latvia, Lebanon, Lithuania, Luxemburg, Malaysia, Malta, Mexico, Morocco, Mauritius, the Netherlands, New Zealand, Nigeria, Norway, Oman, Pakistan, Peru, Philippines, Poland, Portugal, Qatar, Romania, Russia, Serbia, Saudi Arabia, Singapore, Slovenia, South Africa, South Korea, Spain, Sri Lanka, Sweden, Switzerland, Taiwan, Thailand, Trinidad and Tobago, Tunisia, Turkey, Ukraine, United Arab Emirates, the United Kingdom, the U.S.A., Venezuela, and Vietnam. All source data were obtained from the Bloomberg database. We used a monthly time series because it provided a sufficient number of observations to ensure the effectiveness of the tests, and it allowed us to avoid excessive exposure to micro-structure issues (de Moor & Sercu, 2013). We adopted the MSCI indices for all the countries to maintain a consistent return computation methodology because the MSCI indices represent capitalization-weighted benchmarks that are commonly tracked worldwide. Additionally, these indices constitute the basis for numerous futures contracts and ETFs all over the world (see, e.g., MSCI, 2013). Therefore, our decision to adopt the MSCI indices helps to align this research with investment practice. These indices are constructed and managed with the goal of being fully investable from the perspective of the international institutional investor (MSCI, 2014a), and they cover approximately 85% of stock market capitalizations in the countries they represent (MSCI, 2014b). If an MSCI index was not available for a country, the second choice for an index was the Dow Jones; the third choice was the STOXX.

The returns were computed based on capitalization-weighted net total return indices. In other words, the returns were adjusted for corporate actions (i.e., splits, reverse splits, issuance rights, and others) and cash distributions to investors (i.e., dividends). The net convention of the indices means that the dividends were calculated on an after-tax basis. We used this approach to control for different tax rates on dividends in different countries. The sample period ran from January 1999 to March 2015, as available (there were 195 monthly observations). The total sample included equity markets from 78 countries; in addition, both existing and discontinued indices (e.g., MSCI Venezuela) were used to avoid a survivorship bias. A stock market was included in the sample in month t when it was possible to compute returns on a given strategy with all the necessary data (i.e., its return in month t, its capitalization at the end of month t-1, and the metric necessary to sort the countries for the portfolios' formation at the end of month *t*-1).

The initial index values and capitalizations were collected in local currencies; however, we acted in accordance with Liew and Vassalou (2000) and Bali, Cakici and Fabozzi (2013) who argued that comparisons using different currency units could be misleading. This argument is particularly true in emerging and frontier markets where inflation and risk-free rates are occasionally very high and differ significantly across markets. Therefore, we adopted the approach of Liu, Liu and Ma (2011), Bekaert, Harvey and Lundblad (2007), and Brown, Du, Rhee and Zhang (2008) and denominated all data in U.S. dollars (USD) such that we could obtain polled international results. To be consistent with the USD approach, the excess returns were computed over returns on a Bloomberg generic U.S. 1-month T-bill.

Examined Portfolios

We researched the performance of portfolios formed on single and double rankings of four different variables. The choice of sorting metrics was motivated by the outcomes of previous research, and we selected four recent studies on country-selection strategies that were the most reliable and the best documented.

First, a number of authors including Macedo (1995), Kim (2012), Asness et al. (2013), and Zaremba (2015a) have argued that value strategies, which were used to sort indicators such as the book-to-market ratio, the EP ratio, or the dividend yield, help to forecast future returns. Zaremba and Konieczka (2016) have found that, among various value metrics, the EP ratio is the most robust to changes in portfolio weighting schemes or return computation conventions. Thus, the first variable we employed was the EP ratio. To calculate the country-level EP ratio, we divided the weighted-average market value of all the companies in a given index by the weighted average cumulative earnings in the prior four quarters. We weighted the companies' metrics according to the index methodology. Finally, to avoid the look-ahead bias and to assess returns in month *t*, we formed portfolios based on a lagged EP ratio from the end of month *t*-4.

Second, one of the most broadly discussed country-level strategies is momentum (Asness et al. 2013; Balvers & Wu, 2006; Bhojraj & Swaminathan, 2006; Zaremba 2015a). The Achilles' heel of this strategy is the fact that it appeared to work very well for equally-weighted country portfolios and for capitalization. However, regarding liquidity-weighting, its performance appeared to be much worse (Zaremba & Konieczka, 2016). Nevertheless, due to its popularity and extensive interest from both academics and practitioners, we decided to include momentum in this study. Zaremba and Konieczka (2016) have found that the cross-country momentum strategy works best for the 12-month sorting period; therefore, we utilized this approach. Furthermore, we skipped the standard last month to disentangle the impact of short-term reversal (Jegadeesh, 1990; Lehmann, 1990). In summary, for portfolios formed at the end of the month *t*-1, the lagged momentum return was the gross index cumulative return over the period *t*-12 to *t*-2.

Third, Zaremba (2015a) as well as Zaremba and Konieczka (2016) have investigated a few country-selection strategies based on quality, inspired by Asness et al. (2014). Some of these strategies yielded promising results, but the most robust results appeared to be those based on the turnover ratio. Thus, we have also used the turnover ratio as a component strategy in this study. Thus, at the end of each month, we divided the aggregated turnover throughout the month by its total market capitalization of the given index. Next, we averaged the values over months *t*-12 to *t*-1 to obtain the turnover ratios that we used to rank the countries. The higher the turnover ratio, the higher is the market liquidity. Based on the evidence found in Zaremba and Konieczka (2016), we expected that more liquid markets would be characterized by lower returns.

The fourth component strategy was based on the skewness of past returns. Zaremba and Nowak (2015) have hypothesized that, due to the implications of the prospect theory by Tversky and Kahneman (1992), investors overvalue right-skewed return distributions and undervalue left-skewed return distributions. Thus, the country equity markets with a high positive skewness with respect to their prior returns should perform more poorly than markets with a large negative skewness. Zaremba and Nowak (2015) have found convincing evidence that confirms this supposition, showing that country-selection strategies based on skewness could be more profitable than traditional strategies that are based on value, size, and momentum effects. To explain this, we re-examined this strategy, in close accordance with the approach of Zaremba and Nowak (2015). In other words, we sorted countries based on the skewness of their distributions of monthly excess gross returns over the months t-24 to t-1. We expected that countries with higher skewness would have lower returns.

To form portfolios from single sorts, all stock market indices were ranked against one of their underlying metrics at the end of each month t-1: the EP ratio, momentum, the turnover ratio, or skewness. To preserve a consistent method across all four strategies, we always sorted the countries from the lowest to the highest metric. Next, we defined the 20th, 40th, 60th, and 80th percentiles as breakpoints; from this, we formed five sub-groups. Finally, the indices in the respective sub-groups were weighted according to their market capitalization to form portfolios. It is common in country-level studies to equal-weight the indices in portfolios. However, this approach has two important disadvantages. First, it overstates the importance of small and illiquid markets where it may be difficult to invest. Second, the returns on equally-weighted portfolios may be distorted by so-called returns on rebalancing or returns on diversification (Willenbrock, 2011). To overcome these difficulties, we weighted the indices according to their market capitalization. In other words, we weighted the returns in month t according to the total stock market capitalization at the end of month t-1. We subsequently added differential portfolios, in other words, zero-portfolios, that were long/short portfolios: 100% long in the quintile of markets with the highest metric, and 100% short in the quintile of markets with the lowest metric.

The portfolios from simultaneous sorts on two variables were designed in a similar fashion as the portfolios from single sorts. However, in this case, we did not sort the markets based on their skewness or the turnover ratios. Instead, we sorted the markets based on their reverse skewness or reverse turnover ratios, that is, we multiplied them by -1. The reason for this is that we wanted to align all the variables such that the higher variables represented a higher expected return. Each month we ranked the markets on two separate variables; for example, we ranked on momentum and the EP ratio, from the lowest to the highest. We then averaged both rankings and formed portfolios based on the combined ranking. The remainder of the procedure was identical to the portfolios that were based on single sorts.

When calculating the returns on portfolios, we aggregated the arithmetic returns in a cross-sectional fashion to form portfolios, and we subsequently converted them into log returns for statistical interfering.

Performance Evaluation

Examining multi-country international portfolios requires an appropriate asset pricing model. Such a model should comply with the perspectives of an international investor who is motivated to invest in foreign indices-based instruments (e.g., ETFs or futures contracts). In this paper, we used two models. To begin, we employed a country-level CAPM model (Sharpe, 1964). In this approach, which was proposed by Zaremba (2015a), the global market portfolio was composed of all the country portfolios in the sample weighted according to their capitalizations. Next, we attempted to consider other cross-sectional asset pricing effects, such as value, size, and momentum. However, we did not apply global stock-level asset pricing factors because this would be inconsistent with the assumption that investors allocate money to index-based vehicles. Conversely, we did not use country-level asset pricing factors such as Zaremba (2015a) has done, because it is irrational to test certain cross-national anomalies in pricing models where they are an integral component. Therefore, in addition to the country-level CAPM model, we determined whether the quantitative country selection strategies extend the frontier for a U.S. stock-level investor, and we took advantage of the four-factor model by Carhart (1997) based on the U.S. stock-level data. The stock-level data originated from the AQR data library (AQR, 2016).

In accordance with Fama and French (2012), all of the regression parameters were estimated using OLS regressions, which is consistent with the remarks of Cochrane (2005) who has regarded this method as more robust than GLS. Furthermore, t-statistics corresponding to each parameter were estimated using bootstrap standard errors to ensure that there was no distributional assumption. Moreover, to determine whether the intercepts of a group of portfolios statistically differ from 0, they were evaluated with the common GRS test statistic, as suggested by Gibbons, Ross and Shanken

(1989). The test's null hypothesis assumes that all the intercepts (five in total) are equal to 0, with the alternative hypothesis assuming the contrary.

The GRS test for statistic weaknesses is an indication of the significant outperformance of certain portfolio sets, and it operates irrespective of the structure of the returns or their monotonicity. Therefore, to examine whether the excess returns (intercepts) are systematically increasing (for the EP and momentum) or decreasing (for skewness and turnover) in addition to the increase in the underlying variable, we also used the monotonic relation (MR) test introduced by Patton and Timmermann (2010). This test is a simulation-based test where the basic hypothesis is that there is no monotonic pattern in excess returns or intercepts (i.e., their values do not increase in addition to a decreasing variable), with an alternative hypothesis stating that such a pattern does exist. The precise testing procedure is described by Patton and Timmermann (2010). Each MR test in this paper was based on 10,000 random draws, and the test was applied to both raw excess returns and intercepts from factor models.

Robustness Checks

We performed a battery of robustness checks. First, we used two alternative weighting schemes: equal-weighting and liquidity weighting. As we noted previously, it is common in country-level studies to equal-weight the indices in portfolios (e.g., Asness et al., 2013). We used this approach to verify the robustness and to enable comparison with other studies that often also examine equally-weighted portfolios. Nonetheless, as we noted before, we were aware of this approach's disadvantages and potentially unrealistic assumptions. Second, occasionally, the capitalization-weighting approach may not fully reflect the varying level of liquidity across countries. This weakness is very important because many cross-sectional anomalies may stem from liquidity constraints (Jacobs, 2015; Pedersen, 2015). In fact, Novy-Marx and Velikov (2014) as well as Zaremba and Konieczka (2015) have argued that a precise adjustment for liquidity may seriously impede the profitability of certain strategies. Therefore, we also used a third weighting scheme: liquidity weighting. We used the average dollar turnover in months t-12 to t-1 as a proxy for stock market liquidity, and we weighted each of the countries accordingly.

Second, we re-examined all the strategies using gross returns (i.e., returns not adjusted for taxes on dividends). We used this approach because it is commonly employed in international studies; however, we found it to be less useful than the net approach. On the one hand, the net approach better reflects the investment practice. On the other hand, Zaremba and Konieczka (2016) have shown that returns on certain strategies, such as cross-country dividend yield investing, may become obliterated after adjusting for taxes on dividends. An important benefit of examining the strategies based on gross returns is that, in this case, we have access to older financial data. Consequently, the study period for this type of robustness check was lengthened to include data from May 1995–March 2015 (239 monthly observations).

Third, we used two different base currency conventions: euro (EUR) and Japanese yen (JPY). In other words, we performed all computations once again with the financial and market data converted to EUR and JPY. In these two cases, we detected no significant departure from our base USD outcomes; therefore, for brevity, we did not report the results of this robustness check in detail.

Fourth, it is common in cross-sectional studies to re-examine anomalies on the subsets of the full research period. However, in our case, the study period was relatively short; therefore, we eliminated this type of robustness check. Due to the limited availability of data, we did not investigate the earlier years to avoid small sample bias.

Fifth, we re-examined the performance of the strategies from double-sorts within sub-periods. We divided the research period into approximate halves (i.e., before December 31, 2006, and after this date). Next, to show that the performance in both sub-samples was not the result of specifically chosen cut-off dates, we also applied two alternative nearby dates as a basis for the division. The two dates selected were related to important market events: the Dow-Jones peak on October 11, 2007, and the Lehman Brothers bankruptcy on September 16, 2008.

Finally, we replicated the strategies formed from pairs of variables within emerging and developed markets. This check was additionally motivated by the observations of Harvey et al. (2004) and Dimic, Orlov and Piljak (2015), who have argued that the pricing

Table 1. Excess Returns on Portfolios from Sorts on Single Variables

	Low	2	3	4	High	H-L	MR	GRS
			Earnings-to-price ratio					
Mean	-0.15	0.40	0.80	0.27	**1.12***	**1.18****	47.1	
	(-0.35)	*(0.74)*	*(1.47)*	*(0.59)*	***(1.93)***	***(2.79)***		
Volatility	6.31	7.37	7.30	7.93	8.15	6.69		
Sharpe ratio	-0.08	0.19	0.38	0.12	0.48	0.61		
α_{CAPM}	**-0.65****	-0.21	0.22	-0.30	0.50	**1.06****	49.6	13.4
	(-2.22)	*(-0.69)*	*(0.69)*	*(-0.72)*	*(1.34)*	***(2.33)***		
α_{4F}	-0.53	0.08	0.33	-0.13	0.60	**1.04****	40.1	24.5
	(-1.48)	*(0.19)*	*(0.85)*	*(-0.25)*	*(1.33)*	***(2.28)***		
			Momentum					
Mean	0.62	0.68	0.18	0.53	0.28	-0.64	51.2	
	(1.02)	*(1.26)*	*(0.45)*	*(1.11)*	*(0.58)*	*(-1.13)*		
Volatility	7.47	7.27	7.22	7.48	7.23	7.47		
Sharpe ratio	0.29	0.33	0.09	0.25	0.13	-0.29		
α_{CAPM}	0.10	0.11	-0.33	-0.07	-0.29	-0.67	44.1	89.5
	(0.23)	*(0.43)*	*(-0.89)*	*(-0.16)*	*(-0.83)*	*(-1.21)*		
α_{4F}	0.32	0.32	-0.23	0.05	-0.14	-0.76	58.8	84.8
	(0.85)	*(0.87)*	*(-0.54)*	*(0.13)*	*(-0.31)*	*(-1.43)*		
			Turnover ratio					
Mean	0.76	0.35	0.37	0.55	-0.08	**-1.10*****	29.8	
	(1.43)	*(0.79)*	*(0.73)*	*(1.55)*	*(-0.08)*	***(-2.89)***		
Volatility	7.31	6.59	7.16	5.04	5.35	5.17		
Sharpe ratio	0.36	0.18	0.18	0.38	-0.05	-0.74		
α_{CAPM}	0.02	-0.14	-0.16	0.16	-0.47*	**-0.75*****	71.5	3.7
	(0.77)	*(-0.37)*	*(-0.40)*	*(0.69)*	*(-1.70)*	***(-2.65)***		
α_{4F}	0.3	-0.02	0	0.23	-0.37**	**-0.94****	46.0	3.3
	(0.81)	*(-0.07)*	*(0.01)*	*(1.34)*	*(-2.42)*	***(-2.52)***		
			Skewness					
Mean	**1.52*****	0.30	0.14	0.66	0.54	**-1.17****	56.5	
	(2.99)	*(0.58)*	*(0.39)*	*(1.17)*	*(1.04)*	***(-2.42)***		
Volatility	6.65	7.48	7.20	8.19	7.38	6.69		
Sharpe ratio	0.79	0.14	0.07	0.28	0.25	-0.61		
α_{CAPM}	**0.96*****	-0.28	-0.42	0.02	-0.04	**-1.18****	46.4	0.5
	(3.57)	*(-0.77)*	*(-1.33)*	*(0.09)*	*(-0.13)*	***(-2.55)***		
α_{4F}	**1.20*****	-0.18	-0.24	0.30	0.08	**-1.31*****	54.4	0.1
	(3.48)	*(-0.44)*	*(-0.71)*	*(0.66)*	*(0.21)*	***(-2.81)***		

Note. This table reports the means, standard deviations, Sharpe ratios, and intercepts from the CAPM and the four-factor model of excess net returns on quintile capitalization-weighted portfolios sorted by the earnings-to-price ratio, the momentum, the turnover ratio, and the skewness. "Low" denotes markets with the lowest variable, and "High" denotes markets with the highest variable. "H-L" (high minus low) is a zero-cost portfolio that is long in the high-variable markets and short in the low-variable markets. MR and GRS are p-¬values from MR (Patton & Timmermann, 2010) and GRS (Gibbons et al., 1989) tests. The means, standard deviations, intercepts, and p-values are expressed as percentages. The numbers in brackets are t-statistics based on bootstrap standard errors, and the significance at the 10% level is in bold characters. *, **, and *** indicate values that are significantly different from 0 at the 10%, 5%, and 1% levels, respectively. The Sharpe ratios are based on annualized data.

relationship may be different in developed and emerging markets. In this test, in accordance with the MSCI approach, we also consider the dynamic classification changes. We assigned markets to the developed markets category in month *t* when they were classified in this way in a given period of MSCI (see MSCI (2015)). All of the remaining markets (i.e., those classified by MSCI as emerging, frontier, or stand-alone) were categorized in month *t* as emerging markets.

Results and Discussion

This section presents the results of our research. First, we re-examined the strategies from single sorts. Next, we investigated the portfolios based on merged rankings and determined whether they outperformed the single-variable portfolios.

Table 1 presents the performance of portfolios from sorts on single metrics: the EP ratio, momentum, the turnover ratio, and skewness. Three of these indicators were found to be potentially important for international investors: the EP ratio, the turnover ratio, and skewness. In each of these cases, the average return on a zero-portfolio had a sign that is consistent with our expectations, and it is significantly different than 0. The absolute monthly mean returns for all of these metrics exceeded 1%, and the abnormal returns were not fully explained by either the global CAPM or the U.S. four-factor model. Consequently, the intercepts from these models were positive and significantly different than 0. The absolute CAPM alphas varied from 0.75% for the turnover ratio to 1.18% for skewness. The absolute four-factor alphas were 1.04%, 0.94% and 1.31% for the long/short portfolios from sorts on the EP ratio, the turnover ratio, and skewness, respectively. The Sharpe ratios for the zero-portfolios were relatively large in absolute terms, 0.61 for the EP ratio and skewness and -0.74 for the turnover ratio. Naturally, the low Sharpe ratio for the zero portfolio (the intercepts and mean returns as well) was not a problem, because an investor can easily build an identical short version of this by simply shorting the liquid markets and going long in the illiquid markets. The reason why the last strategy outperformed the others in terms of Sharpe ratios is because of its lower volatility. The standard deviation of monthly excess returns was 5.17%, which was lower than the other two country selection methods. Interestingly, the GRS tests suggested no significant expansion of the efficient frontier for the EP ratio. The GRS hypothesis was only rejected for portfolios from sorts on skewness and the turnover ratio.

Although in each of the three above-described cases the top portfolio outperformed the bottom portfolio, the general cross-sectional pattern of returns was uneven and far from linear. In fact, the null hypothesis was rejected for none of the metrics investigated by the MR test. In other words, we did detected no vivid monotonicity in excess returns on portfolios based on ranked country indices. The abnormal performance of a zero-portfolio apparently stemmed from the returns on the market with extreme underlying metrics. For example, the turnover ratios were the most liquid markets that had particularly large negative abnormal returns. Conversely, in the case of skewness, the superior performance of the long/short portfolios was mainly driven by impressive returns in the country equity markets with the most left-skewed past-return distributions.

Our investigation of portfolios from sorts on the three described indicators were in accordance with the previous findings. We confirmed that ranking stocks based on the EP ratio, the turnover ratio, and skewness may be helpful when designing profitable country-selection strategies.

Finally, the fourth anomaly that we examined, the inter-market momentum, was the most disappointing for international investors. Similar to Zaremba and Konieczka (2016), we found that momentum is not a suitable basis for building country-level capitalization-weighted portfolios. The GRS and the MR tests' hypotheses were not rejected, and the excess returns on zero-portfolios displayed no abnormal performance. Zaremba and Konieczka (2016) have argued that the reason for the poor performance of such country-level momentum portfolios may lie in the weighting scheme. Zaremba (2015a) as well as Zaremba and Konieczka (2016) have shown that the country-level momentum effect is strongest within small markets. Consequently, if the weighting scheme emphasizes the large markets with the lowest or negative momentum returns, the overall performance of the strategy may also be poor.

The returns on the country-level factor strategies examined in this study were not strongly correlated with each other (Table 2). The long-only and short-

Table 2. Correlation Coefficients for Country-Level Strategies Based on a Single Sorting Variable

	Long leg			Short leg			Long minus short		
	Mom	TR	Skew	Mom	TR	Skew	Mom	TR	Skew
EP	**0.65*** **	**0.60*** **	**0.72*** **	**0.64*** **	**0.64*** **	**0.68*** **	0.05	-0.08	0.10
	(11.91)	**(10.39)**	**(14.36)**	**(11.49)**	**(11.48)**	**(12.72)**	(0.63)	(-1.13)	(1.45)
Mom		**0.57*** **	**0.76*** **		**0.61*** **	**0.61*** **		**-0.28*** **	-0.12
		(9.61)	**(16.21)**		**(10.63)**	**(10.70)**		**(-4.04)**	(-1.64)
TR			**0.81*** **			**0.59*** **			**-0.16** **
			(19.35)			**(10.04)**			**(-2.29)**

Note. This table reports the correlation coefficients of the return on portfolios from sorts on the earnings-to-price ratio ("EP"), the momentum ("Mom"), the reverse turnover ratio ("TR"), and the reverse skewness ("Skew"). The numbers in brackets are t-statistics based on bootstrap standard errors, and the significance at the 10% level is in bold characters. *, **, and *** indicate values that are significantly different from 0 at the 10%, 5%, and 1% levels, respectively. This table reports the correlation coefficients for top-quintile portfolios ("Long leg"), bottom quintile portfolios ("Short leg"), and top-minus-bottom long/short portfolios ("Long minus short").

only portfolios naturally revealed correlation (correlation coefficients in a range of 0.57–0.72), but this was mainly due to a common market risk factor. When we considered the zero-portfolios, the correlations were predominantly close to 0. Moreover, the returns on the turnover ratio strategy were negatively correlated with the returns on zero-portfolios formed on skewness and momentum. The absolute values of the coefficients were low (-0.16 and -0.28 respectively), but they were significantly different than 0. Interestingly, we found no significant correlation between momentum and the EP ratio strategy. This observation to an extent contradicted the main conclusions of Asness et al. (2013) who have examined value and momentum strategies across a broad range of asset classes and have found that their returns are usually negatively correlated. Nonetheless, these authors have tested equally weighted portfolios within a sample of 18 country equity indices. Therefore, the discrepancies may simply stem from differences in sample size and methodology.

The low correlation among the strategies examined here is particularly important for global investors. This low correlation clearly indicates that it would be beneficial to form a portfolio of various country-level strategies. The low correlation would help to mitigate risk by diversification and reduce the volatility of the returns. In summary, the results show that reasonable investors should build portfolios with strategies from single sorts to maximize the return-to-risk ratio of their investments.

Table 3 shows the performance of strategies from single sorts with alternative return computation conventions and weighting schemes. For brevity, we presented only the characteristics of zero-portfolios and the corresponding MR tests' p-values. Not all the strategies appeared equally robust to the changes we observed. The two most robust strategies were based on skewness and the EP ratio; this was consistent with the previous work of Zaremba and Konieczka (2016) and Zaremba and Nowak (2015). The raw and abnormal returns on country portfolios from sorts on the EP ratio were consistent with our expectations, and they were significantly different than 0 for nearly all variants. The sole exception was the equally weighted portfolio based on gross returns. In this case, the alphas and the returns remained consistent with the expectations, but they were not statistically significant.

The portfolios from sorts on skewness were characterized by similar performance in all the specifications. With the exception of equal-weighting, all of the remaining weighting schemes had negative and significant intercepts from factor models and raw returns.

For both strategies described, the Sharpe ratios of alternative weights were relatively high in absolute

Table 3. Excess Returns on Portfolios from Sorts on Single Variables: Alternative Weighting Schemes and Return Conventions

	Equally weighted portfolios (gross returns)		**Equally weighted portfolios (net returns)**		**Capitalization-weighted portfolios (gross returns)**		**Liquidity-weighted portfolios (gross returns)**		**Liquidity weighted portfolios (net returns)**	
	H-L	MR	H-L	MR	H-L	MR	H-L	MR	H-L	MR
					Earnings-to-price ratio					
Mean	0.34	**8.5**	**0.48***	**0.7**	**1.04****	37.6	**1.00*****	**2.1**	**0.75*****	11.2
α_{CAPM}	0.31	15.1	**0.42***	**1.5**	**0.99****	40.1	**0.93****	**5.6**	**0.60****	35.4
α_{4F}	0.26	21.7	0.40	**0.2**	**0.89****	41.3	**0.87****	22.9	**0.64****	37.3
Sharpe ratio	0.30		0.46		0.50		0.59		0.60	
					Momentum					
Mean	**0.67*****	**0.0**	**0.47****	19.1	-0.39	34.2	0.38	**1.9**	-0.06	44.4
α_{CAPM}	**0.71****	**0.0**	**0.53***	**6.0**	-0.39	36.4	0.40	**3.2**	-0.09	27.3
α_{4F}	**0.55***	**0.4**	0.37	37.2	-0.61	33.3	0.08	**8.5**	-0.24	65.4
Sharpe ratio	0.50		0.37		-0.17		0.22		-0.04	
					Turnover ratio					
Mean	-0.44	77.6	**-0.79****	**1.5**	-0.59	35.8	-0.06	89.3	-0.50	23.7
α_{CAPM}	-0.31	84.0	**-0.65***	**7.7**	-0.34	**6.2**	-0.05	95.4	-0.38	43.8
α_{4F}	-0.55	69.1	**-0.81****	**3.7**	-0.56	27.1	-0.07	90.4	-0.40	27.3
Sharpe ratio	-0.29		-0.56		-0.38		-0.04		-0.41	
					Skewness					
Mean	**-0.39***	46.4	**-0.42****	**5.5**	**-1.45*****	11.5	**-0.99*****	7.3	**-0.74****	12.6
α_{CAPM}	-0.36	70.1	-0.38	**7.4**	**-1.48*****	**3.7**	**-1.03*****	5.0	**-0.74****	12.4
α_{4F}	-0.25	84.6	-0.34	14.0	**-1.43*****	13.8	**-1.01*****	4.6	**-0.80*****	12.4
Sharpe ratio	-0.40		-0.44		-0.73		-0.86		-0.64	

Note. This table reports the means, Sharpe ratios, and the intercepts from the CAPM and the four-factor model of excess returns on quintile portfolios sorted by the earnings-to-price ratio, the momentum, the turnover ratio, and the skewness. "H-L" (high minus low) is a zero-cost portfolio that is long in the high-variable markets and short in the low-variable markets. MR and p-¬values are from the MR test (Patton & Timmermann, 2010). The means, intercepts, and p-values are expressed as percentages. The numbers in brackets are t-statistics based on bootstrap standard errors, and the significance at the 10% level is in bold characters. *, **, and *** indicate values that are significantly different from 0 at the 10%, 5%, and 1% levels, respectively. The Sharpe ratios are based on annualized data.

terms, although they were markedly lower for equal-weighting schemes than for capitalization-weighting schemes. Interestingly, the portfolios from sorts on the EP ratio and skewness displayed a degree of monotonicity in their returns. The evidence was not very strong, but it was nonetheless notable. The null hypotheses of the MR tests were rejected for nearly half of the intercepts and returns we examined (i.e., monotonicity was detected).

The case of momentum appeared particularly interesting. Although the country-level momentum was extensively documented in the literature, it appeared to work well only for equally weighted portfolios. When the gross returns on equal-weighted portfolios were considered, we found very high and significant returns and alphas for the zero-portfolio. Furthermore, the MR tests indicated vivid monotonicity in returns. However, when we considered alternative weighting

Table 4. Excess Returns on Portfolios from Sorts on Combined Pairs of Variables

Panel A: The earnings-to-price ratio and momentum, the earnings-to-price ratio and the turnover ratio, the earnings-to-price ratio and skewness, and the momentum and the turnover ratio

	Low	**2**	**3**	**4**	**High**	**H-L**	**MR**	**GRS**
				Earnings-to-price ratio & momentum				
Mean	0.12	-0.12	0.57	0.47	**0.89***	0.61	12.5	
	(0.20)	*(-0.21)*	*(1.11)*	*(0.91)*	***(1.86)***	*(1.61)*		
Volatility	6.53	7.14	7.58	7.48	7.66	6.98		
Sharpe ratio	0.06	-0.06	0.26	0.22	0.40	0.30		
α_{CAPM}	-0.41	-0.67	0.02	-0.08	0.32	0.58	17.2	23.6
	(-1.40)	*(-2.00)*	*(0.06)*	*(-0.19)*	*(0.89)*	*(1.19)*		
α_{4F}	-0.21	-0.51	0.19	0.02	0.37	0.43	24.2	55.0
	(-0.52)	*(-1.45)*	*(0.37)*	*(0.10)*	*(0.93)*	*(0.86)*		
				Earnings-to-price ratio & turnover ratio				
Mean	0.00	0.48	-0.01	0.28	**1.25****	**1.26*****	58.6	
	(0.11)	*(1.19)*	*(0.04)*	*(0.41)*	***(2.05)***	***(2.67)***		
Volatility	5.27	6.09	6.60	8.53	8.43	6.51		
Sharpe ratio	0.00	0.27	-0.01	0.11	0.51	0.67		
α_{CAPM}	-0.39	0.02	-0.49	-0.44	**0.47***	**0.86****	73.8	17.2
	(-1.44)	*(0.11)*	*(-1.51)*	*(-1.22)*	***(1.84)***	***(2.19)***		
α_{4F}	**-0.31***	0.2	-0.37	-0.16	**0.78***	**1.09*****	74.4	**2.8**
	(-2.14)	*(0.79)*	*(-1.06)*	*(-0.34)*	***(1.84)***	***(2.60)***		
				Earnings-to-price ratio & skewness				
Mean	-0.05	0.48	0.50	0.83	**1.06****	**0.95****	**0.3**	
	(-0.14)	*(1.01)*	*(1.06)*	*(1.48)*	***(1.96)***	***(2.04)***		
Volatility	6.64	6.93	7.96	7.52	7.32	6.46		
Sharpe ratio	-0.03	0.24	0.22	0.38	0.50	0.51		
α_{CAPM}	**-0.57***	-0.05	-0.14	0.26	0.5	**0.92****	**2.8**	20.6
	(-1.78)	*(-0.17)*	*(-0.30)*	*(0.74)*	*(1.47)*	***(2.17)***		
α_{4F}	-0.43	0.14	0.11	0.31	0.63	**0.90****	**1.6**	29.8
	(-1.14)	*(0.43)*	*(0.24)*	*(0.77)*	*(1.59)*	***(2.03)***		
				Momentum & turnover ratio				
Mean	-0.05	0.70	0.60	0.15	0.74	**0.75***	48.0	
	(-0.02)	*(1.29)*	*(1.24)*	*(0.33)*	*(1.48)*	***(1.95)***		
Volatility	5.88	7.37	6.45	7.13	7.85	5.67		
Sharpe ratio	-0.03	0.33	0.32	0.08	0.33	0.46		
α_{CAPM}	-0.46	0.16	0.1	-0.4	0.03	0.47	63.9	35.4
	(-1.47)	*(0.43)*	*(0.39)*	*(-1.18)*	*(0.21)*	*(1.45)*		
α_{4F}	-0.36	0.38	0.24	-0.28	0.27	0.6	62.3	20.5
	(-1.61)	*(1.09)*	*(0.75)*	*(-0.77)*	*(0.73)*	*(1.52)*		

Panel B: Momentum and skewness, and the turnover ratio and skewness

	Low	2	3	4	High	H-L	MR	GRS
			Momentum & skewness					
Mean	0.06	0.08	0.64	0.66	0.70	0.41	**0.5**	
	(0.08)	*(0.14)*	*(1.56)*	*(1.21)*	*(1.34)*	*(0.79)*		
Volatility	7.43	7.41	6.11	7.14	7.33	6.73		
Sharpe ratio	0.03	0.04	0.36	0.32	0.33	0.21		
α_{CAPM}	-0.49	-0.48	0.2	0.09	0.1	0.37	**4.8**	42.0
	(-1.29)	*(-1.33)*	*(0.68)*	*(0.23)*	*(0.43)*	*(0.84)*		
α_{4F}	-0.35	-0.32	0.32	0.3	0.21	0.33	**3.9**	45.3
	(-0.78)	*(-0.84)*	*(0.98)*	*(0.77)*	*(0.56)*	*(0.71)*		
			Turnover ratio & skewness					
Mean	-0.28	0.09	**0.87****	0.49	0.98	**1.21****	36.0	
	(-0.51)	*(0.28)*	***(1.99)***	*(0.86)*	*(1.61)*	***(2.51)***		
Volatility	6.11	6.53	6.29	8.52	8.04	6.04		
Sharpe ratio	-0.16	0.05	0.48	0.20	0.42	0.70		
α_{CAPM}	**-0.74****	-0.38	0.41	-0.16	0.23	**0.91****	71.6	**3.7**
	(-2.36)	*(-1.12)*	*(1.37)*	*(-0.39)*	*(1.07)*	***(2.37)***		
α_{4F}	**-0.63****	-0.3	0.44	0.09	0.54	**1.12*****	33.3	**2.3**
	(-2.48)	*(-0.91)*	*(1.34)*	*(0.23)*	*(1.31)*	***(2.64)***		

Note. This table reports the means, standard deviations, Sharpe ratios, and intercepts from the CAPM and the four-factor model of excess net returns on quintile capitalization-weighted portfolios sorted in pairs of the following variables: the earnings-to-price ratio, the momentum, the reverse turnover ratio (the turnover ratio multiplied by -1), and the reverse skewness (the skewness multiplied by -1). The markets are ranked according to two separate variables, and the portfolios are formed based on the sum of ranks in both rankings. "Low" denotes markets with the lowest variables, and "High" denotes markets with the highest variables. "H-L" (high minus low) is a zero-cost portfolio that is long in the high-rank markets and short in the low-rank markets. MR and GRS are p-¬values derived from MR (Patton & Timmermann, 2010) and GRS (Gibbons et al., 1989) tests. The means, standard deviations, intercepts, and p-values are expressed as percentages. The numbers in brackets are t-statistics based on bootstrap standard errors, and the significance at the 10% level is in bold characters. *, **, and *** indicate values that are significantly different from 0 at the 10%, 5%, and 1% levels, respectively. The Sharpe ratios are based on annualized data.

schemes, the positive abnormal returns disappeared and in certain cases became negative (although not significantly different than 0). Thus, our outcomes were similar to Zaremba and Konieczka (2016).

The strategy based on the turnover ratio ranks best for equal-weighted portfolios when net returns were considered. For capitalization- and equal-weighted portfolios that were based on gross returns, the alphas remained negative (but they were no longer significantly different than 0), and the Sharpe ratios were markedly decreased. Moreover, the returns on zero-portfolio portfolios nearly disappeared completely when the returns were liquidity-weighted. This observation was similar to Zaremba and Konieczka (2016). The underlying reason for this could be that the source of return for the turnover-based strategy stems from markets that are less liquid. In fact, the turnover-based weighting scheme minimized its influence on portfolio performance and overemphasized liquid markets, which perform the weakest.

Table 4 presents the performance of strategies from sorts on pairs of variables. The portfolios based on averaged rankings of momentum and the EP ratio did not reveal a significant cross-sectional pattern. The zero-portfolios were not characterized by significant abnormal returns, and the MR and GRS tests' p-values strongly exceeded 10%. Again, our results in this case were different than those of Asness et al. (2013). However, this finding is not extremely astonishing because the momentum itself was an unprofitable strategy.

The zero-portfolios from sorts on the EP ratio and the turnover ratio performed very well. The mean monthly return was 1.26%, and the intercepts from the global CAPM and U.S. four-factor models were 0.86% and 1.09%, respectively (all the numbers were significantly different than 0). The abnormal returns were largely driven by the great performance of the top-ranked markets. Finally, the MR test suggested no monotonicity. In other words, the results appeared to be due to the impressive performance in extreme markets rather than in a stable monotonic cross-sectional pattern.

The performance of portfolios from simultaneous sorts on the EP ratio and skewness was also remarkable. Not only were all intercepts on zero-portfolios positive and significantly different than 0, the MR test clearly suggested the monotonicity of the returns. However, the GRS tests were not rejected.

The strategy based on momentum and the turnover ratio did not prove to be very useful for investors. Although the raw returns on the long/short portfolios were, on average, positive and significantly different than 0, the abnormal performance here is explained by the asset pricing models employed by this study. When we explain the global market risk or U.S. value, the size and momentum effect of the alphas were no longer significantly different than 0. Furthermore, the MR and the GRS tests' hypotheses were not rejected in any of these cases.

The performance of strategies based on momentum and skewness was also unsatisfactory. Although the high-ranked countries appeared to perform somewhat better than the low-ranked countries (with higher returns and intercepts from the asset pricing models), the scale of outperformance was low and insignificant. Although the MR test suggested monotonicity in the returns, the GRS tests were not rejected.

Finally, the portfolios derived from sorts on combined rankings according to the turnover ratio and skewness appeared to pose a very attractive strategy. The top markets outperformed the bottom markets, and the returns on the long/short portfolios were, on average, 1.21% per month. The intercepts from the asset pricing model were significant and positive, ranging from 0.91% to 1.12%. Although the MR test's p-values indicate no monotonicity, which confirmed the initial suppositions that the abnormal returns originated from markets with extreme underlying metrics, both the GRS tests related to the CAPM and the four-factor model indicated a significant shift in the efficient frontier.

A review of the six strategies from double-sorts reported in Table 4 led to two interesting conclusions. First, the rankings that used momentum as one of the sorting variables did not perform very well. None of the examined variances produced significant and positive intercepts from factor models apparently because the momentum strategy works poorly for capitalization-weighted portfolios. Second, although the performance of the remaining strategies was remarkable, the performance does not appear to be superior to the strategies from the sorts on single variables. For example, the Sharpe ratio of the zero-portfolios was often higher than for both zero-investment portfolios based on the constituent strategies than for the composite strategy. In each case, one of these strategies actually performed better. This thesis holds even if we use CAPM or the four-factor model alpha as a measure of abnormal performance. As always, one the constituent strategies performed better. This observation cast doubt concerning the validity of building portfolios based on averaged rankings. If the underlying strategies performed better on a stand-alone basis, it appears more reasonable to build a portfolio of strategies that is based on single variables rather than to blend two variables into one strategy. This argument may be particularly important; given the results in Table 2, strategies from single sorts were not correlated with each other. In a portfolio, it would be possible to diversify away a portion of the volatility.

To further test the robustness of the results reported in Table 4, we re-examined the performance of the six portfolios with cross-sectional and time-series subsamples (i.e., within developed and emerging markets, see Table A1 in the appendix) and with the earlier and latter halves of the sample (see Table A2 in the appendix). Basically, these tests confirmed the profitability of the strategies examined; the zero-investment portfolios delivered predominantly positive returns within the sub-samples. Nevertheless, in accordance with the observations of Harvey (2004), we observed that the pricing relationship was generally stronger within the emerging markets. Furthermore, the returns were visibly lower within the latter sub-periods of the main sample. The underlying source of this time-series variation could be explored in future studies.

Table 5 describes the performance of portfolios based on the average ranking of two variables that used alternative weighting-schemes and return conventions. Two combinations appeared particularly convincing: the EP ratio with skewness and the turnover ratio with skewness. In this variant, most of the mean raw returns and intercepts from asset pricing models were positive and significantly different than 0. Moreover, in many cases, the MR tests strongly confirmed the monotonic cross-sectional patterns in the sets of portfolios that were examined. Furthermore, particular combinations were characterized by exceptionally high Sharpe ratios. For example, the Sharpe ratio of the equally weighted portfolio from simultaneous sorts on the turnover ratio and skewness (i.e., the net return convention) was 0.88, which was greater than any of the strategies from single sorts. Nonetheless, considering the entire set of robustness tests, we found no strong evidence that sorting simultaneously on two cross-sectional strategies leads to a significant improvement in performance. Basically, the levels of the Sharpe ratios and the alphas in Tables 4 and 5 were similar to those in Tables 1 and 3 and revealed no significant improvement. In other words, the examination of the outcomes in Table 5 confirmed the conclusions from Table 4.

The results of the final mean-variance spanning tests are presented in Table 6. Basically, the outcomes suggest that strategies based on pairs of variables do not perform better than strategies based on single variables. When we consider our base approach, net returns on capitalization-weighted portfolios, none of the strategies from simultaneous sorts on two variables significantly augmented the efficient frontier made by the two separate underlying strategies. The intercepts are occasionally positive and occasionally negative; however, in none of the cases were they significantly different from 0. Furthermore, the investigation of portfolios with alternative weighting schemes and tests based on gross returns do not alter the overall picture. With a few exceptions, most of the intercepts did not differ significantly from 0, and no significant pattern could be detected for any of the combinations. In other words, combining two strategies into one does not lead to much improvement in performance when compared with separate component strategies. In fact, given the very low or negative correlation among the strategies examined in this study, investors would be better off building a portfolio of separate component strategies than blending them into one unified strategy.

Concluding Remarks

The research presented investigated the performance of blended country-level quantitative strategies. Among the re-examined strategies from sorts on single variables, we found that three strategies proved to be useful tools for international investors; these were the strategies based on the EP ratio, the turnover ratio, and skewness. Furthermore, strategies based on the combined rankings of the EP ratio with skewness and the turnover ratio with skewness were also characterized by attractive alphas and Sharpe ratios. However, the blended strategies did not outperform the portfolios based on single metrics. Consequently, we argue that, given the low correlation among the returns on single-variable strategies, investors would be better off building a diversified portfolio of independent strategies rather than blending them into a single approach. These observations are important for fund pickers and money managers who have a global investment mandate.

Our study has two limitations of potentially large importance. First, we did not consider transaction costs, and Novy-Marx and Velikov (2014) as well as Zaremba and Konieczka (2015) have shown that these costs can be potentially harmful for certain cross-sectional strategies. Second, our study period encompassed the global financial crisis. This important global event may have influenced the results in an unexpected manner.

Future studies on the issues discussed in this paper should further explore the properties of the strategies examined. Such research could be pursued in several directions. First, one of the disadvantages of the

Table 5. Excess Returns on Portfolios from Sorts on Combined Pairs of Variables: Alternative Weighting Schemes and Return Conventions

	Equally weighted portfolios (gross returns)		**Equally weighted portfolios (net returns)**		**Capitalization-weighted portfolios (gross returns)**		**Liquidity-weighted portfolios (gross returns)**		**Liquidity weighted portfolios (net returns)**	
	H-L	MR	H-L	MR	H-L	MR	H-L	MR	H-L	MR
					Earnings-to-price ratio & momentum					
Mean	**0.48****	23.9	0.32	63.6	**0.62***	**0.4**	**0.51***	**2.7**	0.14	20.6
α_{CAPM}	**0.47***	28.8	0.28	70.9	0.62	**0.6**	0.49	**7.7**	0.02	56.7
α_{4F}	0.29	37.0	0.13	79.1	0.39	**1.9**	0.32	23.6	-0.04	35.3
Sharpe ratio	*0.44*		*0.28*		*0.32*		*0.39*		*0.11*	
					Earnings-to-price ratio & turnover ratio					
Mean	0.23	45.7	**0.66***	10.1	0.70	79.6	0.23	95.8	0.65	91.4
α_{CAPM}	0.10	61.4	0.51	30.4	0.41	86.3	-0.02	98.2	0.31	97.0
α_{4F}	0.22	61.8	**0.60***	32.3	0.67	82.6	0.18	95.8	0.50	94.7
Sharpe ratio	0.14		0.51		0.34		0.12		0.39	
					Earnings-to-price ratio & skewness					
Mean	**0.68*****	30.6	**0.60*****	17.1	**0.97****	**0.1**	**0.94*****	**0.0**	**0.46***	46.4
α_{CAPM}	**0.66*****	50.8	**0.56****	25.2	**0.95****	**0.3**	**0.94*****	**0.0**	0.41	53.6
α_{4F}	**0.54****	68.8	**0.47****	41.1	**0.87***	**0.3**	**0.83*****	**0.0**	0.34	53.1
Sharpe ratio	0.70		0.64		0.48		0.76		0.44	
					Momentum & turnover ratio					
Mean	0.47	**3.4**	**0.61****	**0.2**	0.59	54.3	0.46	75.0	**0.58****	52.6
α_{CAPM}	0.43	**6.0**	**0.56***	**0.8**	0.40	55.0	0.33	84.1	0.42	63.7
α_{4F}	0.51	**5.8**	**0.57****	**0.4**	0.51	60.7	0.42	79.6	**0.51***	56.9
Sharpe ratio	0.25		0.48		0.27		0.24		0.43	
					Momentum & skewness					
Mean	**0.65****	**3.6**	**0.44***	19.4	0.80	**4.4**	**0.60***	27.7	0.25	13.4
α_{CAPM}	**0.67****	**2.7**	**0.46***	17.9	**0.82***	11.2	**0.68****	27.5	0.31	14.1
α_{4F}	**0.47***	33.3	0.30	45.8	0.56	19.0	0.45	39.2	0.19	20.4
Sharpe ratio	0.55		0.38		0.38		0.44		0.19	
					Turnover ratio & skewness					
Mean	**0.63***	**4.1**	**0.88*****	**1.2**	**0.92***	**0.7**	0.54	**0.9**	**0.68***	**0.9**
α_{CAPM}	**0.52***	10.9	**0.79*****	**7.1**	**0.70***	**3.7**	0.44	**4.2**	**0.56***	**8.2**
α_{4F}	**0.61***	**7.5**	**0.90*****	**0.8**	**0.85****	**1.8**	**0.54***	**1.0**	**0.72****	**0.6**
Sharpe ratio	**0.47**		0.88		0.51		0.38		0.53	

Note. This table reports the means, Sharpe ratios, and intercepts from the CAPM and the four-factor model of excess returns on quintile portfolios sorted in pairs of the following variables: the earnings-to-price ratio, the momentum, the reverse turnover ratio (the turnover ratio multiplied by -1), and the reverse skewness (skewness multiplied by -1). The markets are ranked according to two separate variables, and the portfolios are formed based on the sum of the ranks in both rankings. "H-L" (high minus low) is a zero-cost portfolio that is long in the high-variable markets and short in the low-variable markets. MR and p-¬values are derived from the MR test (Patton & Timmermann, 2010). The means, intercepts, and p-values are expressed as percentages. The numbers in brackets are t-statistics based on bootstrap standard errors, and the significance at the 10% level is in bold characters. *, **, and *** indicate values that are significantly different from 0 at the 10%, 5%, and 1% levels, respectively. The Sharpe ratios are based on annualized data.

Table 6. Mean-Variance Spanning Tests of Portfolios from Sorts on Pairs of Variables

	EWG	EWN	CWG	CWN	LWG	LWN
Earnings-to-price ratio & momentum	-0.12	**-0.28***	0.40	0.40	0.04	-0.10
	(-0.81)	**(-1.83)**	(1.27)	(1.14)	(0.14)	(-0.44)
Earnings-to-price ratio & turnover ratio	-0.12	-0.03	0.08	0.21	0.01	0.09
	(-0.68)	(-0.24)	(0.21)	(0.66)	(0.02)	(0.29)
Earnings-to-price ratio & skewness	**0.39****	0.19	-0.15	-0.06	0.29	-0.01
	(2.58)	(1.25)	(-0.40)	(-0.22)	(1.08)	(0.00)
Momentum & turnover ratio	0.17	0.12	**0.74***	0.25	**0.71***	0.44
	(0.42)	(0.58)	**(1.99)**	(0.91)	**(1.86)**	(1.73)
Momentum & skewness	0.08	-0.03	**0.83***	0.55	0.02	0.03
	(0.51)	(-0.15)	**(1.95)**	(1.23)	(0.06)	(0.22)
Turnover ratio & skewness	0.25	**0.45***	0.23	0.43	0.36	0.39
	(1.01)	**(2.08)**	(0.63)	(1.35)	(1.19)	(1.44)

Note. This table reports the intercepts from mean-variance spinning tests. The dependent variables are the return on H-L quintile portfolios (presented and described in Table 4) from sorts on pairs of the following variables: the earnings-to-price ratio, the momentum, the reverse turnover ratio (turnover ratio multiplied by -1), and the reverse skewness (the skewness multiplied by -1). The markets are ranked according to two separate variables, and the portfolios are formed based on the sum of the ranks in both rankings. The explanatory variables include excess returns on H-L portfolios (presented and described in Table 1) for the two constituent strategies for each double-rank strategy. The numbers in brackets are t-statistics based on bootstrap standard errors, and the significance at the 10% level is in bold characters. *, **, and *** indicate values that are significantly different from 0 at the 10%, 5%, and 1% levels, respectively. The Sharpe ratios are based on annualized data. The returns on portfolios are designed and calculated by six methods: equally weighted portfolios based on gross returns ("EWG"), equally weighted portfolios based on net returns ("EWN"), capitalization-weighted portfolios based on gross returns ("CWG"), capitalization-weighted portfolios based on net returns ("CWN"), liquidity-weighted portfolios based on gross returns ("LWG"), and liquidity weighted portfolios based on net returns ("LWN").

computations performed is the lack of consideration provided to cost-functions and cross-country capital mobility constraints. These aspects should be examined more carefully in future studies, specifically because they may constitute a possible explanation of the examined effect. Second, further examination is warranted on the effect of certain market-specific issues such as the level of development, integration, investors' structure, and openness. Third, certain studies suggest that various market anomalies may be influenced by seasonal effects such as the January effect. This phenomenon is defined as the tendency of stocks to perform better in January than in the remaining months of the year. This issue was investigated by Horowitz, Loughram and Savin (2000) for size, Davis (1994) for value, Loughran (1997) for the momentum effect, and Yao (2012) and Waszczuk (2013) for both value and momentum. It would be interesting to explore whether the country-level anomalies also revealed seasonal patterns. Fourth, Jacobs (2015) has recently examined whether stock-level anomalies are better explained by time-varying limits to arbitrage or sentiment. It would be valuable to repeat this exercise at the country-level because such a study could provide additional confirmation that our outcomes are sentiment driven. Finally, certain papers have suggested that the performance of stock-level anomalies could be forecasted with various variables. For example, Cohen, Polk and Vuolteenaho (2001) and Liu and Zhang (2005) have tested the utility of the so-called value spread as a predictor of future returns on value strategies. If such tools could also be applied at the country level, they could be very beneficial for international investors.

References

Adler, M. & Dumas, B. (1983). International portfolio choice and corporation finance: *A synthesis. Journal of Finance*, 38(3), 925-984. http://dx.doi.org/10.2307/2328091

AQR (2016). AQR Data Sets. Retrieved from http://www.aqr.com/library/data-sets/betting-against-beta-equity-factors-monthly/data

Asness, C. S., Frazzini, A. & Pedersen, L. H. (2014, June 19). quality minus junk. Retrieved from SSRN: http://ssrn.com/abstract=2312432 or http://dx.doi.org/10.2139/ssrn.2312432

Asness, C. S., Moskowitz ,T. J., & Pedersen, L. H (2013). Value and momentum everywhere. *Journal of Finance*, 68(3), 929-985. http://dx.doi.org/10.1111/jofi.12021

Bali, T. G., Cakici, N., & Fabozzi, F. J. (2013). Book-to-market and the cross-section of expected stock returns in international stock markets. *The Journal of Portfolio Management*, 39(2), 101-115. http://dx.doi.org/10.3905/jpm.2013.39.2.101

Balvers, R. & Wu, Y. (2006). Momentum and mean reversion across national equity markets. *Journal of Empirical Finance*, 13(1), 24-48. http://dx.doi.org/10.1016/j.jempfin.2005.05.001

Bekaert, G., & Harvey, C. R. (2000). Foreign speculators and emerging equity markets, *Journal of Finance*, 55(2), 565-613. http://dx.doi.org/10.1111/0022-1082.00220

Bekaert, G., Harvey, C. R., & Lundblad, C. (2007). Liquidity and expected returns: Lessons from emerging markets. *Review of Financial Studies*, 20(6), 1783-1831. http://dx.doi.org/10.1093/rfs/hhm030

Bhojraj, S. & Swaminathan, B. (2006). Macromomentum: returns predictability in international equity indices. *Journal of Business*, 79(1), 429-451. http://dx.doi.org/10.1086/497416

Brown, A., Du, D. Y., Rhee, S., & Zhang, L. (2008). The returns to value and momentum in Asian markets. *Emerging Markets Review*, 9(2), 79-88. http://dx.doi.org/10.1016/j.ememar.2008.02.001

Carhart, M. M. (1997). On persistence in mutual fund performance. *The Journal of Finance*, 52(1), 57-82. http://dx.doi.org/10.1111/j.1540-6261.1997.tb03808.x

Chaieb, I. & Errunza, V. (2007). International asset pricing under segmentation and PPP deviations. *Journal of Financial Economics*, 86(2), 543–578. http://dx.doi.org/10.1016/j.jfineco.2006.06.008

Cochrane, J. H. (2005). *Asset pricing*. Princeton, NJ: Princeton University Press.

Cohen, R.B., Polk, C. & Vuolteenaho, T. (2001). The value spread (Working Paper No. 8242) National Bureau of Economic Research. Retrieved from http://www.nber.org/papers/w8242. http://dx.doi.org/10.3386/w8242

Cooper, I., Sercu, P., & Vanpée, R. (2013). The equity home bias puzzle: A survey. *Foundations and Trends in Finance*, 7(4), 289-416. http://dx.doi.org/10.1561/0500000039

Davis, J. (1994). The cross-section of realized stock returns: the pre-Compustat evidence. *The Journal of Finance*, 49(5), 1579-1593. http://dx.doi.org/10.2307/2329263

de Moor, L. & Sercu, P. (2013). The smallest firm effect: An international study. *Journal of International Money and Finance*, 32, 129-155. http://dx.doi.org/10.1016/j.jimonfin.2012.04.002

Dimic, N., Orlov., V., & Piljak, V. (2015). The political risk factor in emerging, frontier, and developed stock markets. *Finance Research Letters*, 15, 239-245. http://dx.doi.org/10.1016/j.frl.2015.10.007

Errunza, V. & Losq, E. (1985). International asset pricing under mild segmentation: Theory and test. *The Journal of Finance*, 40(1), 105-124. http://dx.doi.org/10.1111/j.1540-6261.1985.tb04939.x

Fama, E. F. & French, K. R. (2012). Size, value, and momentum in international stock returns. *Journal of Financial Economics*, 105(3), 457-472. http://dx.doi.org/10.1016/j.jfineco.2012.05.011

Gibbons, M. R., Ross, S. A., & Shanken, J. (1989). A test of the efficiency of a given portfolio. *Econometrica*, 57(5), 1121-1152. http://dx.doi.org/10.2307/1913625

Goetzmann, W. N., Li, L., & Rouwenhorst, G. (2005). Long-term global market correlations. *The Journal of Business*, 78(1), 1-38. http://dx.doi.org/10.1086/426518

Harvey, C. (2000). The drivers of expected returns in international markets. *Emerging Markets Quarterly*, 4(3), 32-49.

Harvey, C. R. (2004). Country risk components, the cost of capital, and returns in emerging markets. In S. Wilkin (Ed.), *Country and political risk* (pp. 71-102). London, UK: Risk Books.

Harvey, C. R., Liu, Y. & Zhu, H. (2015, February 3). … and the cross-section of expected returns. Retrieved from SSRN: http://ssrn.com/abstract=2249314 or http://dx.doi.org/10.2139/ssrn.2249314

Hester, W. (2013). Fed leaves punchbowl, takes away free lunch (of international diversification). Hausman Funds Investment Research & Insight. Retrieved from: http://www.hussmanfunds.com/rsi/intldiversification.htm

Horowitz, J. L., Loughram, T., & Savin, N. E. (2000). Three analyses of the firm size premium. *Journal of Empirical Finance*, 7(2), 143-153. http://dx.doi.org/10.1016/s0927-5398(00)00008-6

Hsu, J. & Kalesnik, V. (2014). Finding Smart Beta in the Factor Zoo. Retrieved from https://www.researchaffiliates.com/Our%20Ideas/Insights/Fundamentals/Pages/223_Finding_Smart_Beta_in_the_Factor_Zoo.aspx.

Jacobs, H. (2015). What explains the dynamics of 100 anomalies? Journal of Banking and Finance, 57, 65-85. Retrieved from SSRN: http://ssrn.com/abstract=2564706 or http://dx.doi.org/10.2139/ssrn.2564706

Jegadeesh, N. (1990). Evidence of predictable behavior of security returns. *The Journal of Finance*, 45(3), 881–898. http://dx.doi.org/10.2307/2328797

Keppler, M. & Encinosa, P. (2011). The small-country effect revisited. *The Journal of Investing*, 20(4), 99-103. http://dx.doi.org/10.3905/joi.2011.20.4.099

Keppler, M. & Traub, H. (1993). The small-country effect: Small markets beat large markets. *The Journal of Investing*, 2(3), 17-24. http://dx.doi.org/10.3905/joi.2.3.17

Kim, D. (2012). Value premium across countries. *The Journal of Portfolio Management*, 38(4), 75-86. http://dx.doi.org/10.3905/jpm.2012.38.4.075

Lehmann, B. N. (1990). Fads, martingales and market efficiency. *The Quarterly Journal of Economics*, 105(1), 1–28. http://dx.doi.org/10.2307/2937816

Liew, J. & Vassalou, M. (2000). Can book-to-market, size and momentum be risk factors that predict economic growth? *Journal of Financial Economics*, 57(2), 221-245. http://dx.doi.org/10.1016/s0304-405x(00)00056-8

Liu, M., Liu, Q., & Ma, T. (2011). The 52-week high momentum strategy in international stock markets. *Journal of International Money and Finance*, 30(1), 180-204. http://dx.doi.org/10.1016/j.jimonfin.2010.08.004

Loughram, T. (1997). Book-to-market across firm size, exchange, and seasonality: is there an effect? The *Journal of Financial and Quantitative Analysis*, 32(3), 249-268. http://dx.doi.org/10.2307/2331199

Liu, N. & Zhang, L. (2005). The Value Spread as a Predictor of Returns (Working Paper No. 11326). National Bureau of Economic Research. Retrieved from http://www.nber.org/papers/w11326, http://dx.doi.org/10.3386/w11326

Macedo, R. (1995). Country-selection style. In J. Lederman, J. & R. A. Klein (Eds.), *Equity style management: evaluating and selecting investment styles* (pp. 333-355). Burr Ridge, IL: Irwin Professional Publishing.

MSCI (2013). Exchange Traded Products Based on MSCI Indices Q3 2013. Retrieved from https://www.msci.com/resources/pdfs/Exchange_Traded_Products_Based_on_MSCI_Indices.pdf

MSCI (2014a). MSCI Global market accessibility review. Retrieved from: http://www.msci.com/resources/products/indexes/global_equity_indexes/gimi/stdindex/MSCI_Global_Market_Accessibiliy_Review_June2014.pdf

MSCI (2014b). MSCI global investable market indexes methodology. Retrieved from http://www.msci.com/eqb/methodology/meth_docs/MSCI_Aug14_GIMIMethod.pdf

MSCI (2015). MSCI Market Classification. Retrieved from https://www.msci.com/market-classification

Novy-Marx, R. & Velikov, M. (2014). A Taxonomy of Anomalies and their Trading Costs. (Working Paper No. 20721). National Bureau of Economic Research. Retrieved from http://www.nber.org/papers/w20721

Novy-Marx, R. (2013). The other side of value: The gross profitability premium. *Journal of Financial Economics*, 108(1), 1–28. http://dx.doi.org/10.1016/j.jfineco.2013.01.003

Patton, A. J. & Timmermann, A. (2010). Monotonicity in asset returns: New tests with applications to the term structure, the CAPM, and portfolio sorts. *Journal of Financial Economics*, 98(3), 605–625. http://dx.doi.org/10.1016/j.jfineco.2010.06.006

Pedersen, L. H. (2015). *Efficiently inefficient: How smart money invests and market prices are determined*. Princeton, NJ: Princeton University Press.

Piotroski, J. D. (2000). Value investing: the use of historical financial statement information to separate winners from losers. *Journal of Accounting Research*, 38, 1-41. http://dx.doi.org/10.2307/2672906

Quinn, D. P. & Voth, H. J. (2008). A century of stock market correlations and international financial openness. *American Economic Review*, 98(2), 535-540. http://dx.doi.org/10.1257/aer.98.2.535

Sharpe, W. F. (1964). Capital asset prices: A theory of market equilibrium under conditions of risk. *The Journal of Finance*, 19(3), 425-442. http://dx.doi.org/10.2307/2977928

Solnik, B. (1974). An equilibrium model of the international capital market. *Journal of Economic Theory*, 8, 500-524. http://dx.doi.org/10.1016/0022-0531(74)90024-6

Solnik, B., & Zuo L. (2012). A global equilibrium asset pricing model with home preference. *Management Science*, 58(2), 273-292. http://dx.doi.org/10.1287/mnsc.1110.1361

Stulz, R. M. (1981a). A model of international asset pricing. *Journal of Financial Economics*, 9(4), 383-406. http://dx.doi.org/10.1016/0304-405X(81)90005-2

Stulz, R. M. (1981b) On the effects of barriers to international investment. *The Journal of Finance*, 36(4), 923-934. http://dx.doi.org/10.2307/2327556

Tversky, A. & Kahneman, D. (1992). Advances in prospect theory: cumulative representation of uncertainty. *Journal of Risk and Uncertainty*, 5(4), 297-323. http://dx.doi.org/10.1007/bf00122574

Waszczuk, A. (2013). A risk-based explanation of return patterns – Evidence from the Polish stock market. *Emerging Market Review*, 15, 186-210. http://dx.doi.org/10.1016/j.ememar.2012.12.002

Willenbrock, S. (2011). Diversification return, portfolio rebalancing, and the commodity return puzzle. *Financial Analyst Journal*, 67(4), 42-49. http://dx.doi.org/10.2469/faj.v67.n4.1

Yao, Y. (2012). Momentum, contrarian, and the January seasonality. *Journal of Banking and Finance*, 36(10), 2757-2769. http://dx.doi.org/10.1016/j.jbankfin.2011.12.004

Zaremba, A., & Konieczka, P. (2015). Are value, size and momentum premiums in CEE emerging markets only illusionary? *Finance a úvěr-Czech Journal of Economics and Finance*, 65, 84-104. http://dx.doi.org/10.2139/ssrn.2375454

Zaremba, A., & Konieczka, P. (2016). Do quantitative country selection strategies really work? *Journal of Investment Strategies*, 5(2), 1-33. http://dx.doi.org/10.2139/ssrn.2606178

Zaremba, A., & Nowak, A. (2015). Skewness preference across countries. *Business and Economic Horizons*, 11(2), 115-130. http://dx.doi.org/10.15208/beh.2015.09

Zaremba, A. (2015a). Country selection strategies based on value, size and momentum. *Investment Analyst Journal*, 44(3), 171-198. http://dx.doi.org/10.1080/10293523.2015.1060747

Zaremba, A. (2015b). Country selection strategies based on quality. Country selection strategies based on quality. *Managerial Finance*, 41(12), 1336-1356. http://dx.doi.org/10.1108/MF-03-2015-0082

Zaremba, A. (2015c). Is there a low-risk anomaly across countries? *Eurasian Economic Review*, 6(1), 45-65. http://dx.doi.org/10.1007/s40822-015-0036-3

Acknowledgments

This study is part of project no. 2014/15/D/HS4/01235, which is financed by the National Science Center of Poland.

Appendix

Table A1. Mean Monthly Net Returns on the Zero-Investment Portfolios Formed on Pairs of Variables within Developed and Emerging Markets

Strategy	Developed markets			Emerging markets		
	Mean	αCAPM	α4F	Mean	αCAPM	α4F
Earnings-to-price ratio & momentum	0.41	0.29	0.29	0.47	0.53	0.39
Earnings-to-price ratio & turnover	0.32	0.28	0.25	0.65	0.37	0.52
Earnings-to-price ratio & skewness	0.52	0.45	0.55	0.42	0.47	0.35
Momentum & turnover ratio	0.30	0.25	0.31	0.73	0.85	0.83
Momentum & skewness	0.51	0.50	0.53	0.50	0.54	0.47
Turnover ratio & skewness	0.20	0.20	0.31	0.97	0.74	1.03
Mean	0.38	0.33	0.37	0.63	0.58	0.60

Note. This table reports the mean monthly net returns on quintile capitalization-weighted zero-investment portfolios formed from sorts on pairs of the following variables: the earnings-to-price ratio, the momentum, the reverse turnover ratio (turnover ratio multiplied by -1), and the reverse skewness (the skewness multiplied by -1). The markets are ranked according to two separate variables, and the portfolios are formed based on the sum of the ranks in both rankings. The portfolios presented here are zero-cost portfolios that are long in the high-rank markets and short in the low-rank markets. αCAPM and α4F are intercepts from the CAPM and the four-factor model, respectively. The means and intercepts are expressed as percentages. We assign markets to the "Developed Markets" category in month t when they are classified in this way for a given period by MSCI (see: https://www.msci.com/market-classification). All the remaining markets (i.e., classified by MSCI as emerging, frontier, or stand-alone) are categorized in month t as "Emerging Markets".

Table A2. Mean Monthly Net Returns on the Zero-Investment Portfolios Formed on Pairs of Variables within a Sub-Period

	First half	Second half	Pre 2007 peak	Post 2007 peak	Pre Lehman	Post Lehman
Earnings-to-price ratio & momentum	0.92	0.30	1.10	0.02	0.92	0.14
Earnings-to-price ratio & turnover	1.48	1.05	1.63	0.82	1.50	0.91
Earnings-to-price ratio & skewness	1.15	0.76	1.41	0.42	1.25	0.51
Momentum & turnover ratio	1.54	-0.02	1.63	-0.30	1.39	-0.21
Momentum & skewness	1.06	-0.22	1.20	-0.53	0.94	-0.39
Turnover ratio & skewness	1.76	0.68	1.77	0.55	1.58	0.65
Mean	1.32	0.42	1.46	0.16	1.26	0.27

Note. This table reports the mean monthly net return on quintile capitalization-weighted zero-investment portfolios formed from sorts on pairs of the following variables: the earnings-to-price ratio, the momentum, the reverse turnover ratio (turnover ratio multiplied by -1), and the reverse skewness (skewness multiplied by -1). The markets are ranked according to two separate variables, and the portfolios are formed based on the sum of the rank in both rankings. The portfolios presented here are zero-cost portfolios that are long in the high-rank markets and short in the low-rank markets. The means and intercepts are expressed as percentages. We calculated the return on the asset pricing factors within various sub-samples. First, we divided the research period into approximate halves (i.e., before December 31, 2006, and then after this date—the first half and the second half). Second, to show that the performance in both sub-samples was not the result of specifically chosen cut-off dates, we also used two alternative nearby dates as a basis for the division. Both dates were related to important market events: the Dow-Jones peak on the October 11, 2007 (i.e., pre-2007 peak, post-2007 peak), and the Lehman Brothers bankruptcy on September 16, 2008 (i.e., pre-Lehman, post-Lehman).

12

How Taxes, Education and Public Capital Influence Economic Growth in Poland

Michał Konopczyński[1]

ABSTRACT

This paper investigates the relationship between economic growth in Poland and selected elements of fiscal policy and private spending on education. We use the Mankiw-Romer-Weil model, augmented with learning-by-doing and spillover-effects and with concepts from the literature on optimal fiscal policy. We demonstrate that, from 2000-2015, economic growth in Poland was primarily driven by rapid improvements in the level of human capital (at 4.4% per annum) coupled with a rapid increase in public capital (6.0%) and secondarily due to the accumulation of private capital (2.1% annually). Simulations of tax cuts suggest that a synchronized reduction of all tax rates by 5 percentage points (pp) in Poland should increase the annual GDP growth rate by approximately 0.32 pp. Increasing (private or public) spending on education by 1 pp of the GDP would increase the growth rate by approximately 0.3 pp. We also analyze the effects of increasing public capital. The stock of public capital in Poland is still below the optimal level, and it may be beneficial to increase investment in public capital at the cost of public consumption (which is intuitively clear) and – to some extent – at the cost of public spending on education.

KEY WORDS: optimal fiscal policy, income taxes, labor taxes, capital taxes, economic growth, human capital, public capital

[1] Uniwersytet Ekonomiczny w Poznaniu - Katedra Ekonomii Matematycznej, Poland

Introduction

In Konopczyński (2014), we developed a simple exogenous growth model to investigate the long-term effects of modifications in fiscal policy. Our model simulated the long-term effects of changes in tax rates and changes in private and public spending on education. However, the model did not include one important factor of growth that (as we demonstrate in this paper) has been a significant driver of the recent impressive growth of the Polish economy: unprecedented acceleration of public investment, mainly in transportation infrastructure: roads and highways, railways, airports, seaports, etc., financed largely by the EU Cohesion Fund. As Kollias and Paleologou (2013) argue: "a range of other economic activities gain from such public spending. In particular, improved transport infrastructure reduces effective distances between different poles of economic activity, between centres of production and consumption, and reduces road congestion bringing about lower travel times and costs for both enterprises and passengers. Increased trade is a strong stimulus of growth." The benefits in Poland are not limited to internal and international trade. Improving public in-

Correspondence concerning this article should be addressed to:
Michał Konopczyński, Uniwersytet Ekonomiczny w Poznaniu - Katedra Ekonomii Matematycznej, al. Niepodległości 10, Poznań 61-875, Poland. E-mail: michal.konopczynski@ue.poznan.pl

frastructure attracts foreign direct investment, which is yet another important factor of growth for Poland.

The main purpose of this paper is to augment our previous model by adding public capital. The augmented model allows for simulating the effects of changes in the level of government investment in public capital. We also update the simulations presented in Konopczyński (2014) regarding tax rates and spending on education.

Our description of public capital follows the so-called "stock approach", in which public capital is regarded as an accumulated stock that depreciates over time. This approach was initiated by Arrow & Kurz (1970) and developed by many researchers, with notable contributions by Futagami Morita and Shibata (1993), Easterly & Rebelo (1993), Turnovsky (1997; 2004), Fisher & Turnovsky (1998), Dasgupta (1999) and many others. More recent contributions include Chen (2007), who focuses on the productive role of roads, railways, airports, seaports, and public transportation. In his model, public capital serves as a substitute to private capital. However, Chen does not distinguish human capital from physical (private) capital. In addition, (in Chen's own words) "the government behaves passively (...). It collects both the labor income taxes and capital income taxes in each period, and then spends the total amount of taxation in accumulating public infrastructure stock". He analyses income taxes only – and there is no tax on consumption.

Another interesting contribution is that of Marrero and Novales (2007), who analyze income taxes and expenditures on public (utility-enhancing) consumption and investment in infrastructure. However, they assume that public and private capital "fully depreciates each period", which makes their model difficult to interpret and virtually impossible to verify empirically. Similarly, to Chen (2007), they abstract from human capital and assume a permanently balanced government budget.

Conversely, human capital is explicitly present in the analysis of Dhont and Heylen (2009), who construct a closed economy model with several types of taxes, public consumption and productive government spending, including education spending, active labor market expenditures, R&D expenditures, and public investment. These types of spending are aggregated and accumulated as human capital, which is one factor of production.

Agénor and Yilmaz (2011) examine several alternative fiscal rules in their endogenous growth model. The government spends money on infrastructure (a stock) and healthcare (a flow). They numerically evaluate the performance of fiscal rules. A similar model combining both types of public spending is presented by Bucci and Bo (2011). In their model, public capital is partly used as an input in the production of final output (a flow) and partly accumulated to increase its own supply in the future (a stock). The share of productive government expenditures devoted to production services can be exogenous or endogenous (the government serves as benevolent social planner). They find that, in the second case, the share of public investment in the GDP is an important determinant of the long-term growth rate. However, their model relies on several simplifying assumptions, e.g., there is only one flat tax (implicitly, because they only consider government expenditures as a share of the GDP), there is no depreciation, no technological progress, no human capital.

One of the most recent theoretical contributions that includes human capital and stock and flow approaches is Escobar-Posada and Monteiro (2015). They present a two-sector model of physical and human capital accumulation in which public goods provide both productive capital and utility-enhancing services. They analyze the impacts of the level of government expenditure and its composition on growth and welfare and derive their respective growth and welfare-maximizing levels. The latest paper that combines stock and flow approaches is Zhang Ru and Li (2016). They derive the optimal tax structure and show that it is equivalent to the optimal public spending composition.

Contrary to most of the aforementioned literature, our analysis is deliberately based on a simple exogenous growth theory for several reasons, listed in Konopczyński (2014). In endogenous growth theory, economic agents are constantly optimizing, adjusting savings and consumption in response to policy changes. In our view, it would be overly optimistic to assume that Central and Eastern European Countries (CEEC's) are already in this type of equilibrium. These countries remain in a transition from centrally planned, Eastern-oriented economies to market-based economies integrated with the West (the EU). Moreover, over the last 25 years, the CEEC's economies have undergone deep structural changes and significant (often sudden) modifications in economic systems and policies. External conditions have also rapidly evolved, with the great (revolutionary) change of the expansion of the EU in 2004.

We consider four types of taxes: on capital, labor, human capital and consumption. Tax revenues are expended on public consumption, education, public capital, with the remainder transferred back to households. The government budget is permanently balanced, which is a standard assumption in most research on optimal fiscal policy. This assumption is fully justified for closed economy models by the well-known Ricardian equivalence.

The paper is organized as follows. Section 1 presents the details of our growth model. Section 2 contains a qualitative sensitivity analysis. In section 3, the model is calibrated based on statistical data on the Polish economy from 2000-2015. Section 4 contains the baseline scenario. Sections 5 and 6 present scenarios of tax cuts and increased educational expenditures by the government and private sector. In section 7, we determine the optimal structure of private investment. Section 8 contains simulations of increased spending on public capital. Section 9 completes the investigation, with an analysis of changes in tax rates accommodated by appropriate changes in expenditures on public capital or education. The robustness of the results is briefly discussed in section 10. The summary synthesizes the main results and offers some critical remarks. Mathematical proofs are included in the appendix.

1. The economy with the government investing in public capital

To incorporate public services into the model, the aggregate production function (2) used in Konopczyński (2014) is generalized as follows:

$$Y = aK^{\alpha}H^{1-\alpha-\beta}(EL)^{\beta}P^{\beta}, \quad 0<\alpha,\beta<1 \tag{1}$$

where K denotes physical capital, H represents human capital, L is raw labor, and P represents **public productive services** provided by the government. Equation (1) implies constant returns to scale in the private inputs, K, H and L. Note that the public services P are complimentary with all private inputs, i.e., an increase in P increases their marginal products. Following the standard approach in the literature, we assume that the exponent on P is equal to β (see, e.g., Barro and Martin, 2004, p. 220).

Many public services are subject to congestion, e.g., roads and highways, seaports and airports, communication infrastructure, water provision and other publicly provided utilities, courts, police and fire services. This problem is especially visible in Poland, which is the subject of the empirical analysis in the second part of this paper. Therefore, following the standard approach in the literature initiated by Barro and Martin (1992), we assume that P is a linear function of the stock of public productive capital K_p per unit of the GDP, i.e.,

$$P = bK_p/Y, \quad b = const.>0 \tag{2}$$

Without loss of generality, parameter b can be normalized to 1 because, after substituting equation (2) into (1) and separating b^{β} from $(K_p/Y)^{\beta}$, we can combine a with b^{β} and replace it with a new constant. Thus, we set $b=1$.

Following Romer (1986) and Barro and Martin (2004), we assume positive externalities related to learning-by-doing and spillover-effects, embedded in the labor-augmenting technology index E, which is proportional to the capital per worker ratio, i.e., $E = xK/L$, where $x = const.>0$. Thus, the production function can be written as

$$Y = AK^{\alpha+\beta}H^{1-\alpha-\beta}P^{\beta}, \tag{3}$$

where $A = ax^{\beta} = const>0$. Therefore, the aggregate output of the economy is described by a Cobb-Douglas function with constant returns to scale for both types of capital (physical and human). The labor supply in the country is growing exponentially:

$$L = L_0 e^{mt}, \tag{4}$$

where $L_0>0$ denotes the initial stock of labor (at $t=0$) and $t \geq 0$ is a continuous time index. Demand for all three factors of production results from the rational decisions of firms maximizing profits in perfectly competitive markets. Let w_K and w_H denote the real rental price of physical capital and human capital, respectively, and let w denote the real wage rate. In the profit maximizing equilibrium, all factors are paid their marginal products, i.e.,

$$MPK = \partial Y/\partial K = \alpha Y/K = w_K = r + \delta_K, \quad (5)$$

$$MPH = \partial Y/\partial H = (1-\alpha-\beta)Y/H = w_H, \quad (6)$$

$$MPL = \partial Y/\partial L = \beta Y/L = w, \quad (7)$$

where δ_K represents the rate of depreciation of capital. Note that the variables w, w_H and $w_K = r + \delta_K$ represent gross rates, i.e., the unit costs of labor, human capital and physical capital from the perspective of the representative firm, respectively.

The public sector (i.e., the government) levies income and consumption taxes. Let τ_L, τ_H, and τ_K denote the average tax rates on labor, human capital and physical capital stock, respectively. Taxes on labor and human capital are levied on gross wage rates, i.e., the government collects $\tau_L w$ and $\tau_H w_H$. The income tax on capital is calculated as follows: $\tau_K(w_K - \delta_K) = \tau_K r$, i.e., the tax is levied on net capital income, defined as gross income minus a depreciation allowance. The total sum of all income taxes is expressed as

$$T_1 = \tau_L wL + \tau_H w_H H + \tau_K rK, \quad (8)$$

In addition, the government collects consumption taxes equal to

$$T_2 = \tau_C C, \quad (9)$$

where C is the aggregate consumption. The total government revenue is $T = T_1 + T_2$. The government maintains a balanced budget in each period, i.e., $G = T$. This assumption is justified by Ricardian equivalence – see, for example, Elmendorf and Mankiw (1998), and it is commonly applied in the literature; see, for example, Lee and Gordon (2005), Dhont and Heylen (2009), and Turnovsky (2009).

The assumption that Poland maintains a balanced budget may appear unrealistic. Waiving this assumption may significantly change the results and implications of the model presented in this paper. An interested reader may refer to the book by Konopczyński (2015), in which we present a detailed analysis of the generalized version of the model used herein by allowing the government to borrow both internally and from abroad.

Public expenditures include four components:

$$G = G_T + G_E + G_C + G_K, \quad (10)$$

where G_T denotes cash transfers to the private sector (social transfers: pensions, various benefits, etc.), G_E represents public spending on education, G_C is public consumption (primarily health care, national defense, and public safety), and G_K denotes public spending on productive capital (e.g., transport and communication infrastructure, public utilities and R&D infrastructure). To assure balanced-growth equilibrium in the model, we must assume that various categories of public spending are proportional to the GDP:

$$G_T = \gamma_T Y, \quad \text{where} \quad 0 < \gamma_T < 1. \quad (11)$$

$$G_E = \gamma_E Y, \quad \text{where} \quad 0 < \gamma_E < 1. \quad (12)$$

$$G_K = \gamma_P Y, \quad \text{where} \quad 0 < \gamma_P < 1. \quad (13)$$

Obviously, $\gamma_T + \gamma_E + \gamma_P < 1$. In a closed economy, the total compensation of all production factors is equal to the output. Therefore, households' disposable income Y_d is equal to the GDP net of taxes, plus transfers. A fraction of that income is saved, and the remainder is consumed; hence, the budget constraint of the private sector is expressed as follows:

$$Y_d = Y - T_1 - T_2 + G_T = C + S. \quad (14)$$

We assume a constant, exogenous rate of savings:

$$S = \gamma Y_d = \gamma(Y - T_1 - T_2 + G_T). \quad (15)$$

Savings are invested in physical and human capital, with a fixed share coefficient $0 < \psi < 1$:

$$I_K = (1-\psi)S, \quad (16)$$

$$I_H = \psi S, \quad (17)$$

From (14), it follows that private consumption is equal to:

$$C = Y_d - S = Y - T_1 - T_2 + G_T - S. \quad (18)$$

Notice that equations (15) and (18) are interconnected because of (9). According to (15), savings depend on consumption and, simultaneously, according to (18) consumption depends on savings. For convenience, we solve this system of equations. Simple algebraic manipulation yields:

$$C = A_1(Y - T_1 + G_T), \text{ where } A_1 = \frac{1-\gamma}{1+\tau_C(1-\gamma)} \quad (19)$$

$$S = A_2(Y - T_1 + G_T), \text{ where } A_2 = \frac{\gamma}{1+\tau_C(1-\gamma)} \quad (20)$$

Henceforth, for simplicity, certain expressions (functions of parameters) are denoted by A_1, A_2, etc. Substituting (8) and (11), and using (5) – (7), equation (20) can be written as:

$$S = A_2[(1-\alpha\tau_K - \beta\tau_L - (1-\alpha-\beta)\tau_H + \gamma_T)Y + \\ + \tau_K\delta_K K]. \quad (21)$$

From equations (15), (16), (17) and (21), it follows that:

$$I_H = \psi S = \psi A_2[(1-\alpha\tau_K - \beta\tau_L - (1-\alpha-\beta)\tau_H + \gamma_T)Y + \\ + \tau_K\delta_K K]. \quad (22)$$

$$I_K = (1-\psi)S = (1-\psi)A_2[(1-\alpha\tau_K - \beta\tau_L - (1-\alpha-\beta)\tau_H + \\ + \gamma_T)Y + \tau_K\delta_K K]. \quad (23)$$

The accumulation of private capital, human capital and public capital is described by the following equations:

$$\dot{K} = I_K - \delta_K K, \quad 0 < \delta_K < 1, \quad (24)$$

$$\dot{H} = G_E + I_H - \delta_H H, \quad 0 < \delta_H < 1. \quad (25)$$

$$\dot{K}_P = G_K - \delta_P K_P, \quad 0 < \delta_P < 1, \quad (26)$$

where δ_i $(i = K, H, P)$ denotes depreciation rates. (Throughout the text, a dot over the symbol for a variable denotes the time derivative, e.g., $\dot{K} = \partial K(t)/\partial t$.) These equations can be transformed to yield the following growth rates:

$$\hat{K} = \frac{\dot{K}}{K} = \frac{I_K}{K} - \delta_K, \quad (27)$$

$$\hat{H} = \frac{\dot{H}}{H} = \frac{G_E + I_H}{H} - \delta_H, \quad (28)$$

$$\hat{K}_P = \frac{\dot{K}_P}{K_P} = \frac{G_K}{K_P} - \delta_P, \quad (29)$$

Substituting (23), equation (27) can be transformed into the following form:

$$\hat{K} = (1-\psi)A_2A_3\frac{Y}{K} + A_4, \quad (30)$$

where

$$A_3 = 1 - \alpha\tau_K - \beta\tau_L - (1-\alpha-\beta)\tau_H + \gamma_T, \quad (31)$$

$$A_4 = [(1-\psi)A_2\tau_K - 1]\delta_K, \quad (32)$$

Similarly, using (12) and (22) in equation (28) yields:

$$\hat{H} = A_5\frac{Y}{H} + A_6\frac{K}{H} - \delta_H, \quad (33)$$

where

$$A_5 = \gamma_E + \psi A_2 A_3, \quad (34)$$

$$A_6 = \psi A_2\tau_K\delta_K, \quad (35)$$

Finally, using (3), the growth rates (30) and (33) can be written as:

$$\hat{K} = (1-\psi)A_2A_3A\left(\frac{K}{H}\right)^{\alpha+\beta-1}P^{\beta} + A_4, \quad (36)$$

$$\hat{H} = A_5A\left(\frac{K}{H}\right)^{\alpha+\beta}P^{\beta} + A_6\frac{K}{H} - \delta_H. \quad (37)$$

It's worth to compare these 'laws of motion' with equations (36) and (37) in Konopczyński (2014). Note that augmenting the model by adding public capital has significantly complicated the dynamics. Finding the balanced-growth equilibrium in Konopczyński (2014) was relatively simple – equating the right-hand sides of equations (36) and (37) therein and (numerically) solving the resulting nonlinear equation for one unknown (the ratio of K/H). Now, it is more complicated because the 'laws of motion' include an additional variable, P, which evolves over time according to the following equation:

$$\hat{P} = \hat{K}_P - \hat{Y}. \tag{38}$$

Fortunately, the following proposition can be easily proven.

Proposition 1 (proof in the Appendix)

Over time, $P \to \frac{b\gamma_P}{\hat{Y}+\delta_P}$, regardless of whether $\hat{Y}$ is constant or changes over time.

This proposition leads to:

Proposition 2 (proof in the Appendix)

In the long run, the economy converges towards the balanced growth path (hereafter denoted by an overbar), with *K*, *H*, K_P and *Y* growing at the same constant rate (the balanced growth rate, BGR). This balanced growth equilibrium is unique and globally asymptotically stable. The steady-state level of public productive services $\overline{P}$ is related to the BGR through the following formula:

$$\overline{P} = \frac{b\gamma_P}{BGR+\delta_P} = const. > 0 \tag{39}$$

To determine the balanced growth equilibrium analytically, one must solve the system of equations $\hat{Y} = \hat{K} = \hat{H} = \hat{K}_P$. The easiest way to do this is to equate the right-hand sides of equations (36) and (37) and consider equation (39). This consideration results in the following system of two equations with 2 unknowns, K/H and *P*:

$$(1-\psi)A_2A_3A\left(\frac{K}{H}\right)^{\alpha+\beta-1}P^{\beta} + A_4 =$$
$$= A_5A\left(\frac{K}{H}\right)^{\alpha+\beta}P^{\beta} + A_6\frac{K}{H} - \delta_H. \tag{40}$$

$$P = \frac{b\gamma_P}{(1-\psi)A_2A_3A\left(\frac{K}{H}\right)^{\alpha+\beta-1}P^{\beta} + A_4 + \delta_P}. \tag{41}$$

Having solved this system of equations, one can calculate the BGR by substituting the resulting value of K/H into either (36) or (37).

The system of equations (40) and (41) can only be solved numerically, after substituting certain values for all parameters. Although it is not possible to derive an explicit formula for the BGR, it is possible (and worthwhile) to perform a qualitative sensitivity analysis to determine the relationship between the parameters of the model and the BGR.

2. Qualitative sensitivity analysis

In this section, we investigate how changes in the parameter values influence the BGR. The analysis is performed in three stages. First, we investigate whether an increase in the value of a parameter (e.g., τ_K or γ_P) increases or reduces the values of expressions A_2, ..., A_6. Second, using formulas (36) and (37), we investigate whether the graphs of functions $\hat{K}(K/H)$ and $\hat{H}(K/H)$ shift up or down. Third, based on these observations, we conclude whether the intersection of these curves, which corresponds to the BGR (see Appendix, fig. A2), moves up or down.

These stages appear identical to those in the model without public productive services – see section 3 in Konopczyński (2014). However, stage 2 is far more complex than that therein, because functions $\hat{K}(K/H)$ and $\hat{H}(K/H)$ depend on *P*. This stage must be decomposed into 3 steps. First, we investigate how the aforementioned graphs shift under an artificial assumption that the steady-state value of *P* is not affected. Second, we investigate how the steady-state value of *P* changes, and how it shifts the graphs of $\hat{K}(K/H)$ and $\hat{H}(K/H)$. Third, we investigate the combined effects of these two shifts.

As an example of this procedure, we present the analysis of the effects of an increase in the rate of savings γ. It's useful to follow all steps in figure 1, starting from the initial graphs of functions $\hat{K}(K/H)$ and $\hat{H}(K/H)$, labeled $\hat{K}^{old}$ and $\hat{H}^{old}$. The intersection of these curves determines the initial value of BGR, labeled BGR^{old}.

An increase in γ increases the values of A_2, A_4, A_5 and A_6, leaving A_3 unchanged. It follows that the graphs of both functions $\hat{K}(K/H)$ and $\hat{H}(K/H)$ shift up, provided that the steady-state value of *P* is unchanged. (In figure 1, these new graphs are labeled $\hat{K}^A$ for initial $\overline{P}$; $\hat{H}^A$ for initial $\overline{P}$). If the steady-state value of *P* remains at its initial level, then the new BGR would increase to the level labeled BGR^A and our analysis would be complete. However, $\overline{P}$ does not remain at its initial level, as a higher BGR implicates a lower $\overline{P}$, in accordance with equation (39). There-

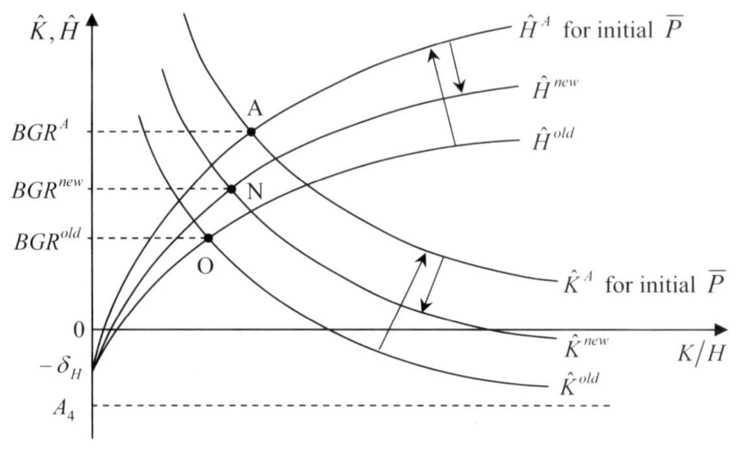

Figure 1. The effects of an increase in the rate of savings γ.

fore, an increase in the BGR reduces $\overline{P}$, which, in accordance with equations (36) and (37) shifts both $\hat{K}(K/H)$ and $\hat{H}(K/H)$ downward to positions labeled $\hat{K}^{new}$ and $\hat{H}^{new}$. This leads to the question: can this downward shift be stronger than the initial upward shift? Can the negative effect of a decrease in $\overline{P}$ entirely offset (or more than offset) the initial positive effect of an increase in the BGR? The answer is: no, it cannot. The next paragraph formally proves this by contradiction.

Let us assume the contrary, i.e., assume that $BGR^{new} \leq BGR^{old}$. Equation (39) implies that $\overline{P}^{new} \geq \overline{P}^{old}$. Recall that we are analyzing the effects of an increase in γ, i.e., $\gamma^{new} > \gamma^{old}$. The last two inequalities imply that $BGR^{new} > BGR^{old}$ because an increase in γ shifts the $\hat{K}(K/H)$ and $\hat{H}(K/H)$ curves up whereas a 'non-reduction' in $\overline{P}$ shifts both curves up or leaves them unchanged. This contradicts our initial assumption. Thus, $BGR^{new} > BGR^{old}$, i.e., an increase in γ unambiguously results in an increase in the BGR.

An increase in the BGR leads to a decrease in $\overline{P}$, i.e., $\overline{P}^{new} < \overline{P}^{old}$. Note that the balanced growth ratio of $\overline{K}/\overline{H}$ will likely change but we do not know the direction of change (it is ambiguous).

The effects of an increase in all other parameters can be traced similarly. In all cases, the initial change (increase/decrease) in the BGR is partially offset by the 'secondary' change (decrease/increase) in $\overline{P}$. The easiest method to prove that this offset is only partial is by contradiction. The results are summarized in table 1.

Notice that increasing any tax rate reduces the BGR and increases $\overline{P}$, with one important exception. The effect of raising the tax rate on capital is ambiguous, as we cannot determine how the $\hat{H}(K/H)$ and $\hat{K}(K/H)$ graphs shift without additional assumptions.

Most of the conclusions are intuitively clear, but some are not. For example, we may have expected a positive relationship between the rate of private savings γ or the rate of public spending on education γ_E and the BGR. To the contrary, the positive relationship between the BGR and the rate of financial transfers to the private sector γ_T requires explanation. Due to the assumption of a permanently balanced government budget, higher transfers to the private sector (with no change in taxes) are automatically offset by reduced public consumption, with no changes in public spending on education or on public capital. These structural changes result in higher disposable income in the pri-

Table 1. Qualitative sensitivity analysis

	$\tau_K \uparrow$	$\tau_H \uparrow$	$\tau_L \uparrow$	$\tau_C \uparrow$	$\gamma \uparrow$	$\gamma_T \uparrow$	$\gamma_E \uparrow$	$\psi \uparrow$	$\gamma_P \uparrow$
A_2	=	=	=	$\downarrow$	$\uparrow$	=	=	=	=
A_3	$\downarrow$	$\downarrow$	$\downarrow$	=	=	$\uparrow$	=	=	=
A_4	$\uparrow$	=	=	$\downarrow$	$\uparrow$	=	=	$\downarrow$	=
A_5	$\downarrow$	$\downarrow$	$\downarrow$	$\downarrow$	$\uparrow$	$\uparrow$	$\uparrow$	$\uparrow$	=
A_6	$\uparrow$	=	=	$\downarrow$	$\uparrow$	=	=	$\uparrow$	=
graph of $\hat{K}(K/H)$	?	$\downarrow$	$\downarrow$	$\downarrow$	$\uparrow$	$\uparrow$	$\downarrow$	$\downarrow$	$\uparrow$
graph of $\hat{H}(K/H)$	?	$\downarrow$	$\downarrow$	$\downarrow$	$\uparrow$	$\uparrow$	$\uparrow$	$\uparrow$	$\uparrow$
BGR	?	$\downarrow$	$\downarrow$	$\downarrow$	$\uparrow$	$\uparrow$	$\uparrow$	?	$\uparrow$
$\overline{P}$	?	$\uparrow$	$\uparrow$	$\uparrow$	$\downarrow$	$\downarrow$	$\downarrow$	?	$\uparrow$
$\overline{K}/\overline{H}$	?	?	?	?	?	?	$\downarrow$	$\downarrow$	?

vate sector. Therefore, private investment in education and physical capital increases whereas government spending on education and public capital remains unchanged. The total effect is unambiguous – the BGR increases and $\overline{P}$ decreases.

The effects of increasing the share parameter ψ are also nontrivial. Recall that ψ represents the share of private savings invested in education. Therefore, increasing ψ increases the rate of human capital accumulation and reduces the rate of physical capital growth. The $\hat{H}(K/H)$ graph shifts up whereas the graph of $\hat{K}(K/H)$ shifts down. Hence, the intersection of these curves unambiguously moves to the left but it is uncertain whether it moves up or down. Again, these shifts are only partially offset by a change (an increase or decrease in $\overline{P}$), which can be proven by contradiction. A higher ψ unambiguously reduces the balanced growth ratio of $\overline{K}/\overline{H}$ – there is more human capital per unit of physical capital. However, the relationship between ψ and the BGR is ambiguous.

The effects of an increase in γ_P, summarized in table 1, require more detailed explanation. Note that an increase in γ_P has no influence on A_2, A_3, A_4, A_5 or A_6. However, an increase in γ_P directly translates into an increase in $\overline{P}$ – see equation (39). Assume that BGR is at its initial level. An increase in $\overline{P}$ shifts the graphs of $\hat{K}(K/H)$ and $\hat{H}(K/H)$ up. (In figure 2, these new graphs are labeled $\hat{K}^A$ for the initial BGR and $\hat{H}^A$ for the initial BGR, respectively). The BGR does not remain at its initial level – it increases. A higher BGR implies a lower $\overline{P}$, in accordance with equation (39). In accordance with equations (36) and (37), this shifts $\hat{K}(K/H)$ and $\hat{H}(K/H)$ down to the positions labeled $\hat{K}^{new}$ and $\hat{H}^{new}$. This shift leads to the question: can this downward shift be stronger than the initial upward shift? Can the (secondary) decrease in the BGR entirely offset (or more than offset) the initial increase in the BGR? The answer is: no, it cannot. Let us prove this by contradiction.

Let us assume the contrary, i.e., assume that $BGR^{new} \leq BGR^{old}$. This implies that $\overline{P}^{new} \leq \overline{P}^{old}$, as the $\hat{K}(K/H)$ and $\hat{H}(K/H)$ curves shift due to changes in $\overline{P}$. Recall that we are analyzing the effects of an increase in γ_P, i.e., $\gamma_P^{new} > \gamma_P^{old}$. Note that these three inequalities contradict each other, which follows from equation (39). Hence, our initial assumption is false. Thus, $BGR^{new} > BGR^{old}$, i.e., an increase in γ_P unambiguously results in an increase in the BGR. It also fol-

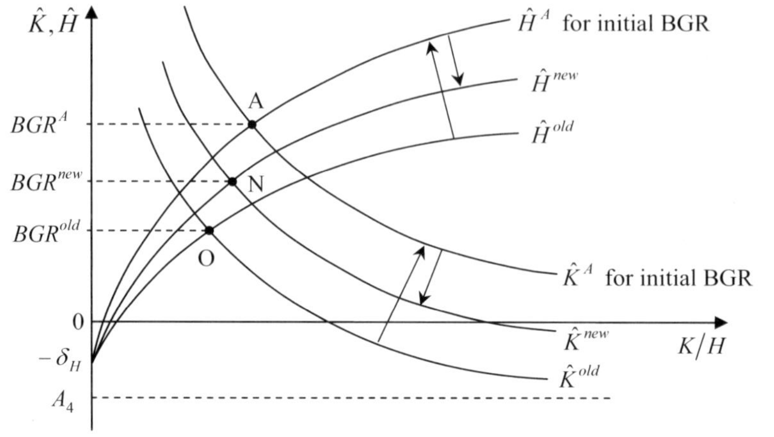

Figure 2. The effects of an increase in γ_P.

lows that an increase in γ_P results in an increase in $\overline{P}$. (Formally, $\overline{P}^{new} > \overline{P}^{old}$). Finally, note that the change in the ratio of $\overline{K}/\overline{H}$ is ambiguous.

Based on table 1, we can formulate the following.

Proposition 3

First, the BGR is an increasing function of the rate of private savings γ, the rate of public transfers γ_T, the rate of public spending on education γ_E, and the rate of government spending on public capital γ_P. Second, the BGR is a decreasing function of the tax rates on labor, human capital and consumption. Third, the relationship between the BGR and the tax rate on capital income and the share coefficient (the percentage of private savings invested in education) are ambiguous.

Although interesting, these *qualitative* results only enhance our desire for *quantitative* results. Moreover, as the BGR cannot be determined analytically, it is not possible to determine *how strongly* changes in the parameters influence the BGR. We know the *direction* of the effect, but we do not know the *size* of the effect. Answering these questions requires calibrating the model and performing numerical analyses. We calibrate the model for Poland and numerically analyze the optimal fiscal policy and private sector parameters. The calibration is based on macroeconomic data for Poland for 2000 – 2015, published by the Eurostat, IMF, OECD, and the Kiel Institute for the World Economy.

3. Model calibration for Poland

Initial stock of private and public capital

Statisticians have difficulty obtaining reliable data on the stock of public capital, even for OECD countries. For example, consider two large, reliable databases constructed by the IMF (IMF 2015) and the KIEL Institute (Kamps 2006). For the majority of OECD countries, the time series reported by both institutions diverges significantly, even for countries such as the United States and Germany (see fig. 3) Moreover, there are large discrepancies although both institutions applied similar definitions of public capital and the same methodology (the Perpetual Inventory Method), started their calculations at the same base year (1860), and applied similar assumptions regarding depreciation patterns over time (in fact, the IMF borrows these assumptions from the KIEL Institute).

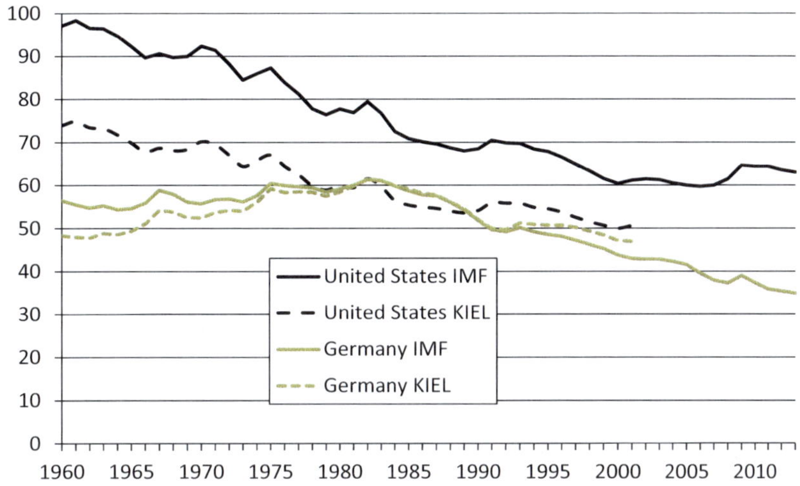

Figure 3. Public capital as a percentage of the GDP.
Source: Adapted from "Making public investment more efficient" by International Monetary Fund (2015). Retrieved from http://www.imf.org/external/np/pp/eng/2015/061115.pdf; "New Estimates of Government Net Capital Stocks for 22 OECD Countries, 1960– 2001" by C. Kamps 2006, IMF Staff Papers, 53(1), 120–50.

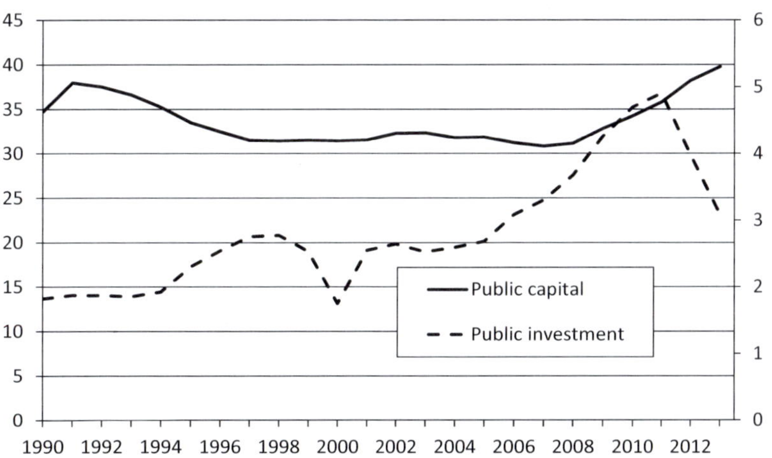

Figure 4. Public capital (left-hand scale) and public investment (right-hand scale) in Poland as a percentage of the GDP.
Source: "IMF Investment and Capital Stock Dataset", by International Monetary Fund (2016). Available at http://www.imf.org/external/np/fad/publicinvestment/

In addition, there are also large differences between countries. For example, according to KIEL, in 2001 (the last year in their database) the stock of public capital (as % of the GDP) varied from less than 40% (in Ireland, Belgium, Canada, UK) to 75% in New Zealand and 120% in Japan. IMF provides statistics for a much wider group of countries, so the differences between countries are even larger (and they persist over time). For example, in 2013, according to IMF, public capital was approximately 35% of the GDP in Argentina, Brazil and Germany and 107% in Japan, 137% in China, and 147% in Malaysia.

Apart from these discrepancies, the databases provided by IMF and KIEL Institute indicate that the ratio of public capital to GDP is not necessarily increasing over time in most OECD countries (as one may expect). In most countries, it has been stable or decreasing in the last 2 decades. This is true for most developed countries, which may indicate that public capital across the world is in decline (perhaps underinvested, as suggested by Dobbs et al. 2013) or is steadily losing importance for economic growth in the richest countries (which is an intriguing empirical question) or both. Let us leave this issue for future research, and turn to Poland.

KIEL does not provide data for Poland but IMF does. Figure 4 presents the overall government investment (gross fixed capital formation) and stock of public capital as a percentage of the GDP.

The evolution of public capital in Poland can be divided into three general phases. During the first phase, which started immediately after political and economic revolution (1989), the stock of public capital deteriorated from approximately 35% of the GDP in 1990 to 31.5% in 1997 due to low investment in public infrastructure, 2.1% of the GDP on average (a sharp increase in 1991 is a statistical effect of the deep recession in 1991 when the GDP decreased by 7% rather than an increase in public capital). In the following decade (1998–2008), the level of public capital remained stable at approximately 31.5% of the GDP. Over the third phase, which started in 2008, Poland enjoyed a significant increase in public investment (mainly due to large EU convergence funds), resulting in unprecedented improvement in public capital that reached 40% of the GDP in 2013.

For our simulations, we assume that the initial stock of public capital is 33% of the GDP and the level of public investment: $\gamma_P = 3.3\%$ (the arithmetic averages for 2000–2013).

Technological parameters

The elasticities of the production function (1) have been estimated in many papers, e.g., Mankiw, Romer, Weil (1992), Manuelli and Seshadri (2005). Studies focusing on Poland include Cichy (2008) and Próchniak (2013). The estimated values are typically close to 1/3; hence, we set: $\alpha = \beta = 1 - \alpha - \beta = 1/3$. As we argued in Konopczyński (2014), the rate of physical capital depreciation is difficult to estimate due to rapid economic transformation that resulted in a large amount of obsolete machinery and infrastructure inherited from the centrally 'planned' economy. In various research papers regarding OECD countries, physical capital depreciation varies from approximately 3.5% to 7%, and we assume that $\delta_K = 5.5\%$. The rate of human capital depreciation has been estimated by Manuelli and Seshadri (2005), Arrazola and de Hevia (2004) and others. Following these authors, we set $\delta_H = 1.5\%$.

There are no statistics regarding the rate of depreciation of public capital in Poland. Therefore, we follow methodology applied by the IMF (2015), which follows assumptions adopted by Gupta et al. (2014). They argue that "country-specific depreciation rates (…) are likely to increase with income assuming that the share of assets with a shorter life spans (such as technology assets) rises with income levels". They assume that public capital in middle income countries depreciates at a rate of 3.51% per year and 4.59% in high income countries. Poland is located somewhere between these two groups, so we set $\delta_P = 4\%$.

Next, we assess the real rate of return on capital (r). From (5), it follows that $r = \alpha \cdot Y/K - \delta_K$. The ratio of Y/K is difficult to estimate for Poland – we exposed major problems in Konopczyński (2014), section 4. The available data for Poland only reflect a share of the productive capital – namely, the "gross value of fixed assets". Therefore, in Konopczyński (2014) we applied the average ratio from the Kiel database, i.e., we set $Y/K = 1/3$. However, we need to alter this number because our model separates public and private capital. Subtracting public capital (33% of the GDP) yields: $Y/K = 1/(3 - K_P/Y) = 1/(3 - 0.3\ ) = 0.375$. Substituting this value into (5) yields the real rate of return on private capital, $r = 6.98\%$. This outcome is very close to most long-term empirical estimates for OECD countries. For example, Campbell, Diamond and Shoven (2001) reported that the average real rate of return on stocks in the U.S. from 1900–1995 was 7%. In our opinion, analogous indicators for the Polish stock market are irrelevant because the Polish stock market is still young and volatile, and thus does not reflect the long-term equilibrium.

Social transfers and the rates of savings and investment

Cash transfers to the private sector (pensions, various benefits, social assistance, etc.) were 15.1% of the GDP from 2000-2015. Thus, we set $\gamma_T = 15.1\%$.

The average rate of savings can be calibrated based on equation 15), which can be transformed into the following formula:

$$\gamma = \frac{S}{Y_d} = \frac{I_K + I_H}{Y - T + G_T} = \frac{I_K/Y + I_H/Y}{1 - T/Y + G_T/Y}. \tag{42}$$

According to Eurostat, the average gross fixed capital formation in Poland from 2000-2015 was 20.3% of the GDP. The average private spending on education from 2000-2011 (the latest data available from Eurostat) was 0.65% of the GDP. The ratio of 'total receipts from taxes and social contributions' to the GDP from 2000-2015 was 33.4% (and very stable). Substituting these numbers into (42) yields $\gamma = 25.64\%$.

The share parameter ψ can be calculated directly from equation (17): $\psi = \frac{I_H}{S} = \frac{I_H/Y}{I_K/Y + I_H/Y} = \frac{0.65\%}{20.3\% + 0.65\%} = 3.10\%$. In Poland, a mere 3.1% of private savings is invested in education. However, private spending on education is probably underestimated in official statistics – Eurostat only considers "school fees; materials such as textbooks and teaching equipment; transport to school (if organized by the school); meals (if provided by the school); boarding fees; and expenditure by employers on initial vocational training". All other private expenses related to education are classified as consumption, e.g., the cost of accommodation, travel, books, etc.

The average public expenditure on education in Poland from 2000-2011 (the latest available data) was 5.20% of the GDP (Eurostat); hence, based on formula (12), we set $\gamma_E = 5.20\%$.

Average tax rates

From 2000-2015, consumption taxes were 12.0% of the GDP. Thus, the ratio of income taxes to the GDP was $T_1/Y = T/Y - T_2/Y = 33.4\% - 12.0\% = 21.4\%$. Eurostat reports 'implicit tax rates' on capital, labor and consumption. In Poland, from 2000-2012 (the latest available data), the average rates were: $\tau_K = 20.5\%$, $\tau_L = 32.8\%$, and $\tau_C = 19.5\%$, respectively. Note that the implicit tax rate on labor is defined as the "*Ratio of taxes and social security contributions on employed labor income to total compensation of employees*". To the best of our knowledge, there are no data on the average tax rates on human capital. As noted in Konopczyński (2014), some researchers suggest that, in countries with highly progressive taxes on personal income, tax rates on human capital must be higher than the tax rates on (raw) labor. However, in Poland, the size of the tax wedge on labor is nearly independent of the level of income, i.e., the effective tax rates on wages are nearly linear. Thus, it is reasonable to assume that the average tax rates on human capital and raw labor in Poland are identical, i.e., $\tau_H = \tau_L$.

Recall that, according to Eurostat, $\tau_L = 32.8\%$. However, if we set $\tau_H = \tau_L = 32.8\%$ and perform the calibration, the model significantly overestimates the total revenue from income taxes (by approximately 7% of the GDP). This problem arises because our concepts of human capital and raw labor are wider than the definitions employed by Eurostat. Eurostat classifies "taxes on income and social contributions of the self-employed" as part of the capital income tax – a detailed explanation can be found in the methodological publication by Eurostat (2010), Annex B. However, self-employed entrepreneurs correspond to our concept of human capital (as well as a part of raw labor). Self-employment is very popular in Poland – there are millions of small, family businesses and many individuals operate single-person firms and provide services for larger enterprises. Note that the tax rate on capital income published by Eurostat is much lower (20.5%) than the tax rate on labor (32.8%). Therefore, in our model, the tax rates on human capital and labor should be somewhere between these two numbers. As there are no additional statistics, we calibrated both rates at this level, at which the model produces a total share of taxes of the GDP that is consistent with statistics (33.4%, see above). Thus, we obtain $\tau_H = \tau_L = 26.6\%$, i.e., rates that are approximately 20% lower than those reported by Eurostat.

The next step in the calibration is computing the expressions A_i. We do not report these values here as they do not have any economic interpretation. Knowing these values and using formula (30), we compute the average capital growth rate from 2000-2015: $\hat{K} = (1-\psi)A_2A_3 Y/K + A_4 = 2.10\%$. Substituting (13) into (29) yields $\hat{K}_P = \frac{\gamma_P}{K_P/Y} - \delta_P$. Substituting the statistical values leads to the following: $\hat{K}_P = \frac{3.3\%}{33\%} - 4\% = 6.0\%$. This implies that the flow of public services was increasing at the following rate: $\hat{P} = \hat{K}_P - \hat{Y} = 6.0\% - 3.66\% = 2.34\%$, which is approximately the private capital growth rate.

From equation (3), it follows that:

$$\hat{Y} = (\alpha+\beta)\hat{K} + (1-\alpha-\beta)\hat{H} + \beta\hat{P}, \tag{48}$$

The average GDP growth rate in Poland from 2000-2015 was 3.66% (geometric mean). We can estimate the human capital growth rate based on the basis of equation (48), from which it follows that

$$\hat{H} = \frac{\hat{Y} - (\alpha+\beta)\hat{K} - \beta\hat{P}}{(1-\alpha-\beta)} = \frac{3.66\% - 2/3 \cdot 2.1\% - 1/3 \cdot 2.34\%}{1/3} =$$

$= 4.43\%$.

These results imply that, from 2000-2015, economic growth in Poland was primarily driven by rapid growth in the stock of human capital coupled with accumulation of public capital (however, the latter was only after 2005, see fig. 1), and secondarily by the accumulation of (private) productive capital. An impressive increase in human capital in Poland is a well-known 'stylized fact', confirmed by a sharp increase in the number of students, PhDs, etc.

For simulations, it is necessary to estimate parameter A. First, from equation (33), we calculate the proportion $K/H = \frac{\hat{H} + \delta_H}{A_5 Y/K + A_6} = 2.7083$. Transforming formula (3) yields

$$A = \frac{Y}{K^{\alpha+\beta}H^{1-\alpha-\beta}P^{\beta}} = \frac{Y}{K}\left(\frac{K}{H}\right)^{1-\alpha-\beta}\frac{1}{P^{\beta}}, \tag{51}$$

which, using (2), can be written as

$$A = \frac{Y}{K}\left(\frac{K}{H}\right)^{1-\alpha-\beta}\left(\frac{K_P}{Y}\right)^{-\beta}, \tag{52}$$

Substituting $Y/K = 1/3$, $K/H = 2.7083$, and $K_P/Y = 0.33$ yields $A = 0.7555$.

To perform the simulations, we assume initial values of the variables K, H, L and K_P. Two of these (K and L) can be determined freely, provided that we confine our interest to the rates of growth and relationships (the proportions) among variables. Therefore, we set $L(0) = 1$ and $K(0) = 267$. This choice is convenient, as the initial GDP is 100, so the initial values of all the other variables are identical to their percentage shares of the GDP. Given $K/H = 2.7083$ and $K_P/Y = 0.33$, it follows that $H(0) = 98.58$ and $K_P(0) = 33$.

In summary, we have the following base set of parameters and endowments:

$$A = 0.7555,\ \alpha = 1/3,\ \beta = 1/3,\ \delta_K = 5.5\%,\ \delta_H = 1.5\%,\ \gamma = 25.64\%,\ \psi = 3.10\%,\ \gamma_E = 5.20\%,\ \gamma_T = 15.1\%,\ \tau_K = 20.5\%,\ \tau_C = 19.5\%,\ \tau_H = \tau_L = 26.6\%,\ L(0) = 1,\ K(0) = 267,\ H(0) = 98.58,\ K_P(0) = 33. \tag{53}$$

4. Baseline scenario

The baseline scenario with the set of parameters (53) reproduces actual statistics on the Polish economy from 2000-2015 and reproduces the factual (average) ratios of the following variables to the GDP: C, I_K, I_H, T_1, T_2, G_T, G_E, G_K as well as the (average) rate of GDP growth. The rates of growth for $t = 0$ generated by the model in the baseline scenario are

$$\hat{Y} = 3.66\%,\ \hat{K} = 2.10\%,\ \hat{H} = 4.43\%,\ \hat{K}_P = 6.0\%.$$

These rates are not equal; hence, the Polish economy is not yet on a balanced growth path. Using the procedure described at the end of section 2, we can numerically obtain the BGR in the baseline scenario, which is 3.70% – slightly higher than the average growth rate from 2000-2015. The process of convergence towards a balanced growth path is presented in figure 5, which illustrates the trajectories of several growth rates in the baseline scenario.

Having augmented the model with public capital, we now update our previous simulations (published in Konopczyński 2014) regarding tax rates and (private and public) spending on education. More importantly, however, the augmented model allows for simulating the effects of changes in the level of public investment into public capital.

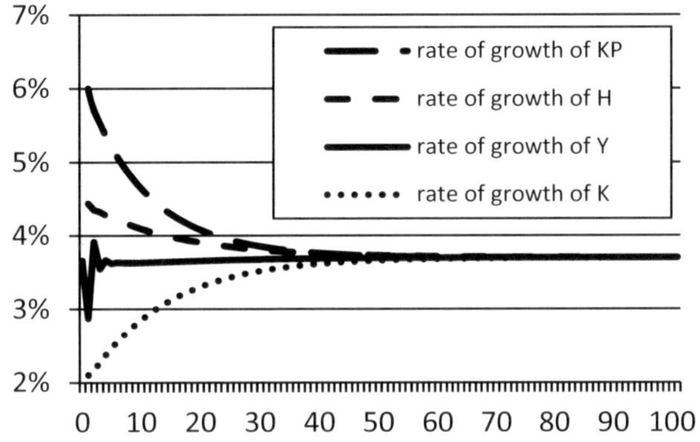

Figure 5. Convergence to a balanced growth path in the baseline scenario.

5. Selected tax-cut scenarios in Poland

As in Konopczyński (2014), let us consider two types of scenarios:

a) reducing a given tax rate by 1 or 5 percentage points (pp),
b) reducing all tax rates by 1 or 5 pp.

Table 2 contains the BGRs calculated under all these scenarios. In all cases, the economy grows faster (on the balanced growth path) than in the baseline scenario. To visualize the long-term (welfare) effects, we also include numbers indicating by how many percent GDP exceeds the baseline GDP after 30 years (in table 2, numbers in bold). These indicators are calculated as follows:

$$\textit{gain after 30 years} = \frac{Y(t=30)\ \textit{in selected scenario}}{Y(t=30)\ \textit{in the baseline scenario}} - 1\,. \qquad (54)$$

In each scenario, the tax rates are reduced at $t = 0$.

Unsurprisingly, the most favorable results are associated with the largest tax cuts, i.e., the scenario of reducing all tax rates by 5 pp. After 30 years, the GDP would be 10.2% higher than that under the baseline scenario. Table 3 shows some structural changes resulting from such a reduction of taxes.

Cutting all tax rates by 5 pp would reduce the overall tax burden from the recent 33.4% to 27.1% of the GDP, which would bring Poland much closer to the levels observed in the United States (approx. 25%), South Korea (26%) and Japan (27%). The immediate effect of the reduction in taxes would be an increase in private sector savings relative to the GDP (from 20.8% to 22.6%), an increase in investment (from 20.2% to 21.9% of the GDP), and an increase in private expenditures on education. The accelerated accumulation of both physical and human capital would shift the economy towards a higher balanced growth path. As a result, the BGR would increase by approximately 0.32 percentage points.

Notably, this scenario is associated with significant structural changes in the economy. Reduced tax receipts while maintaining 15.1% of the GDP for cash social transfers (primarily pensions) and 5.2% of the GDP for public expenditures on education would negatively affect public consumption expenditures. This gap would have to be (partially) offset by

Table 2. Simulation results for Poland - different tax cut scenarios

	1 pp reduction	5 pp reduction
τ_L	3.71% **0.4%**	3.77% **2.2%**
τ_K	3.71% **0.3%**	3.74% **1.3%**
τ_H	3.71% **0.4%**	3.77% **2.2%**
τ_C	3.73% **0.8%**	3.83% **4.1%**
reduction of all tax rates simultaneously	3.76% **1.9%**	4.02% **10.2%**

Table 3. The scenario of simultaneously reducing all tax rates by 5 pp.

the BGR and structural indicators (%)	baseline scenario	reduction of all tax rates by 5 pp
the BGR	3.70	4.02 (the effect after 30 years= +10.2%)
C/Y	60.4	65.4
T/Y	33.9	27.1
S/Y	20.8	22.6
I_K/Y	20.2	21.9
G_P/Y	3.3	3.3
G_E/Y	5.2	5.2
I_H/Y	0.65	0.70
K/Y	2.19	2.30
K_P/Y	0.43	0.41

increased consumption spending in the private sector. As a result of the tax cuts, this would occur naturally. Under the scenario presented in table 3, the share of private consumption of the GDP increases from 60.4% to 65.4%. This would bring the Polish economy structurally closer to that of the United States, where private consumption is approximately 70% of the GDP.

6. Selected scenarios of increasing public and private spending on education

This section contains an update of three scenarios discussed in section 8 of Konopczyński (2014):

A) the government increases public spending on education by 1 pp of the GDP at the expense of public consumption.

Table 4. Scenarios of increasing public and private spending on education

The BGR and structural indicators (%)	Baseline scenario $\gamma_E = 5.20\%$ $\gamma = 25.64\%$ $\psi = 3.10\%$	A Increase in public spending on education by 1 pp of GDP $\gamma_E = 6.20\%$	B Increase in private savings by 1 pp of GDP $\gamma = 26.80\%$ $\psi = 3,10\%$	C Increase in private spending on education by 1 pp of GDP $\gamma = 26.84\%$ $\psi = 7.54\%$
the BGR	3.70	4.00 GDP effect after 30 years **+8.2%**	3.89 GDP effect after 30 years **+5.8%**	4.00 GDP effect after 30 years **+8.3%**
C/Y	60.4	60.3	59.6	59.5
T/Y	33.9	33.9	33.7	33.8
S/Y	20.83	20.81	21.83	21.83
I_K/Y	20.18	20.17	21.15	20.18
G_P/Y	3.3	3.3	3.3	3.3
G_E/Y	5.2	6.2	5.2	5.2
I_H/Y	0.65	0.65	0.68	1.65
K/Y	2.19	2.12	2.25	2.13
K_P/Y	0.43	0.41	0.42	0.41

B) private sector savings increase by 1 pp of the GDP (at the expense of individual consumption), with an unchanged structure of investment expenditures (i.e., an unchanged ψ). As a result, private investment in physical and human capital increase by a total of 1 pp of the GDP.

C) private sector savings increase by 1 pp of the GDP (at the expense of individual consumption) and additional savings are spent solely on education (for this purpose, ψ has been appropriately amended). Private spending on education increases by 1 pp of the GDP at the expense of private consumption.

Table 4 presents the results.

The conclusions are similar to the results obtained in Konopczyński (2014). With respect to the BGR, all three scenarios significantly outperform the baseline scenario. However, the effect of additional spending on education (scenarios A and C) is stronger than the effect of a similar increase in private savings, with additional resources primarily spent on investments in physical capital (97%). It is clearly much better to spend the additional money on education rather than on physical capital. Moreover, comparing scenarios A and C shows that it is relatively unimportant whether the additional funds for education come from a reduction in public or private consumption.

7. The optimal structure of private investment

Investing in human capital (education) is of crucial importance for economic growth. However, as shown in section 2, the relationship between the BGR and the share parameter ψ (the share of private savings spent on education) cannot be established analytically. Therefore, using the baseline scenario as a benchmark, we calculated the BGR corresponding to a range of ψ. Figure 6 pres-

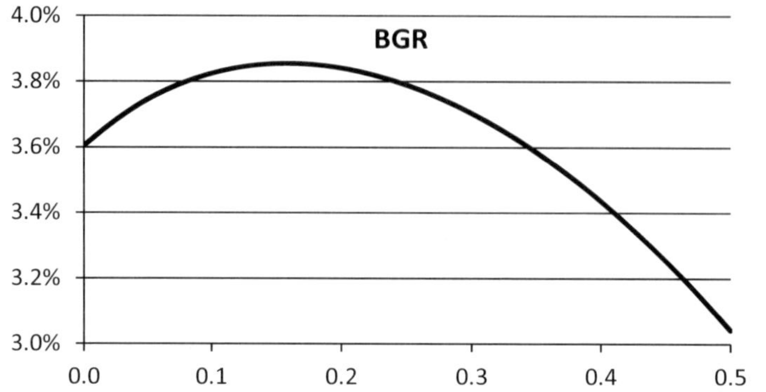

Figure 6. The BGR as a function of the share parameter ψ .

ents the results. The BGR reaches a maximum (3.855%) at $\psi = 16\%$. The current structure of private investment in Poland is far from optimal: households should spend 16% of their savings on education, rather than a mere 3.1%, as Eurostat reports. However, that private spending on education is underestimated in official statistics – a substantial share of it is classified as consumption (e.g., the cost of accommodation, travel, books, etc.).

8. Increasing investment in public capital

Table 5 presents the results of two scenarios:

D) increasing spending on public capital by 1 pp of the GDP at the expense of public consumption.

E) increasing spending on public capital by 1 pp of the GDP at the expense of public spending on education.

These scenarios yield some remarkable conclusions. First, if we assume that increasing expenditures on public capital requires a reduction in public spending elsewhere, these scenarios prove that it's better to cut public consumption rather than public spending on education.

Second, both scenarios significantly outperform the baseline scenario, so the stock of public capital in Poland is still too low. Note that, in both scenarios, the stock of public capital increases from the current level of 40% of the GDP (in 2013) to 52% in scenario D and 55% in scenario E. These scenarios would bring the Polish economy structurally closer to more developed countries, where usually this indicator is 40 to 60%, e.g., according to the IMF, in 2013 it was 63% in the United States, 60% in Italy, 51% in Canada and France, and a mere 35% in Germany. Notably, it was an outstanding 107% in Japan.

Third, it follows from scenario D that it's worth increasing investment in public capital at the cost of public consumption. This proposition is intuitive and does not require deeper analysis; however, it could be politically difficult. In contrast, scenario E implies something far less obvious (and politically controversial): it's worth transferring *certain parts of* public resources in Poland from education to public capital. As a result, the BGR increases significantly. Scenario E assumes that the size of this transfer is 1% of the GDP. We also generalized this scenario and investigated the results of different "shift parameters", from 0% to 2.5% of the GDP. Figure 7 presents the results. The BGR reaches a maximum (3.85%), if the Polish government shifts approx. 1.3% of the GDP from education to public investment. After 30 years, the GDP would be 8.1% higher than that under the baseline scenario.

Table 5. Scenarios of increasing investment in public capital

The BGR and structural indicators (%)	Baseline scenario $\gamma_P = 3.3\%$ $\gamma_E = 5.20\%$	D Shift from public consumption to public capital $\gamma_P = 4.30\%$ $\gamma_E = 5.20\%$	E Shift from spending on education to spending on public capital $\gamma_P = 4.3\%$ $\gamma_E = 4.20\%$
the BGR	3.70	4.20 GDP effect after 30 years **+16.9%**	3.84 GDP effect after 30 years **+6.8%**
C/Y	60.4	60.3	60.4
T/Y	33.9	34.0	33.9
S/Y	20.83	20.80	20.82
I_K/Y	20.18	20.15	20.17
G_P/Y	3.3	4.3	4.3
G_E/Y	5.2	5.2	4.2
I_H/Y	0.65	0.65	0.65
K/Y	2.19	2.08	2.16
K_P/Y	0.43	0.52	0.55

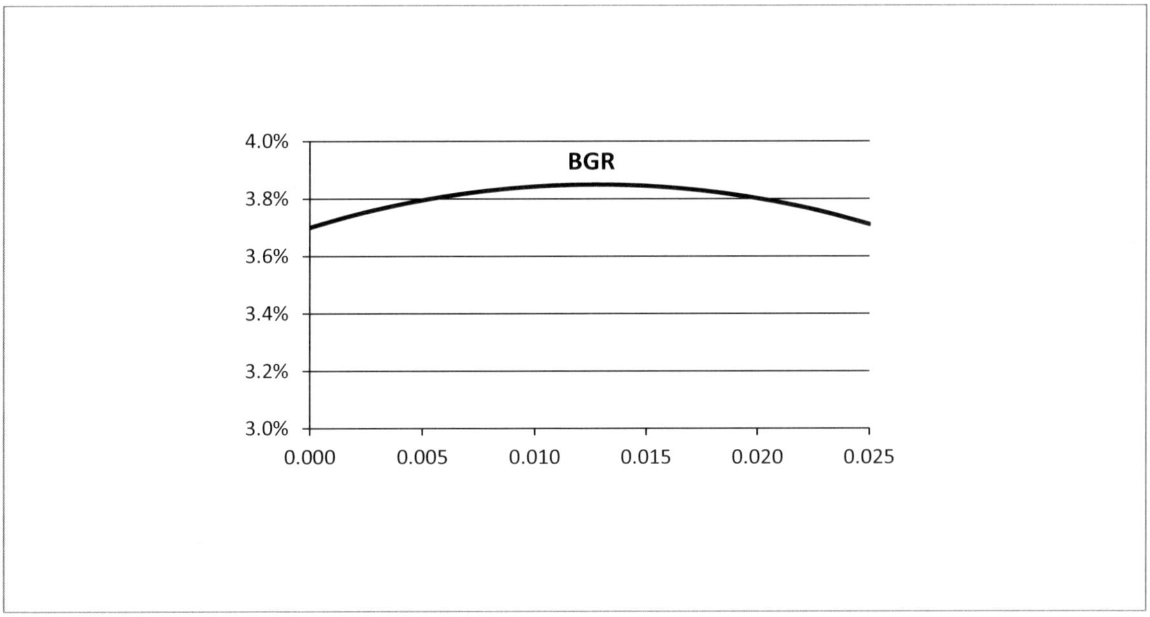

Figure 7. The BGR as a function of the "shift parameter" from public spending on education to public capital.

Table 6. Changes in tax rates accommodated by public capital or public education

The BGR and structural indicators (%)	Baseline scenario $\gamma_E = 5.20\%$ $\gamma_P = 3.3\%$	F The reduction of all tax rates by 1 pp at the cost of public capital $\gamma_E = 5.20\%$ $\gamma_P = 1.75\%$	G The reduction of all tax rates by 1 pp at the cost of public education $\gamma_E = 3.77\%$ $\gamma_P = 3.3\%$	H The increase in all tax rates by 1 pp to the benefit of public capital $\gamma_E = 5.20\%$ $\gamma_P = 4.79\%$	I The increase in all tax rates by 1 pp to the benefit of public education $\gamma_E = 6.61\%$ $\gamma_P = 3.3\%$
the BGR	3.70	2.68 GDP effect after 30 years **–26.0%**	3.26 GDP effect after 30 years **–10.1%**	4.35 GDP effect after 30 years **+22.5%**	4.04 GDP effect after 30 years **+9.3%**
C/Y	60.4	61.6	61.5	59.3	59.4
T/Y	33.9	32.3	32.4	35.3	35.3
S/Y	20.8	21.2	21.2	20.4	20.5
I_K/Y	20.2	20.6	20.5	19.8	19.8
G_P/Y	3.3	1.7	3.3	4.8	3.3
G_E/Y	5.2	5.2	3.8	5.2	6.6
I_H/Y	0.65	0.66	0.66	0.63	0.64
K/Y	2.19	2.52	2.34	2.01	2.08
H/Y	1.12	1.40	0.93	1.00	1.31
K_P/Y	0.43	0.26	0.45	0.57	0.41

9. Changes in tax rates accommodated by public capital or public education

All tax-cut scenarios presented in section 5 assume that lower tax revenue is accommodated by an appropriate reduction in public consumption. As public consumption does not have any productive effect in our model, it is evident that such tax cuts must result in a higher long-term growth rate (the BGR). In this section, we study less obvious scenarios in which reduced tax revenue does not reduce public consumption, rather, other components of public spending are reduced. In all scenarios in this section, we assume that the level of public consumption (as a share of the GDP) is at the baseline steady-state level of 10.3% of the GDP and the government budget is always balanced. Any changes in tax rates are accommodated by an appropriate adjustment in public investment, or public expenditures on education. Table 6 presents the results of four scenarios:

F) simultaneous reduction of all tax rates by 1 pp at the cost of public capital,

G) simultaneous reduction of all tax rates by 1 pp at the cost of public education,

H) simultaneous increase of all tax rates by 1 pp to the benefit of public capital,

I) simultaneous increase of all tax rates by 1 pp to the benefit of public education.

Scenarios F and G clearly show that a reduction in tax rates at the cost of government investment in public capital or education is a very bad idea. In both cases, the BGR drops significantly – due to a huge deterioration in public capital in scenario F (the long-term ratio of public capital to the GDP decreases from 43%

to 26%) and due to significant deterioration in human capital in scenario G (the long-term ratio of human capital to the GDP decreases from 1.12 to 0.93). Notably, although both scenarios F and G are very bad, G is the lesser of the two evils. Thus, if the government is forced to cut public expenditures, it should cut public consumption to benefit the economy – see section 5. If the government is forced to cut expenditures on public capital or education, it should choose the latter as the lesser evil. Although controversial, this conclusion is consistent with scenario E – see section 8 above.

Scenarios H and I are the reverse of F and G, respectively. Rather than cutting taxes, the government raises all tax rates by 1 percentage point in both scenarios and spends the extra revenue on public capital (scenario H) or education (scenario I). Both scenarios outperform the baseline scenario and it's better to invest the extra revenue into public capital rather than education. This conclusion is evidently controversial but is confirmed by scenario E.

10. Robustness of the results

As mentioned in section 7, private spending on education in Poland is likely underestimated in official statistics – a substantial share of it is classified as private consumption. In our calibration, we assumed that the official statistic on private spending on education is accurate, i.e., a mere 0.65% of the GDP. One might suspect that if this ratio was higher, the results and conclusions of this paper might be different. Fortunately, this is not the case. All our simulations (scenarios) are very robust to a change in the level of private spending on education. We verified this by assuming that the private sector spends twice as much on education, i.e., 1.3% of the GDP, and recalibrating the model and re-calculating the scenarios presented above. The baseline scenario and other scenarios were nearly unaffected. For example, a reduction in all tax rates by 5 pp. (table 2) would increase the BGR to 4.03% instead of 4.02%; in scenarios A and C, the BGR would be 3.96% instead of 4.00%; scenarios B and D would be completely unaffected; in scenario E, the BGR would be 3.88% instead of 3.84%; and in scenario F, the BGR would be 2.51% instead of 2.65%.

Summary

We have demonstrated that the economy converges towards a balanced growth equilibrium that is globally asymptotically stable. Despite the simplicity of the model, the balanced growth rate (BGR) can only be calculated numerically, as it requires solving a complex system of two non-linear equations.

The BGR is an increasing function of the rates of private savings, public transfers, public spending on education, and government spending on public capital. The BGR is also a decreasing function of tax rates on labor, human capital and consumption. The relationship between the BGR and the tax rate on capital income and the share coefficient (the percentage of private savings invested in education) are ambiguous. As in Konopczyński (2014), this ambiguity is a property of the theoretical model and implies that these relationships are dependent on specific parameter values. Thus, the relationship between the tax rate on capital and the BGR can be positive or negative depending on the parameter values. The relationship between the tax rate on capital income and the BGR may be positive or negative, depending on a particular set of values of parameters.

Our calibration of the model for Poland leads to several empirical conclusions, which can be summarized as follows. From 2000-2015, economic growth in Poland was primarily driven by a rapid increase in the stock of human capital (at 4.4% per annum) coupled with fast accumulation of public capital (approximately 6% per annum), and secondarily by the accumulation of private capital (2.1% annually). The baseline scenario suggests that Poland will converge to a balanced growth path with the GDP growing at the BGR of 3.7%. However, this rate depends on the long-term (average) values of certain instruments of fiscal policy. For example, reducing income and consumption tax rates by 5 percentage points would increase annual GDP growth by approximately 0.32 percentage points, which would result in a cumulative 10% increase in the GDP after 30 years relative to the baseline scenario (assuming current tax rates). Such a reduction in all tax rates would bring the Polish economy structurally closer to countries such as the United States or South Korea with significantly lower tax burdens (25-27% of the GDP compared to 33% in Poland) and much higher share of individual consumption (approximately 70% of the GDP compared to 60.4% in Poland).

Investing in human capital (education) is essential for economic growth. The conclusions are similar (though not identical) to the results obtained in the model without public capital. An increase in education expenditures by 1 percentage point of the GDP would have a similar long-term effect as simultaneously reducing all tax rates by 5 percentage points. The GDP growth rate would increase by approximately 0.3 percentage points. Whether the additional funding for education comes from a reduction in public or private consumption is irrelevant.

In Poland only 3% of private savings is currently spent on education. We show that, to maximize the BGR, it should be as high as 16%. Therefore, the current structure of private investment in Poland is far from the optimum. However, that private spending on education is likely underestimated in official statistics – a substantial share of it is classified as consumption.

Finally, despite a significant increase in the level of public capital over the last decade, it is still too low. Increasing spending on public capital by 1 pp of the GDP at the cost of public consumption would increase the BGR by 0.5 percentage points. Remarkably, even diverting resources from education to public infrastructure would slightly increase the BGR (by 0.14 percentage points).

Despite the relative methodological simplicity, our analysis provides qualitative and quantitative insights into the positive effects of investing in education and public capital on economic growth in Poland as well as the negative consequences of taxes. Our model captures certain 'stylized facts', especially the rapid accumulation of human capital over the past 2 decades coupled with an equally fast accumulation of public capital over the last decade. However, our model neglects certain phenomena that influence the Polish economy. For example, Poland experienced large inflows of FDI and portfolio investment. Considerable migration from Poland to other EU countries also occurred. These two phenomena are not included in our model and may presumably offset one another to some extent.

References

Agénor, P. R., & Yilmaz, D. V. (2011). The tyranny of rules: fiscal discipline, productive spending, and growth in a perfect foresight model. *Journal of Economic Policy Reform*, 14(1), 69-99. https://doi.org/10.1080/17487870.2010.503086

Arrazola, M., & de Hevia, J. (2004). More on the estimation of the human capital depreciation rate. *Applied Economic Letters*, 11(3), 145-148. https://doi.org/10.1080/1350485042000203742

Arrow, K. J. & Kurz, M. (1970). Public Investment, the Rate of Return and Optimal Fiscal Policy. Baltimore, MD: Johns Hopkins University Press

Barro, R. J., & Martin, X. S. I. (1992). Public Finance in Models of Economic Growth. *Review of Economic Studies*, 59(4), 645-661. https://doi.org/10.2307/2297991

Barro, R.J., & Martin, X. S. I. (2004). *Economic Growth. Second Edition.* Cambridge, MA: MIT Press.

Bucci, A., & Bo, Ch. (2011). On the interaction between public and private capital in economic growth. *Journal of Economics*, 106(2), 133-152. https://doi.org/10.1007/s00712-011-0239-3

Campbell, J., Diamond, P., & Shoven, J. (2001). Estimating the Real Rate of Return on Stocks Over the Long Term. Washington, DC: Social Security Advisory Board.

Chen, B. L., (2007). Factor taxation and labor supply in a dynamic one-sector growth model. *Journal of Economic Dynamics and Control*, 31(12), 3941-3964. https://doi.org/10.1016/j.jedc.2007.01.027

Cichy, K. (2008). Kapitał ludzki i postęp techniczny jako determinanty wzrostu gospodarczego [Human capital and technological progress as determinants of economic growth]. Warszawa: Instytut Wiedzy i Innowacji.

Dasgupta, D. (1999). Growth versus welfare in a model of nonrival infrastructure. *Journal of Development Economics*, 58(2), 359-385. https://doi.org/10.1016/s0304-3878(98)00127-8

Dhont, T., & Heylen, F. (2009). Employment and growth in Europe and the US – the role of fiscal policy composition. *Oxford Economic Papers*, 61(3), 538-565. https://doi.org/10.1093/oep/gpn034

Dobbs, R., Pohl, H., Lin, D-Y., Mischke, J., Garemo, N., Hexter, J.,..., Nanavatty, R. (2013). *Infrastructure productivity: how to save $1 trillion a year*. McKinsey Global Institute.

Easterly W., & Rebelo S. (1993). Fiscal Policy and Economic Growth. *Journal of Monetary Economics*, 32(3), 417-458.

Elmendorf, D. W., & Mankiw, N. G. (1998, March). Government Debt (Working Paper No. 6470). National Bureau of Economic Research. Available at https://ssrn.com/abstract=226215

Escobar-Posada, R. A., & Monteiro, G. (2015). Long-run growth and welfare in a two sector endogenous growth model with productive and non-productive government expenditure. *Journal of Macroeconomics*, 46, 218-234. https://doi.org/10.1016/j.jmacro.2015.09.008

Eurostat. (2010). *Taxation trends in the European Union - Data for the EU Member States, Iceland and Norway*. Retrieved from https://ec.europa.eu/taxation_customs/sites/taxation/files/resources/documents/taxation/gen_info/economic_analysis/tax_structures/2010/2010_full_text_en.pdf

Fisher, W. H., & Turnovsky, S. J. (1998). Public investment, congestion and private capital accumulation. *Economic Journal*, 108(447), 399-413. https://doi.org/10.1111/1468-0297.00294

Futagami, K., Morita, Y., & Shibata, A., (1993). Dynamic analysis of an endogenous growth model with public capital. *Scandinavian Journal of Economics*, 95(4), 607-625. https://doi.org/10.2307/3440914

Gupta, S., Kangur, A., Papageorgiou, C., & Wane, A. (2014). Efficiency-adjusted public capital and growth. *World Development*, 57, 164-178. https://doi.org/10.1016/j.worlddev.2013.11.012

International Monetary Fund. (2015, June). Making public investment more efficient. Retrieved from http://www.imf.org/external/np/pp/eng/2015/061115.pdf

International Monetary Fund. (2016). Investment and Capital Stock Dataset. Available at http://www.imf.org/external/np/fad/publicinvestment/

Kamps, C. (2006). New Estimates of Government Net Capital Stocks for 22 OECD Countries, 1960–2001. *IMF Staff Papers*, 53(1), 120–50.

Kollias, C., & Paleologou, S. M. (2013). Guns, highways and economic growth in the United States. *Economic Modelling*, 30, 449-455. https://doi.org/10.1016/j.econmod.2012.09.048

Konopczyński, M. (2014). How Taxes and Spending on Education Influence Economic Growth in Poland. *Contemporary Economics*, 8(3), 329-348. https://doi.org/10.5709/ce.1897-9254.149

Konopczyński, M. (2015). Optymalna polityka fiskalna w gospodarce otwartej w świetle teorii endogenicznego wzrostu gospodarczego [Optimal fiscal policy in an open economy in the light of the theory of endogenous growth]. Poznań: Wydawnictwo Uniwersytetu Ekonomicznego w Poznaniu.

Lee, Y., & Gordon, R. (2005). Tax structure and economic growth. *Journal of Public Economics*, 89(5-6), 1027-1043. https://doi.org/10.1016/j.jpubeco.2004.07.002

Mankiw, G. N., Romer, D., & Weil, D. N. (1992). A Contribution to the Empirics of Economic Growth. *Quarterly Journal of Economics*, 107(2), 407-437.

Manuelli, R., & Seshadri, A. (2005, June). *Human Capital and the Wealth of Nations*. Paper presented at the meeting of the Society for Economic Dynamics, Budapest, Hungary.

Marrero, G. A., & Novales, A. (2007). Income taxes, public investment and welfare in a growing economy. *Journal of Economic Dynamics and Control, 31*(10), 3348-3369. https://doi.org/10.1016/j.jedc.2006.10.007

Próchniak, M. (2013). To What Extent Is the Institutional Environment Responsible for Worldwide Differences in Economic Development. *Contemporary Economics*, 7(3), 17-38. https://doi.org/10.5709/ce.1897-9254.87

Romer, P. M. (1986). Increasing returns and long-run growth. *Journal of Political Economy* 94(5), 1002-1037. https://doi.org/10.1086/261420

Turnovsky, S. J. (1997). Fiscal Policy in a growing economy with public capital. *Macroeconomic Dynamics*, 1(3), 615-39. https://doi.org/10.1017/s1365100597004045

Turnovsky, S. J. (2004). The transitional dynamics of fiscal policy: long-run capital accumulation and growth. *Journal of Money, Credit, and Banking*, 36, 883-910. https://doi.org/10.1353/mcb.2004.0069

Turnovsky, S. J. (2009). *Capital Accumulation and Economic Growth in a Small Open Economy*. Cambridge, UK: Cambridge University Press.

Zhang, L., Ru, Y., & Li, J. (2016). Optimal tax structure and public expenditure composition in a simple model of endogenous growth. *Economic Modelling*, 59, 352-360. https://doi.org/10.1016/j.econmod.2016.08.005

Acknowledgements

This research has been supported by the Polish National Science Center; grant number 2017/25/B/HS4/02076. The author would like to thank two anonymous referees for their helpful suggestions.

Appendix

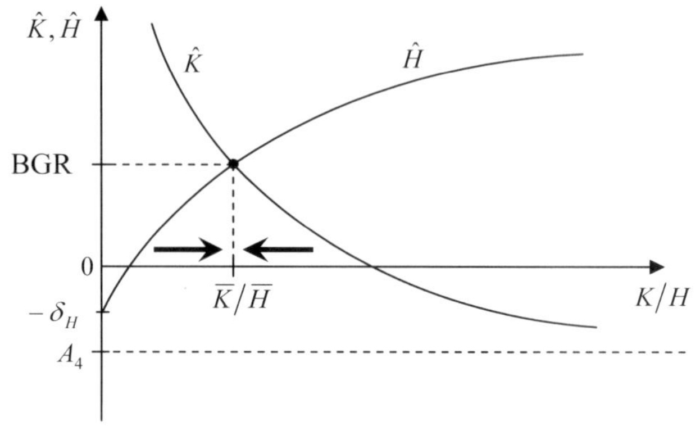

Figure A1. Graphs of the $\hat{K}(K/H)$ and $\hat{H}(K/H)$ functions

Proof of Proposition 1.
By definition, $P = bK_P/Y$, thus $\dot{P} = b\frac{\dot{K}_P Y - K_P \dot{Y}}{Y^2} = b\left(\frac{\dot{K}_P}{Y} - \frac{K_P}{Y}\hat{Y}\right)$. Recall that $\dot{K}_P = G_K - \delta_P K_P = \gamma_P Y - \delta_P K_P$; therefore, $\dot{P} = b\left(\gamma_P - \delta_P \frac{K_P}{Y} - \frac{K_P}{Y}\hat{Y}\right)$, which can be written in following equivalent form:

$$\dot{P} = b\gamma_P - (\hat{Y} + \delta_P)P. \tag{A0}$$

For any given (positive) value of b, δ_P, and $\hat{Y}$, equation (A0) constitutes a linear differential equation of the form $\dot{P} = f(P)$. Figure A0 presents the phase diagram of this equation. Regardless of the initial value of $P(t=0) > 0$, over time, $P \rightarrow \frac{b\gamma_P}{\hat{Y} + \delta_P}$.

Proof of Proposition 2.
Assume that $P = const. > 0$. This assumption allows for proceeding along the lines of the proofs of Propositions 1 and 2 in Konopczyński (2014). Recall that the rates of growth of private capital and human capital are given by equations (36) and (37). Let us determine the signs of all expressions that are marked with symbols A_i. Under the assumptions adopted regarding the signs and the values of tax rates, rates of savings, and other parameters, it can be shown that:

$$A_2, A_3, A_5, A_6 > 0,\ A_4 < 0 \text{ and } A_2 < 1,\ A_6 < 1. \tag{B1}$$

Note that, for a given (constant) value of P, we can treat $\hat{K}$ and $\hat{H}$ as functions of a single variable K/H. These functions are given by equations (36) and (37) and have identical properties to their counterparts in Konopczyński (2014). From (B1), the function $\hat{K}(K/H)$ is decreasing and strictly convex. Moreover, $\hat{K} \xrightarrow[K/H \to 0^+]{} +\infty$, and $\hat{K} \xrightarrow[K/H \to +\infty]{} A_4$. The function $\hat{H}(K/H)$ is increasing, strictly concave, $\hat{H}(K/H = 0) = -\delta_H$, and $\hat{H} \xrightarrow[K/H \to +\infty]{} +\infty$. The graphs of these functions are illustrated in figure A1. Due to the properties of these functions, there is exactly one point of intersection, i.e., there exists exactly one ratio $\overline{K}/\overline{H}$ for which $\hat{K} = \hat{H}$. The values of both functions at this point determine the balanced growth rate (the BGR). The balanced growth state is globally asymptotically stable, as shown in figure A1. In equilibrium, $\hat{K} = \hat{H}$, which, together with (3), implies that $\hat{Y} = \hat{K} = \hat{H}$.

We proved that, *for any given (constant) value of P*, the economy converges to the balanced growth state where $\hat{Y} = \hat{K} = \hat{H}$, which is unique and globally asymptotically stable. Proposition 1 implies that, along the BGR path, $P \rightarrow \frac{b\gamma_P}{\hat{Y} + \delta_p} = const.$ These two facts imply that there is a unique balanced growth equilibrium and that it is globally asymptotically stable. In the steady state:

$$\overline{P} = \frac{b\gamma_P}{\hat{Y} + \delta_p} = const. > 0 \tag{B0}$$

13

Classes in Maximizing Shareholders' Wealth: Irving Fisher's Theory of the Economic Organization in Corporate Financial Economics Textbooks

Tiago Cardao-Pito[1,2]

ABSTRACT Corporate financial economic programs are almost universally featured in economics and management degrees and, therefore, are an essential component of the culture-building process for current and future economists and managers. Nevertheless, these programs are not restricted to financial affairs. A survey of contemporary academic textbooks in corporate financial economics shows that these books are based on promoting Irving Fisher's (1906) specific theory of the organization, which advocates that organizations exist to create wealth for their owners/shareholders. This theory has three key premises. 1) The "correct" equity/stock prices are equal to future cash flows that are payable to the organizations' owners/shareholders. 2) The purpose of the firm and its managers is to maximize the value of the equity/share prices. c) Hence, their purpose is to maximize the cash flows (wealth) payable to owners/shareholders. None of these premises has been clearly demonstrated empirically. Yet, economic and business schools deliver lectures based on this rhetoric every year to thousands of students who will later hold influential roles in society.

KEY WORDS: financialisation, financial economics, finance, Irving Fisher, textbook, economic sociology

[1] ISEG, Universidade de Lisboa, Portugal; [2] Department of Accounting and Finance, University of Strathclyde, UK

Introduction

Academic programs in corporate finance are not just for lecturing and guiding current or future financial executives. Those programs target an entire community of economists, managers, sociologists, and others whose professional lives are connected to real-life organizations. For instance, both a Masters of Business Administration (MBA) student who is interested in sales and a Bachelors of Economics student who is interested in developmental economics will have to pass one or more courses related to corporate finance. Academic degrees in areas such as economics, management, and business administration at all levels of academia generally require at least one course in corporate finance. In his survey of the core curricula of MBA programs at top-ranked U.S. business schools, Navarro (2008) found that all programs included a course in corporate finance. Although often neglected, financial business education plays an important role

Correspondence concerning this article should be addressed to: **Tiago Cardao-Pito** ISEG, University of Lisbon, Rua Miguel Lupi, n.º 20. 1249-078 Lisboa. Portugal E-mail: tcp@iseg.ulisboa.pt

in legitimizing and discussing idealized decisions and actions (Hall & Appleyard, 2012). Indeed, as has been correctly pointed by Jakóbik (2011), theory related to the economy might be one relevant cause of economic crises. Therefore, within the context of corporate finance programs, this study addresses a key phenomenon with implications for economy and society.

Markets and economies depend on cultural meanings (Alexander, 2011). Academic programs in corporate finance may convey to students a specific meaning for organizations. The current paper demonstrates that those academic programs promote: 1) a specific theory of the organization, which defines that the 2) purpose of every organization is to maximize the wealth of their owners/shareholders and, thus, to promote societal financialization, a phenomenon that is generally studied in economic sociology. Societal financialization encompasses the growing importance of financial over nonfinancial activities as a profit source.

Each year, mainstream financial economics is widely lectured to thousands of talented young persons (Fourcade & Khurana, 2013; Navarro, 2008) who will later become top executives, public servants, researchers, politicians, or community leaders, or will perform other prominent societal roles. Some of these students will even join the corporate elite (Jung, 2014; Maclean, Harvey, & Chia 2012; Maclean, Harvey, & Kling, 2014; Mizruchi, 2013; Reed, 2012; Thomas, 1984; Zald, & Lounsbury, 2010). As suggested by Goshal (2005), flawed theories may harm good management practices. Short of learning about alternative theories and methods, students may become the most incisive ambassadors for a dogma of financialization. For these reasons, academic books and lectures in finance/financial economics are part of a relevant societal process that enhances the trajectory of contemporary societies towards financialization.

To elucidate this process, the current paper presents the results of a survey of a sample of leading textbooks on corporate finance taught at contemporary business and economic schools. The findings provide the first demonstration that textbooks in corporate finance/financial economics actively promote the financialization of contemporary societies, a phenomenon generally studied in economic sociology but not in corporate finance classes.

This article is organized as follows. In the next section, the paper presents a theoretical review of Irving Fisher's theory of the organization and its potential link to societal financialization. The third section describes the research questions, while the fourth section discusses the methodology and sample of academic textbooks in corporate finance that were studied in this paper. The fifth section presents the major findings obtained from this sample. The findings are discussed and conclusions are presented in the final section of the paper.

Theoretical Review

Irving Fisher's Theory of the Organization

During most of his life, Irving Fisher was a very popular and prominent American economist. However, his reputation was deeply disturbed by the post-1929 crisis and resulting economic contraction. Fisher had written that such a crisis would be highly unlikely (Allen, 1993; Fisher, 1929; Fox, 2009), and he lost a large amount of his own invested money when the stock market collapsed (Allen, 1993; Bryer, 2013; Dimand, 2007; Fox, 2009; Galbraith, 1977).

During his lifetime, Fisher's reputation and financial stability never fully recovered from those events (Allen, 1993; Bryer, 2013; Fox, 2010; Dimand, 2007; Galbraith, 1977).

Fisher's theory of organizational value and purpose was created many years before 1929. The procedures of valuating investments through projections of future cash flows and discount rates existed before Irving Fisher. For instance, they were used by Simon Stevin of Bruges as early as 1582 (Parker, 1968) and Bohm-Bawerk in 1903. However, Fisher was the first author to associate discounted cash flow methods to the overall market value of organizations (Fisher, 1882; 1906; 1929; 1930a; 1930b; Parker, 1968; Stigler, 1950). In Fisher's view of the firm, organizational value can be found by discounting projections of future cash flows payable to owners of financial securities. In other words, value is determined through predictions of how much cash will flow in the future to the owners of the capital, adjusted by a rate to correct for the temporary monetary worth (from a current-day perspective, inflation will depreciate the nominal worth of future cash flows). Frequently, this form of computation is called the net present value (NPV). Fisher's framework claims to describe prices and values. Cash flows generated in the future (they may go until eternity) discounted by some rate would be equal to an organization's value and would allow the identification of its "correct" stock prices. Accordingly, one would need to project the (unpredictable) future to compute the organizational value and utility functions, imagining future sales, costs, assets, liabilities, etc.

Mainstream economists praise Irving Fisher for being the first person to examine the measurability of the utility function and its relevance to demand theory (Miller, 1988; Stigler, 1950). Indeed, the utility function that is commonly used in contemporary mainstream economics can be traced back to Fisher's work. However, it is not the case that the discounted cash flow method was forgotten from Fisher's time until Modigliani and Miller's (1958) work. Other scholars used or discussed discounted cash flow models before Modigliani and Miller (e.g., Coase, 1952; Gort, 1951a, Gort, 1951b; Samuelson, 1937). Nonetheless, Modigliani, and Miller's (1958) article is often credited as the starting point for contemporary mainstream financial economics (e.g., Harris & Raviv, 1991; Myers, 2001; Titman, 2002). The only surviving author, Merton Miller, received the Prize in Economic Sciences in Memory of Alfred Nobel for this work in 1990.

It is puzzling, then, that Modigliani and Miller (1958) make no reference to Irving Fisher in their work. Only much later would Miller (1988, p. 103) assume that he and Modigliani had adopted Fisher's view of the firm, in which the corporation is a "black box" into which operating activities are placed. Miller explains that he and Modigliani opted for:

Irving Fisher's view of the firm—now the standard one in [mainstream] financial economics, but then just becoming known—[that] impounds the details of technology, production, and sales in a 'black box' and focuses on the underlying net cash flow. The firm for Fisher was just an abstract engine transforming current consumable resources, obtained by issuing securities, into future consumable resources payable to the owners of the securities (Miller, 1988, p. 103).

Moreover, Fisher was mostly concerned with capital and not directly concerned with organizations. Hence, Fisher had direct views of capital, revenue, wealth, and utility, but did not exposit a direct view of organizations. However, the Fisherian view can be used to present a concrete theory to explain why organizations exist, and a Fisherian view of organizations can be developed (Cardao-Pito, 2017a).

Fisherian notions of the organization and corporate value are, in themselves, rhetorical claims that are used to defend the idea that the purpose of the firm is to maximize shareholder value. This relationship is built through a syllogism involving three premises:

1. "Correct" stock prices are equal to the future cash flows that are payable to the owners/shareholders of the firm.
2. The purpose of firm and its managers is to maximize the value of share prices.
3. Hence, one can conclude that the purpose of the firm is to maximize the cash flows (wealth) that are payable to owners/shareholders, and that firms must be organized towards this primary goal.

These three premises are dogmatic in nature because they have never been empirically demonstrated. For instance, there is no systematic evidence that stock prices are equal to the future cash flows that are payable to owners/shareholders (Bougen & Young, 2012; Callen, 2015; Mouck, 1992; Shiller, 1981; 1984). Furthermore, using quantitative tools to suggest the "correct" stock prices and firm values may give a pretense of accuracy to estimates that are highly speculative and uncertain (Cardao-Pito, 2012).

Fisherian Ideas and Promotion of the Shareholder Value View

According to Cardao-Pito (2017a; 2017b), Fisher's view of organizations provides theoretical support for the financialization of contemporary societies, which refers to the growing importance of financial activities as a source of profits (e.g., Azkunaga, San-Jose, & Urionabarrenetxea, 2013; Baud & Duran, 2012; Bay & Schinckus, 2012; Blasiak, 2010; Cardao-Pito, 2017a; Davis, 2009; Epstein, 2005; Falkowski, 2011; Hiss, 2013; Krippner, 2005; 2011; Milberg, 2008; Stockhammer, 2008; Zwan, 2014). At the core of financialization is the idea that organizations should be managed as though maximizing the shareholders' financial wealth is the only possible or legitimate goal (e.g., Aglieta, 2000; Boyer, 2005; Bigio, 2010; Brocklehurst, Grey, & Sturdy, 2010; Davis, 2009; Fiss & Zajac, 2004; Goldstein, 2012; Goutas & Lane, 2009; Jones & Nisbet, 2011; Lazonick & O'Sullivan, 2000; Mizruchi, 2013; Morgan & Takahashi, 2002; Prechel & Morris, 2010; Stockhammer, 2008, Tengblad, 2004; Thompson & Harley, 2007; Tomaskovic-Devey & Lin, 2011; Zorn, 2004; Zwan, 2014). However, it is not clear how societal financialization and shareholder value postulates ever became so widely accepted within the corridors of power (Allon & Redden, 2012; Montgomerie & Williams, 2009; Cardao-Pito, 2017a). As noted by Davis (2009, p. 87), what would have sounded like a radical provocation in the 1970s—that firms exist mainly to maximize shareholders' wealth—had become the "common sense of corporate America (and other countries) by the 1990s". Furthermore, these findings show that whereas organizational theory seems averse to the problematization of its core research object—namely, the organization (Lopdrup-Hjorth, 2015)—a very persuasive albeit feeble theory of the organization is being promoted in business and economic schools.

Thus, the current paper contributes to the study of conditions that enhance the process of financialization. In recent decades, leading business and economic schools may have spread a creed of financialization through their programs in corporate finance/financial economics that are yearly lectured to thousands of students.

Research Questions

This research project pursues three research questions. The first question regards whether Fisher's view of organizations is found in corporate finance textbooks. Modigliani and Miller (1958) are generally credited with launching the field of corporate financial economics (e.g., Harris & Raviv, 1991; Myers, 2001; Titman, 2002), but Fisher's view precedes their work by many decades. The discovery that these textbooks use the Fisherian view would elucidate the origins of a very influential economic theory and would demonstrate that corporate finance textbooks are not merely about financial decisions (i.e., because they would be promoting a theory about organizational purpose). The second research question concerns Cardao-Pito's (2017a; 2017b) hypothesis that the Fisherian framework argues that the purpose of organizations is to maximize the wealth of owners/shareholders, which, in turn, is a key component of the financialization of contemporary societies. This study investigates whether corporate finance textbooks explicitly state that an organization's purpose is to maximize shareholder/owner wealth. The answer to this question will provide evidence to support or refute Cardao-Pito's (2017a; 2017b) hypothesis. The third research question regards how intensely textbooks utilize the Fisherian view. The research will examine whether textbooks provide alternative theoretical explanations to the Fisherian view in describing the purpose of organizations.

Methodology and Sample

Methodology

The study will employ two main technologies of qualitative inquiry: survey and qualitative content analysis. In the survey methodology, a sample is used to make inferences about a population (Cardao-Pito, 2016; Sapsford, 2007; Scheuren, 2004). In this study, the population comprises corporate finance classes that are lectured at business and economic schools around the world. Inferences about this population will be made through qualitative content analysis of the course textbooks as the sample. By drawing inferences from a sample of textbooks, rather than directly questioning lecturers or students via questionnaires or the Internet, this study will avoid some common problems in survey research (e.g., issues of nonresponse or bias). Inferences produced in this paper assume that the textbook contents accurately reflect the contents of lectures made by the books' authors, who are either invited or tenure-track faculty in finance/financial economics. For example, Stephen Ross, the author of one textbook in the sample (Ross, Westerfield, & Jaffe, 2004), is a professor of financial economics at MIT. This research assumes that the content of his corporate finance course aligns with the content of his textbook. The same assumption applies to the lectures of authors of other textbooks in the sample.

Content analysis is a research strategy for making inferences by objectively and systematically identifying specific characteristics of messages (Holsti, 1969; Krippendorff, 1980; Stemler, 2001; Tipaldo, 2014). This research strategy employs a systematic and replicable technique for condensing many words of text into fewer content categories based on explicit coding rules (Berelson, 1952; Krippendorff, 1980; Weber,

1990; Stemler, 2001). For the current study, coding was produced to address the three research questions presented in the previous section. Content analysis can be used to obtain reproducible results for other researchers who investigate the same sample (i.e., corporate finance textbooks). The aim of this study is to achieve trustworthy findings through credibility, dependability, conformability, transferability, and authenticity (Elo, Kääriäinen, Kanste, Pölkki, Utriainen, & Kyngäs, 2014).

Sample of Academic Textbooks in Corporate Finance

Criteria for inclusion of a textbook in the sample are as follows. First, the book must be an academic textbook in the English language that covers the subject of corporate finance. Most of the textbooks in the sample have exam-type exercises at the end of each chapter. Second, the book must be a contemporary edition (published in the 21st century). Third, to avoid redundancy, the sample should only contain one book by each author. The sample was built by using Amazon (www.amazon.com) and academic libraries.

The sample encompassed 36 textbooks written by 65 different authors. A search on Amazon demonstrates that this sample is much smaller than the population of all textbooks about corporate finance written in English and currently lectured at economic and business schools. Appendix A identifies the sample books. These books have three types of authors. Type 1 authors are *faculty members at top-100 business and economic schools, as ranked by Financial Times' 2013 Global MBA ranking*. These 22 authors (33.8% of all authors) include a subset of authors who are associated with schools ranked in the top 10, such as London Business School (University of London), MIT, Wharton School of Business (University of Pennsylvania), and INSEAD. Type 2 authors are *faculty members at business and economic schools other than those described in Type 1*. This group of 31 authors (47.6%) still reaches relevant audiences of students in preeminent schools around the world, such as the Norwegian University of Science and Technology, London School of Economics and Political Science, California Institute of Technology, Leeds School of Business, and others. Type 3 authors are *consultants/investment advisors*. These 12 authors (18.5%) are regularly invited to lecture at universities, and their books are included in academic libraries.

The sample contains nine books that were among the 20 bestselling "corporate finance" books on Amazon in December 2013. The number of books in this category was limited by the criterion of not including more than one book by any one author in the sample. Several authors have multiple books among the top 20 bestsellers in corporate finance (e.g., Brealey, Myers, 2003; Ross, Westerfield, & Jaffe, 2004). These nine bestselling books can be seen as leading books in the field. It can be assumed that these nine books are not only used by their authors but by academic programs at many universities around the world. Five books in the sample were ranked between the top-21 and top-50 bestselling books. Another 22 books were not featured among the top-50 bestselling books in corporate finance on Amazon as of December 2013; however, this fact does not mean that they do not reach substantial audiences.

All books in the sample were recently published in the 21st century. However, it would be incorrect to situate these books only in the 21st century, as editions of some of the leading books have been published since the 1980s. As reported in Table 1, Brealey and Myers (2003) is the 7th edition of a book that was first published in 1981. Likewise, Ross, Westerfield, and Jaffe (2004) is the 7th edition of a book that was initially published in 1988. Given the longevity of these books, they cannot be considered as mere management fads or sets of buzzwords, as studied by Cluley (2013), Sorge and Witteloostuijn (2004), or Abrahamson and Fairchild (1999).

Findings

Corporate Finance Textbooks are based upon Fisher's Theoretical Concept of Organizational Value and Market Price

Regarding the first research question, the findings in Table 2 show that all of the sample books (mean = 1, standard deviation [SD] = 0) promote the discounted cash flow model to explain firm valuation and market prices, ideas that were introduced by Irving Fisher (1882; 1906; 1929; 1930a; 1930b) and reintroduced to financial economics by Franco Modigliani and Merton Miller (1958). The number of chapters used to explain Fisher's theoretical concept varies from book to book,

Table 1. Example of the longevity of two successful books in Corporate Finance

Authors	1st Edition	2nd Edition	3rd Edition	4th Edition	5th Edition	6th Edition	7th Edition
Brealey and Myers	1981	1984	1988	1991	1996	2000	2003
Ross, Westerfield and Jaffe	1988	1990	1993	1996	1999	2002	2004

Table 2. Analysis of the first research question: Are the books based upon Fisher's concept of organization value and market price?

Type of book	N	Mean	Standard Deviation	Minimum	Maximum
Books based on Fisher's framework	36	1.000	0	1	1
Number of book chapters used to explain Fisher's concept of value and market price	36	5.722	2.146	1	10
Does the book identifies Fisher as the author of value and market price concept?	36	0.194	0.401	0	1

ranging from 1 to 10 chapters (mean = 5.722, SD = 2.146 chapters).

These findings confirm that the books and the academic programs supported by these books are based on Irving Fisher's concept of organizations. Hence, although the genesis of contemporary corporate finance theory is generally attributed to Modigliani and Miller (1958) (e.g., Harris & Raviv, 1991; Myers, 2001; Titman, 2002), this reference is not correct. Only a relatively small proportion of the sample books acknowledge Irving Fisher as the author of the subjacent notions of the firm and firm value (mean = 0.194). The other books take these concepts as a given. The few books that do reference Fisher as the conceptual author do so mostly in footnotes or "further recommended reading" sections. This elimination of original sources may be regarded as rhetorically powerful because it gives students the erroneous impression of consensus about Fisherian concepts, such as the meanings of NPV and corporate value and, as shown in the next section, the purpose of corporations.

Corporate Finance Textbooks Explicitly State that an Organization's Purpose Is to Maximize the Wealth of Shareholders/Owners

Most books in the sample are not satisfied with merely *implying* that maximizing shareholder value must be the primary purpose of every organization. Indeed, 0.75 (75%) of all books in the sample (SD: 0.439) deliver a written statement in the first two chapters that the purpose of every firm must be to maximize shareholders' value (wealth), and that this goal is superior to any other possible goal for the firm. It seems reasonable to assume that this same statement is reproduced by lecturers in classrooms from the first or second week of classes. Table 3 gives evidence of these statements from bestselling books in corporate finance.

The 0.25 of all textbooks that do not make similar specific claims in the introductory chapters convey the same ideas by adopting the Fisherian concept of firm value. On the basis of this information, we can identify an explanation for the rapid diffusion of a theoretical background that supports financialization of contemporary societies.

Major Themes Addressed in the Sample Books

To complement the answers to the two previous research questions, Figure 1 describes the major themes

Table 3. Analysis of the first research question: Are the books based upon Fisher's concept of organization value and market price?

Book	Quote
Brealey and Myers (2003, p. 5)	*"As we will see in the next chapter, the fundamental financial objective of the firm is to maximize the value of the cash invested in the firm by its stockholder. "*
Ross, Westerfield and Jaffe (2005, p. 15)	*"It is necessary to precisely identify who controls the corporation. We shall consider the set-of-contracts viewpoint. This viewpoint suggests the corporate firm will attempt to maximize shareholder's wealth by taking actions that increase the current value per share of existing stock (shares) of the firm."*
Berk and DeMarzo (2014, p. 10)	*"In theory, the goal of a firm should be determined by the firm's owners. A sole proprietorship has a single owner who runs the firm, so the goal of a sole proprietorship are the same as the owner's goal. But in organizational forms with multiple owners, the appropriate goal of the firm – and thus of its managers – is not as clear. Many corporations have thousands of owners (shareholders). Each owner is likely to have different interests and priorities. Whose interests and priorities determine the goals of the firm? Later in the book we will examine this question with more detail. However, you might be surprised to learn that the interests of shareholders are aligned for many, if not most, important decisions. That is because regardless of their own personal financial position and stage in life, all the shareholders will agree that they are better off if management makes decisions that increase the value of their shares. "*
Adair (2011, p. 17)	*"The major goal of a corporation's financial manager should be to maximize the value per share of the existing stock, though 'maximizing shareholder wealth' or 'maximizing stock price' are other common ways to state this same goal. As we will see, this goal also motivates the capital budget decision rules that we have discussed briefly in the last chapter – firms will only accept projects if they add [shareholder] value to the firm. "*
Damodaran (2001, p. 11–12)	*"In the introductory chapter, we noted that the objective in corporate finance is to maximize the value of the firm. Investment, financing, and dividend decisions, we stated, should be directed towards this objective. In this chapter, we recast this objective more narrowly. To see why, consider how a firm, especially one that is publicly traded, is structured. The stockholders of the firm hire managers to run the firm for them. Managers make the decisions on which investments to take, how to finance them, and much to return to stockholders. The firm borrows money either from banks or issuing bonds; these lenders enter into agreements with the firm, specifying what assets the firm will offer as security on the borrowing and what the firm can and cannot do in the future periods. Although the firm includes both equity investors and lenders, we could argue that the lenders can protect themselves contractually and that managers should therefore focus on maximizing the wealth of those who hired them in the first place – the stockholders. Thus, the objective is narrowed from maximizing firm value to maximizing stockholder value or stockholder wealth."*

addressed in at least one specific chapter in the sample books. All of the books have at least one chapter introducing mainstream financial economics and another chapter explaining the Fisherian model for valuating the firm (i.e., NPV framework). All of the books have at least one chapter discussing the relationship between return and risk, which can be simplified as the relationship between the projection of future cash flows and discount rates in the Fisherian view. Almost all of the books (0.97) use those tools to make predic-

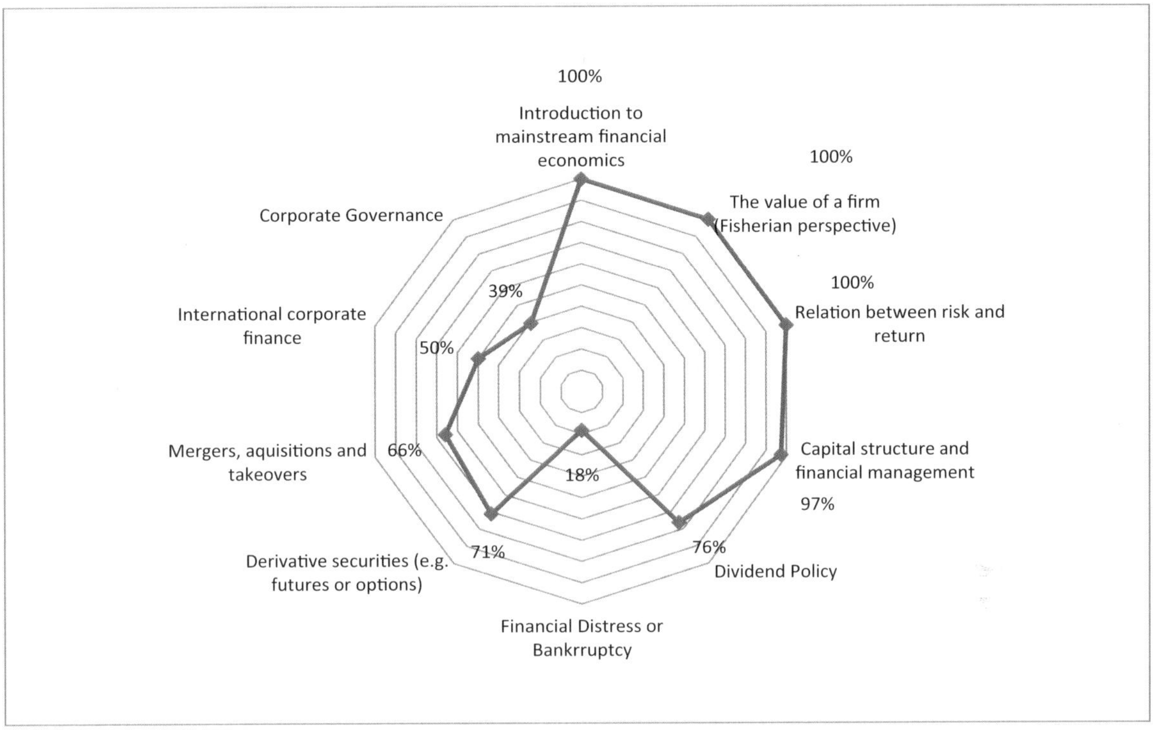

Figure 1. Major themes addressed in the sample books with at least one specific chapter

tions about the capital structure of firms, which are entirely based on the NPV concept. Moreover, 0.76 of the books use the same tools and theories to give directions about the dividends and other payments that firms ought to pay to their owners/shareholders.

Several of the books have chapters that address other interconnected topics that can be addressed within the Fisherian framework. The theme of derivative securities (e.g., options and future contracts) is increasingly popular, with 0.71 of all books dedicating at least one chapter to this concept. Derivative securities are generally used to develop the Fisherian valuation of firm but with slightly more complicated mathematical formulas than are typically associated with this type of securities.

A chapter discussing firm mergers, acquisitions, and takeovers through a Fisherian lens is included in 0.66 of all books. These operations are typically considered as good choices when the Fisherian NPV is positive and poor choices otherwise. Half (0.50) of the books have a chapter discussing issues in international corporate finance, noting that currency exchange and other international risks affect the Fisherian projection of future cash flows and discount rates. Additionally, 0.39 of all books address the issue of corporate governance, generally from the viewpoint of owners/shareholders. Although the sample books are about corporate finance, only 0.18 of them include a specific chapter about financial distress and bankruptcy, important preoccupations for financial managers of real-life firms. Indeed, the risk of bankruptcy and lack of solvency could be the most relevant risks that financial managers face (Broll, Sobiech, & Wahl, 2012). However, these themes are addressed only at some length within other chapters.

Corporate Finance Textbooks Ignore Alternative Theoretical Explanations to the Fisherian View of Organizational Purpose

As described in Table 3, the sample books do not make connections with other social sciences, treating mainstream financial economics as though it were sufficient to explain all existing economic phenomena. Although all of these books were published recently, none of them has even one specific chapter

Table 4. Analysis of the Third research question: Do the Textbooks Provide Alternative Theoretical Explanations to the Fisherian View Regarding Organizational Purpose?

	Does the book have at least a chapter related to:	N	Mean	Standard Deviation	Minimum	Maximum
1	Economic sociology	36	.000	.000	0	0
2	Other social sciences	36	.028	.167	0	1
3	Behavioral economics/finance	36	.194	.401	0	1
4	Discussing limits of Fisher's theoretical concepts	36	.083	.280	0	1
5	Alternative valuation methods	36	.472	.506	0	1

that presents or discusses links to economic sociology where organizational studies would be included. Hence, these books miss the phenomenon of societal financialization that is generally studied in economic sociology. One should not expect to find either classic or contemporary theories about organizations in these books—apart, of course, from the Fisherian view of organizations. Only one book makes connections to other social sciences (0.028), namely the study of the law, but that anomaly might be because its author is a faculty member at New York Law School.

In 0.194 of books, at least one chapter is dedicated to behavioral economics. This field can be considered as a variation of mainstream economics, in which the Fisherian utility function is modified by behavioral, psychological, environmental, or other factors. Nearly half (0.472) of the sample books have a chapter comparing the Fisherian tools for firm valuation with other traditional, ratio-based methods. However, all of these books conclude that the NPV framework is, by far, the best method.

Only 0.083 of books contain a specific chapter addressing the limitations of Fisherian notions, such as whether they might be ethically questionable or problematic to interests of other corporate stakeholders (e.g., customers, workers, suppliers, communities, governments, etc.). However, even those few books that mention ethics are very far from dismissing the Fisherian notions as highly unethical.

Finally, no book in the sample includes any other theory to explain the purpose of organizations other than the Fisherian concept. In this regard, the sample exhibits a high degree of homogeneity. Although many business schools have endeavored to include programs in ethics in their broad curricula, they increasingly risk creating a gap between their upbeat rhetoric around ethics education and their actual MBA curriculum (Rasche, Gilbert, & Schedel, 2012). These findings exemplify the concrete case of programs in corporate finance.

Conclusion

Corporate finance classes are currently included in most programs awarding degrees in management or economics. Hence, they are part of the culture-building process of future and current managers and economists. We must not ignore the organizational theory that is being conveyed to students in those classes. Given the isolation of academic disciplines at contemporary universities, one could be wrongly persuaded that finance classes are merely studying and discussing financial decisions.

This paper demonstrates that the origin of contemporary financial economic programs lays not in Modigliani and Miller (1958), but in Irving Fisher's view of the organization (Fisher, 1882; 1906; 1929; 1930a; 1930b). Furthermore, this study shows that academic programs in corporate finance/financial economics are actively conveying a specific organizational theory to students, which may have important consequences for how students perceive organizations. This theory tells students that the only stakeholders who are really relevant to organizations are the owners/shareholders. This observation is relevant for business schools. For instance, suppose that a certain school is trying to implement a program in business ethics and social responsibility to alert and teach students about an important theme for organizational activities and responsible management. The school must be aware that lecturers in corporate finance classes are promoting a creed of shareholder value to the same students.

In corporate finance classes, the Fisherian formula that is used seems straightforward to lecture in classrooms. It has three premises: 1) "correct" stock prices are equal to future cash flows that are payable to owners/shareholders, and 2) the purpose of firm and its managers is to maximize the value of share prices. Therefore, 3) the purpose of the firm is to maximize cash flows payable to owners/shareholders, and firms must be organized towards this primary goal. Although none of these premises has been clearly demonstrated empirically, they seem to be lectured as dogma.

The textbooks in this sample generally make no connection to other social sciences, contradictory findings, or counterarguments. The Modigliani-Miller-Fisher framework is lectured in the form of "practical applications" (i.e., of increasing shareholder value), with exam-type exercises at the end of each chapter. The dogmatic approach by which these textbooks express their message is of special relevance because their underlying organizational theory is based upon premises that have never been clearly proven. If none of those premises is true, then the entire theory that supports maximizing shareholder value collapses. The same implications apply to the financialization of contemporary societies. Corporate finance textbooks must, at minimum, raise the possibility that these three premises might not be correct.

We may need a new commitment to rigor and inquiry, and may need to challenge key assumptions of the canon embraced by business and economic schools (Montgomerie & Williams 2009; Samuelson, 2006). Problems studied in corporate finance might rank among the most important questions in economics and management. How can an organization progress without adequate management of its financial sources? What activities should an organization invest in? How do markets function and react to firms' activities? Should an organization pay more, less, or no dividends, or alternatively make more, less, or no reinvestments? These examples illustrate just a few of the many fundamental questions studied in finance. One must not confuse the importance of such financial questions with the domain of answers containing the Modigliani-Miller-Fisher framework. Scholars who are not entrenched in mainstream economics must try to address these same important questions.

References

Abrahamson, E., & Fairchild, G. (1999). Management fashion: Lifecycles, triggers, and collective learning processes. *Administrative Science Quarterly, 44*(4), 708-740.

Adair, T. (2011). *Corporate finance demystified.* NYC, NY: Mcgraw-Hill.

Aglieta, M. (2000). Shareholder value and corporate governance: Some tricky questions. *Economy and Society, 29*(2), 146-159.

Allen, R. (1993). *Irving Fisher: A biography.* Cambridge, MA: Blackwell.

Azkunaga, J. A., San-Jose, L., & Urionabarrenetxea, S. (2013). The impact of financial globalization and financialization on the economy in the current crisis through banking corporate governance. *Contemporary Economics, 7*(3), 79-94.

Alexander, J. C. (2011). Market as narrative and character: For a cultural sociology of economic life. *Journal of Cultural Economy, 4*(4), 477-488.

Allon, F., & Redden, G. (2012). The global financial crisis and the culture of continual growth. *Journal of Cultural Economy, 5*(4), 375-390.

Baud, C., & Durand, C. (2012). Financialisation, globalization and the making of profits by leading retailers. *Socio Economic Review, 10,* 241-266.

Bay, T., & Schinckus, C. (2012). Critical Finance Studies: An Interdisciplinary Manifesto. *Journal of Interdisciplinary Economics, 24,* 1-6.

Berelson, B. (1952). *Content Analysis in Communication Research.* Glencoe, Ill: Free Press.

Berk, J. B., & DeMarzo, P. M. (2014). *Corporate finance.* London, UK: Pearson.

Bigio, J. E. (2010). Reforming the European scene. *Contemporary Economics, 4*(3), 5-22.

Blasiak, W. (2010). The global economic crisis and the global accumulation of capital. *Contemporary Economics, 4*(2), 35-51.

Bohm-Bawerk, E. (1903). *Recent Literature on Interest 1884-1899.* NYC, New York: Macmillan.

Bougen, P., & Young, J. (2012). Fair value accounting: Simulacra and simulation. *Critical Perspectives on Accounting, 23,* 390–402.

Boyer, R. (2005). From shareholder value to CEO power: The paradox of the 1990s. *Competition and Change, 9*(1), 7-47.

Brealey, R., & Myers, S. (2003). *Principles of corporate finance*. NYC, NY: Mcgraw-Hill.

Bryer, R. (2013). Americanism and financial accounting theory – Part 3: Adam Smith, the rise and fall of socialism, and Irving Fisher's theory of accounting. *Critical Perspectives on Accounting, 24*(7-8), 572–615.

Brocklehurst, M., Grey, C. & Sturdy, A. (2010). Management: The work that dares not speak its name. *Management Learning, 41*(1), 7-19.

Broll, U., Sobiech, A. & Wahl, J. E. (2012). Banking firm, equity and value at risk. *Contemporary Economics, 6*(4), 50-53.

Callen, J. L. (2015). A selective critical review of financial accounting research. *Critical Perspectives on Accounting, 26,* 157-167.

Cardao-Pito, T. (2012). Intangible flow theory. *American Journal of Economics and Sociology, 71*, 328-353.

Cardao-Pito, T. (2016a). Survey methods in heterodox economic research. In F. Lee, B. Cronin (Eds.), *Handbook of research methods and applications in heterodox economics* (pp. 110-134). London, UK: Edward Elgar.

Cardao-Pito, T. (2016b). A law for the social sciences regarding us human beings. *Journal of Interdisciplinary Economics, 28*(2), 202-229.

Cardao-Pito, T. (2017a). Fisher-Modigliani-Miller organisational finance theory and the financialisation of contemporary societies. Manuscript in preparation.

Cardao-Pito, T. (2017b). Organizations as producers of operating product flows to members of society. *Sage Open, 7*(3), 1-18.

Cluley, R. (2013). What makes a management buzzword buzz? *Organization Studies, 341*(1), 33-43.

Coase, R. (1952). Business Organisation and the Accountant. The Accountant, October-December. Reprinted in shortened form in Buchanan. J. M. and Thirlby, G. F.

(Eds.), L.S.E. Essays on Cost (pp. 95-132). London, UK: Weidenfeld and Nicolson.

Damodaran, A. (2001). *Corporate finance: Theory and practice*. New York, NY: Wiley.

Davis, G. (2009). Managed by the markets. Oxford, UK: Oxford University Press.

Dimand, R. (2007). Irving Fisher and financial economics: The equity premium puzzle, the predictability of stock prices, and intertemporal allocation under risk. *Journal of the History of Economic Thought, 29*(02), 153-166.

Elo, S., Kääriäinen, M., Kanste, O., Pölkki, T., Utriainen, K., & Kyngäs, H. (2014). Qualitative content analysis: A focus on trustworthiness. *SAGE Open, 4*(1), https://doi.org/10.1177/2158244014522633

Epstein, G. (2005). Introduction: Financialization and the world economy. In G. Epstein (Ed.), *Financialization and the world economy* (pp. 3-16). Northampton, UK: Edward Elgar.

Falkowski, M. (2011). Financialization of commodities. *Contemporary Economics, 5*(4), 4-17.

Fisher, I. (1892[1925]). *Mathematical investigations in the theory of value and prices*. New Haven, Connecticut: Yale University Press.

Fisher, I. (1906). *The nature of capital and income.* NYC, NY: Macmillan.

Fisher, I. (1929, December 30). Will stocks stay up in 1929? *New York Herald Tribune*, pp. 28-29.

Fisher, I. (1930a.) *The rate of interest.* NYC, NY: Macmillan.

Fisher, I. (1930b). *The theory of interest.* NYC, NY: Macmillan.

Fiss, P., & Zajac, E. (2004) The diffusion of ideas over contested terrain: The nonadoption of a shareholder value orientation among German firms. *Administrative Science Quarterly, 49*(4), 501-534.

Fourcade, M., & Khurana, R. (2013). From social control to financial economics: the linked ecologies of economics and business in twentieth century America. *Theory and Society, 42*(2), 121–159.

Fox, J. (2009). *Myth of the rational market*. NYC, NY: Harper Business.

Galbraith, K. (1977). *The age of uncertainty*. Orlando, FL: Houghton Mifflin.

Goldstein, A. (2012). Revenge of the managers labor cost-cutting and the paradoxical resurgence of managerialism in the shareholder value era, 1984 to 2001. *American Sociological Review, 77*, 268-294.

Gort, M. (1951a). The planning of investment: A study of capital budgeting in the electric power industry. I. *The Journal of Business of the University of Chicago, 24*(2), 79–95.

Gort, M. (1951b). The planning of investment: A study of capital budgeting in the electric power industry. II. *The Journal of Business of the University of Chicago*, *24*(3), 181-202.

Goshal, S. (2005). Bad management theories are destroying good management practices. *Academy of Management Learning and Education*, *41*, 75-91.

Goutas, L., & Lane, C. (2009) The translation of shareholder value in the German business system: A comparative study of DaimlerChrysler and Volkswagen AG. *Competition and Change, 13*(4), 327-346.

Hall, S., & Appleyard, L. (2012). Financial business education: The remaking of gendered investment banking subjects in the (post-crisis) City of London. *Journal of Cultural Economy*, *5*(4), 457-472.

Harris, M., & Raviv, A. (1991). The theory of capital structure. *Journal of Finance*, *46*, 297-355.

Holsti, O. R. (1969). *Content analysis for the social sciences and humanities*. Reading, MA: Addison-Wesley.

Hiss, S. (2013). The politics of the financialization of sustainability. *Competition and Change*, *17*(3), 234-247.

Jakóbik, W. (2011). Theory of Economy as the Original Cause of the World Crisis. *Contemporary Economics*, *5*(2), 4-15.

Jones, B., & Nisbet, P. (2011). Shareholder value versus stakeholder values: CSR and financialization in global food firms. *Socio-Economic Review*, *9*, 287-314.

Jung, J. (2014). Political contestation at the top: Politics of outsider succession at U.S. corporations. *Organization Studies, 35*, 727-764.

Lazonick, W., & O'Sullivan, M. (2000). Maximizing shareholder value: A new ideology for corporate governance. *Economy and Society*, *29*(1), 13-35.

Lopdrup-Hjorth, T. (2015). Object and objective lost? Organization-phobia in organization theory. *Journal of Cultural Economy*, *8*(4), 439-461.

Krippner, G. (2005). The financialization of the American Economy. *Socio-Economic Review, 3*, 173-208.

Krippendorff, K. (1980). *Content analysis: An introduction to its methodology*. Newbury Park, CA: Sage.

Krippner, G. (2011). *Capitalizing on crisis: The political origins of the rise of finance. Cambridge*. Cambridge, MA: Harvard University Press.

Maclean, M., Harvey, C. & Kling, G. (2014) Pathways to Power: Class, Hyper-Agency and the French Corporate Elite. *Organization Studies, 35*, 825-855.

Maclean, M., Harvey, C., & Chia, R. (2012). Reflexive practice and the making of elite business careers. *Management Learning*, *43*(4), 385-404.

Montgomerie, J., & Williams, K. (2009). Financialised capitalism: After the crisis and beyond neoliberalism. *Competition and Change, 13*(2), 99-107

Milberg, W. (2008). Shifting sources and uses of profits: sustaining US financialization with global value chains. *Economy and Society, 37*, 420-451.

Miller, M. (1988). The Modigliani-Miller propositions after thirty years. *Journal of Economic Perspectives*, *2*, 99-120.

Mizruchi, M. (2013). *The fracturing of the American corporate elite*. Cambridge, MA: Harvard University Press,

Modigliani, F., & Miller, M. (1958). The cost of capital, corporation finance and the theory of investment. *American Economic Review*, *43*, 261-297.

Modigliani, F. (1988). MM – Past, Present and Future. *Journal of Economic Perspectives*, *2*, 149-158.

Morgan, G., & Takahashi, Y. (2002). Shareholder value in the Japanese context. *Competition and Change*, *6*(2), 169-191.

Mouck, T. (1992). The rhetoric of science and the rhetoric of revolt in the story of positive accounting theory. *Accounting, Auditing and Accountability Journal*, *5*(4), 35-56.

Myers, S. (2001). Capital structure. *Journal of Economic Perspectives, 15*, 81-102.

Navarro, P. (2008). The MBA core curricula of top-ranked U.S. Business Schools: A study in failure? *Academy of Management Learning and Education*, *71*, 108-123.

Parker, R. (1968). Discounted cash flow in historical perspective. *Journal of Accounting Research*, *6*, 58-71.

Prechel, H., & Morris, T. (2010). The effects of organizational and political embeddedness on financial malfeasance in the largest U.S. Corporations: Dependence, incentives, and opportunities. *American Sociological Review*, *75*, 331-354.

Rasche, A., Gilbert, D., & Schedel, I. (2012). Cross-disciplinary ethics education in MBA programs: Rhetoric or reality? *Academy of Management Learning and Education, 121*, 71-85.

Reed, M. (2012). Masters of the universe: Power and elites in organization studies. *Organization Studies, 33*, 203-221.

Ross, S., Westerfield, R., & Jaffe, J. (2004). *Corporate Finance.* Chicago, Ill.: Mcgraw-Hill.

Sapsford, R. (2007). *Survey Research* (2nd ed.). London, UK: Sage.

Samuelson, P. (1937). Some Aspects of the Pure Theory of Capital. Quarterly *Journal of Economics, 51*, 1937.

Samuelson, J. (2006). The new rigor: Beyond the right answer. *Academy of Management Learning and Education, 53*, 356-365.

Scheuren, F. (2004). *What is a survey?* Alexandria, VA: American Statistical Association.

Shiller, R. (1981). Do stock prices move too much to be justified by subsequent changes in dividends? *American Economic Review, 71*, 421–435.

Shiller, R. (1984). Stock prices and social dynamics. *Brookings Papers on Economic Activity, 2*, 457–498.

Sorge, A., & Witteloostuijn, A. (2004). The (non)sense of Organizational Change: An essai about universal management hypes, sick consultancy metaphors, and healthy organization theories. *Organization Studies, 25*, 1205-1231.

Stemler, S. (2001). An overview of content analysis. *Practical Assessment, Research & Evaluation, 7*(17), 1-6. Retrieved from http://PAREonline.net/getvn.asp?v=7&n=17

Stigler, G. (1950). The development of utility theory. II. *Journal of Political Economy, 58*, 373-396.

Stockhammer, E. (2008). Some stylized facts on the finance-dominated accumulation regime. *Competition and Change, 12*(2), 184-202.

Tengblad, S. (2004). Expectations of alignment: Examining the link between financial markets and managerial work. *Organization Studies, 25*, 583-606.

Thomas, A. (1984). The Value of MBA's? The fitting role of Business Schools. *Management Learning, 15*(3), 201-208.

Thompson, P., & Harley, B. (2007). Beneath the radar? A critical realist analysis of 'The Knowledge Economy' and 'Shareholder Value' as competing discourses. *Organization Studies, 289*, 1369-1378.

Tipaldo, G. (2014). *L'analisi del contenuto e i mass media* [The analysis of the content and the mass media]. Bologna, IT: Il Mulino.

Titman, S. (2002). The Modigliani and Miller theorem and the integration of financial markets. *Financial Management, 31*, 101-115.

Tomaskovic-Devey, D., & Lin, K-H. (2011). Income dynamics, economic rents, and the financialization of the U.S. economy. *American Sociological Review, 76*, 538-559.

Weber, R. P. (1990). *Basic Content Analysis* (2nd ed.). Newbury Park, CA: SAGE.

Zald, M., & Lounsbury, M. (2010). The wizards of Oz: Towards an institutional approach to elites, expertise and command Posts. *Organization Studies, 31*, 963-996.

Zorn, D. (2004). Here a chief, there a chief: The rise of the CFO in the American firm. *American Sociological Review, 69*, 345-364.

Zwan, N. (2014). Making sense of financialization. *Socio-Economic Review, 12*, 99-129.

Acknowledgements

Joao Silva Ferreira; Julia Smith; Patrick McColgan; Andrew Marshal; Christine Cooper; the ADVANCE Research Center at ISEG; and the Portuguese national funding agency for science, research and technology (FCT) Project-UID/SOC/04521/2013.

14

Making work pay: increasing labour supply of secondary earners in low income families with children

Anna Kurowska[1], Michał Myck[2], Katharina Wrohlich[3]

ABSTRACT In-work support through the tax-benefit system has proved to be an effective way of increasing the labor supply of lone mothers and first earners in couples in a number of OECD countries. At the same time, these instruments usually create negative employment incentives for secondary earners. This in turn reduces the potential of in-work support to address the joint objectives of higher employment and lower poverty levels. In this paper, we present a simulation exercise to examine labor supply implications of a diverse set of possible reforms to the main elements of tax and benefit support for families with children. We set the analysis in the context of the Polish tax and benefit system and show how an adequate combination of increased generosity of support with the introduction of a "double earner" premium may result in an increased labor supply of first and second earners in couples. The simulated reactions are concentrated in the lower half of the income distribution, thus increasing the potential of in-work support to alleviate poverty.

KEY WORDS: labor supply, tax-benefit system, microsimulation, family policy

[1] University of Warsaw - Institute of Social Policy, Poland; [2] Centre for Economic Analysis CenEA, Poland; [3] German Institute for Economic Research, DIW-Berlin, Germany

Introduction

Over the past few decades, in-work support has been introduced in many OECD countries with the objective to jointly address the goals of poverty reduction and increase employment, and it has been shown that these policies have positive effects on the labor supply of lone mothers and primary earners in couples (see, e.g., Blundell, 2000; Brewer, Duncan, Shephard & Suarez, 2006). However, such in-work financial support often goes along with strong negative work incentives for secondary earners (see, e.g., Brewer et al., 2006; Eissa & Hoynes, 2004; Haan & Myck, 2007). This is because 'classic' in-work support such as the Earned Income Tax Credit (EITC) in the US or the Working Families' Tax Credit (WFTC) in the UK are means-tested at the family level. As a result, these instruments may generate strong income effects on secondary earners, while high taper rates on their employment income imply high marginal tax rates. These in turn result in disincentive effects at the extensive and intensive margin, respectively.

Correspondence concerning this article should be addressed to: **Anna Kurowska**, University of Warsaw - Institute of Social Policy, Nowy Świat 67, room 110, Warszawa 00-927, Poland. E-mail: a.kurowska@uw.edu.pl

To avoid these negative incentives for secondary earners, some countries have introduced individual-based in-work credits, e.g., Belgian 'Employment Bonus', (Bargain, Caliendo, Haan, & Orsini, 2010) or subsidies to social security contributions of low-income employees, e.g., German 'Mini-Jobs', (Steiner & Wrohlich, 2005). While these schemes help to avoid high marginal tax rates on secondary earners, they may still discourage them from taking up work due to income effects and are generally less efficient in targeting poverty, as some of the low-wage workers live in medium or high-income households.

Recent policy has focused on families with children in Poland, resulting to a large extent from one of the lowest fertility rates in OECD countries, has led to an introduction of a number of policies that increased in-work incomes of families with children. These include a generous income tax credit for families with children in 2007 and its extension in 2014 with increased generosity for low-income families as well as a recent reform that changed a point withdrawal system in means-tested family benefits into tapered reduction. On top of these, April 2016 saw an introduction of a major reform of support for families (the so-called 500+ Program), which implemented a universal benefit of 500 PLN per month for the second and subsequent children aged 0-17 with a means-tested top up for first children for low income families. Until now, however, successive governments have not considered any instruments aimed specifically at two-earner households, and the point withdrawal of the 500+ benefits will add to second earner disincentive effects. As we show in this paper, it is the focus of support on second-earners that can effectively lead to a combination of improvement in the material conditions of low-income families and employment among parents. To illustrate this, we use the example of the Polish system of support for families with children as it was implemented in 2009 (i.e., before the extended child tax credit, the withdrawal taper in family benefits and the 500+ program) and examine the potential ways to improve its implications for labor market incentives with a particular focus on the ways to encourage employment of secondary earners. In our analysis, we shed new light on the issue highlighting the trade-offs involved. Similar to Figari (2015), the exercise conducted in this paper goes beyond the well-documented trade-off between equity and labor market objectives (Adam & Browne 2010; Blundell, Duncan, McCrae, & Meghir 2000; Duncan & Giles, 1996; Immervoll & Barber 2006; Immervoll, Kleven, Kreiner, & Verdelin, 2011; Jara & Tumino 2013) and addresses the less prominent concerns, namely, the need to balance first and second earner incentives and labor supply effects by the level of household income. The analysis focuses on family-level rather than individualized financial support given the less precise targeting of support toward low-income households in the latter case (e.g., Bargain & Orsini, 2006; Figari 2015). All the modeled alternatives have been calibrated in such a way that they are ex post (i.e., after labor supply adjustments) equally costly to the state budget. We concentrate our analysis on couples with children for three important reasons. First, the negative work incentives of in-work support concern second earners in couples (and not lone mothers). Second, the gender employment gaps in Poland, as in many other countries of Central and Eastern Europe (CEE), are strongly related to the demographic structure of the household and childcare responsibilities and are particularly visible among men and women with children (Myck, Kurowska & Kundera, 2013; Kurowska, Myck & Wrohlich, 2012). Third, poverty in Poland and other CEE countries is particularly high among families with children (European Commission, 2008).

The paper is structured as follows. In Section 2, we provide a brief background on the system of financial support for families with children in Poland as it operated in 2009. Section 3 describes the data we use and the modeling approach, while in Section 4 we present the results of the simulations. Section 5 offers conclusions and policy implications.

2. Background for microsimulations: system of financial support for families in Poland (2009)

The Polish system of financial support for families with children comprises two principal components: the means-tested Family Benefits (FB), and a non-refundable Child Tax Credit (CTC). The first element is composed of the basic Family Allowance (FA) with additional supplements.[1] Eligibility criteria for Family Benefits assess family income with reference to

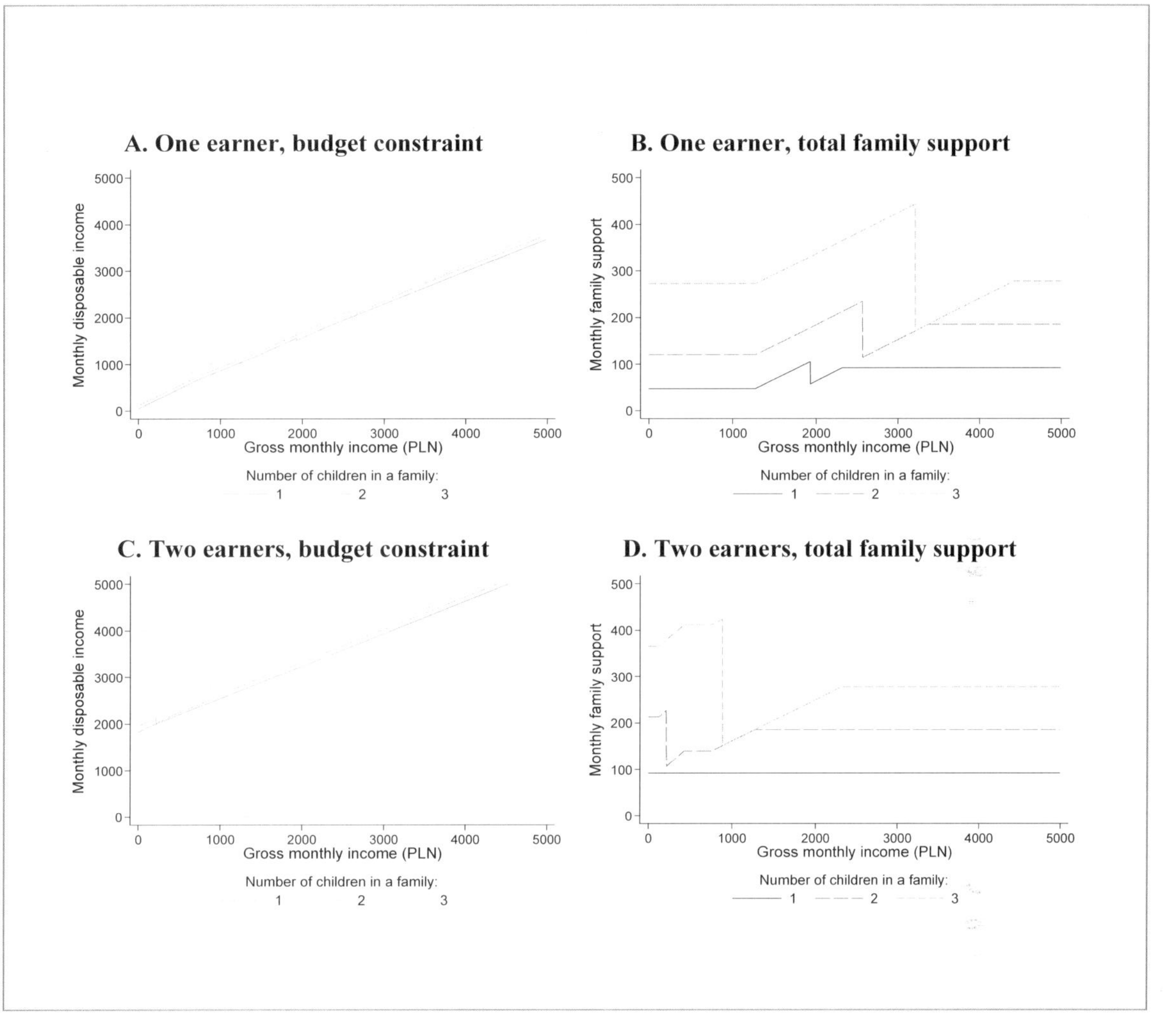

Figure 1. Gross income and family support – 2009
Source: Authors' calculations using the SIMPL microsimulation model (V4S3_12). For second earner's figures, earnings of the first earner are fixed at 2,326.31 PLN (equivalent to 75% of gross monthly mean wage in 2009).

a threshold, which – prior to the reform in 2015 – once exceeded makes the family ineligible to claim the benefits. Such a 'point withdrawal' of benefits implies very high effective marginal tax rates and has significant implications for average effective rates of tax (see Myck et al., 2013; Myck et al., 2015). The CTC is available to families with children who are subject to progressive income taxation. Eligibility to the credit is conditional on sufficient level of taxable income and starts approximately at the level of annual income corresponding to full time employment at the minimum wage. In 2009, the maximum value of the credit per child was 92,70 PLN (€20,70[2]) per month, and it was not withdrawn for high-income families. Low-to-middle income families can combine receiving support from both sources. The FB and the CTC are assessed on the basis of joint family income, and as such, imply the well-known consequences in the form of discouraging employment of secondary earners in couples (e.g., Bargain & Orsini, 2006, Brewer et al., 2006; Blundell et al., 2000; Duncan & Giles, 1996; Haan & Myck, 2007; Immervoll et al., 2011). Research on the consequences of such features using data for other countries suggests that they play an important role in determining the pattern of employment among couples (Dearing, Hofer, Lietz, Winter-Ebmer, & Wrohlich, 2007; Steiner & Wrohlich, 2005).

The described features of the 2009 system are illustrated in Figure 1A, where we show the budget constraint for a single earner couple with one, two and three children, and in Figure 1B, which for the same families shows the relationship between gross income and monthly total family support – the sum of the FB and the CTC. The corresponding relationship for the second earner in couples with children is given in Figures 1C and 1D. As we see in the case of the figures for single earners, the combination of FB and CTC results in similar levels of support given to low and high-income families. The highest amounts of support are paid to families with incomes just below the FB eligibility threshold where they can claim part of the CTC and still receive the full amounts of Family Benefits (in the case of single earner couples, this occurs at the level of 1,930 PLN for families with one child, 2,570 PLN for families with two children and 3,210 PLN for families with three children). The general structure of family support in 2009 was retained until 2014 when the CTC was made more generous to the lowest income families through the possibility of claiming it not only against income tax but also against social insurance contributions. Additionally, the government implemented tapered withdrawal of Family Benefits, which came into force in 2016. However, neither of these reforms introduces any specific second-earner incentives.

3. Data and Methods

3.1 The Polish Household Budget Survey

We base our analysis on the data from the Polish Household Budget Survey (PHBS) for 2009. This survey is conducted annually by the Polish Central Statistical Office and covers detailed information on demographics, incomes and household expenditure. The 2009 PHBS database includes information on a representative sample of 37,412 private households (107,967 individuals).

For the purpose of our analysis, we choose couples in labor supply flexible households (men aged 18-59; women 18-54; not self-employed or student; not receiving disability or retirement pensions). The final sample comprises 10,623 couples, of which 76% have at least one child and 11% three or more children. In the baseline scenario, 62.4% are two-earner couples.

3.2 Simulated reform scenarios: employment support through financial incentives

To address the research questions outlined in the introduction and to illustrate the implication of changes in financial incentives for families, we design four alternative reform scenarios: two implementing changes to the system of Family Benefits and two introducing modifications to the functioning of the CTC. The exercise is constructed in such a way that the policies are easily implementable extensions of existing instruments and for each policy area, they include an increase in the generosity of the system or combine increase in generosity with a "double earner" premium. With regard to comparability of the policy effects, the modeled changes have been calibrated in such a way that they are ex post (i.e., after labor supply adjustments) equally costly to the government (approximately 0.5bn PLN, i.e., €110mn).

The following reforms are analyzed:

- **System 1:** introduction of tapered withdrawal of FB at the rate of 55% (same as the rate of the UK's WFTC) instead of the current point withdrawal;
- **System 2:** introduction of tapered withdrawal of FB (at 55%) combined with a "double earner" premium in the form of extended withdrawal threshold conditional on the work of both parents (they need to earn at least 80% of the national minimum wage (NMW, equal to 1276 PLN, €285,50 euro, per month in 2009));
- **System 3:** increase in the maximum value of the CTC from 92.70 PLN per month per child to 107 PLN per month;
- **System 4:** introduction of a "double earner" premium through the CTC in the form of an additional value of the CTC (92.70 PLN per month) for couples where both parents earn at least 175% of the NMW.

The implications of these reforms for the level of support through the two elements of the system for stylized households are presented in Figure 2. In Systems 1 and 2, the common feature is that the point with-

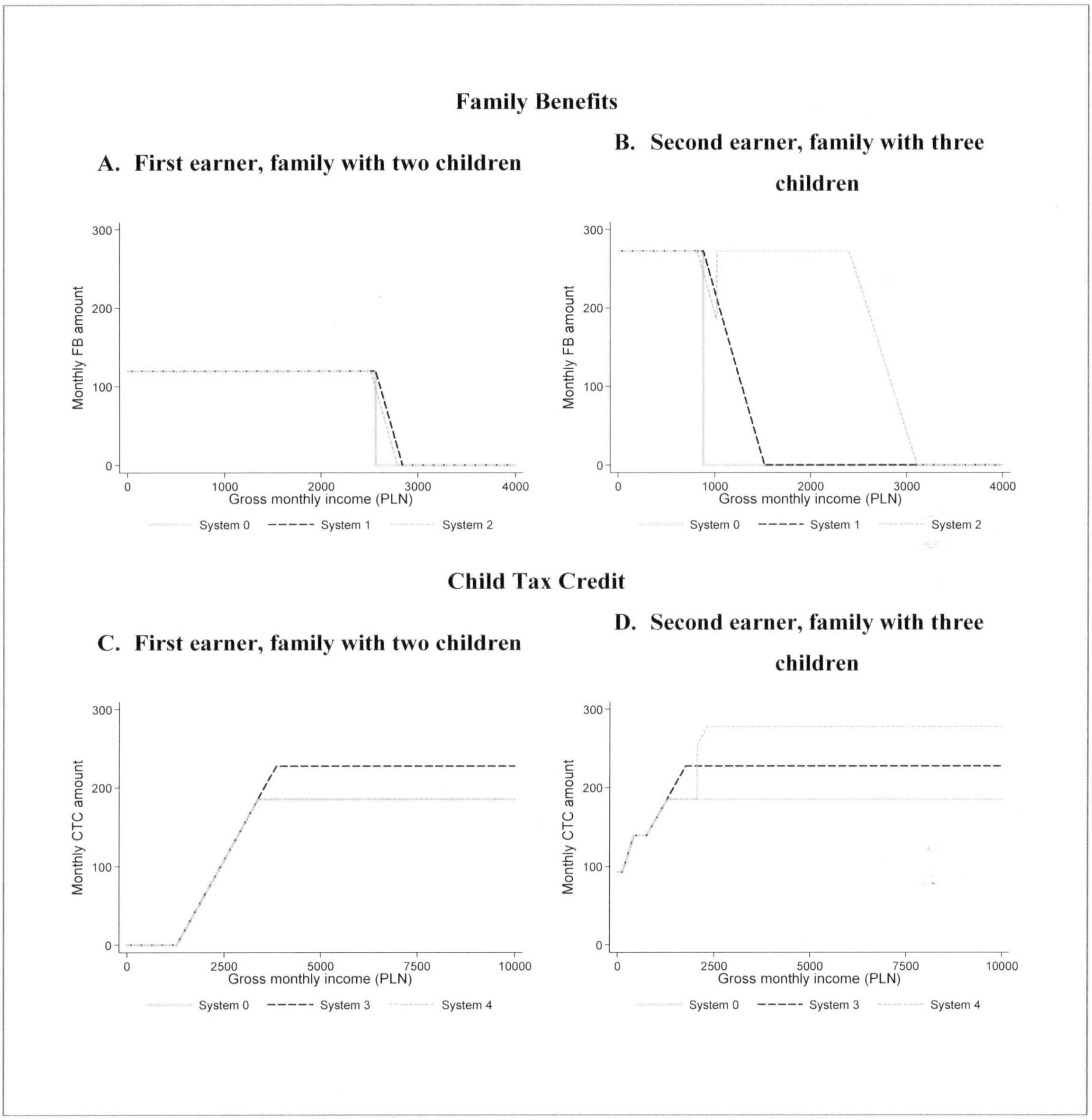

Figure 2. Level of support under the base and reformed scenarios

Source: Authors' calculations using the SIMPL microsimulation model (V4S3_12). For second earner's figures, earnings of the first earner are fixed at 2,326.31 PLN (equivalent to 75% of gross monthly mean wage in 2009).

drawal of benefits at the level of net monthly income of 504 PLN per person is substituted with gradual withdrawal of the benefits. Figure 2B shows how the "double earner" premium of System 2 is designed to operate. With the first earner employed at 2,330 PLN per month, initially the benefits begin to be withdrawn when the second earner's gross salary crosses the threshold of 810 PLN. However, when they reach the required level of 80% of the NMW (approximately 1020 PLN), the "double earner" premium kicks in, and the withdrawal threshold is increased to 2,400 PLN. This implies that this family continues to receive Family Benefits up to the level of income of the second earner of 3,110 PL per month (to equate

Table 1. Labor supply participation elasticities

	Own net wage	Cross net wage	Total net wage
Men	0.287	-0.026	0.272
Women	0.696	-0.053	0.659

Source: Adapted from "Stability of elasticity estimates in the context of significant changes in labour market incentives" by Myck (2014). Retrieved from http://www.cenea.org.pl/images/stories/pdf/working_papers/Myck_CenEA_WP0114.pdf.

the costs of System 2 and System 1, the baseline withdrawal threshold in System 2 is reduced from 504 to 494 PLN per person). Figures 2C and 2D demonstrate the operation of Systems 3 and 4. Under System 3, the one-earner family with two children (Figure 2C) begins to see benefits of higher levels of the tax credit once gross earnings exceed 3,380 per month, while the two-earner family with three children when the monthly gross earnings of the second earner exceed 1,280 PLN. Under System 4 the two-earner couple with three children will see their CTC level jump to 255 PLN per month once the second earner exceeds the required threshold of 175% of NMW (2,230 PLN). As we see in Figure 2D, the "double earner" premium, even in the case of a family with three children, is higher compared to the additional level of the credit for each of the children in the family resulting from the design of System 3. The "double earner" earnings thresholds under Systems 2 and 4 have been designed in such a way that they affect different sections of the earnings distribution and account for other elements of the system in such a way that they target a sufficiently large proportion of families.

3.3 Modeling labor supply response to the simulated reforms

To model the labor supply response to the simulated reforms, we apply the standard static discrete choice labor supply model along the lines of van Soest (1995), Blundell et al. (2000), Steiner & Wrohlich (2005) and Haan & Myck (2007). Due to lack of information on precise hours worked in the data, we model the labor supply choice between not working, working part time and working full time. Incomes in the modeled labor market scenarios are computed using the microsimulation model SIMPL.[3] The utility function is quadratic in household consumption (c_i) and includes dummy variables for participation (w_i^m and w_i^f for men and women respectively), part time dummies (pt_i^m and pt_i^f) and their interactions. The deterministic part of the utility function takes the following form:

$$U_{ij}\left(c_{ij}, w_{ij}^m, w_{ij}^f\right) =$$

$$= \beta_{1i}c_{ij} + \beta_2(c_{ij})^2 + \beta_{3mi}w_{ij}^m + \beta_{3fi}w_{ij}^f + \beta_{4m}pt_{ij}^m + \beta_{4f}pt_{ij}^f +$$

$$+\gamma_{1f}c_{ij}w_{ij}^f + \gamma_{1m}c_{ij}w_{ij}^m + \gamma_{2f}c_{ij}pt_{ij}^f + \gamma_{2m}c_{ij}pt_{ij}^m + \gamma_{3m}w_{ij}^m w_{ij}^f \quad (1)$$

and parameters β_{1i}, β_{3mi} and β_{3fi} are allowed to vary with characteristics (taste shifters). Our estimates account unobserved heterogeneity through estimating a mass point on $\beta_{ci.}$ The budget constraint is determined by wages (ω_i), work status (w_{ij}), out-of-work incomes (y_i), household characteristics (X_i) and the tax and benefit function (ϕ):

$$c_{ij} = \phi\left[\omega_i^m, \omega_i^f, w_{ij}^m, w_{ij}^f, X_i, y_i\right]. \quad (2)$$

4. Results: labor supply estimates and employment effects

The simulated average labor supply elasticities separately for men and women are presented in Table 1 (for estimation details and derivation of elasticities, see Myck, 2014). The own net wage elasticity for women is positive and more than two times higher for women than for man. For both genders, the cross net wage elasticity is negative, but small and again stronger for women than for men.

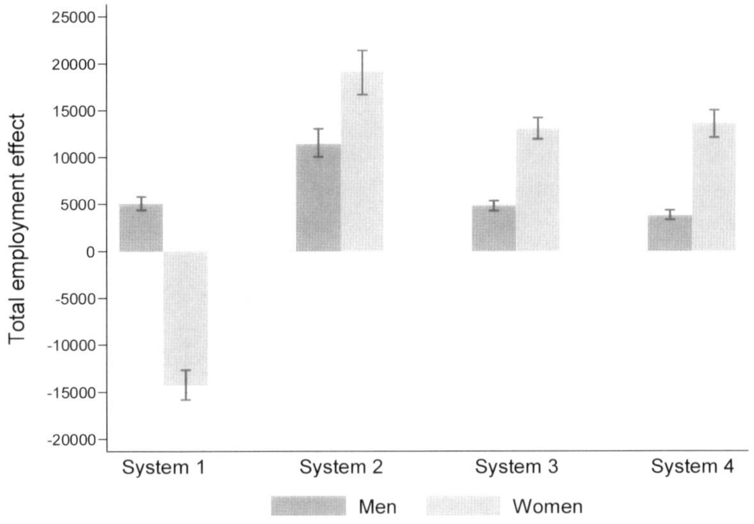

Figure 3. Employment effects of modeled reforms
Source: own calculations based on PHBS-2009 data and SIMPL microsimulation model.

Table 2. Labor supply effects of modeled reforms

	System 1	System 2	System 3	System4
In thousands:				
Men	5.0	11.4	4.8	3.8
Women	-14.3	19.2	13.0	13.6
Total:	-9.3	30.6	17.8	17.4
As percentage of parents in couples:				
Men	0.17	0.38	0.16	0.13
Women	-0.48	0.64	0.44	0.46
Total:	-0.16	0.51	0.30	0.29
Total by income quintile (in thousands):				
Q1	0.0	16.1	4.1	0.8
Q2	-3.2	9.2	4.7	1.8
Q3	-3.8	3.1	4.7	3.3
Q4	-1.6	1.6	3.0	5.0
Q5	-0.7	0.4	1.3	6.5

Source: own calculations based on PHBS-2009 data and SIMPL microsimulation model. Absolute values computed using grossing up weights provided by the Central Statistical Office.

The labor supply effects of the reforms are presented in Figure 3 and Table 2 separately for men and women. In the first reform scenario, the tapered withdrawal of Family Benefits, designed to ease the very high effective marginal tax rates, increases the labor supply of men (in most cases, first earners) but at the same time, diminishes the labor supply among women with a negative net effect of approximately 9,000 individuals, which is approximately 0.2% of all parents in couples. This is a classic example of the well-documented negative second earner effect of greater generosity of means tested support and has the well-known implication of increasing the proportion of one-earner households. The latter effect is due to, on the one hand, increased activity in no-earner couples, and on the other hand, the reduced labor supply among two-earner households

However, the negative labor supply effects among women are fully overturned under System 2 reform, which combines tapered FB withdrawal with a "double-earner" premium (see Figure 3). The total labor supply effect is approximately 31,000 individuals, i.e., approximately 0,5% of parents in couples, and the labor supply of women increases by approximately 19,000 (0.6% of mothers in couples).

The two reforms of support through the Child Tax Credit (System 3 and 4) have similar total effects on the labor supply of approximately 4000 for fathers (0.15%) and 13000 for mothers (0.45%). The labor supply effects of these reforms, however, affect different sections of the household income distribution. This is depicted in the second panel of Table 2, where for each reform we document the labor supply changes by baseline income quintile. In the case of System 3, the effect on the labor market is concentrated in the lower and middle quintiles, while System 4 affects the labor supply of households primarily in higher quintiles.

The quintile distribution of labor supply reactions sheds additional light on the effects of Systems 1 and 2. Labor supply reductions in the case of System 1 are concentrated in the second and third quintile, i.e., in the parts of the distribution where low income double earner families are located, while the positive reaction to System 2 comes primarily from the lower end of the distribution, and in particular, from the first quintile.

5. Conclusions

We have presented an exercise in simulating labor supply reactions of a diverse set of hypothetical reforms to the system of financial support for families with children, which bring a number of general implications for designing tax-benefit systems. As has been demonstrated earlier (e.g., Brewer et al., 2006, Eissa & Hoynes, 2004; Haan & Myck, 2007), increases in the generosity of means-tested support without specific second earner premiums results in the overall reduction of the labor supply among couples, although such reforms usually reduce the number of so-called workless households. In this article, we have shown how an adequate combination of the increase in the generosity of the tax-benefit system with the introduction of a "double earner" premium may balance the employment incentives for first and second earners and concentrate the labor supply effects in the lowest quintile of the income distribution. Naturally, as in the case of all labor supply simulations, there may be additional constraints, which might influence the actual effects of specific policies if implemented in reality. These include such aspects as existence of suitable employment positions, hours constraints, benefit take-up issues or the availability of childcare (Bargain et al., 2010; Brewer et al., 2006; Haan & Wrohlich, 2011; Wrohlich, 2011). More specific and extended labor supply models based on much more detailed data would be necessary to address these concerns, although it seems that most of them would apply equally strongly to the different hypothetical scenarios modeled in our exercise.

In our labor supply exercise, the small negative effects of the introduction of a tapered withdrawal of Family Benefits, simulated in the Polish tax and benefit system of 2009, turn strongly positive once a "double-earner" premium is implemented on top of it while holding the cost of the modeled reforms constant. The resulting labor supply effects are in the range of 31000 individuals and could increase employment of men by approximately 0.3pp and that of women by 0.5pp. The majority of the generated labor supply response is concentrated among households from the bottom quintile of the income distribution. In contrast, the "double earner" premium implemented in the Child Tax Credit, which benefits middle and high-income families, has a much lower effect on the labor supply and affects employment mainly in the higher part of the income distribution. This is due to the way in which the CTC eligibility is allocated and due to the modeled requirements for the levels of income of both partners to qualify for the premium.

The presented exercise shows that a redesign of low-income support for families with children with explicit rewards for two-earner couples could be an efficient way to increase the labor force participation rates of mothers. Designing "double earner" premiums as elements of low-income means-tested support could be a successful means to reduce child poverty through the combination of direct support and higher labor market activity among parents.

References

Adam, S., & Browne, J. (2010). Redistribution, Work Incentives and Thirty Years of UK Tax and Benefit Reform. *Institute for Fiscal Studies* (Working Paper 10/24). Retrieved from https://www.ifs.org.uk/wps/wp1024.pdf

Bargain, O., & Orsini, K. (2006). In-work policies in Europe: Killing two birds with one stone. *Labour Economics*, *6*(13), 667-693.

Bargain, O., Caliendo, M., Haan. P., & Orsini, K. (2010). Making work pay in a rationed labor market. *Journal of Population Economics*, *1*(21), 323-351.

Blundell, R.W. (2000). Work incentives and in-work benefit reforms: A review. *Oxford Review of Economic Policy*, *16*(1), 27-44.

Blundell, R., Duncan, A., McCrae, J., & Meghir, C. (2000). The labour market impact of the working families' tax credit. *Fiscal Studies*, *21*(1), 75–103.

Brewer, M., Duncan, A., Shephard, A., & Suarez, M. J. (2006). Did working families tax credit work? The impact of in-work support on labour supply in Great Britain. *Labour Economics*, *13*(6), 699-720.

Dearing, H., Hofer, H., Lietz, C., Winter-Ebmer, R., & Wrohlich, K. (2007). Why are mothers working longer hours in Austria than in Germany? A comparative microsimulation study, *Fiscal Studies*, *28*(4), 463-495.

Domitrz, A., Myck, M., Morawski, L., & Semeniuk A. (2013). Dystrybutywny wpływ reform podatkowo-świadczeniowych wprowadzonych w latach 2006-2011 [Distributive Effect of Tax and Benefit Reforms Implemented in the Period 2006-2011]. *Bank i Kredyt [Bank & Credit]*, *44*(3), 261-286.

Duncan, A., & Giles, C. (1996). Labour supply incentives and recent family credit reforms. *The Economic Journal*, 106(434), 142-155.

Eissa, N., & Hoynes, H. (2004). Taxes and the labor market participation of married couples: The earned income tax credit. *Journal of Public Economics*, *88*(9-10), 1931-1958.

European Commission (2008). *Child poverty and well-being in the EU. Current status and way forward.* Belgium: Office for Official Publications of the European Union.

Figari, F. (2015). From housewives to independent earners: How the tax system can help women to work in a context of strong familialism. *Journal of Social Policy*, *44*(1), 63-82.

Haan, P., & Myck, M. (2007). Apply with caution: Introducing UK-style in-work support in Germany. *Fiscal Studies*, *28*(1), 43-72.

Haan, P., & Myck, M. (2010). Safety net still in transition: labour market incentive effects of social support in Poland and Germany. *Bank i Kredyt [Bank & Credit]*, *41*(3), 5–34.

Haan, P., & Myck, M. (2012). Multi-family households in a labour supply model: a calibration method with application to Poland. *Applied Economics*, *44*(22), 2907 - 2919.

Haan, P., & Wrohlich, K. (2011). Can child care encourage employment and fertility? Evidence from a structural model. *Labour Economics*, *18*(4), 498-512.

Immervoll, H., & Barber, D. (2006). Can parents afford to work? Childcare costs, tax-benefit policies and work incentives (Discussion Paper No. 1932). Institute for the Study of Labor. Retrieved from http://ftp.iza.org/dp1932.pdf

Immervoll, H., Kleven, H. J., Kreiner, C. T., & Verdelin, N. (2011). An evaluation of the tax-transfer treatment of married couples in European countries. *Journal of Public Economics*, *95*(11-12), 1485-1500.

Jara, H., & Tumino, A. (2013). Tax-benefit systems, income distribution and work incentives in the European Union. *International Journal of Microsimulation*, 1(6), 27-62.

Levy, H., Morawski, L., & Myck, M. (2012). *EUROMOD Country Report – Poland.* ISER, University of Essex. Retrieved from https://www.iser.

essex.ac.uk/files/euromod/country-reports/CR_PL2006-09_Final_12-2-2012.pdf

Kurowska, A., Myck, M., & Wrohlich K. (2012). Family and labor market choices: Requirements to guide effective evidence-based policy (Discussion Paper No. 6846). Institute for the Study of Labor. Retrieved from http://ftp.iza.org/dp6846.pdf

Morawski, L., & Myck, M. (2010). 'Klin'-ing up: Effects of Polish tax reforms on those in and on those out. *Labour Economics*, *17*(3), 556-566.

Morawski, L., & Myck, M. (2011). Distributional effects of the child tax credit in Poland and its potential reforms. *Ekonomista [Economist]*, 6, 815-831.

Myck, M. (2014). Stability of elasticity estimates in the context of significant changes in labour market incentives (Working Paper 01/14). Centre for Economic Analysis. Retrieved from http://www.cenea.org.pl/images/stories/pdf/working_papers/Myck_CenEA_WP0114.pdf

Myck, M., Domitrz, A., Morawski, L., & Semeniuk, A. (2015). Financial incentives to work in the context of a complex reform package and growing wages: the Polish experience 2005-2011. *Baltic Journal of Economics*, *15*(2), 99-121.

Myck, M., Kurowska, A., & Kundera, A. (2013). Financial support for families with children and its trade-offs: balancing redistribution and parental work incentives. *Baltic Journal of Economics*, *13*(2), 61-85.

Steiner, V., & Wrohlich, K. (2005). Work incentives and labour supply effects of the ‚mini-jobs'-reform in Germany. *Empirica*, *32*(1), 91-116.

Van Soest, A. (1995). Structural models of family labor supply: A discrete choice approach. *Journal of Human Resources*, *30*(1), 63-88.

Wrohlich, K. (2011). Labor supply and child care choices in a rationed child care market (Discussion Paper No. 1169). DIW Berlin, German Institute for Economic Research. Retrieved from https://www.diw.de/documents/publikationen/73/diw_01.c.388164.de/dp1169.pdf

Endnotes

1 *For details of the Polish tax and benefit system, see, e.g., Domitrz, Myck, Morawski & Semeniuk (2013), Levy, Morawski & Myck (2012) or Morawski & Myck (2010, 2011).*

2 *Throughout the paper, we use the exchange rate from June 31, 2009: €1 = 4.47 PLN.*

3 *For details concerning the model and for examples of its earlier applications, see, e.g., Bargain et al. (2010), Haan & Myck (2010; 2012), Morawski & Myck (2010; 2011).*

Acknowledgments:

This article was written with financial support from the Foundation for Polish Science (Parent-Bridge Program) as part of the project "Joint influences of family and labor market policies on labor market participation and fertility decisions of men and women" directed by Anna Kurowska. Data used in the analysis have been provided by the Polish Central Statistical Office (GUS), which takes no responsibility for the analysis and interpretation of the results. We are grateful to Michał Kundera for assistance with microsimulation analysis. The usual disclaimer applies.

Permissions

All chapters in this book were first published in CE, by University of Finance and Management, Warsaw; Vistula University; hereby published with permission under the Creative Commons Attribution License or equivalent. Every chapter published in this book has been scrutinized by our experts. Their significance has been extensively debated. The topics covered herein carry significant findings which will fuel the growth of the discipline. They may even be implemented as practical applications or may be referred to as a beginning point for another development.

The contributors of this book come from diverse backgrounds, making this book a truly international effort. This book will bring forth new frontiers with its revolutionizing research information and detailed analysis of the nascent developments around the world.

We would like to thank all the contributing authors for lending their expertise to make the book truly unique. They have played a crucial role in the development of this book. Without their invaluable contributions this book wouldn't have been possible. They have made vital efforts to compile up to date information on the varied aspects of this subject to make this book a valuable addition to the collection of many professionals and students.

This book was conceptualized with the vision of imparting up-to-date information and advanced data in this field. To ensure the same, a matchless editorial board was set up. Every individual on the board went through rigorous rounds of assessment to prove their worth. After which they invested a large part of their time researching and compiling the most relevant data for our readers.

The editorial board has been involved in producing this book since its inception. They have spent rigorous hours researching and exploring the diverse topics which have resulted in the successful publishing of this book. They have passed on their knowledge of decades through this book. To expedite this challenging task, the publisher supported the team at every step. A small team of assistant editors was also appointed to further simplify the editing procedure and attain best results for the readers.

Apart from the editorial board, the designing team has also invested a significant amount of their time in understanding the subject and creating the most relevant covers. They scrutinized every image to scout for the most suitable representation of the subject and create an appropriate cover for the book.

The publishing team has been an ardent support to the editorial, designing and production team. Their endless efforts to recruit the best for this project, has resulted in the accomplishment of this book. They are a veteran in the field of academics and their pool of knowledge is as vast as their experience in printing. Their expertise and guidance has proved useful at every step. Their uncompromising quality standards have made this book an exceptional effort. Their encouragement from time to time has been an inspiration for everyone.

The publisher and the editorial board hope that this book will prove to be a valuable piece of knowledge for researchers, students, practitioners and scholars across the globe.

List of Contributors

Marcin Wnuk
Adam Mickiewicz University, Department of Work and Organizational Psychology, Poland

Anselm Komla Abotsi
University of Education, Winneba - Department of Economics Education, Ghana Arts Centre, Accra, Ghana

Yiing Jia Loke
Universiti Sains Malaysia - School of Social Sciences, Malaysia

Esther Calderon-Monge
Faculty of Economics and Administration of Business, University of Burgos, Spain

Ivan Pastor-Sanz
Faculty of Economics and Administration of Business, University of Valladolid, Spain

Jan Vlachý
Czech Technical University in Prague - Masaryk Institute of Advanced Studies, Czech Republic

Qaiser Rafique Yasser
University Malaysia Sarawak, Malaysia

Abdullah Al Mamun and Marcus Rodrigs
University of Newcastle - Newcastle Business School, Australia

Chai J Sia and Rayenda Brahmana
Universiti Malaysia Sarawak - Faculty of Economics and Business, Malaysia

Gesti Memarista
Universitas Kristen Petra - Faculty of Economics, Indonesia

Denisa Gajdová and Helena Majdúchová
University of Economics in Bratislava, Slovakia

Wiesław Dębski
University of Finance and Management in Warsaw - Management and Finance, Poland

Bartosz Świderski and Jarosław Kurek
Warsaw University of Life Sciences - Faculty of Applied Informatics and Mathematics, Department of Applied Informatics, Poland

Ozren Rafajac
Polytechnic of Rijeka, Croatia

Marinko Skare
Juraj Dobrila University of Pula, Croatia

Adam Zaremba
Poznan University of Economics and Business, Poland

Michał Konopczyński
Uniwersytet Ekonomiczny w Poznaniu - Katedra Ekonomii Matematycznej, Poland

Tiago Cardao-Pito
ISEG, Universidade de Lisboa, Portugal
Department of Accounting and Finance, University of Strathclyde, UK

Anna Kurowska
University of Warsaw - Institute of Social Policy, Poland

Michał Myck
Centre for Economic Analysis CenEA, Poland

Katharina Wrohlich
German Institute for Economic Research, DIW-Berlin, Germany

Index

O

P

R

S

T

V

X